China's Industrial State-owned Enterprises
Between Profitability and Bankruptcy

China's Industrial State-owned Enterprises
Between Profitability and Bankruptcy

Carsten A. Holz

World Scientific
New Jersey • London • Singapore • Hong Kong

Published by

World Scientific Publishing Co. Pte. Ltd.
5 Toh Tuck Link, Singapore 596224
USA office: Suite 202, 1060 Main Street, River Edge, NJ 07661
UK office: 57 Shelton Street, Covent Garden, London WC2H 9HE

British Library Cataloguing-in-Publication Data
A catalogue record for this book is available from the British Library.

CHINA'S INDUSTRIAL STATE-OWNED ENTERPRISES
BETWEEN PROFITABILITY AND BANKRUPTCY

Copyright © 2003 by World Scientific Publishing Co. Pte. Ltd.

All rights reserved. This book, or parts thereof, may not be reproduced in any form or by any means, electronic or mechanical, including photocopying, recording or any information storage and retrieval system now known or to be invented, without written permission from the Publisher.

For photocopying of material in this volume, please pay a copying fee through the Copyright Clearance Center, Inc., 222 Rosewood Drive, Danvers, MA 01923, USA. In this case permission to photocopy is not required from the publisher.

ISBN 981-238-332-8

Printed in Singapore.

To Thomas P. Lyons

Preface

The fate of China's industrial state-owned enterprises (SOEs) has occupied the minds of economists inside as well as outside China for the past two decades. The data certainly look grim. Between 1978 and 1997, losses in industrial SOEs rose twentyfold. By 1998, approximately 20% of all industrial SOEs had partly or fully stopped production. Capacity utilization in more than half of all industrial SOEs was below 60%. One-third of all employees in industrial SOEs had been made redundant. While in 1990 industrial SOEs in only three of the thirty major industrial sectors were running aggregate losses, by 1997 there were aggregate losses in fully 25 of the then 39 sectors. Yet by 2001, the number of industrial sectors in which SOEs were running aggregate losses was down to four.

These facts raise a number of questions. First, why did the profitability of industrial SOEs decline so drastically during the first two decades of China's economic reforms? Did competition drive down profitability, was labor remuneration excessive, or was a high liability-asset ratio to blame? What can we learn about the causes of the decline from industrial SOEs' profit and loss account? Once we know the causes of the decline in industrial SOE profitability over the past more than two decades, what are the implications for industrial SOE profitability in the future?

Second, how do industrial SOEs compare with industrial non-SOEs? Is profitability in industrial non-SOEs so much higher than in industrial SOEs that a change in the ownership form of industrial SOEs is called for? What explains the difference in industrial SOE vs. non-SOE profitability? Are differences in profitability the outcome of continued differential government policies or of systemic deficiencies in SOEs?

Third, are profit rates equal across all industrial SOEs, or do we need to distinguish between specific groups of industrial SOEs, or even individual enterprises? Does sector, location, size, or ownership level matter? If profit rates are not equal, why not, and what are the implications of unequal profit rates for industrial SOE reform?

Finally, what has the Chinese government done to improve industrial SOE profitability? In 1998, the central government initiated a three-year SOE reform program. Has it achieved its objectives? Which government reform policies succeeded, and which did not? What are the current impasses in industrial SOE reform, and what are the prospects for their resolution?

Understanding the determinants and characteristics of industrial SOE profitability is important, because profitability matters. Profitability matters, because in the long run it determines the economic viability of an enterprise. Industrial SOE profitability also affects employment, government finances, and the health of the banking system. In as far as low industrial SOE profitability triggers industrial SOE reform measures, which in turn are intricately linked to other reforms ranging from social security reform to financial sector reforms, industrial SOE profitability ultimately has implications for the entire transition process.

Carsten A. Holz
December 2002

Contents

Preface vii
List of Tables xv
List of Figures xix

1. Introduction 1
   Efficiency May Be an Interesting Concept 2
   ... But It Is Profitability That Matters 3
   Industrial SOE Profitability in the Literature 5
   The Issues in This Book 8
   Acknowledgments 11

2. Data 13
   The Directly Reporting Industrial SOEs 13
      Defining the Object of Analysis 13
      Industrial SOEs in Perspective 22
      Sectoral and Regional Classification of Industrial SOEs 26
   Profit and Profitability Measures 31
      Profit 31
      Profitability in the Literature 33
      Profitability in This Book 35
   Data Sources 39
   Appendix 1: Value-added 42
   Appendix 2: Depreciation 43
   Appendix 3: Labor Remuneration 47

Wages 47
Social Welfare Expenditures for Current Employees 50
Pensions and Social Welfare Expenditures for Retirees 52

**Part I Explaining the Reform Period Decline in Industrial
SOE Profitability** 55

3. Tracing the Decline in Industrial SOE Profitability through
   the Profit and Loss Account 57
   Industrial SOE Profitability Trends 58
   Explaining the Decline in Industrial SOE Profitability
   Over Time 62
       1980s 62
       1990s 70
   Incentives to Misreport Profit 78
   Operating Surplus 82
       Data and Time Trends 82
       Explaining the Difference in the Time Trends of
       Operating Surplus and Profit 86
   Conclusions 92

4. The Impact of Competition and Labor Remuneration on
   Profitability 95
   Competition and Excessive Labor Remuneration Are Not
   Alternative Hypotheses 98
       Intermediate Competition Indicator 99
       Intermediate Labor Remuneration Indicator 101
       Potential Interaction between Competition and Labor
       Remuneration 103
   Competition as a Uni-causal Explanation of Profitability 105
       Market Share and Profitability 106
       The Relationship between the Market Share and the
       Intermediate Competition Indicator 111
   Excessive Labor Remuneration as an Alternative
   Explanation of Profitability 113

Analysis Using Nationwide Data 115
Analysis Using Provincial-Level Data 119
Explaining Profitability 123
Conclusions 128

5. The Impact of the Liability-Asset Ratio on Profitability 131
Explaining the Time Trend of the Industrial SOE
Liability-Asset Ratio 134
   The Data 134
   The Rise in the Liability-Asset Ratio During the
   Reform Period Reflects the Process of Transition 139
   The Liability-Asset Ratio of China's Industrial SOEs
   Is Not Excessive in Domestic and International
   Comparisons 142
Linking the Liability-Asset Ratio to Profitability 144
   Accounting Link between the Liability-Asset Ratio
   and Profitability 144
   Testing the Link Between the Liability-Asset Ratio and
   Profitability Measures 147
   Resolving Potential Endogeneity Problems 152
Conclusions 159

Part II Industrial SOE Profitability in Perspective 161

6. SOEs versus Non-SOEs 163
Profitability Patterns of SOEs versus Non-SOEs 164
   SOEs versus the Aggregate of Non-SOEs 165
   Distinguishing among Non-SOEs 169
Selection Bias 174
Explaining the Profitability Gap between Industrial SOEs
and Non-SOEs 178
   Difference in the Rate of Circulation Taxes 180
   Difference in Capital Intensity 186
      Costs of a High Level of Capital Intensity 186
      Causes of High SOE Capital Intensity 190
Conclusions 194

7. Profitability across Industrial SOEs 197
    Individual Profitability Patterns 200
        Industrial sectors 200
        Provinces 204
        Size 207
        Ownership 209
    Multivariate Analysis 212
        Provincial-Level Industrial SOE Profitability 213
        Within-Province Sectoral Industrial SOE Profitability 220
    Sectoral Profitability Patterns 221
        Sectoral Profitablity Trends 223
        Polarization Across Sectors 226
        Implications of Sectoral Industrial SOE Profitability for
        Provincial-Level Aggregate Industrial SOE Profitability 233
        Polarization Within Sectors 237
        Performance and Exit 238
    Conclusions 239

8. Recent Industrial SOE Reform Policies 243
    The 1998–2000 Industrial SOE Reform Program 244
        The Modern Enterprise System 245
        Turning Around Large and Medium Industrial SOEs 246
        Enlivening Small Industrial Enterprises 247
        Dismissal of Industrial SOE Staff and Workers 249
        SOE Equity and Liabilities 256
        SOE Bankruptcy 258
        Implications 261
    Enhancing Enterprise Management 264
        Property Rights Reform versus the Modern Enterprise
        System 265
        Price Competition 270
        Supervision and Personnel Appointment 273
        Implications 281
    Outlook 284

9. Conclusions 289
    Main Findings 289
    Implications for Privatization 295
        The Issue of Privatization in the Literature 296
        The Arguments Against Privatization of Large and
        Medium Industrial SOEs in China 300
    Key Issues in Industrial SOE Reform 304
        The Driving Factors Behind Industrial SOE Reform 304
        Obstacles to Industrial SOE Profitability 308
        Management Distractions 312
    Summing Up 314

References 317
Index 343

List of Tables

Table 2.1	Enterprise Categorization (with data for Shaanxi Province, 2000)	17
Table 2.2	Directly Reporting Industrial Enterprises, 1999 and 2000	21
Table 2.3	Sectoral Shares in Industrial SOEs' Value-added	28
Table 2.4	Coverage of Sectoral Data in Provincial Statistical Yearbooks	31
Table 2.5	Statistical Yearbook Sources for Output, Balance Sheet, and Profit and Loss Account Data	40
Table 2.6	Estimated Depreciation of Industrial SOEs	45
Table 2.7	Derivation of the Economy-wide Industrial SOE Depreciation Rate from Provincial-level Industrial SOE Data, 1992–2000	46
Table 2.8	Labor Remuneration in Industrial SOEs	48
Table 3.1	Profitability of Industrial SOEs, 1978–2000	60
Table 3.2	Composition of Sales Revenue of Industrial SOEs, 1978–2000	64
Table 3.3	Impact of Changes in Accounting Procedures, Tax System and Depreciation Rules on Profit	72
Table 3.4	Composition of Value-added in Industrial SOEs, 1978–2000	84
Table 4.1	Significance Level of Market Share in Explaining Industrial SOE Profitability	112
Table 4.2	Impact of Market Share on Industrial SOE Intermediate Competition Indicator	113

Table 4.3	Correlation Coefficients of Individual Components of Labor Remuneration with the Intermediate Labor Remuneration Indicator or Profitability in Industrial SOEs	116
Table 4.4	Impact of Labor Remuneration on the Intermediate Labor Remuneration Indicator for Industrial SOEs across Provinces, 1993–1997	120
Table 4.5	Impact of Labor Remuneration on the Intermediate Labor Remuneration Indicator for Industrial SOEs across Provinces, 1999–2000	121
Table 4.6	Impact of Competition and Labor Remuneration on Industrial SOE Profit per Unit of Equity across Provinces, 1993–2000	124
Table 4.7	Impact of Intermediate Competition and Labor Remuneration Indicators on Industrial SOE Profit per Unit of Equity, 1993–2000	126
Table 4.8	Contribution of Intermediate Competition and Labor Remuneration Indicators to Change in Profitability of Industrial SOEs, 1994–2000	128
Table 5.1	Liability-Asset Ratios	135
Table 5.2	Liability-Asset Ratios of Directly Reporting Industrial Enterprises, 1995	142
Table 5.3	Impact of the Liability-Asset Ratio on Industrial SOE Profitability, 1995	150
Table 5.4	Impact of the Liability-Asset Ratio on Industrial SOE Profitability, 1993–2000	153
Table 5.5	Impact of the Liability-Asset Ratio on Industrial SOE Profitability after Accounting for Endogeneity, 1993–2000	156
Table 6.1	Profitability of Industrial SOEs, 1978–2000	166
Table 6.2	Profitability of Industrial Non-SOEs, 1978–2000	167
Table 6.3	Financial Performance of Enterprises with Independent Accounting System at the Township Level and Above, 1995	171
Table 6.4	Financial Performance of SOEs and Other Ownership Groups within the Directly Reporting Industrial Enterprises, 1996–2000	172

Table 6.5	Profitable vs. Loss-making Industrial SOEs and Non-SOEs in Five Provinces, 1998–2000	179
Table 6.6	Sales-related Taxes	181
Table 6.7	Circulation Taxes and Capital Intensity of SOEs vs. Non-SOEs across Industrial Sectors	182
Table 6.8	Capital Intensity	187
Table 6.9	Adjusting SOE Profitability to Match Non-SOEs' Capital Intensity and Circulation Tax Rates	189
Table 7.1	Availability of Data on Industrial SOE Profitability	199
Table 7.2	Industrial SOE Profitability across Sectors and Provinces, 1986–2000	202
Table 7.3	Degree of Monopolistic Pricing Power and Industrial SOE Profitability	203
Table 7.4	Profitability across Size and Ownership Level of Industrial SOEs, 1995	209
Table 7.5	Correlation Coefficients of Industrial SOE Profitability across Ownership and Size, Selected Provinces 1993–2000	212
Table 7.6	Patterns of Province-wide Industrial SOE Profit per Unit of Equity, 1993–2000	214
Table 7.7	Patterns of Province-wide Industrial SOE Losses per Unit of Gross Profit, 1993–2000	215
Table 7.8	Patterns of Within-Province Industrial SOE Profitability, 1993–2000	222
Table 7.9	Industrial SOE Sectoral Profitability Clusters, 1993 through 1997	225
Table 7.10	Sectors with Highest and Lowest Industrial SOE Profitability, 1993–2000	226
Table 7.11	Performance of Industrial SOEs in Selected Sectors	228
Table 7.12	Sector-specific Industrial SOE Performance, 1997 and 2000	229
Table 7.13	Profitable vs. Loss-making Industrial SOEs, Selected Provinces 1998–2000	240
Table 8.1	Small Industrial SOEs across Provinces, 1997 vs. 2000	250

List of Figures

Figure 2.1	Enterprise Coverage in Industry Statistics	15
Figure 2.2	Value-added Shares	22
Figure 2.3	Share of Staff and Workers in Industrial SOEs as Share of Staff and Workers in (i) State-owned Material Production Sectors, and in (ii) All State-owned Units	25
Figure 2.4	Profit and Loss Account	32
Figure 3.1	Profitability of Industrial SOEs, 1978–2000	61
Figure 3.2	Economic Cycles	66
Figure 3.3	Price Indices and Interest Rates	67
Figure 3.4	Industrial SOE Market Share and Price Liberalization	68
Figure 3.5	Operating Surplus and Profit as Shares of Value-added	87
Figure 3.6	Value-added and Profit	88
Figure 4.1	Impact of Competition and Labor Remuneration on Profitability	100
Figure 4.2	Impact of Competition on Industrial SOE Losses per Unit of Gross Profit across Sectors, 1995 vs. 1986	109
Figure 4.3	Impact of Competition on Industrial SOE Losses Per Unit of Gross Profit across Provinces, 1995 vs. 1986	110
Figure 5.1	Industrial SOE Liability-Asset Ratios and Profitability across Sectors, 1995	132
Figure 5.2	Linking the Liability-Asset Ratio to Profitability Measures	145
Figure 6.1	Non-SOE Profitability Divided by SOE Profitability	168

1
Introduction

While the reform of industrial state-owned enterprises (SOEs) gave cause to muted optimism only a few years ago, by the end of the 1990s the view of industrial SOE reform both in and outside China was predominantly pessimistic.

In 1994, Thomas Rawski (1994a, p. 50) struck a positive note when he concluded that "the initial outcome of China's reform efforts shows that state firms burdened with all the trappings of socialist planning can be moved in the direction of market-oriented and entrepreneurial behavior." By 1998, however, Jeffrey Sachs (1998, pp. 13 and 19) argued that "at the center of the nation's economy, the large enterprises are mostly money-losing, protected, and rarely subject to judgment. Now China has reached the stage where it cannot delay the process any longer because there are too many problems. The losses are too great; the financial loss resulting from the money-losing state sector is too serious." And "in the long run for state enterprise reform, China must go along the way of privatization, and I think history is moving in that direction." Nicholas Lardy (1998, p. 22) concluded tentatively on the question of if the economic performance of the state sector had improved "that reforms to date have failed in large portions of the state-owned sector and that their ultimate success will depend on the willingness of the Chinese Communist Party to embrace privatization."

Chinese policy makers also saw the urgent need for reform, albeit not for privatization. While industrial SOE reform has been an ongoing process since 1978, President and Chinese Communist Party General Secretary Jiang

Zemin at the 15th Party Congress in September 1997 announced a three-year reform program to improve the financial performance of SOEs.

Efficiency May Be an Interesting Concept ...

The pessimistic Western view of China's SOEs is supported by findings that efficiency in China's industrial SOEs is stagnating. An initial series of production function estimations indicated that there was little total factor productivity growth in the early 1980s. Later production function estimations revealed high total factor productivity growth in the mid- and late 1980s, but total factor productivity growth of industrial SOEs gradually fell behind that of enterprises under other ownership forms in many of these estimations. By the late 1990s, it became accepted wisdom that after an initial boost to total factor productivity when industrial reform started in the mid-1980s, SOE efficiency levels had begun to stagnate. More and more studies found zero or negative total factor productivity growth, especially in the later reform years.[1]

Total factor productivity is of interest for two reasons. First, in neoclassical growth theory, changes in total factor productivity together with factor accumulation explain economic growth; high total factor productivity growth, *ceteris paribus*, leads to high economic growth. With total factor productivity often interpreted as technological progress (or efficiency), the development of total factor productivity in industrial SOEs over time reveals the capability of industrial SOEs to innovate. Second, a comparison of total factor productivity growth in industrial SOEs with that in industrial non-SOEs reveals which ownership group achieves a higher degree of technological progress.

While these may be interesting research issues, the method of analysis

---

[1] Examples of total factory productivity studies, conducted using a variety of datasets and covering different time periods, are Chen Kuan et al. (1988), David Dollar (1990), Xiao Geng (1991), Gary Jefferson, Thomas Rawski, and Zheng Yuxin (1992 and 1996), Robert McGuckin et al. (1992), Theodore Groves et al. (1994), Gregory Chow (1994), Wing-Thye Woo et al. (1994), Vincent Mok (1996), F.C. Perkins (1996), Huang Yiping and Ron Duncan (1997a), Martin Raiser (1997a), Kong Xiang, Robert Marks, and Wan Guanghua (1999), James Laurenceson and Joseph Chai (2000), Gary Jefferson et al. (2000), Zhang Anming, Zhang Yimin, and Ronald Zhao (2001), and Sean Dougherty and Robert McGuckin (2001).

has its limitations. Measuring total factor productivity typically involves the assumption of the existence of an *aggregate* production function, which in a particular functional form comes with further assumptions, such as constant labor and capital shares and constant returns to scale. The fact that different ownership groups could be operating in administratively separated product categories has not received any attention. Total factor productivity itself does not necessarily reflect technological progress; all it does is capture changes in output that cannot be attributed to factor accumulation, usually the accumulation of labor and capital.

... But It Is Profitability That Matters

In contrast, profitability has direct real-world relevance. Profitability is crucial for enterprise survival. Losses immediately reduce an enterprise's net worth. In an SOE, this implies that the government is losing its assets. It may also mean that new capital injections by the government are necessary for the enterprise to survive; continued losses in the absence of new capital contributions lead to insolvency. Bankruptcies invariably damage the state banks' balance sheets when SOE debts cannot be recovered.

Enterprises with a low or even negative level of profitability, even while still solvent, may furthermore run into numerous difficulties due solely to their level of profitability. For example, banks could be reluctant to lend to loss-making SOEs in anticipation that these SOEs will one day turn insolvent and that their outstanding loans would not be fully recovered. A credit crunch may affect an SOE's current production and thus accelerate its profitability decline. Similarly, suppliers would likely be reluctant to supply inputs on credit.

In an economy with a poorly developed system of financial intermediation, profit accumulation is a major source of funding for expansion. In China, approximately one-half of industrial SOE investment is financed through internal enterprise funds. Enterprises with low profitability may be in urgent need of innovation. But if these low-profitability enterprises are severely constrained in their access to external funding, much if not all of their investment in innovation must be financed through their own funds. Given their low profitability, these funds are unlikely to be sufficient. In short, low profitability may lead to a vicious cycle of deteriorating financial performance.

Low-profitability enterprises may furthermore quickly lose their best employees. Plummeting employee morale could lead to asset stripping in expectation of future bankruptcy. Foreign investors with new technologies that could improve the firm's profitability may be difficult to attract. Capital- and technology-intensive products of a firm with low profitability may be shunned if potential purchasers fear that after-sales services and the supply of spare parts are in doubt.

Industrial SOE profitability then matters in that its particular value has implications for industrial SOEs' ability to maintain normal production or increase their size of operation. If the decline in industrial SOE profitability is the result of one-time transition effects and if the process of transition is close to completion, low industrial SOE profitability may be less of a problem than if the decline in profitability is due to a systemic deficiency of industrial SOEs. The causes of the long-term decline in SOE profitability need to be understood.

Furthermore, second, the industrial SOE profitability level is of interest, similar to the case of total factor productivity in efficiency analysis, when profitability levels differ across ownership forms. Differences in the profitability levels of enterprises under different ownership forms have potential implications for government policies regarding SOEs. Before judging the government's policies, the characteristics of the differences in profitability need to be understood.

Third, within the aggregate industrial SOE sector, different groups of industrial SOEs may enjoy different profitability levels. Identification of the patterns, and an understanding of what causes them, has direct implications for SOE reform policies as well as investment strategies. Thus, from an economy-wide perspective, a high profitability level in a particular industrial sector signals investment opportunities to investors. But if profitability levels are not determined by the market, later changes in government policy could have the consequence that much of the earlier investment has, in the long run, been mis-allocated.

Finally, recent industrial SOE reforms provide some information on if the decline in industrial SOE profitability can be reversed. Upcoming industrial SOE reforms provide some indication of the likely aggregate performance of industrial SOEs in the future. But closer inspection of the management arrangements in SOEs reveals a number of shortcomings that may have persistently negative effects on industrial SOE profitability.

Profitability has no place in neat mathematical production function formulations. The widespread assumption of perfect competition implies that economic profit must be zero, i.e., that accounting profitability must, once adjusted for risk, be comparable to the return on other investments (such as bank deposits). Perfect competition does not allow for differences in profitability levels across enterprises, ownership forms, or industrial sectors.

Efficiency is vaguely related to profitability. Total factor productivity measures the quantitative change in output not accounted for by quantitative changes in inputs, where "quantitative" implies monetary values expressed in base-year prices. In total factor productivity analysis, the range of inputs is limited and actual estimation involves a range of assumptions. The same inputs that are used in total factor productivity analysis also affect profitability, but, in the case of profitability analysis, the price effects are included. Furthermore, the profit and loss account of industrial SOEs allows the identification of *all* immediate determinants of industrial SOE profitability through an identity. No assumptions are required beyond the definition of profit and profitability. Profitability is thus the more comprehensive measure. An enterprise may be highly efficient compared to other enterprises, or its efficiency may increase rapidly over time, but if it is not profitable, it is unlikely to survive.[2]

Industrial SOE Profitability in the Literature

The literature on the profitability of China's industrial SOEs invariably deals with the decline over time and the current low level of industrial SOE profitability.[3] Typically, the decline in industrial SOE profitability is noted

---

[2] In contrast to total factor productivity, furthermore, profitability data are readily available. Profit is the residual of sales revenue in the profit and loss account once various cost items have been deducted. Profitability equals profit divided by equity. Equity is the residual in the balance sheet once liabilities have been subtracted from assets. Total factor productivity not only needs to be estimated, but the variables needed for the estimation are beset by a host of difficulties. For a discussion on some of the data shortcomings in total factor productivity estimations, see Gary Jefferson et al. (1999), pp. 131–136.

or the profitability of industrial SOEs compared with that of industrial enterprises under other ownership forms. An attempt is made to explain the decline in industrial SOE profitability or the difference in the profitability of industrial SOEs compared with non-SOEs, and recommendations for further industrial SOE reform are offered. Statistical testing of explanations is rare.

The quantitative analysis that goes beyond correlations tends to focus on two explanations of the decline in the profitability of industrial SOEs over time. The first explanation is that the increase in competition during the reform period has driven down monopoly rents in the state sector. The alternative explanation is "excessive" labor remuneration. These two hypotheses are viewed as competing with each other, but the literature has not reached a final verdict that resolves the discussion.[4]

Much of the quantitative analysis in the literature is furthermore based on survey data. None of the surveys is reported to have been based on a nationwide random sample, and, where details on the sampled enterprises are provided, they attest to a narrow sectoral or regional focus; the number of years covered by surveys tends to be small. In contrast, balance sheet as well as profit and loss account data are now available for the years 1993 through 2000 on the aggregate of nationwide industrial SOEs as well as the aggregate of industrial SOEs in individual industrial sectors, provinces, and industrial sectors within provinces.[5] A more limited set of data is available for the earlier reform years from 1978 through 1992.

One theoretical issue that underlies much of the discussion of industrial SOE profitability (or productivity) in the literature is corporate governance problems. The agency problem in the case of China's SOEs is twofold:

---

[3] See, for example, Barry Naughton (1992), Song Qun et al. (1992), Gary Jefferson and Thomas Rawski (1995), Fan Gang and Wing-Thye Woo (1996), Joseph Chai and George Docwra (1997), Frances Perkins (1999), Gary Jefferson et al. (1999), Huang Yiping, Wing-Thye Woo, and Ron Duncan (1999), Zhu Tian (1999), Dic Lo (1999), Yuk-shing Cheng and Dic Lo (2002), and Zhang Anming, Zhang Yimin, and Ronald Zhao (2002).

[4] See, for example, Huang Yiping and Ron Duncan (1997b and 1999) or Martin Raiser (1997a); these authors base their regressions on enterprise-specific survey data. The conclusions are contradictory in that the former favor excessive labor remuneration, and the latter decides in favor of competition.

[5] A rare example of the use of (limited) profit and loss account data in the literature is Robert Ash and He Liping (1998).

managers act as agents of government bureaucrats, and government bureaucrats act as agents of the state. In practice, control mechanisms are lacking in both instances, and incentive mechanisms for the agents are poor or non-existent. Under the alternative arrangement of private ownership, the owner is legally entitled to any residual income and thus has a powerful motivation to maximize long-run profits. One obvious remedy for industrial SOE corporate governance problems is radical property rights reform.[6]

Edward Steinfeld (1998) argues that a property rights perspective is not appropriate in studying China because property rights in China are too dispersed (and potentially held by the wrong institutions) and because relevant institutions such as functioning property rights markets are still lacking. Without such institutions, the restructuring of property rights as envisaged by the 1993 company law remains for the most part meaningless. Edward Steinfeld therefore suggests an alternative analytical approach that focuses on the softness of the budget constraint. He argues that while reforms cut government departments lose and decentralized property rights, accountability was not decentralized; the top priority of SOE reform should therefore be the introduction of hard budget constraints across the economy. Cao Yuanzheng, Qian Yingyi, and Barry Weingast (1999) similarly stress the importance of a hard budget constraint and point out that increasingly hard budget constraints are forcing local governments to resort to a variety of measures, including privatization, to resolve the problems of their loss-making enterprises.[7]

Like Edward Steinfeld, Justin Lin, Cai Fang, and Li Zhou (1998, 1999, 2001) note that reform has led to a decentralization of property rights with an increase in enterprise autonomy. They view the agency problem in the case of Chinese SOEs as particularly severe due to three SOE idiosyncrasies. The SOEs' differential social responsibilities, their current capital intensity,

---

[6] For the point on the twofold agency problem, see Zhu Tian (1999). Other literature focusing on corporate governance aspects include Qian Yingyi (1994 and 1996), World Bank (1997), On Kit Tam (1999), OECD (2000), and Stoyan Tenev and Zhang Chunlin (2002).

[7] David Li and Liang Minsong (1998) explain the soft budget constraint through three, primarily corporate governance deficiencies: politicians' influence on enterprises' behavior, creditors' lack of information and lack of commitment not to refinance bad projects, and insiders' or managers' control rights.

and the remaining price distortions that many SOE products face all make the playing field uneven. SOEs with low profitability invariably will point out that they are disadvantaged in comparison with other enterprises due to different, historically given starting conditions. Because of the information asymmetry between enterprises and owners, the state finds it impossible to distinguish between policy-induced losses and losses due to managerial incompetence. The major task facing Chinese reformers is therefore to make the playing field level.[8]

The Issues in This Book

I do not question the plausibility of the corporate governance issues advanced in the literature to explain the decline in industrial SOE profitability and industrial SOEs' poor performance relative to industrial non-SOEs. Rather, I attempt to use the copious amounts of quantitative data now available to investigate the causes of the decline in industrial SOE profitability, the reasons for the profitability gap between industrial SOEs and non-SOEs, and the characteristics of industrial SOE profitability today.

Numerical data and historical facts tell their own story about the factors that led to the decline in industrial SOE profitability, the factors that determine the performance of industrial SOEs compared with enterprises under other ownership forms, as well as the factors that shape profitability patterns across industrial SOEs. Governance issues, including softness of the budget constraints and SOE idiosyncrasies, are relevant and might be driving many of those factors that are identified in this book as crucial in answering the questions on the trends and patterns of industrial SOE profitability. But these broad theoretical arguments miss many of the finer details that directly explain the trends and patterns of industrial SOE (and non-SOE) profitability in China.

Once these profitability trends and patterns are better understood, and

---

[8] Chen Aimin (1998), in a case study of six SOEs in Chongqing, also elaborates further on the importance of the differential burdens imposed on SOEs through their social responsibilities (as well as on other corporate governance problems). The industrial SOE idiosyncrasies are widely noted across the literature but rarely investigated in further detail.

once the 1998–2000 industrial SOE reform program has been evaluated, the corporate governance issues discussed in the literature appear to lose some of their importance. Perhaps they are not that important in the analysis of the financial performance of China's industrial SOEs, after all, or not that important any more as in the earlier reform years. Focusing all attention on one of the corporate governance issues may not be that fruitful in explaining what is happening on the ground in China.

This book is divided into two parts. The three chapters in the first part explore and explain the decline in industrial SOE profitability over time. The three chapters in the second part focus on industrial SOE profitability in the most recent years. The following chapter, Chapter 2, which precedes the first part of the book, clarifies a number of data issues and defines the key variables used in this book.

Chapter 3 makes full use of industrial SOE profit and loss account data to reveal how changes in individual accounting items led to the changes in residual profit over time. The pattern of the decline is far from regular, inviting investigation into the causes of the irregularities. Since accounting profit may not be the best measure of industrial SOE performance, an alternative indicator in the form of operating surplus (based on the national income accounts) is also constructed and its time trend is compared to that of profit.

Chapter 4 investigates the two main, alternative hypotheses in the literature that purport to explain the decline in industrial SOE profitability, namely the hypothesis of a decline in monopoly rents as enterprises under other ownership forms gained market share over time vs. the alternative hypothesis of excessive labor remuneration. Two decades of data and a few insights into the logical relationship between variables allow the discussion to be resolved.

Chapter 5 examines the more recent claim, mainly by Chinese policy makers, that industrial SOEs' rapidly increasing debt burden during the reform period translates into low profitability. Theoretically, the causality can have either sign, positive or negative, depending on the assumptions chosen. Empirical analysis controlling for the endogeneity of profitability is able to identify the sign of the causality.

The second part of the book asks three different questions about industrial SOE profitability in recent years. Do non-state industrial enterprises outperform industrial SOEs, and if so, why? What are the patterns of industrial SOE profitability across different industrial SOEs? What are the most recent industrial SOE reform measures, and have they been successful?

Chapter 6 compares the profitability of industrial SOEs to the profitability of enterprises under other ownership forms. At first sight, the performance of industrial non-SOEs, especially of private enterprises, is clearly superior to that of industrial SOEs. Yet, upon closer inspection, the differences in profitability can be explained by just two factors, which in turn can be traced to historical facts and policy preferences.

Chapter 7 explores the characteristics of industrial SOE profitability today by distinguishing among four characteristics of industrial SOEs: their size, ownership level, sectoral classification, and location. In a perfectly competitive market, none of these characteristics should matter. Profit rates, adjusted for risk, should equalize across these characteristics. Yet, in China they do not. Some characteristics are more conducive to high profitability than are others.

Chapter 8 presents and evaluates the most recent industrial SOE reform measures, in particular the 1998–2000 three-year SOE reform program. While improving industrial SOE profitability — one of the main reform objectives — has been somewhat successful, the overall process of industrial SOE reform is still incomplete and ongoing. The reform process is increasingly turning to narrow governance issues, without, however, being able to resolve a number of inconsistencies.[9]

The conclusions summarize the findings. Based on the findings, first, the implications for property rights reform are explored. Second, the driving factors behind industrial SOE reform over the past two decades are identified and evaluated regarding their implications for future industrial SOE reforms. Finally, corporate governance issues are revisited in light of the findings presented in this book.

---

[9] This book does not offer a historical overview over industrial SOE reform during the reform period since 1978, but refers to historical issues as needed. For historical overviews, see, for example, Gene Tidrick and Chen Jiyuan (1987), Li Hong (1990), William Byrd (1992), Yu-shan Wu (1994), Donald Hay et al. (1994), and Gao Shangquan (1996, Chapter 5). For case studies, which illustrate some of the historical issues, see, for example, William Byrd (1992), Edward Steinfeld (1998), or Chen Aimin (1998). Yi-min Lin (2001) interweaves topic-focused analysis with case studies.

Acknowledgments

A number of passages, accounting for about one-third of this book, have previously appeared in four different journal articles. These four articles are: "Identifying the Patterns of Profitability Across Chinese State-owned Enterprises: Which Industrial State-owned Enterprises in China Are Profitable?," *Journal of Asian Business 17*, no. 2 (2001): 33–62; "The Impact of the Liability-Asset Ratio on Profitability in China's Industrial State-owned Enterprises," *China Economic Review 13*, no. 1 (2002): 1–26; "The Impact of Competition and Labor Remuneration on Profitability in China's Industrial State-owned Enterprises," *Journal of Contemporary China 11*, no. 32 (Aug. 2002): 515–38; "Long Live China's State-owned Enterprises: Deflating the Myth of Poor Financial Performance," *Journal of Asian Economics 13*, no. 4 (July/August 2002): 493–529.

The book has profited from extensive comments by anonymous reviewers of the journal articles in the first instance and from a round of consolidation when the book was written. The original passages in the journal articles have been significantly rewritten, rearranged, and updated. A number of arguments were thoroughly rethought and then altered or developed further. All quantitative analyses extend through 2000, the most recent year for which detailed, systematic data are available, with a few occasional data points for 2001 and early 2002.

While helpful comments were received from numerous fellow researchers and seminar participants, my greatest debt is due to Thomas P. Lyons and Henry Wan, Jr., for pointers in the right direction when I needed them and for their frequent encouragements to complete this book.

I am also grateful to five research assistants who at various points of time have helped with data collection and data entry. These are Billy Kwan Hoi Shun, Lam Lam, Michael Lee Kar Wah, Chung Siu Fung, and Choi Kai Hang. Dr. Virginia Unkefer of the Hong Kong University of Science and Technology's grants administration has made this book readable. Juliet Ley Chin Lee of World Scientific Publishing Company has been a very patient and highly supportive editor. The Hong Kong University of Science & Technology has provided funding for some of the research through a Direct Allocation Grant.

2
Data

This chapter explains the enterprise classification system for China's industry, defines profit and profitability, and documents the main data sources. The first section identifies industrial SOEs as a sub-category of all industrial enterprises reporting directly to China's statistical departments; directly reporting industrial enterprises in turn are a sub-category of all industrial enterprises. The second section defines "profit" and explores the various choices of profitability indicators. The third section lists the major data sources. Three appendices document how missing values on key variables used in the following chapters were estimated.

The Directly Reporting Industrial SOEs

Defining the Object of Analysis

Detailed output, balance sheet, and profit and loss account data are available for industrial SOEs with *independent* accounting system. Data on industrial SOEs with *dependent* accounting system cover the industrial activities of units that are not classified as *industrial* firms but, for example, as constructions firms. The gross output value data that are available for all industrial activities of SOEs show that the industrial SOEs with independent accounting system capture more than 95% of all industrial output by SOEs. In 1978, industrial SOEs with independent accounting system produced 96.44% of the industrial gross output value of all state-owned units, and in 1997 95.97%; this share remained constant at 96% to 97% in the two decades between 1978 and 1997.[10] Since no separate profit and loss account data are available on industrial activities in non-industrial units, the focus in what follows is on industrial SOEs with independent accounting system only. The limitation to industrial SOEs with independent accounting system is common practice in the literature.[11]

Industrial SOEs with independent accounting system constitute one ownership category within the larger group of directly reporting industrial enterprises, i.e., those industrial enterprises that report regularly to the statistical bureaus and on which data are published annually in the *Statistical Yearbook*. Until 1997, the directly reporting industrial enterprises comprised all "industrial enterprises with independent accounting system at the township level and above." By definition, SOEs are organized at the county level or above; all industrial SOEs with independent accounting system are thus included in the industrial enterprises with independent accounting system at the township level and above. Non-state industrial enterprises ("industrial non-SOEs") then comprise all industrial enterprises with independent accounting system at the township level and above that are not state-owned. They thus do not include the few industrial non-SOEs with dependent accounting system that operate as part of a non-state non-industrial enterprise organized at township level or above, or as part of a non-state industrial enterprise which itself is not organized at the township level or above. Through the restriction on the level of jurisdiction, they also exclude self-employed individuals (*getihu*) working in industry and the collective-owned industrial enterprises on village level (Figure 2.1).

The industry statistics provide detailed output, balance sheet, and profit and loss account data on the aggregate of industrial enterprises with independent accounting system at the township level and above, as well as on the sub-categories SOEs, collective-owned enterprises, foreign-funded enterprises, enterprises with investment by Hong Kong, Macao and Taiwanese entrepreneurs (HKMT enterprises), and, since 1993, shareholding enterprises (i.e., shareholding companies, the aggregate of

---

[10] Calculated from *Seventeen Years of Reform*, p. 146; *Statistical Yearbook 1998*, pp. 435 and 454; *1997*, p. 413. Beginning with 1998, no data are available on all industrial SOEs.
[11] See, for example, Gary Jefferson and Thomas Rawski (1994), Nicholas Lardy (1998), or Gary Jefferson et al. (2000).

limited liability companies and stock companies). The value-added of these sub-categories in 1995 fell 1.39% short of the total; further data (available for 1995 only) show that this residual comprises private enterprises (0.26%), i.e., individual-owned enterprises with more than seven employees, domestic joint operation enterprises (1.01%), i.e., joint ventures between two or more domestic enterprises, and a category "others" (0.12%).[12]

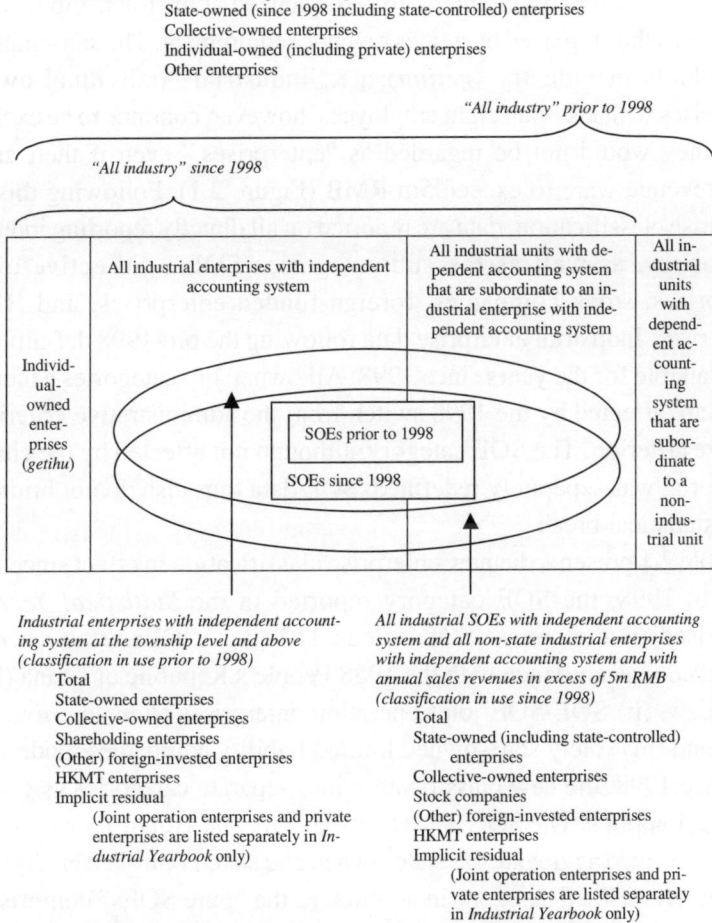

Figure 2.1 Enterprise Coverage in Industry Statistics

---

[12] For the breakdown of the residual, see *Industrial Census 1995*, Vol. 1, p. 47.

In 1998, statistical reporting on industrial enterprises with independent accounting system at the township level and above ceased. Detailed output, balance sheet, and profit and loss account data have since 1998 been reported in the *Statistical Yearbook* for a newly defined group of directly reporting industrial enterprises, the group of "industrial SOEs with independent accounting system and non-state industrial enterprises with independent accounting system and with annual sales revenue in excess of 5m RMB."[13] The administrative requirement, to be organized at the township level and above, was thus replaced by a sales revenue requirement. The self-employed individuals in industry (*getihu*), i.e., industrial "individual-owned" enterprises with less than eight employees, however, continue to be excluded since they would not be regarded as "enterprises," even if their annual sales revenue were to exceed 5m RMB (Figure 2.1). Following this new enterprise classification, data are reported on all directly reporting industrial enterprises, as well as the sub-categories SOEs, collective owned enterprises, stock companies, foreign-funded enterprises, and HKMT enterprises. Industrial enterprise data following the pre-1998 definition are not available for the years since 1998. All ownership categories except the SOEs are affected by the 1998 switch from the administrative criterion to the size criterion. The SOE category, although not affected by the changes in criteria, was separately redefined. SOE data thus also do not bridge the 1998 statistical break.

Table 2.1 presents the new enterprise classification in effect since 1998. Prior to 1998, the SOE category reported in the *Statistical Yearbook* comprised (i) the "pure" SOEs (code 110), i.e., SOEs established and registered in accordance with the 1988 People's Republic of China (PRC) SOE Law, (ii) SOE-SOE joint operation enterprises (*lianying qiye*, code 141), and (iii) solely state-owned limited liability companies (code 151).

Since 1998, the new classification into separate categories as given in Table 2.1 applies. The SOE data reported in the *Statistical Yearbook* cover a newly defined aggregate of "state-owned and state-controlled enterprises." This newly defined category in addition to the "pure SOEs" comprises all

---

[13] The Renminbi (RMB) is China's currency unit. The term "yuan" is a numeral and was omitted throughout. Thus "5 million units of RMB" is rendered as "5m RMB."

Table 2.1 Enterprise Categorization (with data for Shaanxi Province, 2000)

Code	Category	2000 Number of ent.	2000 VA (b RMB)	2000 VA (%)	1998 VA (%)
100	**Domestic enterprises**	2427	36.47	88.76	88.37
110	SOEs	1353	18.89	45.97	60.64
120	Collective-owned enterprises	429	2.02	4.93	7.49
130	Employee shareholding companies	98	0.37	0.90	1.27
140	Joint operation enterprises	32	0.20	0.49	0.71
141	State-owned	14	0.09	0.22	0.23
142	Collective-owned	10	0.07	0.18	0.35
143	State- and collective-owned	6	0.03	0.07	0.11
149	Others	2	0.01	0.02	0.02
150	Limited liability companies	233	4.93	11.99	10.76
151	Solely state-invested	28	1.68	4.09	4.23
159	Others	205	3.25	7.90	6.53
160	Stock companies	124	9.24	22.47	5.95
170	Private enterprises	158	0.83	2.01	1.56
171	Private sole proprietorships	67	0.28	0.67	0.52
172	Private partnerships	14	0.07	0.16	0.35
173	Private limited liability companies	66	0.40	0.98	0.65
174	Private stock companies	11	0.08	0.19	0.04
190	Other enterprises				
200	**HKMT-invested enterprises**	62	1.93	4.69	5.35
210	Joint equity ventures	51	0.74	1.80	2.32
220	Contractual joint ventures	2	1.02	2.48	2.54
230	Wholly HKMT-owned enterprises	7	0.15	0.36	0.45
240	HKMT stock companies	2	0.02	0.05	0.04
300	**Foreign-invested enterprises**	64	2.69	6.55	6.28
310	Chinese-foreign equity joint ventures	58	2.67	6.50	6.13
320	Chinese-foreign contractual joint ventures	5	0.02	0.04	0.11
330	Wholly foreign-owned enterprises	1	0.00	0.01	0.03
340	Foreign-invested stock companies				0.00
Total		2427	41.09		
	"State-owned and state-controlled enterprises" (separately reported)	1633	32.67	79.50	77.61

Ent.: Enterprises.
VA: Value-added.
Sources: NBS (1999), p. 11; *Shaanxi tongji nianjian 1999*, pp. 322f.; *2001*, pp. 319f., 324f.

shareholding companies (limited liability companies and stock companies) in which the state has a controlling share; data on these shareholding companies are included in full. The post-1997 SOE definition furthermore includes data on all other enterprises in which the state has a share (including those companies in which the state has a less than controlling share); data on these enterprises are included in proportion to the state's equity share, where the share of legal persons in paid-in capital is ignored for the purpose of the calculation.[14] (SOE-SOE joint operation enterprises fall into the latter category and thus continue to be fully included in the reported SOE data.)

The following equation summarizes the coverage issues for industrial SOEs.

"SOEs" following the post-1997 definition (in publications often but not always called "state-owned and state-controlled enterprises") =
    pre-1998 definition SOEs, i.e.,
        pure SOEs (since 1998 code 110),
        SOE-SOE joint operation enterprises (code 141), and
        solely state-owned limited liability companies (code 151),
+ all (other) shareholding companies (i.e., limited liability companies and stock companies) in which the state has a controlling share,
+ all (other) enterprises or shareholding companies in which the state has a stake, with the economic data counted towards the SOE category in proportion to the state's equity share, where the share

---

[14] For details on the 1998 statistical break, see Carsten Holz and Yi-min Lin (2001a). For comparison, the number of industrial SOEs in 1997 was 74,388, while the number of state-owned and state-controlled enterprises in 1998 was 64,737; the average industrial SOE created value-added worth 12.35m RMB in 1997 (17.11m RMB for the revised SOE category in 1998), collected sales revenue of 37.62m RMB (51.85m RMB), and had average annual net fixed assets worth 32.95m RMB (49.26m RMB). The number of industrial enterprises with independent accounting system at the township level and above in 1997 was 468,506 (vs. 165,080 SOEs plus non-SOEs with independent accounting system and with annual sales revenue in excess of 5m RMB in 1998); the average industrial enterprise created value-added worth 4.23m RMB in 1997 (11.77m RMB in 1998), collected sales revenue of 13.54m RMB (38.86m RMB), and had average annual net fixed assets worth 8.49m RMB (26.74m RMB). The 1998 deflator for value-added of all industrial activities in China was negative 5.29% (*Statistical Yearbook 1998*, pp. 432f., 435; *1999*, pp. 55, 57, 432f., 435).

of legal persons in paid-in capital is ignored for the purpose of the calculation.[15]

The *Statistical Yearbook 1999* provides data on industrial SOE gross output value in 1996 and 1997 following the new classification. These revised 1996 and 1997 SOE gross industrial output value data can consequently be compared with such data following the pre-1998 classification.[16] The SOE gross industrial output value following the new classification exceeded SOE gross output value following the old classification by 27.54% in 1996 and by 23.91% in 1997 (*Statistical Yearbook 1998*, p. 433; 1999, p. 423).

The *Industrial Yearbook 2001* offers data on the newly defined SOE category "state-owned and state-controlled enterprises" as well as, separately, on pure SOEs. Only economy-wide data and only values for a very few variables are available on the pure SOEs. The 42,426 pure SOEs in 2000 accounted for 79.32% of the number of "state-owned and state-controlled enterprises" (53,489), 52.35% of the value-added, 59.17% of profit and taxes, and 29.76% of profit (*Industrial Yearbook 2001*, pp. 48f., 53).[17]

---

[15] The term "(other)" means that solely state-owned limited liability companies are not double-counted in the group of pre-1998 definition SOEs and then as shareholding companies in which the state has a controlling share; the same holds for the SOE-SOE joint operation enterprises vis-a-vis the enterprises in which the state has a stake.

[16] The comparison is complicated by the fact that in the table in which the yearbook provides SOE gross output values for 1996 and 1997 following the new classification, pre-1996 values cover all industrial SOEs regardless of type of accounting system, while the 1998 data cover only industrial SOEs with independent accounting system. It is therefore not clear whether the retrospectively revised 1996 and 1997 values cover all industrial SOEs regardless of type of accounting system, or only the industrial SOEs with independent accounting system (and those industrial SOEs with dependent accounting system that are part of industrial SOEs with independent accounting system). In the following, it is assumed that the retrospectively revised 1996 and 1997 gross output values cover all industrial SOEs regardless of type of accounting system.

[17] Some provincial statistical yearbooks offer detailed data on all individual categories (as listed in Table 2.1). This allows the construction of values on the SOE category as defined prior to 1998. For example, in Shaanxi Province in 2000, the pure SOEs accounted for 91.43% of the value-added of a reconstructed pre-1998 SOE category, SOE-SOE joint operation enterprises for 0.44%, and solely state-owned limited liability companies for 8.13% (see also Table 2.1). The contribution of SOE-SOE joint operation enterprises is invariably extremely small across the provinces for which the data are available, while the contribution of solely state-owned limited liability companies also tends to be in the single digit percentage range.

The *Statistical Yearbook 2001* is the only source that offers an extensive (but not complete) breakdown of the various ownership sub-categories for the two variables enterprise number and gross industrial output value, and only for the years 1999 and 2000. Table 2.2 presents the data. In 2000, pure SOEs accounted for only 23.53% of the gross industrial output value of all directly reporting industrial enterprises. SOE-SOE joint operation enterprises accounted for another 0.27%, and solely state-invested limited liability companies for 5.27%. Pre-1998 definition SOEs, i.e., the sum of these three values, thus accounted for 29.06% of gross industrial output value, compared to the 47.34% for the newly defined SOE category (of state-owned and state-controlled enterprises).

Due to the statistical break, comparisons of pre-1998 data with data since 1998 are not possible; but 1998 through 2000 data by themselves are comparable. If the SOEs are reported according to the 1998 definition, the various sub-categories of the directly reporting industrial enterprises are no longer mutually exclusive; the state's non-controlling share in non-state enterprises is now included in the SOE category, but also double-counted in whatever other category that enterprise is included in.[18]

In the following, the term "SOEs" will denote both the pre-1998 category of (industrial) SOEs as well as the since 1998 newly defined category of (industrial) SOEs. Whenever reference is made to pre-1998 data, the term "SOEs" follows the pre-1998 definition, and whenever reference is made to post-1997 data, the term "SOEs" follows the post-1997 definition. In the few deviations from this rule, the deviation is explicitly noted. The term "pure SOEs" is used to denote the SOEs registered in accordance with the 1988 PRC SOE Law (the category with code 110 in Table 2.1). Similarly, the term "industrial enterprises" (or "all enterprises") usually denotes the directly reporting industrial enterprises. In the few instances where it doesn't (such as in some of the following paragraphs), the full term "directly reporting industrial enterprises" is contrasted with "all industry."

---

[18] Because state-controlled companies are fully counted as SOEs, the aggregate size of SOEs is exaggerated. (For details on the 1997–1998 statistical break, see Carsten Holz and Yi-min Lin, 2001a).

Table 2.2 Directly Reporting Industrial Enterprises, 1999 and 2000

	Number of enterprises (in % of total)		Gross industrial output value (in % of total)	
	1999	2000	1999	2000
Domestic enterprises	83.44	82.54	73.93	72.61
(Pure) State-owned enterprises	31.26	26.05	30.56	23.53
Collective-owned enterprises	26.28	23.23	17.07	13.90
Employee shareholding companies	6.26	6.66	3.57	3.38
Joint operation enterprises	1.71	1.54	1.24	1.05
State-owned	0.29	0.26	0.31	0.27
Collective-owned	0.51	0.45	0.34	0.29
State- and collective-owned	0.67	0.59	0.44	0.34
Residual: Others	0.24	0.24	0.15	0.15
Limited liability companies	6.00	8.11	9.67	12.75
Sole state-invested	0.63	0.75	4.36	5.27
Residual: Others	5.37	7.36	5.31	7.48
Stock companies	2.76	3.12	7.22	11.78
Private enterprises	9.01	13.59	4.46	6.09
Other enterprises	0.15	0.23	0.15	0.13
HKMT(-invested) enterprises	9.74	10.12	12.37	12.34
Foreign-invested enterprises	6.82	7.34	13.70	15.05
Additional information:				
State-owned and state-controlled enterprises	37.83	32.84	48.92	47.34
Implicit: Pre-1998 definition SOEs	32.18	27.06	35.23	29.06
Implicit: Difference between above two	5.65	5.78	13.70	18.28

The total number of directly reporting industrial enterprises in 1999 was 162,033, and their gross industrial output value was 7270.704b RMB. The corresponding values for 2000 are 162,885 and 8567.366b RMB.

"State-owned and state-controlled enterprises" in the third-to-last row of the table is the newly defined (post-1997 definition) SOE category. The last row of the table represents the difference between the newly defined SOE category and the pre-1998 definition SOE category.

Source: Statistical Yearbook 2001, p. 401.

Industrial SOEs in Perspective

Data are available to contrast industrial SOEs with all SOEs, on the one hand, and with all directly reporting industrial enterprises, on the other hand. All directly reporting industrial enterprises can also be compared to all of industry. To start from the aggregate, Figure 2.2 compares the value-added of the directly reporting industrial enterprises to that of all of industry.[19]

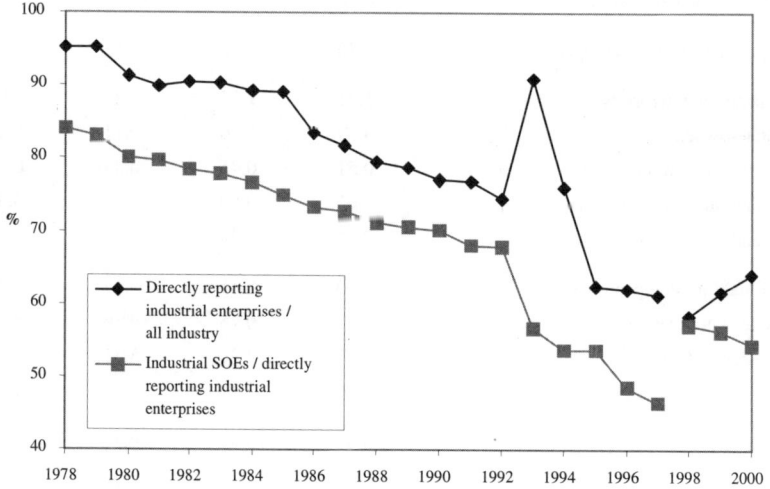

The definition of directly reporting industrial enterprises changed in 1998 (see text).
Sources: See appendix to this chapter; *Statistical Yearbook 2001*, p. 49.

Figure 2.2   Value-added Shares (in %)

While the directly reporting industrial enterprises in 1978 accounted for more than 90% of industrial value-added, by 1999 this share had sunk to about 60%. A similar pattern holds for the share of industrial SOE gross output value in the gross output value of all industry, not shown in the

---

[19] For all industry, data are only available on value-added, gross output value, number of enterprises, and employment.

figure.[20] Much of the decline in the output share value of the directly reporting industrial enterprises is explained by the growth of the group of self-employed individuals in industry ("individual-owned industrial enterprises") and those private industrial enterprises not included in the group of directly reporting industrial enterprises. In 1999, all individual-owned and private enterprises in industry together accounted for 18.18% of the gross output value of industry (*Statistical Yearbook 2000*, p. 409); no separate value-added data on these two ownership groups are available.[21]

The 15% rise in the share of value-added data of the directly reporting industrial enterprises in 1993, with a subsequent and similar fall in 1994, appears highly questionable. The concept of value-added was introduced in 1993 only, with value-added data on the directly reporting industrial enterprises (and their subcategory industrial SOEs) available since 1992 (retrospectively). Enterprises may have experienced difficulties compiling data on this newly introduced variable in the early years. (Value-added data on the directly reporting industrial enterprises for the years prior to 1992 are estimates obtained as described in the appendix.)

The redefinition of the group of directly reporting industrial enterprises in 1998 ended the downward trend of the share of directly reporting industrial enterprises in the value-added of all industry. The replacement of the administrative criterion for inclusion by a size criterion implies that all industrial enterprises with independent accounting system and annual sales revenue in excess of 5m RMB are consistently captured. The slight increase in the share between 1998 and 2000 reflects relatively rapid growth in the average size of the directly reporting industrial enterprises.

Within the group of directly reporting industrial enterprises, the share of SOEs in the value-added of the directly reporting industrial enterprises fell from more than 80% in 1979 to only about 45% in 1997, but then recovered to 60% once the new rule on data aggregation took effect in 1998 (Figure 2.2). The share in gross industrial output value since 1983,

---

[20] Industrial gross output value has been revised and redefined over time, but these changes should affect the directly reporting industrial enterprises and all other industrial enterprises equally. (On such revisions and redefinitions, see Carsten Holz and Yi-min Lin, 2001b.)

[21] Only gross output value data and enterprise numbers are available for this group of individual-owned and private industrial enterprises. Year 2000 data are not available.

not shown in the figure, is always a few percentage points lower, but it follows the same time pattern. Industrial SOE value-added in 1993 appears to be less of an outlier than the value-added of all directly reporting industrial enterprises, since the ratio continues to drop rather than increase in 1993.

Industrial SOEs constitute only a small share of all state-owned units. A comparison between industrial SOEs and all state-owned units is only possible based on employment data. Figure 2.3 shows the number of staff and workers in state-owned industry as a share of the staff and workers in all state-owned units.[22] This share remained almost constant at about 40% between 1978 and 1997. In 1998, it fell to 30% when industrial staff and workers who were not actually in their posts, i.e., who were still attached to the enterprise but not working in the enterprise any more, were no longer included. Furthermore, the industrial SOE employment data after 1997 continue to follow the pre-1998 SOE definition, but many industrial SOEs have in recent years (particularly since 1998) adopted the "modern enterprise system," which usually implies the transition into a state-controlled shareholding company. The 1998–2000 employment data do not include employees in state-controlled shareholding companies, unless such firms were solely state-invested limited liability companies, and the data thus underestimate the true employment rates in state-owned and state-controlled industry.

---

[22] It is not clear whether the employment data on staff and workers that are available cover industrial enterprises with independent accounting system or industrial enterprises regardless of type of accounting system. The table in the *Statistical Yearbook* with employment data on all state-owned units includes figures for year-end industrial employment in 1996 and 1997 that exceed the annual average employment in industrial SOEs with independent accounting system in these years according to the *Industrial Yearbook* (*Statistical Yearbook 2000*, p. 126; *Industrial Yearbook 1998*, p. 81). With employment falling over the years, year-end data should be smaller than average annual data. The fact that they are not suggests that the employment data on staff and workers in state-owned units may cover industrial enterprises regardless of type of accounting system.

The term "staff and workers" in general refers to all persons drawing a salary from enterprises and institutions, but excludes retired persons who were rehired, teachers in self-organized (unofficial) schools, and foreigners (*Statistical Yearbook 2000*, p. 162).

All employment by state-owned units includes the staff and workers in such units as government agencies, the Party organization, and scientific research institutes. Industrial SOEs can also be compared to all state-owned material production units, which, besides industry, comprise agriculture, construction, geological prospecting and water conservancy, transportation and telecommunications, and commerce and catering.[23] Staff and workers in industrial state-owned units since 1978 account for 50–60% of employment in all state-owned material production units.

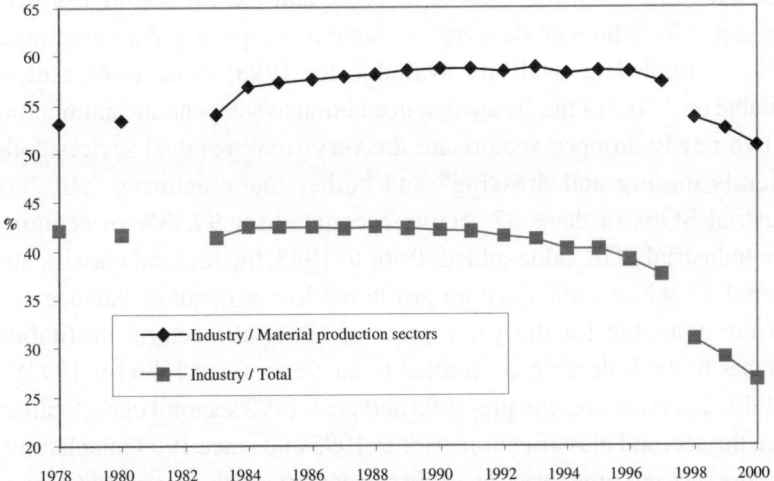

For 1979, 1981, and 1982, data are only available according to a different classification system. "Industrial SOEs" in all years follow the pre-1998 definition of industrial SOEs. Their staff and workers since 1998 exclude those staff and workers who are still part of the unit, but not actually engaged in any activity of the unit.
Sources: Statistical Yearbook 1994, pp. 94f.; 2000, pp. 126f.; 2001, pp. 118f.

Figure 2.3 Share of Staff and Workers in Industrial SOEs as Share of Staff and Workers in (i) State-owned Material Production Sectors, and in (ii) All State-owned Units (in %)

---

[23] Industry comprises (i) mining and quarrying, (ii) manufacturing, and (iii) electricity, gas, and water production and supply. Apart from employment in material production units, total employment in state-owned units also includes staff and workers in (i) social services, (ii) health care, sports and social welfare, (iii) education, culture and arts, radio, film and television, (iv) scientific research and technological services, (v) government agencies, Party agencies, and social organizations, and (vi) "other" units.

Sectoral and Regional Classification of Industrial SOEs

Aggregate data on industrial SOEs are available for the economy in total, with a further distinction by sector and by region (province) in most years. Detailed data according to sector are available since 1986. The sectoral classification in use during the period 1985 through 1992 covered 30 sectors, accounting for 94.36% of economy-wide SOE value-added in 1992. For the years 1993 through 1997, aggregate SOE data are available on 39 industrial sectors, accounting for 99.48% of economy-wide industrial SOE value-added in 1993, for 99.40% in 1995, and for 99.55% in 1997. The only sector for which no data are available is weapons and ammunition.

No sectoral data at all are available for 1998; since 1999, data are available on 37 out of the 40 sectors; in addition to weapons and ammunition, the two newly dropped sectors are the very small residual sectors "other minerals mining and dressing" and "other manufacturing." In 2000, industrial SOEs in these 37 sectors accounted for 99.53% of economy-wide industrial SOE value-added. Prior to 1985, the sectoral classification covered 13 sectors, but since no profit and loss account or balance sheet data are available for the years prior to 1986, all sectoral profitability analyses in the following are limited to the years since 1986 (or 1993).

Table 2.3 compares the pre-1993 and post-1992 sectoral classifications. Since the sectoral classification prior to 1993 and since 1993 match only in part, any sectoral time series analysis can cover only the years 1986 through 1992, and then, separately, 1993 through 1997. Due to the accounting reform in 1992, the variables on which data are available up through 1992 differ from those since 1993; the sectoral break conveniently occurs at the same time as the break in balance sheet variables. The statistical break in enterprise classification in 1998, furthermore, implies that the 1993–1997 data on industrial SOEs (or the directly reporting industrial enterprises) are not comparable to those of 1999–2000.

The 1995 industrial census offers detailed data on SOEs in 37 out of the 40 sectors (first-digit industry classification), as well as on their sub-sectors (second-digit and third-digit industry classification). These 37 industrial sectors in terms of value-added accounted for 99.26% of the nationwide SOE total in 1995; not included in the 37 sectors are the two very small sectors "other minerals mining and dressing" and "other manufacturing."

Detailed sub-sectoral data at the second-digit and third-digit classification level (but no sectoral data) are otherwise available only from *China's Industrial Markets Yearbook 1997* and *China Markets Yearbook* of 1999, 2000 and 2001 with data for the years 1995, 1996, 1998 and 2000; but the sub-sectoral coverage is incomplete, the number of variables very limited, and the enterprise classification also underwent the 1997–1998 statistical break.

Parallel to the sectoral classification, aggregate provincial-level SOE data are available in the *Statistical Yearbook* except for 1998. As in the sectoral case, a number of variables of interest in profitability analysis are covered since 1986. Hainan was first listed as a separate province from Guangdong in 1988 and Chongqing from Sichuan in 1997. In time series analysis of the years 1986 through 1992, Hainan is folded back into Guangdong for the years since 1988. Similarly, in time series analysis of the years 1993 through 1997, Chongqing is folded back into Sichuan.

The statistical yearbooks of most provinces also contain data on the 37 or 39 sectors of industry in the particular province. The sectoral classification is the same as nationwide, but the covered variables differ from province to province. Second- or third-digit sub-sectoral data for provinces are not available except in the individual provincial volumes of the 1995 industrial census.

The 1998 statistical break also occurs in the provincial statistical yearbooks, but not in all provinces immediately. The National Bureau of Statistics (NBS, prior to 1998 called the State Statistical Bureau) requires provincial statistical bureaus to provide industrial enterprise data according to the enterprise categories listed in Table 2.1. Data on the newly defined SOE category ("state-owned and state-controlled enterprises") since 1998 should be provided separately. While the *Statistical Yearbook* reports only on a subset of all major enterprise categories, some provincial statistical yearbooks report on all major enterprise categories, as well as on all sub-categories (as listed in Table 2.1 with some data for Shaanxi). The range of variables covered in some provincial statistical yearbooks since 1998 is excellent. Other provincial yearbooks drop all enterprise sub-categories, or even reduce the classification system to "state-owned economy," "collective-owned economy," and "others."

Table 2.3 Sectoral Shares in Industrial SOEs' Value-added (in %)

Sectoral classification since 1993		1993	1992
1	Coal Mining and Dressing	4.09	4.51
2	Petroleum and Natural Gas Extraction	7.75	6.95
3	Ferrous Metals Mining and Dressing	0.25	0.31
4	Nonferrous Metals Mining and Dressing	0.76	0.75
5	Non-metal Minerals Mining and Dressing	0.88	[a]0.40
6	Other Minerals Mining and Dressing	0.00	
7	Logging and Transport of Timber and Bamboo	1.15	1.18
8	Food Processing	4.37	
9	Foods Production	1.21	3.61
10	Beverages	2.34	2.67
11	Tobacco (Processing)	5.69	6.64
12	Textiles	5.37	5.76
13	Garments and Other Fiber Products	0.39	
14	Leather, Fur, Down and Related Products	0.32	
15	Timber, Bamboo, Cane, Palm Fiber & Straw Products	0.35	0.22
16	Furniture	0.06	0.06
17	Paper	0.60	
18	Printing and Record Media	0.88	
19	Cultural, Educational and Sports Goods	0.13	
20	Petroleum Processing and Coking	4.32	[b]4.19
21	Chemical Raw Materials and Products	5.45	[c]7.24
22	Medical and Pharmaceutical Products	1.82	
23	Chemical Products	0.82	[d]1.88
24	Rubber	0.79	1.17
25	Plastics	0.42	0.44
26	Non-metal Mineral Products	5.55	[e]4.93
27	Ferrous Metals Smelting and Pressing	14.06	10.03
28	Nonferrous Metals Smelting and Pressing	2.32	2.22
29	Metal Products	0.98	0.86
30	Ordinary Machinery	4.02	
31	Special Purpose Equipment	3.11	
32	Communication and Transport Equipment	5.67	4.92
33	Electric Equipment and Machinery	2.38	2.56
34	Electronic and Telecommunication Equipment	1.72	1.95
35	Instruments, Meters, Cultural & Office Machinery	0.67	0.65
36	Other Manufacturing	0.29	
37	Electricity, Steam and Hot Water Prod. & Supply	7.69	8.48
38	Gas Production and Supply	0.11	
39	Tap Water Production and Supply	0.69	0.71
40	Weapons and Ammunition	n.a.	n.a.
Additional sectors in sectoral classification of 1986-92			
	Fodder		0.24
	Coking, coal gas and coal products		0.18
	Machinery		8.63
Share of all sectors in total		99.48	94.36

Five 1986-92 categories have slightly different names: (a) construction materials and other non-metal minerals mining and dressing, (b) petroleum processing, (c) chemicals, (d) chemical fibers, (e) construction materials and other non-metal mineral products.
Sources: Statistical Yearbook 1993, p. 426; *1994*, p. 388.

Thus, while in some provincial statistical yearbooks data are available on pure SOEs, SOE-SOE joint operation enterprises, solely state-invested limited liability companies, and "state-owned and state-controlled enterprises," in others no data on "state-owned and state-controlled enterprises" are available. In many cases, it is not discernible whether the SOEs listed are only the pure SOEs (the most likely case) or include the SOE-SOE joint operation enterprises and solely state-invested limited liability companies.[24] But for many provinces, the difference between pure SOEs and the pre-98 definition SOEs is small. SOE-SOE joint operation enterprises across all provinces tend to be of very negligible size compared to the pure SOEs, while solely state-invested limited liability companies may produce value-added equivalent to a few percentage points of pure SOEs' value-added.

---

[24] The reasoning why the undefined SOEs are most likely only the pure SOEs is as follows. In 1999, 15 provincial statistical yearbooks (out of 31) reported data on pure SOEs, another 15 provincial statistical yearbooks reported data on an undefined category of SOEs that could be either pure SOEs or pre-1998 definition SOEs, and 23 provincial statistical yearbooks reported data on all state-owned and state-controlled enterprises. The data on all state-owned and state-controlled enterprises are also available for all provinces in the *Statistical Yearbook 2000*. (The *Statistical Yearbook 1999* does not provide provincial data for 1998 and ensuing comparisons are therefore not possible for 1998.)

The arithmetic mean ratio across the 15 provinces on which the value-added of pure SOEs is reported — dropping the problematic value for Tianjin as explained in the next note means only data on 14 provinces are used — of the value-added of all state-owned and state-controlled enterprises to the value-added of the pure SOEs is 1.42. But the mean ratio of the value-added of all state-owned and state-controlled enterprises to the value-added of the undefined SOEs (either pure SOEs, or pre-1998 definition SOEs) across the eight provinces on which also value-added on all state-owned and state-controlled enterprises but not on pure SOEs are available — dropping the problematic values for Hainan and Tibet as explained in the next note means only data on six provinces are used — is 1.59. Including four additional provinces for which value-added data on state-owned and state-controlled enterprises are only available in the *Statistical Yearbook*, changes this ratio to 1.57. If the provinces on which data are reported for the pure SOEs were not to differ significantly from the provinces on which data are reported only for the undefined category (of either pure SOEs or pre-1998 definition SOEs), and if the undefined category were to cover pre-1998 definition SOEs, then the latter ratio should be smaller than 1.42. The fact that it is larger suggests that the undefined category covers even fewer enterprises than the pure SOEs. This is impossible. The smallest group of SOEs is the group of pure SOEs.

It is also impossible to check the coverage of the provincial-level data provided on "state-owned and state-controlled enterprises." Presumably, the NBS receives highly detailed data on all categories in Table 2.1 from the provincial statistical bureaus (with many more variables on which data are collected but not published, such as the different equity ownership categories within each enterprise category) and can then calculate the values for the "state-owned and state-controlled enterprises" itself; the presentation of aggregate provincial industrial data in the *Statistical Yearbook* is consistent with the data in the provincial statistical yearbooks in those provinces which report on state-owned and state-controlled enterprises.[25]

While the enterprise coverage is not uniform across provinces, each provincial statistical yearbook consistently provides data on numerous standardized variables (output, balance sheet and profit and loss account data) for the particularly defined group of SOEs that it uses.

Table 2.4 summarizes the SOE coverage in the (within-province) sectoral industrial statistics in provincial statistical yearbooks since 1998. (The coverage is unproblematic in the years prior to 1998.) Out of the 31 provinces, six do not report detailed sectoral data for the years 1998 through 2000; of these six, Gansu reports the enterprise number and gross output value only. The 26 provinces that report sectoral data report these data on different SOE categories. In 1998, eight provinces reported sectoral data on the pure SOEs, two on state-owned and state-controlled enterprises, 14 on pure SOEs or pre-1998 definition SOEs (unclear, but most likely pure SOEs), and one on an undetermined SOE category. In 2000, only two provinces reported sectoral data on the pure SOEs, 18 on state-owned and state-controlled enterprises, one on the pre-1998 definition SOEs, and three on either pure SOEs or pre-1998 definition SOEs (unclear, but most likely pure SOEs).[26]

---

[25] Three exceptions in the year 1999 are Tianjin, Hainan and Tibet. The value-added of all state-owned and state-controlled enterprises in Tianjin as reported in the provincial statistical yearbook amounts to only 87.15% of the value-added of the same enterprise group reported in the *Statistical Yearbook 2000*. For Hainan, the share is 76.55%, and for Tibet, 106.55%. In all the other 19 provinces for which the provincial statistical yearbooks report value-added of all state-owned and state-controlled enterprises, the data fully match the data reported in the *Statistical Yearbook* 2000 (except for what appears to be rounding errors of usually just a fraction of one percentage point).

[26] In 2000, a very few provinces reported sectoral data separately for the category state-owned and state-controlled enterprises as well as for the category pure SOEs. These were counted as reporting sectoral data on state-owned and state-controlled enterprises (i.e., following the new definition).

Table 2.4 Coverage of Sectoral Data in Provincial Statistical Yearbooks (number of provinces)

Definition of SOE category	1998	1999	2000
Pure SOEs	8	5	2
Pre-1998 definition SOEs	0	1	1
Unclear whether pure SOEs or pre-1998 definition SOEs[a]	14	4	3
State-owned and state-controlled enterprises	2	14	18
Undetermined	1	1	0
No sectoral data available	6	6	6

[a] For most if not all provinces in this group, the coverage is likely to be "pure SOEs." The provinces are listed in this group rather than with the first group of pure SOEs, because the data provided are insufficient to ascertain that the SOE-SOE joint operation enterprises and the solely state-invested limited liability companies are included with the joint operation category and the limited liability company category, respectively.

Profit and Profitability Measures

Profit

Aggregate profit (*zong lirun*) reported in Chinese statistics is the residual of sales revenue after deducting various cost items and adding other income sources (Figure 2.4). Since 1993, sales costs, sales fees, sales taxes and surcharges, a small category "others," administrative charges, and financial charges have been subtracted from sales revenue, while other net business profit, investment returns, and net non-business revenue are added in order to determine the value of profit.

As the various items that are deducted from or added to sales revenue change over time, so does profit. Items change over time not only because the transactions they reflect change over time, but also due to redefinitions of the individual profit and loss account categories. The accounting system established in 1980 underwent minor revisions in 1985 and 1989, before a largely new accounting system was adopted in 1993. Prior to 1993, profit included items such as employee bonus funds, which, in the 1993 reform of the accounting system, were shifted into cost items (bottom of Figure 2.4). Similarly, any change in depreciation rules affects sales costs and thereby the residual profit. Changes in profit over time are therefore not only due to economic factors. The following chapter details some of the changes in the accounting system since the mid-1980s.

Since 1993:
Sales revenue (since 1994 net of value-added tax)
[in industrial SOEs with independent accounting system in 1995, as share of sales revenue (below likewise): 1.0000]
- sales costs (costs incurred in the production of those products actually sold) [0.7902]:
    * materials
    * transportation, mailing, repair, storage, insurance
    * wages and other labor expenses (for employees engaged in actual production)
    * depreciation
- sales fees (including wages and other labor expenses on sales employees) [0.0228]
- sales taxes and surcharges (since 1994 net of value-added tax) [0.0301]
- others [implicitly: 0.0024]
= *sales profit* [0.1544]
- administrative charges (including wages and other labor expenses for administrative personnel) [0.0964]
- financial charges [0.0553]
+ other net business profit (other business income - other business expenses) [implicit: 0.0127]
= *business profit* [0.0153]
+ investment returns [0.0042]
+ net non-business revenue (non-business revenue - non-business expenses) [implicit: 0.0059]
= *profit* [0.0255]
    in case of an individual enterprise: positive (profit) or negative (loss)
    across all enterprises = *gross profit* (profit of profitable enterprises) [0.0500]
      + *losses* (negative profit of loss-making enterprises) [-0.0245]
- income tax (on positive profit only) [0.0111]
= **net profit, or post-tax profit** [0.0138]
- special funds contribution: profit adjustment tax, and energy and communication key construction fund tax (both terminated in 1994)
+ undistributed profit from previous year and adjustments to previous year's profit
- adjustments to previous year's income taxes
= **profit for distribution**
+ reduction in profit reserves to compensate for current-year losses
- additions to profit reserves (general profit reserve, and "public" profit reserve with employee bonus and welfare funds)
- profit for distribution
= *undistributed profit*

Reference: "profit and taxes" (separately reported) [0.1101]

Prior to 1993:
Sales revenue - sales taxes - sales production costs (- sales fees) - technology transfer fee
= *product sales profit* + other sales profit + net non-business revenue - resource tax - usage fee on fixed funds and working funds (until 1989)
= *profit* - approximately twenty items (including profit to be submitted to government or superordinate department, since 1984 largely in form of income tax and adjustment tax)
= *retained profit* to be allocated to the (i) new product trial fund, (ii) production development fund, (iii) reserves, (iv) employee welfare fund, and (v) employee bonus fund

Sources: *Industrial Census 1995*, Vol. 1, pp. 51-53; FM (5 Jan. 1985, 21 April 1989, 31 Dec. 1992).

Figure 2.4   Profit and Loss Account

Aggregate profit is the sum of the positive profit of profitable enterprises and the negative profit (losses) of loss-making enterprises. When data on the losses of loss-making enterprises are separately available, this allows the calculation of the (positive) profit of profitable enterprises, in the following labeled "gross profit."

Profit includes income taxes. The separately reported measure "profit and taxes" (*lishui zong'e*) is the sum of profit plus "sales-related taxes" (circulation taxes), which in turn comprise "sales taxes and surcharges" (*xiaoshou shuijin ji fujia*) and the since 1994 separately listed value-added tax (*zengzhishui*).

Profitability in the Literature

Profit is frequently related to fixed assets in a measure that resembles a neoclassical profit rate. For example, Thomas Rawski (1994b), Huang Yiping and Ron Duncan (1997b), and James Laurenceson and Joseph Chai (2000) relate profit to year-end net fixed assets. Yuk-shing Cheng and Dic Lo (2002) relate profit and taxes to net fixed assets. Gary Jefferson and Thomas Rawski (1995 and 1996), Martin Raiser (1997a), and Dic Lo (1999) relate profit to net fixed assets plus average working capital. Barry Naughton (1992) and Fan Gang and Wing-Thye Woo (1996) relate profit plus taxes to net fixed assets plus average working capital.

The latter profit rate, profit plus taxes relative to net fixed assets and average working capital, was also reported in the *Statistical Yearbook* from the early 1980s until 1997 as the "funds profitability rate" (*zijin lishuilu*). An often unnoticed severe statistical break in this profit rate occurred between 1991 and 1992. The rate was first defined in 1990 (for 1990 data) as profit plus taxes relative to the average annual net fixed assets plus the average annual *fixed-quota* working capital. In 1992, the second half of the denominator was redefined as 'average annual *total* working capital,' an increase in the denominator by approximately one-third. In 1993, 'average annual total working capital' turned into 'average annual current assets,' which presumably reflects a change in labeling only.

The pre-1992 indicator is thus not comparable with the indicator in 1992 or the indicator since 1993. The published profit rate, which can be constructed based on the items it comprises, furthermore did not correctly match the definition in 1990 and 1991.[27] If, rather than using the published indicator, the profit rate is calculated based on its individual components, there is also a statistical break in 1992 since no consistent working capital data are available for the 1980s and 1990s.

Data on "net fixed assets" are even more problematic. "Net fixed assets" are calculated by adding the price of each newly acquired fixed asset to the cumulative price of previously acquired fixed assets net of depreciation. Some authors, such as Chen Kuan et al. (1988) and Gary Jefferson (1992), have attempted to correct for changes in the price level over time, but as Wing-Thye Woo et al. (1994) show, the deflators available to do so inspire little confidence. While fixed asset data are not regularly corrected for changes in the price level over time, in 1993 the State Council asked all SOEs for a one-time re-evaluation at market prices of all their fixed assets purchased before the end of 1993 (SC, 3 May 1993), an event that appears to have been missed in the literature that uses net fixed asset data in the calculation of profit rates.

Beyond these data issues, all four profit rates used in the literature also suffer from a methodological problem. A profit rate that comprises profit plus taxes relative to net fixed assets and working capital may be highly appropriate for the socialist economy in which (i) all funds for investment in fixed assets and fixed-quota working capital are provided by the government and (ii) the enterprise pays for these funds by handing over its annual surplus to the government as a combined taxes and profit transfer. Since the early 1980s, both assumptions are no longer satisfied in China. Banks began to extend their first investments in fixed asset loans in 1979; at the same time, the government's fixed-quota working capital

---

[27] On the profit rate definitions, see *Statistical Yearbook 1991*, p. 449; *1993*, p. 472; *1994*, p. 416. For SOEs, the average annual total working capital in 1992 was 1.98 times the average annual value of fixed-quota working capital (*Statistical Yearbook 1993*, pp. 427 and 430). Calculating the 1990 and 1991 profit rate of industrial SOEs using the individual items it comprises reveals that the reported profit rate in fact uses year-end net fixed assets rather than average annual net fixed assets. For 1992, when the profit rate was redefined, independent data on average annual net fixed assets are lacking and the reported profit rate thus cannot be checked; using the year-end net fixed assets yields an industrial SOE profit rate that is smaller than the reported one, suggesting that the definition may now match the reported figure. In 1993, the reported industrial SOE profit rate matches the definition.

appropriations began their steady decline to virtually zero today. The 1983–1985 tax reform instituted a clear distinction between profit and taxes, with taxes being paid by enterprises independent of ownership form.

Profit constitutes the return to equity holders, not the return on debt (liabilities). But the sum of some measure of working capital (current assets) and net fixed assets is an approximation of the total assets, i.e., equity *plus* debt. If the denominator reflects total assets, then the numerator, besides profit, must include the return on debt, i.e., interest payments (financial charges). When profit is understood as reflecting the return to equity holders, financial charges are the return on debt; profit plus financial charges are the return to equity and debt holders, i.e., the return on total assets.[28]

Second, any change in circulation taxes, such as the value-added tax, changes the value of a profitability indicator that includes taxes in the numerator. Thus, if the government triples the rate of the value-added tax, the value of a profitability indicator that includes "profit plus taxes" in the numerator may rise drastically. Yet a meaningful measure of profitability over time should not be a function of tax rates. Including circulation taxes makes sense only for a comparison between SOEs and non-SOEs when the actual rate of circulation taxes differs across ownership forms.

Due to the data problems underlying these profitability indicators and due to their questionable meaning, the four profitability indicators used in the literature appear unsuitable measures of industrial SOE profitability. Below, other profitability indicators are introduced that avoid some of these shortcomings.[29]

Profitability in This Book

The most appropriate profitability indicator is "return on equity," i.e., profit per unit of equity. Return on equity is the return obtained by the owners of the firm in exchange for providing equity. Profit in the aggregate is the

---

[28] Similarly, there is no reason to believe that equity is equal to net fixed assets, which could justify using only net fixed assets in the denominator, as the first two profit rates listed above do.

[29] The long-term time trends of the four traditional profitability indicators come close to those of the (preferred) profitability indicators introduced below. The use of more appropriate profitability indicators could but need not necessarily challenge conclusions reached in the literature based on long-term profitability trends using these "traditional" indicators.

profit of profitable enterprises ("gross profit") less the losses of loss-making enterprises. Any change in circulation tax rates or corporate income tax rates has no impact on profit. Circulation taxes should be included only for cross-ownership comparisons (if actual tax rates differ across ownership forms). Equity data are available for the years since 1993, which means that profit relative to equity can be calculated for the years since 1993.

If the focus were on the return to creditors in addition to owners, then the appropriate profitability indicator is 'profit plus financial charges' relative to assets (equity plus liabilities).[30] A "social" return on assets could further include circulation taxes in the numerator, to capture the return to owners, debt-holders, and the government.[31] These two indicators can also be calculated for the years since 1993, when asset data first became available. For earlier years, assets could be approximated using year-end net fixed assets plus average annual fixed-quota working capital (available until 1992); 1992 data suggest that, in the late 1980s and early 1990s, the approximated assets fell one-quarter to one-third short of actual assets.[32]

---

[30] The published data on financial charges are net data, i.e., interest payments and other fees on liabilities less interest receipts from bank deposits. Since interest income already contributes to profit, a measure of gross financial charges would be preferable; such a measure, however, is not available. The published (net) financial charges may not be too different from gross financial charges. Bank loans to all enterprises tend to be three times larger than enterprises' deposits at banks (see, for example, *Statistical Yearbook 2000*, p. 401), and interest rates on enterprise deposits are well below those on loans to enterprises. Provincial-level industrial SOE data for the years 1998 through 2000 occasionally include data on interest payments; these tend to fall only 5–10% *short* of the (net) financial charges; this implies that the "other fees" on liabilities must be quite high. In 1995, industrial SOE interest payments were equal to 87.56% of financial charges (*Industrial Census 1995*, Vol. 1, p. 51). No data at all are available on non-interest fees related to liabilities. In the following, interest payments and other fees on liabilities will be approximated by financial charges.

[31] Since 1998, the *Statistical Yearbook* has published a social return on assets, labeled "total asset contribution rate" (*zong zichan gongxian lu*). It is defined as profit plus taxes plus interest payments per unit of average annual assets (*Statistical Yearbook 2000*, p. 463). Across sectors, for industrial SOEs, data on this indicator are available since 1999 only (across provinces since 1998).

[32] In 1992, total working capital was about twice the volume of fixed-quota working capital and approximately equal to net fixed assets (*Statistical Yearbook 1993*, pp. 419 and 430). The approximation of assets still ignores long-term investments and a residual group of intangible assets, deferred assets, other long-term assets and deferred taxes.

The return on assets and the social return on assets for the years through 1992 are thus overestimated.[33]

An alternative indicator for earlier years when equity and asset data are not available is losses of loss-making enterprises relative to profit of profitable enterprises, i.e., losses per unit of gross profit. Losses per unit of gross profit splits aggregate profit into its two sub-categories and standardizes one by the other. It is an extremely sensitive measure of profitability.[34] If the profitability of both profitable and loss-making enterprises deteriorates, the numerator rises and the denominator falls, yielding a sharp increase in the indicator. SOE loss data are available economy-wide and across sectors and provinces for the years 1986 through 1991 and 1995. For all other years, only economy-wide SOE loss data are available.

The losses per unit of gross profit indicator has a drawback in that enterprise mergers may lead to inconsistencies in aggregate profit data. For example, if a loss-making and a profitable enterprise merge, the aggregate losses per unit of gross profit indicator is likely to fall because the percentage (downward) change in the aggregate losses numerator is likely to be larger than the percentage (downward) change in the aggregate gross profit denominator. Aggregate profit remains unchanged and the return on equity or assets is thus not affected.

Since profit is the residual of sales revenue after deducting (and adding) various items, profit can also be meaningfully related to sales revenue. With some (limited) data available on the various profit and loss account items, the immediate causes of any change in profit can be identified. To avoid a statistical break in sales revenue caused by a change in taxes reported

---

[33] If the revaluation of net fixed assets requested by the State Council in 1993 was actually completed in 1993, then 1992-93 constitutes a statistical break in two respects. First, since 1993 data on total assets are available; data on total assets prior to 1993 are approximated. Second, (total) assets since 1993 comprise *revalued* net fixed assets; net fixed assets data in the years prior to 1992 are valued at the original purchasing price less depreciation.

[34] Losses relative to gross profit is not so much a profit rate as a loss rate. While reversing the ratio would yield a profit rate (gross profit relative to losses), the fact that losses tend on average to be smaller than gross profit, and often around zero, implies that this ratio would easily become very (if not infinitely) large.

as part of sales revenue, sales revenue in the following unless otherwise noted is always net of all circulation taxes.[35]

However, relating profit to sales revenue is also problematic because this indicator responds to purely financial restructuring. For example, suppose the interest rate on liabilities were the same as the rate of profit per unit of equity. If equity were to be doubled and liabilities were to be reduced correspondingly, profit per sales revenue would, *ceteris paribus*, double. (Profit doubles because fewer interest payments are subtracted from sales revenue, raising the residual profit. There is no reason why sales revenue should change.) But nothing has changed except the financing structure. When the return on liabilities equals the return on equity, a reliable profitability indicator should not change in response to a change in the financing structure; profit relative to equity, the preferred profitability indicator, indeed remains unchanged.

To summarize, the types of profitability measures used in the analyses below are:

(i) Profitability per se: profit per unit of equity, or profit plus circulation taxes per unit of equity (for cross-ownership comparisons); equity data are only available since 1993.

(ii) Return on assets: 'profit plus financial charges' per unit of assets, with the denominator in the years prior to 1993 approximated by net fixed assets plus fixed-quota working capital. A "social" return on assets further includes circulation taxes in the numerator.

(iii) Losses per unit of gross profit (data available for all years in the reform period).

(iv) Sales-based profitability: profit (or profit plus circulation taxes) relative to sales revenue, with data available for all years in the reform period.

---

[35] Up through 1993, sales revenue included, among others, the value-added tax, business tax, and product tax. Since 1994, sales revenue excludes the value-added tax, business tax, and product tax, but now includes the consumption tax. Value-added tax is now reported as a separate item. This implies a statistical break in sales revenue between 1993 and 1994 with an approximately four percentage point reduction unless sales revenue net of all sales-related taxes (circulation taxes) is used (Carsten Holz and Yi-min Lin, 2001b).

Data Sources

The data used in this book are obtained primarily from the various annual issues of the *Statistical Yearbook*, the *Industrial Yearbook*, and provincial statistical yearbooks. The 1995 industrial census (*Industrial Census 1995*) provides sub-sectoral data for 1995, while the few available copies of the *China Markets Yearbook* (and *China's Industrial Markets Yearbook*) contain similar types of data on 1995, 1996, 1998 and 2000. A number of other statistical publications provide additional data. The sources of all data are usually documented below with the use of the data. To avoid lengthy and repetitive lists of numerous issues of the *Statistical Yearbook*, sometimes only "*Statistical Yearbook*" in general is cited without further details. In this case, Table 2.5 provides a summary reference to the data on all directly reporting industrial enterprises and on industrial SOEs across the different volumes of the *Statistical Yearbook*. All data are aggregate data, whether economy-wide data, sectoral or provincial data, within-province sectoral data or within-province data grouped according to various other criteria.

Aggregate data have four significant advantages over survey data. First, none of the survey data on industrial SOEs used in the literature are based on nationwide random samples and may thus contain sectoral, regional, size or other biases. Large differences in sectoral and regional aggregate profitability levels documented in Chapter 7 imply a high likelihood of severe bias if surveys are not based on random samples.

Second, the number of years covered by any particular survey tends to be small. In contrast, balance sheet as well as profit and loss account data are now available for the years 1993 through 2000, including data on nationwide industrial SOEs in the aggregate as well as on SOEs (again, in the aggregate) in individual industrial sectors, provinces, and industrial sectors within provinces. A more limited set of data is furthermore available for the earlier reform years from 1978 through 1992.

Third, enterprise survey data are likely to be less accurate than enterprise-specific data underpinning the official aggregate data on directly reporting industrial enterprises. Directly reporting industrial enterprises regularly submit standardized reports to the statistical departments. The variables on which these reports are made are exceedingly well defined. The best a survey can do is to obtain data as accurate as these regular reports. If

Table 2.5 Statistical Yearbook Sources for Output, Balance Sheet, and Profit and Loss Account Data (page numbers in the specific yearbook)

Year in title	Year covered	Directly reporting industrial enterprises by ownership category/ sector[a]	by province	Industrial SOEs by sector	by province
1986	1985	242	n.a.	243	n.a.
1987	1986	263f., 310f.	312f.	314f.	316f.
1988	1987	320f., 373f.	375f.	377f.	379f.
1989	1988	271f., 273f., 292f., 320f.	275, 322f.	324f.	275, 326f.
1990	1989	419-22	423, 440	441f.	423, 443
1991	1990	399-402	403-6	407-8	403, 409
1992	1991	411-4	415, 418f.	420f.	415, 422-3
1993	1992	417-20	421, 424f.	426f.	421, 428f.
1994	1993	378-81	385-7	388-91	392-4
1995	1994	388-91	384-7	392-5	384, 396-8
1996	1995	414-7	410-3	418-21	410, 422f.
1997	1996	424-7	420-3	428-31	420, 432f.
1998	1997	444-7	440-3	448-51	440, 454f.
1999	1998	432-5	429-31	n.a.	n.a.
2000	1999	414-7	420-2	424-7	430-2
2001	2000	410-3	416-8	420-3	426-8

[a] The tables on sectoral data for all (directly reporting) industrial enterprises beginning with the 1988 data also include a breakdown according to ownership category. Nationwide data on SOEs are thus available in the sectoral table for all industrial enterprises, in the sectoral table on industrial SOEs, and in the provincial table on industrial SOEs.

Each yearbook only includes data covering the year preceding the year in the yearbook title. Beginning with the *Statistical Yearbook 1990*, all variables tend to be covered in one table (with rare exceptions); in the earlier years output data and the number of enterprises tend to be listed in separate tables. Occasionally, time series data are offered for a very few variables. Sectoral and provincial tables each also give the nationwide total. Since 1998, SOE data cover SOEs under the new definition (i.e., state-owned and state-controlled enterprises). Nationwide 1999 and 2000 data for SOEs in the pre-1998 definition are available for a very few variables in the *Industrial Yearbook 2001*, pp. 48–53.

To give two examples of the variables and ownership categories covered, the *Statistical Yearbook 1990* with data for 1989 covers the following variables: number of enterprises, gross output value of industry, net output value of industry, sales revenue, original value of fixed assets, net value of fixed assets, average annual fixed-quota working capital, depreciation, profit, profit and taxes, and retained profit. The sectoral table on all industrial enterprises also offers an exhaustive breakdown into the ownership categories SOEs, collective-owned enterprises (with the sub-category township-run enterprises), and "other" enterprises. The *Statistical Yearbook 1998* with data for 1997 covers the following variables: number of enterprises, gross output value of industry, industrial value-added, capital, assets, current assets (working capital), annual average current assets (working capital), fixed assets, original value of fixed assets, annual average net value of fixed assets, short-term liabilities, long-term liabilities, equity, sales revenue, sales costs, sales taxes and surcharges, profit, value-added tax, profit and taxes. The sectoral table on all industrial enterprises also offers a non-exhaustive breakdown into the ownership categories SOEs, collective-owned enterprises, shareholding enterprises, foreign-funded enterprises, and Hong Kong or Macao or Taiwanese enterprises; two separately listed categories are "absolutely" and "relatively" state-controlled shareholding enterprises. For a definition of the latter two terms, see Carsten Holz and Yi-min Lin (2001b, p. 46).

enterprises maintain a second set of "true" accounts and report only highly polished data to the statistical departments, they are also unlikely to report the "true" data in other surveys.[36]

Fourth, longitudinal industrial SOE surveys suffer from a potentially high rate of attrition or, if data are collected retrospectively, from potentially severe selection bias as the sampling frame covers only industrial SOEs currently in existence (the "survivors"). Aggregate industrial SOE data, in contrast, covers the whole population at a particular point of time. Even industrial SOEs that are reorganized into holding companies or merged with other SOEs remain part of the population (with the exception of industrial SOEs that were turned into less than solely state-owned limited liability companies or into stock companies prior to 1998).

Redefinitions of variables pose a serious obstacle to time series analysis. Profit underwent its most drastic redefinition in 1993 with the adoption of a new accounting system (explained in more detail in the following chapter). The formal adoption of the System of National Accounts, which replaced the previous Material Product System in 1993, introduced value-added as a new output measure to replace net material product (with retrospective data on the directly reporting industrial enterprises available for 1992). Gross output value data continue to be published, but in 1995, this measure was redefined to exclude the value-added tax.[37]

Data on some variables are not available for industrial SOEs, but can be estimated with what appears to be a sufficiently high degree of reliability. These data include value-added data for the years prior to 1992, depreciation data for the first half of the 1980s and most of the 1990s, and (total) labor

---

[36] Data reported by enterprises to the statistical departments could also be falsified by the statistical departments, in which case a survey that prevents data falsification by the statistical authority could be superior. Data falsification by statistical authorities in China in the case of the directly reporting industrial enterprises is highly unlikely (see Carsten Holz, 2003).

[37] Gross output value data may not always be of the best quality. The gross output values of all industrial enterprise categories — except SOEs — for the years 1991 through 1994 were revised retrospectively following the 1995 industrial census. (No retrospectively revised data on the directly reporting industrial enterprises are available. Presumably, the gross output value of the sub-category of directly reporting industrial SOEs has been correctly reported all along.) See Carsten Holz and Yi-min Lin (2001b) for details on the redefinitions of output variables.

remuneration data across the reform period. All data estimations are described in the appendix to this chapter.

Non-numerical information is obtained from a variety of sources. Central government (including ministerial) regulations are regularly published in the "State Council Bulletin" (*Zhonghua renmin gongheguo guowuyuan gongbao*), while provincial and sub-provincial regulations are published in local bulletins (*zhengbao*). Various law compendia also carry relevant regulations, as does the law database within *China Infobank* (www.chinainfobank.com). The secondary literature includes numerous Chinese and English language journals as well as books.

Appendix 1: Value-added

Data on industrial SOE value-added have been available only since 1992. Each annual value for the years since 1992 is published in the corresponding year's *Statistical Yearbook*. (Some issues of the *Industrial Yearbook* include two years' data.) Earlier data are not revised. The value for 1993 appears highly dubious with its 40.21% rise over the previous year at a time when the deflator implicit in economy-wide industrial value-added rose by only 14.51% (*Statistical Yearbook 2001*, pp. 49, 51). With the introduction of the System of National Accounts only in 1993, it is likely that early value-added data are not fully reliable.

Industrial SOE value-added data for the years 1980, 1982 through 1984, and 1986 through 1991 are estimated by assuming that industrial SOEs follow the same ratio of net material product (on which data are available for these years as well as for 1985 and 1992) to value-added (on which industrial SOE data are not available for these years) as does *all* industry. For all industry, net material product data are available until 1992 and value-added data are available for all years. A comparison of the available industrial SOE value-added data for 1985 and 1992 with the estimated values shows that the estimated values in these two years fall short of the actual values by 2.58% and 2.16%, respectively.

Industrial SOE value-added data for the years 1978, 1979, and 1981 were obtained by first calculating the ratio of all other reform years' industrial SOE value-added to industrial SOE gross output value. This ratio exhibits a steady downward trend. The ratio for 1981 was obtained by dividing the difference between the 1980 and 1982 ratio by half and adding this amount to the 1980 ratio. The same interval adjustment was then applied to the 1980 ratio in order to obtain the 1997 ratio, and similarly from the 1979 ratio the 1978 ratios. The three ratios finally were multiplied with the relevant industrial SOE gross output values.[38]

Value-added data on all directly reporting industrial enterprises are missing in the same years as they are missing for the industrial SOEs. The missing values were obtained in similar fashion as for SOEs, with one exception. Since the 1978 gross industrial output value of the directly reporting industrial enterprises is not available, 1978 value-added is calculated differently. First, the ratio of value-added of the directly reporting industrial enterprises to the value-added of all industry was calculated for the years 1979 through 2000; while this ratio exhibits a continuous downward trend in later years, in the early and mid-1980s, this trend is far from stable. Therefore, the 1979 ratio was assumed to hold for 1978 and was then applied to 1978 value-added of all industry to obtain the 1978 valued-added of the directly reporting industrial enterprises.

Appendix 2: Depreciation

Nationwide aggregate industrial SOE depreciation data are available only for the years 1985 through 1991. For the years 1978 through 1984, nationwide aggregate industrial SOE depreciation is estimated by applying the (arithmetic) average actual depreciation rate of the years 1985 through 1991 to year-end net fixed assets of the years 1978 through 1984. This procedure is straightforward and the data are reported in Table 2.6.

---

[38] The data sources are the following. Industrial SOE value-added 1985: *Industrial Yearbook 1986*, p. 21; 1992-2000: *Statistical Yearbook 1993*, p. 426; *1994*, p. 388; *1995*, p. 393; *1996*, p. 418; *1997*, p. 428; *1998*, p. 455; *1999*, p. 432; *2000*, p. 414; *2001*, p. 410. Industrial SOE net material product 1980: *Statistical Yearbook 1986*, p. 278; 1982-1992: *Industrial Yearbook 1986*, p. 21; *Statistical Yearbook 1984*, pp. 216, 218; *1986*, p. 278; *1987*, p. 263; *1988*, p. 320; *1989*, p. 292; *1990*, p. 419; *1991*, p. 399; *1992*, p. 411; *1993*, p. 426. Industrial SOE gross output value: *Seventeen Years of Reform*, p. 146. Value-added of all industry: *Statistical Yearbook 2000*, p. 53. All industry net material product (1978–92): *Statistical Yearbook 1993*, p. 33.

For the years 1992 through 2000, nationwide aggregate industrial SOE depreciation is estimated based on limited provincial-level industrial SOE depreciation data. The limited provincial-level data are reported in Table 2.7, while the estimated nationwide depreciation rate is included in Table 2.6. The availability of provincial-level data was determined by checking all 31 provincial yearbooks of 1998 (with 1997 data) and identifying those (ten) provinces for which industrial SOE depreciation data are available. The annual provincial yearbooks of each of these ten provinces were then consulted for depreciation and net fixed asset data.

Provincial (industrial SOE) depreciation data are related to year-end net fixed assets (in 1991 and 1992) or to average annual net fixed assets (1993–2000) to obtain a provincial depreciation rate. (Provincial-level year-end net fixed asset data are no longer available for the years after 1992, while provincial-level average annual net fixed asset data are not available for the years prior to 1993.) The provincial depreciation rate was then weighted by the share of the particular province's industrial SOE net fixed assets in the sum of the net fixed assets of industrial SOEs across all provinces for which depreciation data are available. The estimated nationwide industrial SOE depreciation rate is the sum of all weighted provincial depreciation rates (of those among the ten provinces for which depreciation data are available).

This estimation procedure is validated by a comparison with actual 1991 depreciation data. If the 1991 nationwide industrial SOE depreciation rate is calculated based on those provinces only for which 1992 depreciation data are available, the estimated nationwide industrial SOE depreciation rate is 6.30% (instead of the actual 6.08%). If the 1997 selection of provinces is used, the estimated 1991 depreciation rate is 6.15%.

A few provincial yearbooks also list large-scale repairs and maintenance funds. These are typically about one-half to two-thirds the value of depreciation and are not included in the depreciation data.

Table 2.6 Estimated Depreciation of Industrial SOEs

	Net fixed assets (100m RMB)			Depreciation rate (in %)		Depreciation (100m RMB)	
	Year-end	Average annual	Actual	Based on 1985-91 average rate	Based on provincial-level data	Actual	Estimated
1978	2225.7			6.16			137.01
1979	2378.6			6.16			146.42
1980	2528.0			6.16			155.61
1981	2709.3			6.16			166.77
1982	2914.0			6.16			179.37
1983	3161.0			6.16			194.58
1984	3395.5			6.16			209.01
1985	3980.8		6.16			245.23	
1986	4543.8		6.23			283.28	
1987	5242.4		6.18			324.18	
1988	6040.4		6.28			379.35	
1989	7033.2		6.18			434.90	
1990	8088.3		5.97			482.77	
1991	9507.2		6.08		6.15	577.88	
1992	10982.7	10096.37			6.44		707.28
1993	13304.4	11881.27			7.59		901.79
1994	15677.5	13673.41			9.64		1318.12
1995	21363.9	17474.11			9.05		1581.41
1996	23860.7	22140.84			7.63		1689.35
1997	25883.0	24513.64			7.09		1738.02
1998	31429.8	31891.43			6.73		2146.89
1999	35735.1	33938.96			6.63		2126.45
2000	37638.8	36886.64			7.05		2600.77

Depreciation data for the nationwide aggregate of all industrial SOEs are available for the years 1985 through 1991. For all years, year-end net fixed asset data on the nationwide aggregate of all industrial SOEs are available; average annual net fixed asset data are also available since 1993. For 1992, the provincial statistical yearbooks (and the *Statistical Yearbook*) offer only year-end net fixed assets, and for the years since 1993, only average annual net fixed assets are reported. (Nationwide data on year-end net fixed assets for all years are reported only in the *Industrial Yearbook*.) The economy-wide industrial SOE depreciation rate calculated based on the available provincial data in 1992 and all earlier years is based on year-end net fixed assets. For the years since 1993, it is based on average annual net fixed assets. In deriving the absolute economy-wide industrial SOE depreciation values, the depreciation rate is applied to the corresponding nationwide value of net fixed assets.
Sources:
Year-end net fixed assets: *Industrial Yearbook 2001*, p. 24.
Average annual net fixed assets: *Statistical Yearbook*.
Depreciation: *Statistical Yearbook*; *Industrial Yearbook 1986*, p. 21. The arithmetic mean of the 1985 through 1991 actual depreciation rate is 6.16%; for the derivation of the estimated pre-1985 depreciation values this depreciation rate was not rounded to two decimals. For the depreciation rates of the years since 1992 (used in the derivation of depreciation for the same years), see next table.

Table 2.7 Derivation of the Economy-wide Industrial SOE Depreciation Rate from Provincial-level Industrial SOE Data, 1992–2000 (all rates in %)

	1991	1992	1993	1994	1995	1996	1997	1998	1999	2000	Asset share[a]
Beijing	7.10	7.46	5.80	10.40	7.70	7.69	7.27	7.33	7.24	7.13	3.51
Tianjin	6.40										2.91
Hebei	5.92										5.04
Shanxi	6.79										4.01
Neimenggu	5.68										2.07
Liaoning	6.31										8.61
Jilin	5.76						7.07	6.40	6.59	5.03	3.77
Heilongjiang	5.47										5.08
Shanghai	6.71										4.00
Jiangsu	6.83										5.36
Zhejiang	6.62										2.98
Anhui	6.36	6.37			8.27	6.51	5.28	6.87	8.19		2.50
Fujian	5.73										1.69
Jiangxi	6.80										2.12
Shandong	4.63										7.46
Henan	5.31										5.01
Hubei	6.62	7.09	8.78	9.76	9.96	7.58	7.32	6.62	5.78	6.48	4.01
Hunan	6.65	6.92	7.82	10.64	8.25	6.86	6.55	5.50	5.54	6.61	3.44
Guangdong	6.60										4.99
Guangxi	5.53										2.24
Hainan	3.81										0.40
Chongqing											1.79
Sichuan	6.86										4.20
Guizhou	5.64										1.46
Yunnan	6.20										2.18
Tibet	4.61	4.05	4.06	5.69	5.25	4.06	3.92				0.07
Shaanxi	5.64			7.49	8.30	6.92	6.45	5.78	6.78	7.21	2.70
Gansu	5.47	5.20			7.80	6.71	6.37	6.70			2.22
Qinghai	6.15	4.99	4.67	9.44	9.47	6.05	5.69	6.29	5.42	10.24	0.95
Ningxia	5.66										0.57
Xinjiang	4.76	4.96	9.68	9.88	11.96	10.89	10.49	9.55	8.50	8.73	2.66
National[b]	6.08	6.44	7.59	9.64	9.05	7.63	7.09	6.73	6.63	7.05	
NFA[c]	100	17.62	15.27	16.58	19.57	21.77	25.85	20.88	22.81	17.27	

[a] 1997 share of a particular province's industrial SOE average annual net fixed assets in nationwide industrial SOE average annual net fixed assets, for reference only.

[b] 1991: actual nationwide industrial SOE depreciation rate. 1992–2000: Average of industrial SOE depreciation rates across provinces, with the depreciation rate of each province weighted by the share of the province's industrial SOE net fixed assets in the sum of the net fixed assets of industrial SOEs across those of the ten provinces for which depreciation data are available.

For the years through 1997, depreciation data provided in the provincial statistical yearbooks are related to net fixed asset values provided in the *Statistical Yearbook* (rather than in the provincial statistical yearbooks), since some provincial yearbooks provide only depreciation data. For all those provincial yearbooks that also provide net fixed asset data, these values are identical to those offered in the *Statistical Yearbook* (except one instance noted below). For the years since 1998, both depreciation and net fixed asset data are taken from the provincial statistical yearbooks, as the depreciation data for some provinces are more limited in enterprise coverage than the net fixed asset data in the *Statistical Yearbook*.

In the years through 1997, the pre-1998 definition of the category "SOEs" applies (as pure SOEs plus SOE-SOE joint operations and solely state-owned limited liability companies). In 1998, the same definition is used in Hubei. Hunan and Xinjiang use the new and broader (post-1997) SOE definition (as pure SOEs plus all shareholding companies in which the state has a controlling share, and all other enterprises in which the state has a share but with data only in proportion to the state's equity share). All other provinces provide data only on the pure SOEs. In 1999, all provinces used the new, post-1997 SOE definition, except for Beijing, Jilin, Anhui, and Gansu, which cover only the pure SOEs. In 2000, all provinces used the new SOE definition, except for Beijing and Jilin, which cover only the pure SOEs. One single instance of incongruent data are the 1999 data for Gansu; the average annual net fixed assets given in the provincial yearbook for the industrial SOEs exceeds the corresponding value in the *Statistical Yearbook* by 19.19%. Since the *Statistical Yearbook* covers the broadest possible range of SOEs, the value from the provincial yearbook should not exceed the value in the *Statistical Yearbook*.

c   Share of the sum of industrial SOE net fixed assets (NFA) of those of the ten provinces for which depreciation data are available in nationwide industrial SOE net fixed assets. The 1991 and 1992 values are year-end net fixed assets; data on the years since 1993 are average annual net fixed assets.
Sources:
1991: *Statistical Yearbook 1992*.
1992–2000: Provincial statistical yearbooks and *Statistical Yearbook*.

Appendix 3: Labor Remuneration

Labor remuneration comprises three components: employees' wages, social welfare expenditures for current employees, and payments to retirees (pensions and social welfare payments). Much of the data has to be estimated. These estimations are explained in the following. All final data are reported in Table 2.8.

Wages

Wage data comprise all payments to labor independent of whether these payments are made in monetary or non-monetary form. They explicitly include all bonus payments, allowances, and subsidies. (See, for example, *Statistical Yearbook 1992*, p. 141f.) Wage data for the different years are obtained as explained below.

Table 2.8 Labor Remuneration in Industrial SOEs (billion RMB)

	Wages		Social welfare payments for current employees		Estimated pensions (inc. social welfare payments to retirees)	In % of wages: Current soc. welf.	Pensions
	Actual	Estimated	Actual	Estimated			
1978	20.96			1.21	0.65	5.77	3.10
1979	23.65			1.67	1.25	7.06	5.29
1980	27.55			2.27	1.86	8.24	6.75
1981	28.69			2.78	2.08	9.69	7.25
1982	30.30			3.36	2.49	11.09	8.22
1983	31.36			3.93	2.88	12.53	9.18
1984	38.52			5.16	3.91	13.40	10.15
1985	45.97			6.54	5.46	14.23	11.88
1986	55.70		8.25		7.14	14.81	12.82
1987	63.61		9.87		9.00	15.52	14.15
1988	79.23		12.50		11.21	15.78	14.15
1989	91.47		14.56		13.51	15.92	14.77
1990	103.12		17.06		16.21	16.54	15.72
1991	115.14		19.22		19.19	16.69	16.67
1992	133.59		22.14		23.82	16.57	17.83
1993	162.43		24.79		28.98	15.26	17.84
1994	201.30		24.25		39.02	12.05	19.38
1995	242.14		26.31		49.10	10.87	20.28
1996	259.47		28.90		57.82	11.14	22.28
1997	258.82		29.82		63.00	11.52	24.34
1998		267.79		37.33	68.17	13.94	25.46
1999		273.76		37.79	74.49	13.80	27.21
2000		270.01		38.87	78.50	14.40	29.07

For details on the sources of actual values and the calculations underlying the estimated values, see the text.

For the years through 1997, wage bill data cover only "staff and workers" (*zhigong*) rather than all "laborers" (*congye renyuan*). A comparison is possible for 1995, 1999 and 2000. In 1995, the year-end number of all laborers in industrial SOEs exceeded the year-end number of staff and workers in industrial SOEs by 0.69% (*Industrial Census 1995*, Vol. 1, p. 198). In 1999 and 2000, the year-end number of laborers in *all* SOEs exceeded the year-end number of staff and workers in all SOEs by 2.59% and 3.02% (*Statistical Yearbook 2000*, p. 152; *2001*, p. 149); no such comparison data are available for industry only. No attempts are made to adjust any wage bill data to achieve complete employment coverage (all laborers) in the years prior to 1998.

1978–1997

Industrial SOE wage bill data for staff and workers are available in the *Industrial Yearbook 1998*, p. 20.

1998

The statistical yearbooks of ten provinces offer average annual employment data for the newly defined SOE category. These employment data are compared to the data on year-end staff and workers provided in the *Statistical Yearbook 1999*, p. 144, for these provinces. (Data on staff and workers in the *Statistical Yearbook* for the years after 1997 continue to follow the pre-1998 definition of SOEs.) The comparison yields an average multiplier across the ten provinces (with provinces weighted by average annual employment following the new SOE definition) of average annual employment in the newly defined SOE category compared with the pre-1998 definition SOE category. This multiplier is then applied to the nationwide aggregate year-end number of staff and workers (following the pre-1998 definition of SOEs) to obtain an estimate of the total average annual employment in industrial SOEs following the new SOE definition.[39]

This employment number is multiplied by the average wage in state-owned industry to yield the total wage bill. The average wage in state-owned industry is obtained using the data on the year-end number of staff and workers and their average wages, data which are available only separately for the three sub-sectors of state-owned industry, namely (i) mining and quarrying, (ii) manufacturing, and (iii) electricity, gas and water production and supply (*Statistical Yearbook 1999*, pp. 144, 164).

Using the average annual industrial SOE wage of staff and workers following the pre-1998 definition of SOEs to obtain wage data appears justified because the average annual wage of staff and workers in *all state-*

---

[39] The provincial-level data used to estimate nationwide industrial SOE employment in 1998 in some provinces are labeled "staff and workers," and in others "laborers." A comparison of provincial statistical yearbook data with data on average annual industrial SOE laborers offered in the *Industrial Yearbook 2001* for 1999 and 2000 reveals that the labeling is not applied consistently across one of the two sources.

owned units in 1999 and 2000 was, respectively, only 0.49% and 0.84% smaller than the average wage of laborers in *all SOEs* following the new SOE definition (*Statistical Yearbook 2000*, pp. 148, 152; *2001*, pp. 142, 149). (Data on only *industrial* SOEs are not available.)

Using the province-based procedure to estimate average annual employment in SOEs in 1998 following the new SOE definition appears justified since the obtained values for 1999 and 2000 differ from the actual values by only −1.29% and +1.08%. In contrast, actual average annual employment (laborers) in industrial SOEs following the new SOE definition in 1999 and 2000 exceeds the number of year-end staff and workers in industrial SOEs following the pre-1998 SOE definition by 40.74% and 42.90%, respectively.

1999 and 2000

The industrial SOE wage bill is calculated as the average annual number of laborers in industrial SOEs following the new SOE definition multiplied by the annual wage of staff and workers in industrial SOEs following the pre-1998 SOE definition (*Statistical Yearbook 2001*, p. 142; *Industrial Yearbook 2001*, p. 119). The average annual wage of staff and workers in industrial SOEs is calculated based on the year-end number of staff and workers and their average wage in each of the three sub-sectors of state-owned industry.

Social Welfare Expenditures for Current Employees

Social welfare expenditures for current employees comprise medical and hygiene-related expenses, expenses for recreational activities, sports, and propaganda, subsidies for collective welfare facilities (such as communal showers or a barber shop), expenses for communal equipment (such as cutlery for the communal cafeteria, or housing repairs, but not for investment in communal fixed assets), and other expenses related to social welfare, such as (other) insurance payments. (See, for example, *Statistical Yearbook 1999*, p. 786.)

1986-1997

The relevant social welfare data for industrial SOEs are available in the *Statistical Yearbook 1987*, p. 690; *1988*, p. 204; *1989*, p. 151; *1990*, p. 815; *1991*, p. 788; *1992*, p. 806; *1993*, p. 815; *1994*, p. 662; *1995*, p. 686; *1996*, p. 734; *1997*, p. 747; *1998*, p. 796.

1978-1985

First, the 1986 through 1997 social welfare data are expressed as a percentage of the corresponding year's wage bill. The percentages for the years 1986 through 1993 exhibit a very stable and gradual upward trend; between 1993 and 1994, the percentage drops from 15.26% to 12.05%, and thereafter stays at the lower level. The 1986 through 1993 percentages are then regressed on a constant, a time trend, and the absolute value of the annual wage bill (the coefficients are all significant at the 1% or 5% level).[40] The coefficients obtained in the regression are then used to construct 1978 through 1985 social welfare data.

1998 through 2000

A very few provincial statistical yearbooks offer data on both social welfare expenses and the wage bill of industrial SOEs (six provinces in 1998, five in 1999, seven in 2000). These provincial data are used to derive an aggregate ratio of social welfare expenses to the wage bill (with province-specific industrial SOE wage bills as weights), which is then applied to the nationwide industrial SOE wage bill of SOEs following the new SOE definition. The majority of the provincial data are on all industrial SOEs following the new SOE definition, but if social welfare and wage data are available only for SOEs following the pre-1998 SOE definition, or only for pure SOEs, these data are also included. (The difference in the ratios between SOEs in the three definitions are likely to be small.)

---

[40] A number of regressions were run with different sets of regressors, including a quadratic time trend. The final choice of specification was based on the best match in a visual inspection of the actual vs. fitted data. The same procedure applies to the regressions introduced further below in this appendix.

The nationwide ratios of 1998 through 2000 at about 14% are two percentage points larger than the ratios of 1994 through 1997. There is a possibility that the social welfare data in the provincial statistical yearbooks of 1998 through 2000 include social welfare payments to retirees. (Provincial statistical yearbooks do not offer social welfare data for the years prior to 1998, which would allow a double-check.) The calculated 1998 through 2000 data thus may over-estimate the social welfare payments to current employees.

Pensions and Social Welfare Expenditures for Retirees

Pensions and social welfare expenditures for retirees (in the following abbreviated as "pensions") comprise pure pensions, resignation allowances, medical and hygiene-related expenses, funeral expenses, transportation and heating subsidies, as well as other, unspecified items. (See, for example, *Statistical Yearbook 1999*, pp. 765, 786.) Data on pensions in industrial SOEs are not available. What is available are data on total social insurance and welfare funds in all state-owned units for the years 1978 through 1998 and the volume of pensions in these units, for the years 1978, 1980 and 1985 through 1998 (*Statistical Yearbook 1998*, p. 797; *1999*, p. 765).

Subtraction of pensions from all social insurance and welfare payments yields social welfare expenses for current staff and workers in all state-owned units; a thus (through subtraction) obtained value of social welfare expenses for current staff and workers in the year 1997 perfectly matches the same item in a table specifically on social welfare expenses for current staff and workers (*Statistical Yearbook 1998*, p. 796). This latter table offers a breakdown according to sector, and the industry data in this table were used in the previous section.

1986-1997

With data available on (i) social welfare payments to current staff and workers in industrial SOEs for the years 1986 through 1997 and (ii) social welfare payments to current staff and workers in *all* state-owned units for the years 1978, 1980, and 1985 through 1998, the first can be expressed for each year (1986 through 1997) as a ratio of the second. Assuming that the same ratio holds for retirees, multiplying pension payments of all state-owned units by this ratio yields pensions of industrial SOEs.

1978, 1980, 1985

The ratio calculated in the previous paragraph for the years 1986 through 1997 exhibits a distinct, gradual downward trend over the years. Regressing it on a constant and a time trend yields coefficients (both significant at the 0.1% significance level) that are then used to establish the ratio for the earlier years. The thus obtained ratios for the years 1978, 1980 and 1985 are applied to the available data on pensions of all state-owned units in these years to immediately obtain pensions in industrial SOEs.[41]

1979, 1981–1984

The so-far available pension data for industrial SOEs (for the years 1978, 1980, 1985–97) are first expressed as a percentage of the wage bill of industrial SOEs. This percentage exhibits a strong upward trend over the years. Regressing it on a constant and a time trend yields coefficients (both significant at the 0.1% significance level) that are then used to establish the percentage of pensions in the wage bill of industrial SOEs for the years 1979 and 1981 through 1984. Multiplying by the absolute value of the wage bill of industrial SOEs in these years yields the absolute value of pensions in industrial SOEs.

1998 through 2000

Pension data for the years 1986 through 1997 are first expressed as a

---

[41] For 1985, one separate value on all social (insurance and) welfare payments in industry of 12.23b RMB for both current staff and workers and for retirees is available (*Statistical Yearbook 1986*, p. 666). Subtracting the earlier calculated social welfare payments for current staff and workers yields a value of 5.69b RMB for retirees. This value closely matches the value of 5.46b RMB calculated (and used) here.

percentage of the wage bill of industrial SOEs.[42] Regressing this percentage on a constant, a time trend, and a squared time trend yields coefficients that are then used to establish the percentage of pensions in the wage bill of industrial SOEs for the years 1998 through 2000.[43] Multiplying by the absolute value of the wage bill of industrial SOEs in these years yields the absolute value of pensions in industrial SOEs.

---

[42] The earlier years were omitted since pension data for the earlier years are themselves estimates and since the annual changes in the percentages between 1986 and 1997 are not as drastic as in the years 1978 through 1986.

[43] The constant and the coefficient of the squared time trend are both highly significant (0.1% and 1% levels), but the time trend itself is insignificant at the 10% significance level. The combination of time trend plus the squared time trend was chosen over other sets of regressors because it yielded a very accurate match of actual and fitted data.

Part I
Explaining the Reform Period Decline in Industrial SOE Profitability

With the systemic reforms beginning in 1978, the only possible direction that industrial SOE profitability could take was down. In the pre-reform economy, the government determined prices in such a manner that the bulk of all surplus was concentrated in state industry, greatly facilitating the transfer of the economy-wide surplus to the government. Farmers faced mandatory agricultural procurement quotas at low prices. These low food prices allowed the wages in urban industry to be low. With the prices of industrial products set at relatively high levels, the result was a large volume of surplus in state industry. This surplus was transferred to the government budget through taxes and to the enterprises' superordinate government departments in the form of residual profit transfers (extrabudgetary funds). The taxes paid by industry constituted three-quarters of all government budget revenues in 1978. The residual profit transferred from industrial SOEs to their superordinate government departments almost equaled the formal taxes and provided government departments with approximately two-thirds of their extrabudgetary funds. Industrial SOEs in turn received all their investment funds as well as the largest part of their working capital from the government budget and their superordinate government departments.

In the course of the economic reforms, this distorted price structure was gradually adjusted, with initial increases in the procurement prices of agricultural goods, then general price rises for raw materials, and finally adjustments to industrial prices. Industry lost its unique position as the collector of the economy-wide surplus. By 1993, the last year for which data on sector-specific tax payments are available, the tax base had been expanded across the whole economy and industry accounted for little more than one-third of the total government budget revenue; the transfer of profit to government departments largely ended with the tax reform of 1993–1994. As the economy-wide surplus dissipated from industry to all other sectors of the economy, industry profit came under downward pressure.

The following three chapters focus on the decline of industrial SOE profitability throughout the reform period. Chapter 3 documents the decline in industrial SOE profitability and traces the immediate causes of the decline through the industrial SOEs' nationwide aggregate profit and loss account. Chapter 4 investigates the competing hypotheses that industrial SOEs' profit was eroded through competition or that it diminished due to "excessive" labor remuneration. Chapter 5 examines the more recent claim that industrial SOEs' rapidly increasing debt burden during the reform period has translated into low profitability.

3
Tracing the Decline in Industrial SOE Profitability through the Profit and Loss Account

Industrial SOE profitability declined drastically during the reform period. This chapter first documents the decline in the various profitability measures introduced in the previous chapter. It then proceeds to explain the development over time of one particular profitability indicator, namely profit relative to sales revenue. Profit is the residual in the profit and loss account after subtracting (and adding) various items from (to) sales revenue. As the size of these items relative to sales revenue changes over time, so too does the residual profit.

Yet, accounting profit may not be the best measure of financial success. Not only has this measure been repeatedly redefined, but accounting regulations have invariably given enterprises some flexibility in their accounting procedures. Consequently, the volume of profit varies depending on the reporting incentives that enterprises face. These incentives have changed in the course of the economic reform period.

Profit is by definition a value derived following standard accounting practices. Most data used in enterprise accounts are historical values. A preferable profit measure would be economic profit which is based on opportunity costs. Yet opportunity cost calculations for aggregate industry are impossible to figure. One alternative measure to accounting profit that is available is the operating surplus, i.e., the residual of value-added after subtracting labor remuneration, net taxes on production as well as depreciation. While it is not a perfect economic measure of profit, it has the advantage that it is less influenced by changes in accounting practices and by the varying incentives for enterprise managers to over- or underreport accounting profit.

The data suggest that the decline in industrial SOE profitability is primarily a healthy outcome of the economic transition. Large-scale price liberalization in 1988 led to double-digit inflation, which then triggered a period of retrenchment and adjustment with an administratively orchestrated economic downturn in 1989-1990. SOE profitability plummeted. Severe after-effects prevented a recovery in the early 1990s; an increase in competition as more prices were freed and entry barriers across many industrial sectors were lowered did not help. Repeated changes to the definition of profit and rising financial and administrative charges in the early and mid-1990s due to increased market orientation in the financial sector and better accounting practices in enterprises all had a negative impact on profit. The operating surplus declined much less and, in the late 1990s, it was several times higher than accounting profit, suggesting that the decline in profitability indicators based on accounting profit in the 1990s is to some extent an accounting artifact. Many of the causes for the decline in industrial SOE profitability furthermore appear to be transition phenomena and, as such, may have largely run their course. Industrial SOE profitability today is low, but not at the point of entering terminal decline.

The following section presents and interprets the time trends of several industrial SOE profitability indicators. The third section explores the reasons for the deterioration in profit relative to sales revenue over time. The fourth section examines the incentives for enterprises to misreport profit, and the fifth section provides an estimated operating surplus of industrial SOEs as an alternative measure of the development of industrial SOE profitability. The sixth section concludes.

Industrial SOE Profitability Trends

At first sight, the financial performance of industrial SOEs appears to be deteriorating fast. Losses by industrial SOEs increased twenty-fold between 1978 and 1997. Once these losses are adjusted for inflation using the ex-factory price index of industrial products, however, the losses of industrial

SOEs rose only six-fold between 1978 and 1997. Profitability measures exhibited the following patterns in the years 1978 through 2000 (Table 3.1 and Figure 3.1).

(i) The return on equity between 1993 and 1997 declined by approximately six percentage points to 2.09%; if circulation taxes are included, profitability almost halved from 23.13% in 1993 to 14.20% in 1997. The ratio of losses to gross profit in SOEs was stable throughout the 1980s, with even an improvement in the mid-1980s, but it increased by six times in just the two years from 1988 to 1990, with a further doubling between 1993 and 1996. It is only in the years 1999 and 2000 that profitability improved again, with the return on equity recovering to 7.36% and losses relative to gross profit falling by two-thirds.

(ii) The return on (approximated) assets dropped drastically between 1988 and 1990 from 12.37% to 5.96%. In the 1990s, the return on assets first declined modestly, to 3.02% in 1997, before recovering to 4.33% in 2000. The social return on assets exhibits the same time trend.

(iii) Profit per unit of sales revenue declined gradually in the early 1980s, but then precipitously from 14.08% in 1985 to 9.95% in 1988 and 3.66% in 1990. Profitability improved slightly in the following years before falling again, to 1.58% in 1997. Between 1997 and 2000, profitability recovered to 5.87%. If circulation taxes are included, profitability declined from 25.44% in 1985 to 14.18% in 1990 and 10.74% in 1997, with an improvement to 14.32% in 2000.

All profitability measures exhibit three common patterns. First, the general trend of the profitability measures in the reform period is downward. Second, the decline in profitability is not uniform over time. Profitability declined very gradually in the early 1980s, but then plummeted between 1988 and 1990. It remained rather stable in the early 1990s, and then declined slightly further between 1993 and 1997.

Table 3.1 Profitability of Industrial SOEs, 1978–2000

	Losses in 1978 b RMB	Losses / gross profit (%)	Profit / equity (%)	Profit + taxes / equity (%)	Return on assets[a] (%)	Social return on assets[b] (%)	Profit / sales revenue[c] (%)	Profit + taxes / sales revenue[c] (%)
1978	4.21	7.64			16.09	24.70	18.21	28.30
1979	3.58	6.07			16.66	25.31	18.60	28.56
1980	3.36	5.53			16.57	25.35	17.81	27.59
1981	4.50	7.35			15.28	24.15	17.25	27.47
1982	4.66	7.37			14.86	23.89	16.35	26.59
1983	3.15	4.77			15.32	24.12	15.97	25.74
1984	2.58	3.63			16.05	25.44	15.94	26.01
1985	2.89	4.21			14.53	25.17	14.08	25.44
1986	4.67	7.32			12.35	22.38	11.59	22.53
1987	4.85	7.20			12.37	22.12	11.01	21.17
1988	5.66	8.41			12.37	22.64	9.95	19.80
1989	10.50	19.52			10.14	20.13	7.38	17.60
1990	19.53	47.33			5.96	15.19	3.66	14.18
1991	19.35	47.71			5.35	14.29	3.17	13.11
1992	18.23	40.83			5.82	14.57	3.50	12.72
1993	18.02	35.64	7.70	23.13	4.07	9.09	3.89	11.69
1994	16.08	36.79	6.72	23.30	4.85	10.17	3.88	13.47
1995	18.54	49.00	4.10	17.71	4.45	9.10	2.63	11.35
1996	22.28	65.71	2.24	14.87	3.52	7.92	1.57	10.41
1997	23.48	66.01	2.09	14.20	3.02	7.21	1.58	10.74
1998	33.91	68.66	1.96	12.60	2.72	6.52	1.61	10.35
1999	29.19	49.21	3.26	13.34	2.99	6.82	2.86	11.69
2000	20.69	22.63	7.36	17.97	4.33	8.46	5.87	14.32

[a] Return on assets denotes 'profit plus (net) financial charges, per unit of assets,' where assets prior to 1993 comprise only average annual fixed-quota working capital plus year-end net fixed assets. Assets in 1993 are the sum of liabilities and equity. Net financial charges prior to 1993 are approximate. (See explanation with 'sources' below.)

[b] Social return on assets denotes 'profit plus taxes plus (net) financial charges, per unit of assets.' On assets and financial charges, see 'a.'

[c] Sales revenue is net of all sales-related taxes.

Sources:
Losses, profit, and 'profit and taxes:' *Statistical Yearbook 1998*, p. 461; *Industrial Yearbook 2001*, p. 24. Ex-factory price index of industrial products: *Statistical Yearbook 1994*, p. 246; *2001*, p. 297.
Equity and assets: *Statistical Yearbook* (see Table 2.5). Average annual fixed-quota working capital: *Statistical Yearbook 1993*, p. 430; year-end net fixed assets: *Statistical Yearbook 1998*, p. 461.
Financial charges: *Statistical Abstract 1994*, p. 86; *1995*, p. 86; *Industrial Census 1995*, Vol. 1, p. 51; *Statistical Abstract 1997*, p. 106; *1998*, p. 112; *1999*, p. 108; *2000*, p. 113; *2001*, p. 125; *Financial Yearbook* various issues and pages. Except for 1995, data are preliminary data first published in March of the following year. The revised data on financial charges are not published. Data for the years prior to 1993 are approximated as total working capital loans (i.e., loans with less than one year maturity) of state banks to industrial state-owned enterprises (*Financial Statistics 1952-1996*) times the average annual interest rate on working capital loans of six months or less maturity (calculated from various issues of the *Financial Yearbook*); in 1993, the approximated value exceeds the actual value by 4.36%.
Sales revenue, sales taxes and surcharges, and value-added tax: *Seventeen Years of Reform*, p. 146, for years prior to 1991; since 1991: *Statistical Yearbook* (see Table 2.5). Sales-related taxes up through 1993 are obtained as the difference of 'profit and taxes' and profit.

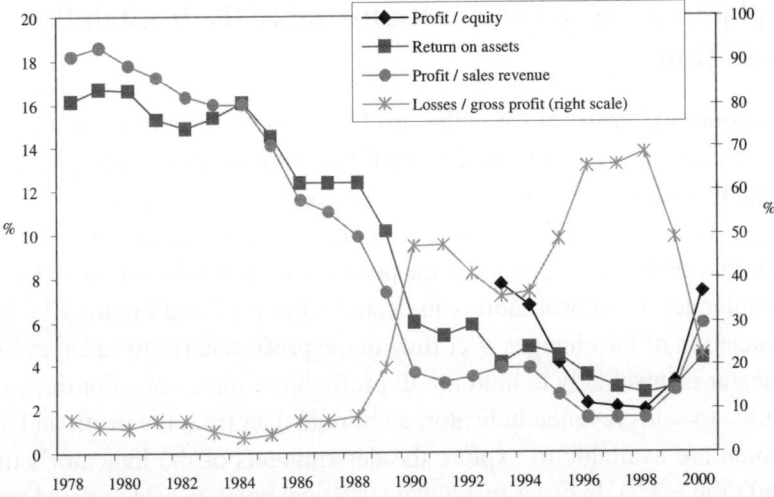

Sources: See Table 3.1.

Figure 3.1 Profitability of Industrial SOEs, 1978–2000

Third, all profitability measures recovered after 1997. This is in part due to the redefinition of the industrial SOE category.[44] The profitability of SOEs as defined prior to 1998 improved in 2000, but by less than that of the newly defined SOE category. Profitability data on SOEs as defined prior to 1998 for the years since 1998 are available only for 1999 and 2000, and only for profit relative to equity; these two values were 1.98% and 4.23%, with the 2000 value thus above the 1997 value, but below the 2000 value when the newly defined SOE category is used.[45]

---

[44] Prior to 1998, the SOE category comprised "pure" SOEs (those organized in accordance with the 1988 SOE regulation) as well as solely state-owned limited liability companies and SOE-SOE joint operation enterprises; since 1998, the SOE category further includes all other shareholding companies in which the state has a controlling share, and all other enterprises (and companies) in which the state has a share, but with data only in proportion to the state's equity share (for details, see Chapter 2).

[45] For the 1999 and 2000 data on the SOE category as defined prior to 1998, see *Industrial Yearbook 2001*, pp. 52f.

Explaining the Decline in Industrial SOE Profitability Over Time

In accounting terms, profit is the residual of sales revenue once all costs have been subtracted (Figure 2.4). Profit relative to sales revenue declined gradually in the early 1980s and then rapidly in the late 1980s; it recovered slightly in the early 1990s, fell again in the mid-1990s, and then improved in the late 1990s. As explained in the previous section, this pattern of decline is similar across all profitability indicators (Table 3.1 and Figure 3.1). Any explanation of the changes over time in the profit relative to sales revenue indicator is thus likely to hold for all profitability indicators. For the profit relative to sales revenue indicator, additional data from the profit and loss account are available to explore the determinants of the indicator's time trend (Table 3.2). In order to avoid a statistical break in sales-related taxes between 1993 and 1994, all sales revenue in the following (as well as in all tables and figures) is net of sales-related taxes.

1980s

Prior to 1993, profit was measured as the residual of sales revenue after subtracting sales costs and other costs. Sales costs as a share of sales revenue began to rise in the mid-1980s and then exploded from 88.07% in 1988 to 98.37% in 1990. Profit fell accordingly (Table 3.2). An explanation of the dramatic rise in sales costs in the late 1980s thus explains the fall in profit.

The years 1989 and 1990 were marked by a severe economic downturn (Figure 3.2). Following strong inflationary pressures in 1988, the State Council issued a blanket prohibition for starting new investment projects and organized a campaign to cut investment under construction that lasted well into 1989.[46] Real sales revenue of SOEs fell by 5.25% in 1989 and stagnated in 1990 (Table 3.2). The accounting system in place at the time required that sales costs cover the costs of production only to the extent that products were actually sold. The rise in the ratio of sales costs to sales revenue thus implies that unit production costs must have risen. An

---

[46] For details, see Carsten Holz (1999).

independent indicator, the production cost reduction index, confirms the rise in unit production costs with a drastic deterioration by 15.59% in 1988 and 22.17% in 1989 (Table 3.2).[47]

Material inputs, labor remuneration, and depreciation are consistently included in sales costs throughout the 1980s and 1990s (Figure 2.4). The cost of material inputs in the mid- to late 1980s rose significantly faster than the sales prices of finished products. The annual increase in the purchasing price index of raw materials, energy and power (*yuancailiao, ranliao he dongli*) was several percentage points above that of the ex-factory price index of industrial products (Figure 3.3).[48] Since most prices of industrial goods were determined by the state throughout the 1980s, the discrepancy in price rises for material inputs compared with those for finished products appears largely the result of the government's pricing policy. (See Figure 3.4 for the share of retail sales and producer goods sold at market prices compared with those at state-determined or state-guidance prices.)

Labor remuneration and depreciation charges may have made only a minor contribution to the rise in sales costs. Table 3.2 shows that, between 1988 and 1990, the wage bill, social welfare expenditures for current employees, and depreciation allowances rose only slightly, altogether by 1.42 percentage points of sales revenue.

---

[47] To calculate the production cost reduction index first requires identification of the set of products that are identical in the two periods covered. For these products, the index is defined as the percentage difference in unit production costs last year vs. this year (*Statistical Yearbook 1993*, p. 472f.).

[48] The rise in input prices is presumably due to the rapid growth in investment throughout the mid-1980s (Figure 3.2). While industrial SOEs that produce raw materials, energy and power gain from higher prices, some (or all) of the extra return may be appropriated by the state (through surcharges) or by commercial intermediaries. It is unlikely that the overall gain to industrial SOEs providing raw materials, energy and power is larger than the overall loss to industrial SOEs caused by smaller increases in the ex-factory price index. The discrepancy between input and output prices may even be larger than the official data suggest. The second half of the 1980s is also the period of the two-tier price system, with (low) state plan prices and (high) market prices for the same good. The official price indices may not properly capture the price rises for industrial inputs that were originally sold at plan prices to intermediaries, who then passed them on at significantly higher prices.

Table 3.2 Composition of Sales Revenue of Industrial SOEs, 1978–2000

Year	Sales-related taxes	As % of sales revenue (net of all sales-related axes)									Reference data				Real sales growth (%)	Turn-over ratio	Prod. cost reduction index
		Profit and loss account data																
		Sales costs	Sales profit	Sales fees	Fin. fees	Adm. fees	Other costs	Profit	Wages	Social welfare	Re-tirees	Subsid. to loss-m. ent.	Depre-ciation	Additions to invent.			
1978	10.09	79.04			(0.63)		2.75	18.21	7.50	0.43	0.23		4.90	3.44		2.67	4.6
1979	9.97	81.94			(0.60)		-0.54	18.60	7.81	0.55	0.41		4.84	6.48	6.71	2.73	0.3
1980	9.79	81.56			(0.66)		0.63	17.81	8.38	0.65	0.57		4.73	4.65	8.08	2.89	-1.1
1981	10.22	82.44			(0.36)		0.32	17.25	8.54	0.83	0.62		4.96	4.61	2.05	2.89	-1.17
1982	10.24	82.61			(0.50)		1.04	16.35	8.29	0.92	0.68		4.91	2.79	9.00	2.97	-0.38
1983	9.77	82.27			(1.02)		1.76	15.97	7.81	0.98	0.72		4.85	3.25	9.86	3.11	0.24
1984	10.08	83.89			(1.28)		0.17	15.94	8.69	1.16	0.88		4.72	2.08	8.90	3.26	-1.97
1985	11.36	87.43		12.44	(1.45)		-1.51	14.08	8.77	1.25	1.04	9.67	4.68	5.24	8.87	3.23	-7.7
1986	10.94	88.04			(1.89)		0.37	11.59	9.35	1.39	1.20	5.45	4.76	2.57	9.39	3.05	-7.34
1987	10.17	87.36			(1.89)		1.64	11.01	8.90	1.38	1.26	5.26	4.53	1.66	11.30	3.23	-7.04
1988	9.85	88.07			(1.93)		1.98	9.95	8.84	1.39	1.25	4.98	4.23	1.12	8.99	3.50	-15.59
1989	10.23	96.13			(3.01)		-3.51	7.38	9.08	1.45	1.34	5.95	4.32	7.65	-5.25	3.07	-22.17
1990	10.52	98.37			(3.14)		-2.03	3.66	9.72	1.61	1.53	5.46	4.55	8.03	1.14	2.65	-7.03
1991	9.93	91.97			(2.76)		4.86	3.17	9.08	1.52	1.51	4.03	4.56	3.46	12.55	2.78	-4.84
1992	9.22	90.33			(2.63)		6.17	3.50	8.74	1.45	1.56	2.91	4.63	2.61	12.91	2.99	-6.5
1993	7.80	83.48	3.96	(12.56)	2.44	6.32	-0.09	3.89	7.73	1.18	1.38	1.96	4.29	-2.64	10.84	1.40	
1994	9.59	80.56	2.03	(17.41)	4.86	9.95	-1.28	3.88	9.43	1.14	1.83	1.71	6.17		-14.93	1.26	
1995	8.72	81.73	2.35	(15.92)	5.71	9.94	-2.36	2.63	9.56	1.04	1.94	1.29	6.25	-0.84	3.18	1.33	
1996	8.84	82.27	2.63	(15.09)	5.48	9.39	-1.35	1.57	9.87	1.10	2.20	1.28	6.42	0.48	0.95	1.27	
1997	9.16	82.76	2.75	(14.49)	5.01	9.14	-1.24	1.58	9.56	1.10	2.33	1.36	6.42	-0.47	3.28	1.18	
1998	8.74	83.18	3.59	(13.23)	4.64	8.63	-1.65	1.61	8.22	1.15	2.09	1.02	6.59	0.17	(25.42)	1.10	
1999	8.83	82.89	4.33	(12.78)	4.03	8.28	-2.40	2.86	7.85	1.08	2.13	0.83	6.09	-1.09	9.74	1.12	
2000	8.45	81.54	3.21	(15.26)	3.00	7.80	-1.40	5.87	6.58	0.95	1.91	0.68	6.34	-4.02	14.46	1.26	

Table 3.2 (continued)

Sources:

Sales revenue, sales costs, and sales profit: *Seventeen Years of Reform*, p. 146; *Statistical Yearbook 1987*, p. 315; *1992*, p. 411; *1993*, p. 417; *1994*, p. 381; *1995*, p. 391; *1996*, p. 417; *1997*, p. 427; *1998*, p. 447; *1999*, p. 435; *2000*, p. 417; *2001*, p. 413. Real sales growth is based on sales revenue (net of sales-related taxes) deflated by the ex-factory price index (*Market Yearbook 1995*, p. 588; Statistical *Yearbook 2001*, p. 297).

Sales-related taxes (calculated either as 'profit plus taxes' less 'profit,' or equivalently as the sum of 'sales taxes and surcharges' and value-added tax): *Industrial Yearbook 1998*, p. 51; *Statistical Yearbook 1994*, p. 381; *1995*, p. 391; *1996*, p. 417; *1997*, p. 427; *1998*, pp. 451, 461; *1999*, p. 435; *2000*, p. 417; *2001*, p. 413.

Sales fees are obtained as a residual (sales revenue net of sales-related taxes, less sales costs and sales profit). Sales fee data available for 1995 in the *Industrial Census 1995*, Vol. 1, p. 51, perfectly match the value obtained as the residual.

Financial and administrative fees (charges): *Statistical Abstract 1994*, p. 86; *1995*, p. 86; *Industrial Census 1995*, Vol. 1, p. 51; *Statistical Abstract 1997*, p. 106; *1998*, p. 112; *1999*, p. 108; *2000*, p. 113; *2001*, pp. 125. Except for 1995, data are preliminary data first published in March of the following year. The revised data on financial and administrative charges are not published. Financial fee data in parentheses are calculated as total working capital loans (i.e., loans with less than one year maturity) of state banks to industrial state-owned enterprises (*Financial Statistics 1952-1996*) times the average annual interest rate on working capital loans of 6 months maturity or less (calculated from various issues of *Financial Yearbook*).

Other costs equal 100% less the columns sales costs, sales fees, financial fees, administrative fees, and profit.

Profit: *Industrial Yearbook 2001*, p. 24.

Subsidies to loss-making enterprises: *Statistical Yearbook 2000*, p. 257; *2001*, p. 247.

Additions to inventories is the difference of gross output value (*Seventeen Years of Reform*, p. 146; *Statistical Yearbook 1985*, p. 376; *1988*, p. 318; *1989*, p. 275; *1990*, p. 419; *1991*, p. 399; *1992*, p. 415; *1993*, p. 421; *1994*, p. 388; *1995*, p. 392; *1996*, p. 418; *1997*, p. 428; *1998*, p. 448; *1999*, p. 432; *2000*, p. 414; *2001*, p. 410) and sales revenue, with 1994 changes in inventories not computable because gross output value in 1994 includes an unknown volume of value-added tax, while sales revenue is net of value-added tax.

Turnover ratio equals sales revenue (net of sales-related taxes) divided by annual average fixed-quota working capital until 1992 (*Statistical Yearbook 1992*, p. 427; *1993*, p. 430), and divided by year-end current assets since 1993 (*Statistical Yearbook 1994*, p. 379; *1995*, p. 389; *1996*, p. 415; *1997*, p. 425; *1998*, p. 445; *1999*, p. 433; *2000*, p. 415; *2001*, p. 411).

Production cost reduction index: *Statistical Yearbook 1993*, p. 437.

For depreciation charges, wages, social welfare payments, and payments to retirees (comprising pensions and social welfare payments), see appendices to Chapter 2.

One item that rose drastically is inventories. SOEs had incentives not to cut production, because any increase in inventories proportionally cut the share of the wage bill and depreciation charges as well as various other administrative charges included in sales costs, thereby boosting profit. Concise data on the inventories of SOEs are lacking. An estimated time series reported in Table 3.2 shows a clear rise in inventories; economy-wide data included in Figure 3.2 also show a rise in inventories.[49] While changes in inventories do not affect current-period sales costs, they still impact on the current-period financial charges if the inventories need to be financed through debt and if this new debt furthermore comes at a high price. A turnover ratio until 1992 calculated as sales revenue (net of sales-

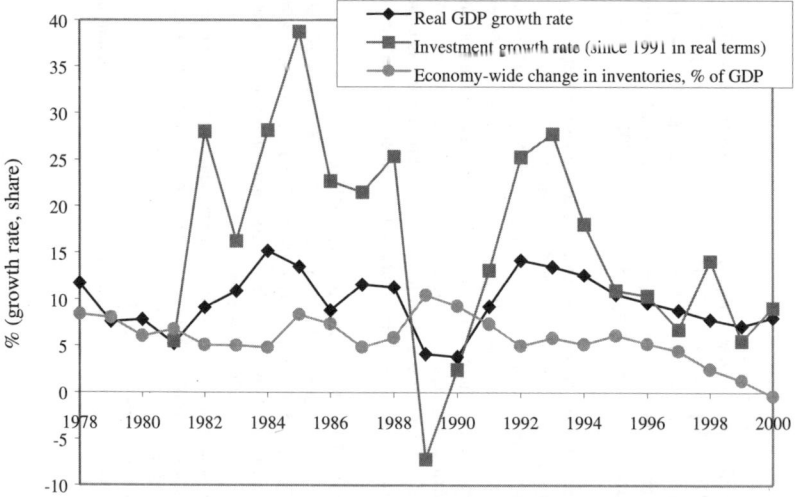

Sources: Real GDP growth rate: Statistical Yearbook 2001, p. 51; investment in current prices: Statistical Yearbook 2000, p. 168; 2001, p. 157; fixed asset investment price index to deflate investment data since 1991: Statistical Yearbook 1993, p. 269; 1994, p. 243; 1996, p. 272; 1998, p. 318; 2000, p. 306; 2001, p. 298; economy-wide inventories and nominal GDP: Statistical Yearbook 2001, pp. 49, 62.

Figure 3.2   Economic Cycles

---

[49] In the absence of inventory data, additions to inventories of industrial SOEs are calculated as the gross industrial output value less sales revenue. This difference also includes additions to semi-finished products and self-produced fixed assets in the particular year.

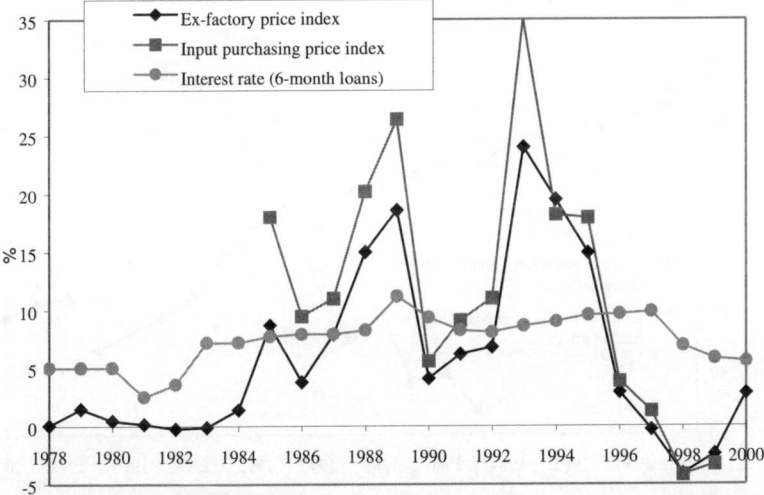

The time pattern of the GDP deflator, retail price index, and the fixed asset price index (available since 1991) are extremely close to that of the ex-factory price index of industrial products.

Sources: Ex-factory price index of industrial products: *Statistical Yearbook 2001*, p. 297; *Market Yearbook 1995*, p. 588; purchasing price index of raw materials, energy and power: *Price Yearbook 1992*, p. 538; *Market Yearbook 1996*, p. 587; *Price Yearbook 1996*, p. 331; *1997*, p. 423; *1998*, p. 348; *1999*, p. 357; *2000*, p. 368; average annual interest rate on working capital loans of up to six months duration: *Financial Yearbook*, various issues.

Figure 3.3   Price Indices and Interest Rates

related taxes) divided by average annual fixed-quota working capital (*ding'e liudong zijin*) shows that, by 1990, a quarter more fixed-quota working capital was required per unit of sales revenue than in 1988 (Table 3.2). Data are available only for government-determined fixed-quota working capital; the need for "excess" working capital (*chao'e liudong zijin*) may have risen even faster.

Financial charges paid by SOEs on working capital loans (loans of maximally one year maturity) were until 1992 included in sales costs and thus no separate data are available. Approximating these financial charges with the (average annual) six-month working capital loan interest rate multiplied by the year-end volume of working capital loans (loans with a maturity of up to one year) of state banks to industrial SOEs, a method that yields a very good match to the official net financial charges in 1993, shows

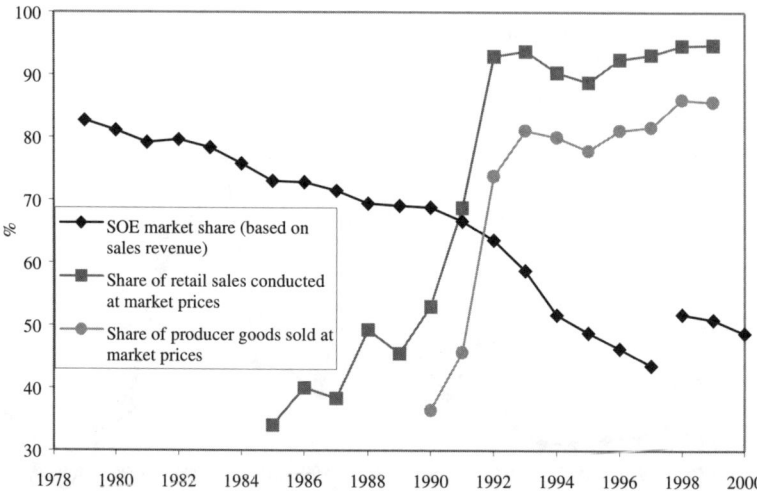

Sources: Industrial SOE market share is the sales revenue of industrial SOEs with independent accounting system divided by the sales revenue of all industrial enterprises with independent accounting system at the township level and above (since 1998 the revenue of all industrial SOEs divided by the sales revenue of all industrial SOEs plus of non-SOEs with annual sales revenue in excess of 5m RMB; all enterprises with independent accounting system); the annual data are published in each issue of the *Statistical Yearbook*, and in *Seventeen Years of Reform*, p. 146. Share of retail sales and producer goods sold at market prices: *Price Yearbook 1991*, p. 466; *1999*, p. 574–577; *2000*, pp. 495–497.

Figure 3.4 Industrial SOE Market Share and Price Liberalization

an increase in the financial charges of industrial SOEs in 1989 and 1990 (data in parentheses in the "financial fees" column in Table 3.2).[50]

"Other costs" capture the difference between sales revenue, net of sales taxes and surcharges as well as sales costs, and profit. The highly negative item "other costs" in 1989 and 1990 implies that items such as net non-business revenue and investment returns were positive. Non-business revenue includes subsidies. In fact, government subsidies to *all* loss-making enterprises reached a volume equivalent to 5.95% of the industrial SOE

---

[50] Actual financial charges paid are likely to be at times much higher than these calculations suggest. Following the rapid price rises in 1988, interest rates on all household deposits with three years or longer maturity were inflation-indexed (10 Sept. 1988 through 1 Dec. 1991). Lending rates were not inflation-indexed and therefore fell below the inflation-indexed deposit rates. Banks then are likely to have charged various extra fees on their loans; SOEs may also have had to resort to additional sources of financing outside the formal financial sector, where lending rates can only have been higher.

sales revenue in 1989 (Table 3.2).[51] Prior to 1993, "other costs" also included all pensions and social welfare payments to retirees. These increased modestly in 1989 and 1990 and thus rendered the item "others" less negative than it would otherwise have been. Similarly, losses incurred due to the government-ordained investment cuts in 1988 and 1989 had a positive effect on the item "others," thus reducing residual profit.

Of all potential causes of the reduction in residual profit, perhaps the most significant in the late 1980s were the over-proportionally rising material input prices (relative to output prices) and higher financial charges as SOEs increased their liabilities to finance their inventory investments. These cost increases are reflected in the ten percentage point rise in sales costs relative to sales revenue. The main cause behind these cost increases appears to be the partial price reform in 1988, i.e., an economic transition factor, with a detrimental impact on in particular SOE input prices. Strong inflationary pressures in 1988 then led to the administratively imposed stabilization process and the economic downturn in 1988 through 1990. SOEs did not cut back production correspondingly, perhaps because increases in inventories were to their temporary advantage. The proportional allocation of production costs to inventories meant that profit did not fall by as much as it would otherwise have, but these rising inventories only created problems to be resolved in the future.[52]

---

[51] After the tax reform of 1983-1985 with the introduction of a formal tax system, subsidies to loss-making SOEs were made explicit beginning in 1985. In 1985, these subsidies to *all* SOEs were equivalent to 16 times the losses of loss-making industrial SOEs, but in the following years, subsidies did not grow in correspondence with losses. In 1986 through 1988, subsidies to all SOEs exceeded the losses of loss-making industrial SOEs six times, but by 1991, subsidies were approximately equal to the losses of industrial SOEs. If industrial SOEs received a share of subsidies at least proportional to their employment share in all SOEs (approximately one-half), then this implies that by 1991 industrial SOEs no longer received enough subsidies to cover their losses.

[52] Changes in the definition of profit (or costs) also directly affect the size of profit. A number of changes in accounting practices in the late 1980s could have led to a reduction in profit (Table 3.3 below), but the data show no significant impact. For example, changes in depreciation rules in 1985 and 1987, by increasing depreciation as a sales cost item, should also have exerted downward pressure on profit; yet depreciation relative to sales revenue did not increase following these changes. Fixed assets are linearly depreciated based on their original purchasing price. Any increase in the average depreciation rate is likely to have been swamped by the rise in the ex-factory prices of industrial goods that underlie nominal sales revenue (and thus by the rise in the denominator of depreciation per unit of sales revenue).

The decline in profit relative to sales revenue prior to 1988 has been more gradual, with no clear, singular explanation, and the early and mid-1980s therefore are not further explored here; rising material input prices, a rising wage bill, and rising financial fees are likely to gradually have eroded the profit of SOEs prior to 1988.

1990s

The developments in the profit and loss account of SOEs in the 1990s are best analyzed by distinguishing between three sub-periods, namely (i) the period 1990 through 1992, (ii) the period 1993 through 1997, with a redefinition of profit and loss account items in 1993, and (iii) the period since 1998, with the change in enterprise coverage in 1998.

In the first sub-period, 1990 through 1992, sales costs as a percentage of sales revenue fell from their high of 98.37% in 1990 to 90.33% in 1992. This should have allowed profit to recover by up to eight percentage points to pre-1988 levels, but profit remained low due to the rise in "other costs" (in the published statistics implied as a residual). These rose from -2.03% in 1990 to 6.17% in 1992.

Sales costs relative to sales revenue may have fallen as drastically as they did in 1991 and 1992 largely due to double-digit growth in real sales revenue. But retrenchment and adjustment policies continued through the years 1990 and 1991, with economic growth lagging behind at below the level of the 1980s. SOE inventories continued to accumulate, albeit at a lower rate. Material input prices still rose faster than the ex-factory price index of industrial products. Only labor remuneration and financial charges (as shares of sales revenue) fell back slightly.

The government initiated numerous measures to improve SOE profitability, with a focus on "cleaning up hidden losses" (*qiankui*). The problems ranged from inventories that could not be sold and should be written off to accounts receivable that would never be received, previous-year losses that had not entered the profit and loss account but had been hidden in various other accounts, and inventory values that exceeded current sales prices. All "hidden" losses of 1992 were to enter the cost accounts in

1992. "Hidden" losses from previous years were to be written off over the next three years, beginning in 1993.[53]

Prior to 1993, corrections to the value of current assets, such as inventories and current accounts receivable, were regarded as non-business expenses; these are included in "other costs." Other "hidden" costs are also likely to be part of the "other costs." This led to the massive increase in other costs from −2.03% of sales revenue in 1988 to 6.17% in 1990; the size of these corrections in 1992 was almost as large as the total annual wage bill. The fact that profit in 1990 through 1992 did not recover thus appears primarily to be due to poor accounting practices in the previous economic downturn.

The second sub-period, 1993 through 1997, began with major changes to the accounting system in the form of a new set of accounting regulations issued on 1 July 1993. These created the new cost categories "sales fees," (net) "financial charges," and "administrative charges."[54] Sales fees were previously fully included in sales costs, while financial charges on working capital and all administrative charges were assigned to each good and then included in sales costs only for those goods that were sold. (For details on the accounting reform, see Table 3.3.) Since 1993, financial and administrative charges are subtracted in full from sales revenue, i.e., they are no longer assigned to inventories.

---

[53] See SC (28 April 1992, 3 May 1993); FM (5 June 1992, 28 Oct. 1992).

[54] Sales fees comprise transportation fees, loading fees, handling fees, packaging fees, insurance fees, travel fees, exhibition fees, security fees, examination fees, intermediaries' fees, labor service fees, advertisement fees, product damage, import-export handling fees, and salaries and welfare benefits of employees in sales. Financial charges cover all expenses incurred by the enterprise in collecting external funds, including net interest expenditures during production periods, exchange losses, foreign exchange handling fees, fees charged by financial institutions, and all other fees incurred in the collection of external funds. Administrative charges comprise all expenses paid by the administrative departments in organizing production, including expenses for company management, labor unions, staff and workers' education, labor insurance, insurance for those unemployed and waiting for jobs, the board of directors, consulting, audits, the courts, sewage, tree planting, (some very minor) taxes, land use, land damage, technology transfer, technological development, losses to intangible assets, the general office, accommodation, losses to accounts receivable, losses to inventories including value corrections as well as damage and scrap. (FM, 30 Dec. 1992, Art. 49, 50, 51.)

Table 3.3   Impact of Changes in Accounting Procedures, Tax System and Depreciation Rules on Profit

	Measure	Impact on profit
1983	Tax: energy and communication key construction fund tax of 10% (in 1989 revised to 25%) levied on enterprise retained profit, enterprise depreciation fund, and other sources (SC, 15 Dec. 1982)	pos.?
1984/85	Tax, first revision of 1980 accounting regulations: prior to 1984, enterprises handed over to government sales-related taxes and virtually all profit; beginning in 1984 most enterprises pay income tax (as well as sales-related taxes) plus an adjustment tax (depending on 1983 profit); profit that is "used" to repay loans is exempt from income tax for some enterprises; the retained profit is allocated to five funds: new product trial fund, production development fund, reserve fund, employee welfare fund, and employee bonus fund; beginning of subsidies to loss-making enterprises as formalized tax system requires re-transfer (SC, 18 Sept. 1984; Li Bo, 1989; FM, 5 Jan. 1985; SC, 5 March 1984; FM, 26 April 1984)	pos.?
1985	Depreciation: for 433 asset categories a fixed number of years for linear depreciation is provided; this revises a 1979 regulation that required the State Planning Commission, the State Economic Commission, and the "relevant" departments to determine depreciation rates (years) for each sector; all depreciation funds are to be retained in the enterprise, in contrast to the 1979 regulation requiring 30% of depreciation funds to be handed up to the superordinate department; a 30% shortened depreciation period applies to key backbone enterprises in the machinery industry (SC, 13 July 1979; SC, 26 April 1985; FM, 19 May 1986; FM, 7 March 1987; FM, 19 Jan. 1990)	?
1986	Tax: the newly established real estate tax and vehicle and boat use tax enter costs (but not as sales taxes and surcharges) (PRC FM Tax Office, 1996; FM, 31 Dec. 1992)	neg.
1987	Depreciation: if the depreciation rate according to asset categories falls below the previously comprehensive depreciation rate determined by the Finance Ministry, the higher comprehensive depreciation rate may be applied until 1990 (then revised to be effective until new depreciation rates are issued, which happened in 1993); (FM, 7 March 1987; FM, 19 Jan. 1990)	neg.?
1988	Tax: the newly established land use tax and stamp tax enter costs (but not as sales taxes and surcharges) (PRC FM Tax Office, 1996; FM, 31 Dec. 1992)	neg.
1989	Second revision of 1980 accounting regulations: bonus payments are to be gradually included as costs (rather than paid out of retained profit); "fixed capital" and "working capital" usage fee (*guding zijin zhanyongfei, liudong zijin zhanyongfei*) are no longer included as costs but paid out of profit; profit now includes a number of new items which presumably were not regulated previously (FM, 5 Jan. 1985; FM, 21 April 1989)	?
1993	New accounting regulations: switch from "total cost method" (*wanquan chengbenfa*) to "production cost method" (*zhizao chengbenfa*) with drastic reduction in items to be charged against profit:	
(i)	interest payments on fixed asset loans newly included as cost (previously paid out of profit; penalty interest continues to be paid out of profit); together with interest on working capital loans listed in a new cost account 'financial charges'	neg.

Table 3.3 (continued)

	Measure	Impact on profit
(ii)	pensions now enter costs in the new cost category "administrative charges" rather than as non-business expenses (no impact on profit)	
(iii)	technological development fees now fully enter costs (previously in part covered by production development fund, within profit)	neg.
(iv)	all bonus payments are to be included in costs (can be implemented gradually)	neg.
(v)	changed scope of welfare costs to be included in costs vs. in profit (all current expenses are to enter the cost accounts at up to 14% of wages and salaries, all welfare-related fixed asset purchases are to be paid out of profit)	neg.?
(vi)	travel fees and entertainment fees newly enter costs	neg.
(vii)	depreciation period shortened by up to one-half (on average by 20-30%); enterprise can choose from a range of years	neg. neg.
(viii)	previously, financial and administrative charges were assigned to inventories; the new method requires financial and administrative charges to be fully entered as costs in the interval in which they accrue; this implies that existing inventories need to be reevaluated and the reduction in value be budgeted as a one-off cost	

(SC, 26 April 1985; FM, 21 April 1989; FM, 30 Dec. 1992; FM, 31 Dec. 1992; FM, 17 May 1993; FM, 30 May 1993; FM, 10 June 1993; Li Xianzhong and Zhang Yongguo, 1995)

1993	Depreciation: the chemical industry can choose depreciation periods that are up to 30% shorter than the stipulated ones (FM, 6 Sept. 1993)	neg.
1994	Tax: reduction in the maximum corporate income tax rate from 55% to 33%, introduction of new taxes and expansion of the value-added tax; a reallocation of taxes from local governments to the center may induce an increase in locally levied fees; the end of the energy and communication key construction fund tax, the adjustment tax, and the possibility to "use" profit before income tax to repay loans (the latter to be implemented gradually); enterprises supposedly no longer hand over part of their profit to government departments, yet the relevant accounting category still exists (FM, 27 Aug. 1994)	?
Ongoing,	accounting: several of the above measures are implemented gradually across enterprises: transfer of bonus payments from profit to costs; the pension burden (administrative charges) rises as the relative number of retired staff and workers increases; range of possible depreciation rates allows enterprises to switch to faster depreciation[a]	neg.
Ongoing,	subsidies: price subsidies to enterprises are included in non-business revenue (FM, 21 April 1989), and subsidies for policy losses are listed as a separate item between investment returns and non-business revenue (FM, 10 June 1993); any change in subsidies thus affects profit	neg.

[a] Zhang Zuocai (1999) reports that in 1996 and 1997 an examination of 840,000 units (enterprises and other work units) found 16% of the units not to have established proper accounts, and the accounts of another 16.2% of the units to be severely flawed. In industry, the percentage is likely to be lower, but implementation of the new accounting system was probably not completed in 1993; for example, enterprises under the enterprise responsibility system were to adopt the new accounting system in full only once their responsibility contract had expired.

Numerous other changes to accounting practices, the tax system, and depreciation rules are also listed in Table 3.3. The changes have in common an unambiguous reduction in profit relative to sales revenue, either by shifting items originally designated as profit into the cost category or by raising costs exogenously. Thus, for example, interest payments on fixed asset loans are now newly treated as financial charges rather than being counted as part of the residual profit. Bonus payments to labor are now regarded as costs rather than as an item within the residual profit. Current expenses on staff social welfare are now capped at 14% of wages and salaries, and these current expenses are regarded as costs (only fixed asset purchases for staff social welfare purposes continue to be paid out of profit). The depreciation period for fixed assets was shortened by up to one-half (on average 20–30%), thus increasing costs. Although these measures were taken in 1993 and 1994, implementation of some items could be stretched over the following years, while for other items, implementation simply did not happen immediately as envisaged.

With the introduction of the three new profit and loss account items (sales fees, financial charges, and administrative charges), sales costs fell from 90.33% of sales revenue in 1992 to 83.48% in 1993 and then remained remarkably stable throughout the mid-1990s. "Other costs" similarly fell in 1993, as some previous "other cost" items, such as pensions and special write-offs on current assets, were now included in administrative charges. Financial charges and administrative charges together rose rapidly between 1993 and 1995 by almost seven percentage points, before falling back slightly. By 1992, profit as a share of sales revenue at 3.50% was at such a low level that the increases in financial and administrative charges despite a slight reduction in sales costs and other costs since 1993 drove profit to just 1.58% of sales revenue in 1997. A number of factors account for the rises in the various charges.

In the economic downturn of 1989–1990, SOEs had accumulated inventories equivalent to perhaps 8% of sales revenue for each year, with further inventory accumulation in 1991 and 1992. Inventories of finished products had been assigned financial and administrative charges, whereas, according to the new 1993 accounting regulations, financial and administrative charges were to enter the profit and loss account in full in the period in which they occurred; these accumulated financial and administrative charges thus now had to be written off. Pre-1992 corrections were to be entered as administrative charges over three years beginning in 1993. The impact of these write-offs on administrative charges in the year 1993 cannot be determined because 1992 data are not available. Administrative charges rose in 1994 from their 1993 "base year" value and remained at their new, high level in 1995, before falling back slightly in 1996 and 1997.[55]

Rising interest rates in the mid-1990s helped to keep financial charges high. Following Deng Xiaoping's tour through South China in early 1992, real investment soared (Figure 3.2) and material input prices again rose faster than the ex-factory price index of industrial products (Figure 3.3). Inflation reached double-digit levels in 1993 through 1995 and loan interest rates rose to close to ten percent for six-month working capital loans and stayed high even after inflation abated (Figure 3.3).[56] Bank lending remained strong as a rapid rise in supplier credit led to a chain of triangular debt with severe implications for production, which had to be resolved through new bank loans.[57] A turnover ratio since 1993 calculated as sales revenue (net of

---

[55] Administrative charges may have remained high because enterprises that linked their total wage bill to their "economic efficiency" now included any increase in wages as administrative charges (FM, 10 June 1993), rather than paying such additional wages out of retained profit as before. Furthermore, pension payments, newly included in administrative charges in 1993, rose by one percentage point (of sales revenue) between 1993 and 1997.

[56] Interest rates on household deposits of three years maturity or longer were again inflation-indexed from 11 July 1993 until May 1997, thus exceeding loan credit interest rates. Enterprises that were unable to secure loans at the low real lending rates had no choice but to incur high-interest borrowing outside the state banks.

[57] The central government started a first campaign to clean up the triangular debt problem in March 1990 (SC, 26 March 1990). It repeatedly intervened with directed credit injections to resolve triangular debt chains in 1991 and 1992, before Prime Minister Zhu Rongji in mid-1993 ordered a clamp-down on the banking system that had been channeling funds into speculative and high-interest uses. A summary report issued in February 1993 provides an overview of the administrative efforts to resolve the triangular debt problem (SC, 9 Feb. 1993). Industrial SOEs incurred ever higher liabilities to suppliers. Sales-related taxes had to be paid even if the payment on the goods had not yet been received by the enterprise itself, leading to an additional need for borrowing. Some enterprises also responded by falling behind in their tax payments to the government. The issue of not paying outstanding taxes first received separate attention, but was soon merged with the triangular debt issue. On the banking system's efforts to resolve the triangular debt problem, see also *Financial Yearbook 1992*, pp. 31, 52, 80, 457, 503f.

sales-related taxes) divided by year-end current assets — the change in the denominator between 1992 and 1993 being dictated solely by data availability — shows a decline by one-fifth between 1993 and 1997, implying ever increasing current assets. With current assets mostly financed through borrowing, the volume of financial charges relative to sales revenue rises.

By 1993, SOEs faced a severe problem of insufficient depreciation funds. With fixed assets being depreciated based on their original prices, the rise in producer goods prices (as indicated by the rise in the ex-factory price index) meant that the accumulated depreciation funds were by far too small to replace obsolete fixed assets. In 1993, the government asked SOEs to re-evaluate all their fixed assets purchased before 1991 to market prices and to raise their depreciation funds correspondingly, thus increasing sales costs, which include depreciation charges (SC, 3 May 1993). Depreciation relative to sales revenue in 1994 rose by almost two percentage points and remained at the new level in the years after. On the other hand, any appreciation of fixed assets would enter non-business revenue and would thus reduce "other costs."

The reallocation of numerous items previously included in "other costs" to the new accounting categories necessarily implied a reduction in other costs in 1993, as did any appreciation of fixed assets; other costs fell by more than six percentage points. Since 1993, other costs, calculated in Table 3.2 as a residual from the few profit and loss account items on which data are available, comprises non-business expenses less non-business revenue, investment returns, and "other" business profit (not captured by "sales profit"). (See also Figure 2.4.) Non-business expenses may still have been relatively large throughout the mid-1990s.[58] The fact that enterprises did not increase inventories significantly after 1992 despite stagnating sales revenue suggests that some production lines may have stopped production. Losses associated with irregular production stops or extraordinary write-offs of fixed assets are included in net non-business expenses.

---

[58] Non-business expenses comprise losses to fixed assets including value corrections as well as damage and scrap and losses incurred in the sale of fixed assets, losses from non-seasonal production stops that are not caused by repairs, school fees for children of employees, extraordinary losses, donations to public social relief activities, and additions to compensation funds and contract violation penalty funds (FM, 30 Dec. 1992, Art. 60).

The sales outlook for SOEs never improved much again. By the mid-1990s, growth in real sales revenue of SOEs was flat.[59] One explanation for the inability to raise output prices and the stagnation in sales revenue is an increase in competition in the mid-1990s. As Figure 3.4 shows, between 1990 and 1992, the share of all retail goods and all producer goods sold at market prices approximately doubled to about eighty percent. Price liberalization allows price competition and it may also be a proxy for the relaxation of administrative barriers to entry in some industries. The share of SOEs in total industrial sales revenue began to slip in 1991, fell rapidly until 1994, and declined further but more gradually in the following years. Many industrial SOEs, heavily battered by the 1989–1990 economic downturn, never had a chance to recover as they began to defend their already low profitability levels against competition.[60] (The issue of competition is explored in more detail in the following chapter.)

In the third sub-period, since 1998, industrial SOEs appear to have turned the corner. While the new coverage of SOEs did not change the SOE profitability level much in 1998, profitability improved both in 1999 and in 2000. The rise in profit relative to sales revenue from 1.61% in 1998 to 5.87% in 2000 was brought about by modest reductions in sales costs, financial charges, and administrative charges. The reduction in sales costs could be due to the elimination of the gap between the input purchasing price index and the ex-factory price index (Figure 3.3), but also to a 1.64 percentage point reduction in the wage bill relative to sales revenue. Social welfare payments to current employees stabilized relative to sales revenue, as did depreciation charges. Financial charges may have fallen by one-third mainly because of interest rate reductions (Figure 3.3).

The reduction in interest rates since 1998 at first sight suggests that the increase in SOE profitability in the late 1990s is in large part due to fortunate events external to SOEs. Non-SOEs, competing with SOEs, faced similarly low interest charges and output prices (and thereby sales revenue) and thus

---

[59] In 1994, real sales revenue fell by almost 15%. There is no obvious explanation for this sharp fall; it could in part be an accounting artifact due to the introduction of the new accounting system in 1993 and the tax reforms in 1994.

[60] Competition from abroad also increased when import tariffs fell in 1995 from an average of 36% to 23%; another reduction to 17% occurred in 1997 (Chen Qingtai, 1998, p. 8).

should similarly have seen their profitability increase. Yet their profitability did not improve as much as that of SOEs (Chapter 6 below).

A more plausible explanation for the rising profitability level in SOEs might be the three-year SOE reform program of 1998 through 2000. Two reform elements had an immediate impact on profitability. One was a drastic reduction in the number of SOE employees, reflected in the falling wage bill. The other element was the slow but steady exit of the worst-performing SOEs. Thus, the general decline of SOE profitability in the mid-1990s concealed a combination of a relatively constant volume of profit in profitable enterprises and rising losses in loss-making enterprises. The three-year SOE reform program especially targeted the worst loss-makers, leading to slightly falling aggregate losses every year, while aggregate profit of profitable enterprises grew rapidly. (The three-year SOE reform program is discussed in more detail in Chapter 8.)

Incentives to Misreport Profit

Accounting regulations invariably grant enterprises some leeway in the determination of profit. The 1993 accounting regulations, for example, give enterprises a choice of five valuation methods for materials (FM, 31 Dec. 1992).[61] In a period of double-digit inflation, a switch from last-in-first-out accounting of materials to first-in-first-out may temporarily raise profit significantly. Similarly, the (limited) choice since 1993 of over how many years to depreciate fixed assets influences the size of residual profit. This raises the question of whether enterprises have incentives to report a small or a large profit.

Beginning in 1979, enterprises were allowed to retain part of their surplus (profit). Once an enterprise had fulfilled various planned targets, such as on output quantity and quality as well as profit, retained profit could be used to make bonus payments to employees. This created incentives to report a large profit. Bonus payments subsequently grew so rapidly — which

---

[61] Once one method has been chosen, it should not be changed arbitrarily (*suiyi*), but the regulation does not mention under what circumstances a change is permissible.

implies an increasing amount of retained profit — that in 1981 the State Council warned against issuing excessive bonus payments and then, in 1984, levied a progressive bonus tax.[62] At the same time, a State Council circular of 1984 created incentives for loss-making enterprises to report a profit. The circular threatened factory directors and managers with disciplinary action and dismissal if they could be blamed for not turning targeted losses into profit (SC, 3 May 1984). Profitability by all definitions thereafter remained relatively stable until the mid-1980s (Table 3.1).

The enterprise contract responsibility system introduced in the first half of 1987 directed enterprises to achieve certain targets in exchange for greater autonomy. The core target was the submission of a fixed amount of profit to the government, equaling the income tax plus the adjustment tax paid in the previous year. Enterprises then paid their taxes but were reimbursed 80% of any taxes paid in excess of the contracted fixed amount. The contracted amount of profit submission was based on the previous year's profit (loss); in extreme cases of profit fluctuation it was based on the previous two to three years' profit (loss). The contract then was valid for at least three years (SC, 27 Feb. 1988). By the end of 1988, 93% of all industrial enterprises had adopted the contract responsibility system (Gao Shangquan, 1996, p. 73).

Enterprises again faced incentives to report high profit. A large amount of retained profit allowed large bonuses and social welfare payments. But due to the economic downturn in 1989, these incentives may not have had much impact. As profit fell, many enterprises were unable to meet their contracted profit submissions. Some contracts were re-negotiated.[63] Otherwise, maintaining high output and increasing inventories temporarily boosted profit as overheads proportionally assigned to inventories lowered sales costs, but this only created problems that had to be solved in the following years.

---

[62] See SC (28 June 1984). In 1978, bonuses accounted for 2.48% of total wages in (all) state-owned units; in 1980 for 9.70%; and in 1985 for 14.51% (*Statistical Yearbook 1998*, p. 158).

[63] This was especially the case for financially weak enterprises; governments more often reduced than raised tax targets and thus allowed losses to be smaller than they otherwise would have been (Chen Qingtai, 1998, p. 2).

By 1992, the government initiated numerous measures to reduce the volume of "hidden" losses and issued enterprise targets for turning losses into profit. The ensuing incentives to misreport profit may have been mixed. On the one hand, enterprise managers could have used the chance to write down their enterprises' assets as extraordinary losses as far as possible, reducing profit. On the other hand, the regulations on loss reduction threatened penalties if targets were not met. In the end, with the rise in triangular debt and therefore high financial charges, many of these targets could simply not be fulfilled.[64]

With the introduction of a modern tax system in 1994, the contract responsibility system with its arrangements of surrendering profit (or "taxes") to the government or to various government departments was phased out. Tax contracting now continues only for a few very large state-owned conglomerates. Under the new tax system, SOEs pay a maximally 33% corporate income tax on their profit, compared with the 55% corporate income tax rate originally introduced in 1984–1985; the adjustment tax as well as the energy and communication key construction fund tax were abolished. The tax burden on profit is thus smaller than before, reducing incentives to hide profit. But the 1993 accounting reform asked enterprises to enter all bonus payments and recurrent social welfare payments as costs; enterprises thus had fewer incentives to report a large profit, which previously would have allowed high bonus payments (out of profit).

In 1995, the government also allowed selected enterprises, which were having difficulties servicing or repaying their capital construction loans originally extended between 1979 and 1988 under the 'switching from budget appropriations to loans' scheme, to relabel these loans as 'state equity' (SC, 12 July 1995). Further measures on debt forgiveness followed,

---

[64] The nationwide target in 1992 for industrial SOEs directly under the budget was to reduce losses by 10% (20% for market-based losses, and no change in policy-induced losses), which was met, but the 1993 target of reducing losses across industrial SOEs by 20% was badly missed (SC, 28 April 1992; *Jingji tizhi gaige neibu cankao*, no. 19, 1993, pp. 3–9).

Yu Lixin (1994) reports that, according to one survey of 50 loss-making enterprises by the China Industry Association, in 1991, 19.4% of all losses were due to policy reasons, 47.8% to macroeconomic reasons, and 32.8% to poor management. By 1993, according to a survey by the State Planning Commission and the State Economic Commission, these percentages in the case of 2586 loss-making enterprises were 9%, 9%, and 81.9%, respectively. Losses could no longer be attributed to systemic or cyclical causes.

culminating in the establishment of four resolution trust companies in 1999 and 2000 to take over the bad loans of the state banks, with about one-third of the transferred loans subsequently turned into state equity. These measures created considerable moral hazard problems even in the early stages when they were only under discussion but not yet implemented. Enterprises reporting losses were rewarded with debt forgiveness or free funding. Managers who took a long-term view thus could underreport profit in order to obtain debt forgiveness for their enterprises. On the other hand, managers who took a short-term view could opt for exaggerated profit in order to further their careers. The overall effect on reported profit is ambiguous. While, in the 1980s, enterprises predominantly faced incentives to overreport profit, by the early and mid-1990s these incentives varied, but perhaps with an overall tendency to lead to the underreporting of profit.

The literature points in the same direction. Di Na (1992, pp. 2f.) paints a picture of wide-spread underreporting of *losses*. Thus a "recent" Finance Ministry study of 257 industrial SOEs in nine provinces found "hidden" (i.e., unreported) losses equivalent to 180% of reported losses. Similarly, a study of 10,580 industrial SOEs conducted by 40 branches of the Industrial and Commercial Bank of China in the second half of 1990 (to cover the first half of 1990) revealed hidden losses equivalent to 172% of reported losses; reported and hidden losses together were equivalent to 56% of the sum of profit and taxes.[65]

In contrast, Thomas Rawski (1999, p. 146), relying on a Chinese source, stated that "a well-informed researcher cites reports indicating that about 60 per cent of the actual profits of state industry went unreported in 1990." By the late 1990s, the tendency to overreport profit appears to have definitely turned. Zhang Weiying (1999, p. 22), claimed, based on personal experiences, that "telling 'good news' was a dominant strategy in pre-reform China. But now the fashion has changed. Today China's SOEs have strong incentives to tell 'bad news.' Although there are some loss-makers which

---

[65] If aggregate data on industrial SOEs in 1990 are relevant to this sample of 10,580 industrial SOEs, then the hidden losses in this sample exceeded the reported profit. (In 1990, the sum of profit and taxes for the aggregate of all industrial SOEs was equal to 3.87 times the profit; *Industrial Yearbook 2001*, p. 24. The hidden losses in the sample enterprises amounted to 10.83b RMB.)

still overreport, most state enterprises underreport profits, because reported profits belong to the state, whereas hidden profits accrue to management." [66]

Operating Surplus

The reliability of accounting profit as a measure of industrial SOE profitability over time is severely challenged by changing accounting rules and changing incentives to misreport profit. Even if over- and underreporting of profit were to cancel out in the aggregate, the revisions to the accounting system, particularly those effective since 1993, would make profit data highly time inconsistent. One alternative profit measure that avoids some of the shortcomings of accounting profit is production-based operating surplus. The operating surplus remains unaffected by most changes in accounting practices, such as a transfer of profit items into cost categories. Any attempt to mis-represent profit by manipulating such accounting items as non-business revenue or expenses similarly does not affect the operating surplus (but affects accounting profit). On the other hand, the operating surplus is not a perfect measure because it does not capture items such as corrections to the value of fixed assets or corrections to the value of inventories but the accounting profit does, which may be desirable to include in a meaningful profit measure.

Data and Time Trends

Operating surplus by definition is the residual of value-added. Value-added (including all taxes) less (i) labor remuneration, (ii) net taxes on production, and (iii) depreciation equals the operating surplus. For the full economy, the relevant data are published, but for industrial SOEs, the income components of value-added must be pieced together.

Labor remuneration according to its official definition comprises wages plus social insurance and welfare payments (NBS, 1997, pp. 200f.). Wages

---

[66] On the other hand, according to the World Bank (1999, pp. 28 and 37), "a 1998 audit of 162 key loss-making enterprises found that losses were twice as high as reported. The audit also revealed unreported profits in the petroleum industry and overstated profits in state petrochemical enterprises."

include official wages, allowances, and all bonus payments, whether monetary or in-kind. Social insurance and welfare payments comprise all such payments to current as well as retired staff and workers (including pensions). With data on total labor remuneration in industrial SOEs not available, these data are constructed as explained in an appendix to Chapter 2.

Net taxes on production consist primarily of sales-related taxes (i.e., "sales taxes and surcharges" and, since 1994, the separately listed value-added tax). Net taxes on production, in addition, include taxes listed as part of the administrative charges, namely road construction fees; sewage fees, water and electricity fees and surcharges; and special payments to the government for tobacco and alcohol. Net taxes on production are net of subsidies for policy losses, subsidies to the grain system (not relevant to industry), and taxes returned to foreign trade enterprises for exported goods, i.e., these three items are subtracted (NBS, 1997, p. 15). Only data on sales-related taxes are available. The other items are likely to be quite small and, furthermore, partly cancel each other out (through the additions and subtractions), with the residual net effect probably being of rather minor size.

Official depreciation data for industrial SOEs are available only for the years 1985 through 1991; estimates of depreciation in all other years are derived in an appendix to Chapter 2. Data on industrial SOE value-added are available only for the years since 1992; estimates of value-added in the years prior to 1992 are also derived in an appendix to Chapter 2. Operating surplus finally is obtained as the residual of value-added after subtracting labor remuneration, sales-related taxes, and depreciation.

Table 3.4 for industrial SOEs reports the percentage shares of the four items that compose value-added over the period 1978 through 2000. The 1993 values are severe outliers due to an implausibly large increase in nominal value-added in 1993, which then consequently affects residual operating surplus; 1993 values are therefore ignored in the following. The 1992 and 1994 value-added data and thus all data on the shares of the constituent items may also be of questionable quality.[67]

---

[67] No time series data of industrial SOE value-added have ever been published. Each annual value is published in the corresponding year's *Statistical Yearbook* only. (Some issues of the *Industrial Yearbook* include two years' data.) Earlier data are thus not revised. With the introduction of the System of National Accounts in 1993, the early value-added data for industrial SOEs appear to be of dubious quality.

Table 3.4   Composition of Value-added in Industrial SOEs, 1978–2000

Industrial SOEs	As share of value-added (in %)					Growth rate of value-added
	Constituent elements of value-added (sum = 100%)				Profit	
	Labor remuneration	Sales-related taxes	Depreciation	Residual: Operating surplus		
1978	17.77	21.95	10.67	49.62	39.61	
1979	19.02	21.59	10.48	48.92	40.28	8.78
1980	21.70	22.04	10.66	45.60	40.10	4.48
1981	22.89	23.45	11.38	42.27	39.56	0.37
1982	23.56	24.41	11.69	40.33	38.96	4.69
1983	22.87	23.48	11.66	42.00	38.40	8.82
1984	24.95	23.41	10.96	40.69	37.02	14.29
1985	25.17	25.88	10.65	38.30	32.05	20.71
1986	29.40	26.94	11.71	31.95	28.53	7.79
1987	30.30	26.71	11.91	31.08	28.91	12.57
1988	31.51	27.03	11.61	29.86	27.30	20.02
1989	33.25	28.65	12.10	26.00	20.67	10.03
1990	36.84	30.11	13.04	20.01	10.48	2.99
1991	36.39	29.84	13.70	20.08	9.53	13.96
1992	34.58	27.13	13.62	24.67	10.30	23.07
1993	29.69	22.49	12.39	35.43	11.22	40.21
1994	33.48	25.90	16.68	23.94	10.49	8.54
1995	38.23	26.59	19.04	16.15	8.01	5.12
1996	39.60	26.59	19.32	14.49	4.72	5.24
1997	38.25	26.97	18.91	15.87	4.65	5.15
1998	33.70	25.69	19.38	21.23	4.74	20.49
1999	31.82	25.40	17.53	25.26	8.22	9.53
2000	28.12	25.19	18.88	27.82	17.48	13.56
Total economy	Labor remuneration	Net production taxes	Depreciation	Operating surplus		
1978	49.66	12.81	9.71	27.82		
1985	52.64	11.99	9.90	24.98		
1990	53.45	13.06	11.68	21.86		
1991	52.20	13.28	12.33	22.26		
1992	50.12	13.38	12.87	23.68		
1993	50.70	13.84	11.64	23.88		
1994	51.16	13.63	11.91	23.26		
1995	52.85	12.85	12.35	21.96		
1996	53.40	12.57	12.80	21.23		
1997	52.79	13.16	13.63	20.42		
1998	53.14	13.40	14.47	18.99		
1999	52.38	13.54	15.07	19.01		
2000	51.38	15.40	14.16	19.06		

Sources:
Value-added: see appendix to Chapter 2.
Wages, social insurance and welfare, sales-related taxes (sales taxes and surcharges, value-added tax), depreciation, profit: see Table 3.2.
Economy-wide value-added and its components: NBS (1998), pp. 87-96, 125-33; *Statistical Yearbook 1998*, p. 66; *1999*, p. 66; *2000*, p. 64; *2001*, p. 60.

The residual operating surplus as a percentage of industrial SOE value-added almost halved between 1978 and 2000. But this decline was far from uniform. In the period 1978 through 1990, the share of the operating surplus declined almost continuously from 49.62% to 20.01%. Approximately two-thirds of the thirty percentage point decline in operating surplus is explained by an increase in labor remuneration, with the other one-third explained by an increase in sales-related taxes; depreciation remained rather constant.

In the early and mid-1990s, the operating surplus decreased further to a low in 1996, before recovering slightly in 1997. The fall in the share of the operating surplus to 14.49% in 1996 was in part due to another increase in the share of labor remuneration to 39.60%, and an almost doubling of the share of depreciation to 19.32%; sales-related taxes following the 1994 tax reform fell back and remained rather constant at 25–27% in the mid- and late 1990s.[68]

With the switch to the new SOE definition in 1998, the share of operating surplus improved by more than five percentage points and continued to rise to 27.82% in 2000. Much of this increase was due to a drastic reduction in the share of labor remuneration from 39.60% in 1996 to 33.70% in 1998 and 28.12% in 2000.

A comparison between industrial SOEs and all economic activities in China (including industrial SOEs) shows that industrial SOEs' operating surplus in 1978 at 49.62% of value-added was almost double the economy-wide average of 27.82% in 1978. This reflects the fact that planners in China maintained a relative price structure conducive to the accumulation of the economy-wide surplus in the industrial sector, which then facilitated

---

[68] Any difference between "net taxes on production" and "sales-related taxes" is likely to have become more positive over time, because subsidies to (all) loss-making enterprises in 1997 were little more than half their 1989 peak values (in absolute terms, unadjusted for inflation), while various fees and surcharges that are included in net taxes on production but for which no data are available are likely to have increased in number and value over time. If net taxes on production in the early reform years exceeded sales-related taxes, the difference is likely to be even larger in the later reform years. If net taxes on production in the early reform years fell short of sales-related taxes, the difference is likely to be smaller in the later reform years, or net taxes on production may have come to exceed sales-related taxes. This implies that a curve depicting the share of operating surplus in industrial SOE value-added over time should have a more negative (or less positive) slope.

appropriation of this surplus by the government. By the early 1990s, the share of operating surplus in value-added of industrial SOEs was equal to the value for the whole economy, suggesting that the special role of industry in the collection of the economy-wide surplus had largely ended. Industrial SOEs, however, continued to pay sales-related taxes as a share of value-added that were almost twice the economy-wide value.

Depreciation as a share of value-added is always a few percentage points higher for industrial SOEs than for the economy as a whole, while the share of labor remuneration even in the peak year 1996 was still more than ten percentage points below the rather constant economy-wide value. These discrepancies are explained by the fact that economy-wide values include agriculture and services, which both require a relatively small stock of fixed assets (in relation to value-added) and thus experience low depreciation, and in which much of the operating surplus tends to be included in labor remuneration.[69]

Explaining the Difference in the Time Trends of Operating Surplus and Profit

If profit is compared to value-added, it follows a strikingly similar pattern to operating surplus until the late 1980s (Table 3.4 or Figure 3.5). Until 1988, profit is almost as large as the operating surplus. But profit then experienced a much sharper drop in the late 1980s and never recovered in the early 1990s. While operating surplus in the early 1990s remained at about 20%, profit remained at about 10%. Operating surplus relative to

---

[69] Labor remuneration in agriculture comprises the income of rural households from employment in collective- or state-owned agricultural enterprises plus the net income (income after expenses) of rural households from private agricultural production, less depreciation (NBS, 1997, p. 26). Most agricultural production is organized by individual households; the calculation of labor remuneration in this household-based agricultural sector does not allow for any operating surplus. Depreciation in an agricultural system with little mechanization should be small. In 1998, taxes, monetary and in-kind payments to the collective, and various fees amounted to just 5.1% of the total net income of rural households (*Zhongguo jingji daobao*, 1 Sept. 1999). Labor remuneration in agriculture expressed as a share of agricultural value-added is thus likely to be around 90%. Agriculture accounted for 18.4% of GDP, compared to industry's 42.1% (*Statistical Yearbook 1999*, p. 56).

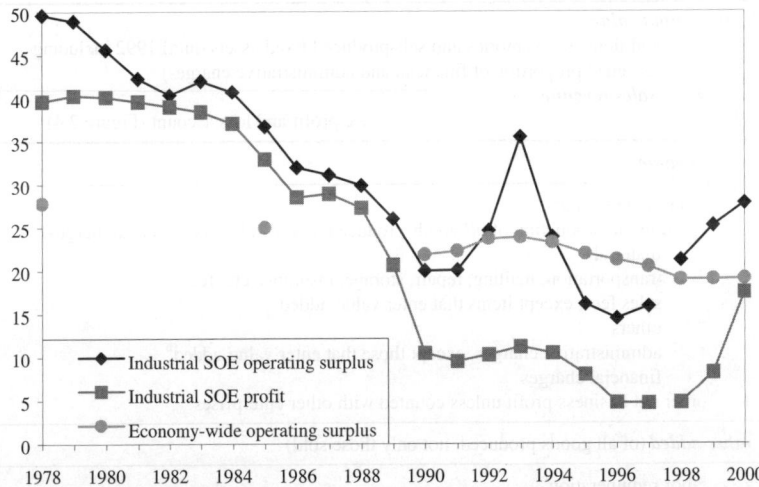

Industrial SOE operating surplus and profit are expressed as percentage of industrial SOE value-added, economy-wide operating surplus as percentage of economy-wide GDP.
Sources: See Table 3.4.

Figure 3.5 Operating Surplus and Profit as Shares of Value-added

value-added then fell by almost twenty percentage points to 16.15% in 1995, while profit relative to value-added fell by only three percentage points to 8.01%. The percentage point difference between operating surplus and profit relative to value-added remained rather constant in the following years, with both ratios falling further until 1997, and then, following the new SOE definition, gradually rising between 1998 and 2000 to 27.82% and 17.48% in 2000.[70]

In explaining the diverging patterns of operating surplus and profit (both relative to value-added) in the years 1988 through about 1991, operating

---

[70] In the U.S., operating profit of the S&P 500 companies between 1987 and 1997 grew at the same rate as economy-wide operating surplus ("national accounts surplus"), but between 1998 and (presumably) 2001, operating profit of the S&P 500 companies doubled, while economy-wide operating surplus stagnated (*The Economist*, "A Survey of International Finance," 18 May 2002, p. 18). This is the reverse of the pattern of industrial SOE profit vs. operating surplus in China since 1990. The U.S. data are interpreted as implying exaggeration of profit. The data on industrial SOEs in China then could be intereppreted as underreporting of profit.

88 China's Industrial State-owned Enterprises: Between Profitability and Bankruptcy

Gross output value[a]
- additions to inventories and self-produced fixed assets (until 1992 including assigned proportion of financial and administrative charges)
= **sales revenue**
    see profit and loss account (Figure 2.4)

Gross output value[a]
- intermediate inputs
  (used in the production of *all* goods produced; net of sales taxes and surcharges)
  * materials
  * transportation, mailing, repair, storage, insurance etc. fees
  * sales fees, except items that enter value-added
  * others
  * administrative charges, except those that enter value-added[b]
  * financial charges
+ other net business profit unless counted with other enterprises

= **value-added** (of all goods produced, not only those sold)

- labor remuneration[c]
- net taxes on production (sales taxes and surcharges + other production-related taxes and surcharges - subsidies)
- depreciation

= **operating surplus**

- subsidies (re-enter as non-business revenue or separate items after business profit)
+ labor remuneration out of profit
+ other net business profit that is not included in this enterprise's value-added
- certain types of administrative charges that were not subtracted out earlier:[b]
    40% of trade union fees
    additions to provisions for asset losses, losses from failed experiments, as well as production losses due to seasonal repairs
    insurance against natural disasters
    "hygiene" and tree planting fees
- production- and sales-related taxes imputed to additions to inventories (unless subtracted out through inclusion in net taxes on production)[a]
- imputed profit for additions to inventories[a]

= **business profit**

+ investment returns
+ net non-business revenue (non-business revenue - non-business expenses)

= **profit**

a In contrast to the profit and loss account, gross output value and value-added are based on all products produced. Material and transportation fees, etc., in the derivation of value-added thus cover the expenses for all products produced, not only for those sold. According to the regulations of the National Bureau of Statistics on how to calculate value-added, gross output value is valued at the ex-factory price, i.e., the sales price (NBS, 1997, pp. 7 and 32). NBS (1997, pp. 268f.) furthermore explicitly suggests that additions to semi-finished and finished products are not only valued at production costs but that (upward) adjustments be made for not yet paid production- and sales-related taxes since sales revenue, on which the gross output value of those products that were sold is based, includes these taxes. It also suggests to add in a profit margin comparable to that for products actually sold. If

Figure 3.6. continued

this were current practice, then these two items would need to be subtracted again in the transition from operating surplus to business profit (as indicated). NBS (1997, p. 39), in detailing how to derive the operating surplus from business profit, neglects to say so.

b   Administrative charges in the derivation of value-added are net of approximately thirty items that enter the constituent elements of value-added; thus, for example, the wages of administrative personnel enter labor remuneration, technological development fees enter depreciation, and additions to provisions for losses on accounts receivable together with the other three items listed in the lower part of the table enter the operating surplus (NBS, 1997, pp. 253f.). The same source at a different location (NBS, 1997, p. 35) lists seven items to be included in the operating surplus, two of which are the first and third type of administrative charges listed in the lower part of the table. The other five items are: losses from experimental production, losses from seasonal repairs and production stops, fire insurance as part of the total insurance fees, fees levied for planting trees, and cleanliness and hygiene fees. These five items are likely to be included in net non-business revenue since 1993. NBS (1997, p. 253) at the same time, in apparent contradiction, requires the tree planting fee to be included in intermediate inputs.

c   "Labor remuneration" comprises official wages, bonuses and allowances (all paid in money or in goods and services), social welfare expenses including unemployment insurance and medical insurance and expenses, transportation subsidies to and from work, and other quasi-payments to labor.

Sources: *Statistical Yearbook 1998*, p. 95; NBS (1997), primarily pp. 30-41 and 195-201 with an enumeration of all accounting items included in value-added.

Figure 3.6   Value-added and Profit

surplus as a residual of value-added needs to be explicitly linked to profit as a residual of sales revenue. This is done in Figure 3.6. Operating surplus is linked to business profit as follows. Operating surplus (i) minus subsidies for losses, (ii) plus labor remuneration out of profit, (iii) plus that share of other business profit that is not included in the enterprises' value-added, (iv) plus four types of administrative charges, (v) minus adjustments for inventories yields business profit. Business profit (vi) plus investment returns, (vii) plus net non-business revenue equals total profit. This relationship can be used to explain the different development of operating surplus and profit over time.[71]

---

[71] The focus in the following is on "profit" rather than "business profit" since concise data on business profit are not available except for the year 1995. In 1995, business profit was equal to 60.13% of (total) profit, and investment returns equal to another 16.65% (*Industrial Census 1995*, Vol. 1, p. 52); the unspecified residual of 23.22% then consists of net non-business revenue.

In 1988 through 1990, operating surplus relative to value-added declined less than profit relative to sales revenue for possibly three reasons. First, in the calculation of operating surplus (or value-added), inventories are assigned a profit margin comparable to that on products sold (NBS, 1997, pp. 268f.). The profit and loss account, on the other hand, does not consider inventories (item v in the above list).

Second, stagnating sales revenue led to unexpectedly low cash flow, while the extension of new bank loans was severely curtailed in 1990. Inter-enterprise arrears began to accumulate. Inter-enterprise arrears became so predominant that, by 1991, the central government intervened by injecting new loans to resolve the triangular debts.[72] If accounts receivable were to have increased by only 5% of total assets in 1990, and if half of this increase were to have led to additional provisions for losses on accounts receivable (item iv), then these additional provisions would have amounted to approximately 10% of value-added in 1990, more than half the decline in profit relative to value-added between 1998 and 1990.[73]

Third, in 1989 and 1990, net non-business revenue was positive, possibly due to government subsidies for losses. Such subsidies affected operating surplus and profit equally. However, the effects of the State Council's 1988 administrative measures to curtail investment are likely to have affected only profit, not operating surplus. Any losses incurred by the prohibition on the start of new investment projects and the cut in investment projects under construction enter non-business expenses (Li Xianzong and Zhang Yongguo, 1995, p. 225), and thus lower net non-business revenue (item vii) and thereby profit, but have no effect on operating surplus.

---

[72] The State Council organized special sessions to repay approximately one-third of total investment in fixed assets loans caught in triangular debt chains. Special attempts to resolve short-term supplier credit chains remained on a smaller scale due to the very large number of such inter-enterprise arrears (*Financial Yearbook 1992*, pp. 31, 52, 80, 457, 503f.). Short-term bank loans to industrial enterprises in 1989 still increased by 12.07% adjusted for inflation (nominal 30.67%), on a par with earlier years, but then fell 10.16 % (6.06%) in 1990, before recovering in 1991 with a 59.30% (65.50%) rise. For the nominal lending data, see *Financial Yearbook 1992*, p. 456, and for the ex-factory price index of industrial products, see *Market Yearbook 1995*, p. 588, and *Statistical Yearbook 2001*, p. 297.

[73] Total assets are approximated by the sum of net fixed assets and fixed-quota working capital. In 1992, this sum is likely to fall short of total assets by about one-quarter.

The absence of a recovery in profit (but possibly in operating surplus) in the years 1990 through 1993 may be attributable to just one factor, the resolution of the "hidden cost" problem. Corrections to the value of current assets (prior to 1993) entered non-business expenses and thus affected profit but not operating surplus. The drastically rising item "other costs" in Table 3.2 encompasses these non-business expenses.

In the years from about 1993 through 1995, operating surplus may have fared worse than profit relative to value-added. This could be due to the introduction of the new accounting system in 1993. Corrections to the value of current assets (such as inventories or some "hidden losses") are now included as administrative costs, which implies the same negative effect on profit as before, but newly reduces value-added and the operating surplus. A second reason could be the absence since 1993 of large new additions to inventories; this implies that operating surplus can no longer be inflated by profit assigned to newly added inventories.

The data show that operating surplus has remained more stable than profit over time (both relative to value-added). Accounting profit tends to exhibit wider swings; the economic downturn of 1988 through 1990 had a much stronger impact on profit than on operating surplus. Both measures, however, operating surplus and profit, are subject to the same long-term trends. This suggests that time inconsistencies and misreporting of accounting profit may not be so dominant as to render accounting profit a meaningless measure.

The attempts to explain the discrepancy in the trends of operating surplus vs. profit (both relative to value-added) in the years 1988 through 1995 show that operating surplus is not a measure without shortcomings. Operating surplus is a purely production-based measure that does not take into account financial issues or non-business transactions. Thus, it is not affected by the accumulation of inventories that cannot be sold or that have to be written off, by accounts receivable that cannot be collected, or by investment losses. But a meaningful profit measure should focus on the ability of an enterprise to survive, which requires inclusion of purely financial issues. Accounting profit, despite its shortcomings, in particular the time inconsistencies and potential misreporting, may yet be a better measure of profit than operating surplus is.

Conclusions

The profitability of industrial SOEs in China declined severely over the past two decades. This was only to be expected as the economic transition reduced the special role state industry played in accumulating economy-wide surplus.

The pattern of decline has been far from uniform over time. Profitability declined very gradually in the early 1980s, but then plummeted between 1988 and 1990. It remained rather stable in the early 1990s, and then declined slightly further between 1993 and 1997. Since 1998, industrial SOE profitability has been on the rise again, partly, but not solely, due to the redefinition of the industrial SOE category.

The available data on the aggregate profit and loss account of industrial SOEs allows a year-by-year examination of the long-term downward trend of profit relative to sales revenue. The main explanatory factor appears to be the economic transition. Reform shocks in 1988 through 1993 — an attempt at radical price reform, then an administratively ordained economic downturn, followed by successful price reform in a more favorable environment — led to a temporary deviation from the trend. Transition effects are also apparent in (i) the adoption in 1993 of a new accounting system better suited to yield a meaningful measure of profit, (ii) a gradual phasing out of government support measures for industrial SOEs, including subsidies for loss-making enterprises and readily available bank loans at artificially low interest rates (occasionally below the inflation rate), (iii) an increase in competition mainly throughout the 1990s as industries were opened to new entrants and prices were freed, and (iv) the three-year industrial SOE reform program of 1998 through 2000. The latter targeted large and medium-sized loss-making industrial SOEs and included reductions in industrial SOE employment to alleviate the long-term overstaffing of industrial SOEs with the consequent negative impact on residual profit. (The issue of competition and "excessive" labor remuneration are taken up in more detail in the following chapter.)

The quality of accounting profit data may not be outstanding, but it appears sufficiently good to condone the use of accounting profit in the evaluation of industrial SOE profitability. Throughout the 1980s, industrial SOEs predominantly faced incentives to overreport profit, yet, in the 1990s, incentives varied, assuaging any suspicion of systematic misreporting of profit across all industrial SOEs. Operating surplus, the alternative profitability measure, confirms the long-term trend in accounting profit, with discrepancies in the time pattern of the two measures during the years 1988 through 1995 explained by their different contents.

Many of the transition effects may have run their course. Subsidies to loss-making industrial SOEs have largely been replaced by government appropriations financing the exit of loss-making enterprises. Bank loans are no longer readily available to enterprises independent of their performance and loan interest rates are now well above deposit rates and the inflation rate. Most industrial sectors have been opened to domestic competition as well as to imports, with WTO accession only representing the final step in a long series of market-opening measures.

One yet unfinished transition item is the de facto limitation of the dismissal of excess labor in many industrial SOEs, along with social welfare and pension burdens. But even here much progress has been made. Industrial SOE employment has been falling sharply ever since 1997 (with details provided in Chapter 8). Consequently, the wage bill of industrial SOEs (following first the pre-1998 definition of industrial SOEs, and since 1998 the new definition of industrial SOEs) has been constant since 1996 (Table 2.8 on labor remuneration in the appendix to Chapter 2). Social welfare payments to current staff and workers have been capped at 14% of the wage bill. (This limit was exceeded slightly in the estimated data for 2000 presented in Table 2.8.) Pension obligations have since 1998 been held at approximately 20% of wages, payable to an enterprise-external fund. Table 2.8 shows that pensions together with social welfare payments to retirees — the latter from available data on all state-owned units tend to account for approximately one-third of all payments to retirees — have been rising rapidly throughout the reform period and were equivalent to almost 30% of the wage bill in 2000. But even a further rise in payments to retirees implies only a small increase in aggregate labor remuneration.

4
The Impact of Competition and Labor Remuneration on Profitability

Chapter 3 considered the decline in industrial SOE profitability by examining the development of the various items in the profit and loss account over time. Previous scholarship has proposed two alternative explanations for this phenomenon. The first is an increase in competition over time and the second is "excessive" labor remuneration. Both explanations were implicitly included in the analysis presented in the previous chapter, with the increase in competition affecting sales revenue, and labor remuneration constituting a major element of sales costs. This chapter further examines the impact of competition and labor remuneration on industrial SOE profitability.

Barry Naughton (1992) argues that a reduction in barriers to entry has led to a reduction in SOE monopoly rents. He finds that while average profit rates declined by 8.4% between 1980 and 1989, this decline was due solely to a decline in profitability in the sectors that initially had above-average profit rates. But these are also the sectors with the lowest barriers to entry. Competition in the sectors where it is allowed and feasible is eroding monopoly profits, leading to a convergence of profit rates across all sectors.[74] Barry Naughton's view is echoed by Gary Jefferson and Thomas

---

[74] An auxiliary hypothesis is that profit rates in the non-SOE sectors, taken to be rural industries, should initially be high as these enterprises entered high-profit sectors that were formerly closed to them, but that competition would then drive down their profitability, too. Barry Naughton (1992) finds that the data also confirm this hypothesis. In his later work, Barry Naughton (1995) repeats and further elaborates on the argument of profit rate convergence.

Rawski (1994, p. 60): "our own calculations show that profitability within the state industry is lowest in provinces where the output of non-state industry has grown most rapidly."[75]

Fan Gang and Wing-Thye Woo (1996), as well as Huang Yiping and Ron Duncan (1999), deny that competition is the cause of the decline in SOE profitability. Fan Gang and Wing-Thye Woo present nationwide SOE profit rate and market share data for 27 sectors in 1989 and 1992 to argue that the collapse of SOE profitability occurred across all branches of industry independent of the degree of entry by non-SOEs. They show that in four of the five cases where the SOE market share was unchanged, the profit rates were lower in 1992. A regression of the change in the profit rate on the change in the market share yields an insignificant relationship. Barry Naughton's conclusion thus appears not to hold for the years 1989 through 1992. Huang Yiping and Ron Duncan use annual data from a survey of 421 selected SOEs in four sectors over the years 1980 through 1994 to regress total profit on twenty explanatory variables, several of which measure policy changes, such as the implementation of the manager responsibility system.[76] From the fact that almost none of the policy variables has a significant positive impact on profit, the authors conclude that their "study strongly rejects the popular argument that the worsening financial performance of China's SOEs during the reform period was mainly due to increased competition."

Fan Gang and Wing-Thye Woo (1996) as well as Jeffrey Sachs and Wing-Thye Woo (1997) propose "excessive" labor remuneration as alternative explanation for the 'disappearing profits.' Using aggregate data on 300 large and medium-sized sample state enterprises for each of the years 1984 through 1988, Fan Gang and Wing-Thye Woo show that direct

---

[75] For the calculations, see also Gary Jefferson and Thomas Rawski (1995). Martin Raiser (1997a) also presents evidence in favor of the competition hypothesis.

[76] Huang Yiping and Ron Duncan report that the survey they use was conducted by the Institute of Economics, Chinese Academy of Social Sciences, and covers about 800 enterprises, more than 600 of which had data for each year of the period. Of these 600 enterprises, the 421 enterprises in the four sectors of food processing, textiles, building materials, and machinery and electronics (out of 40 sectors in the official categorization of industries) were chosen. It is not stated whether the survey is a random sample, what the regional distribution of the enterprises is, and how the sectoral distribution was obtained.

income rose faster than net output value in all years.[77] The same is true for indirect income; between 1984 and 1988, welfare funds increased by 240%, non-production expenditures (presumably enterprise consumption) by 234%, and net management costs by 165%, all exceeding the overall growth of net output value.[78] Labor remuneration is excessive in that its growth rate exceeds that of net output.[79]

Excessive labor remuneration need not rule out a negative impact of competition on industrial SOE profitability. None of the studies tests its hypothesis in a multivariate setting that controls for changes in other variables, including in the variable that, according to the alternative hypothesis, matters.[80]

Both Barry Naughton as well as Fan Gang and Wing-Thye Woo furthermore define the profit rate as profit and taxes divided by net fixed assets and working capital. Their data are identical to those published in the *Statistical Yearbook* of the corresponding years (there labeled "profit and taxes relative to funds," *zijin lishuilu*). But this official profit rate prior to 1992 does not match these authors' definition; a severe statistical break then occurred between 1991 and 1992. Before 1992, current assets (or

---

[77] No further information on this survey is available. The survey is reported to cover the year 1989, but the 1989 data are not used.

[78] The argument as presented remains one of plausibility, bare of statistical tests. No correlation coefficients are calculated to explore further the relationship between profitability and direct income growth across the 300 enterprises.

[79] Another definition of "excessive" would be that labor remuneration exceeded the marginal product value of labor, an altogether different issue. The authors do not consider whether a rise in labor remuneration does not reflect a gradual move towards equalization of labor remuneration with the value of the marginal labor product. If, as outlined in the introduction to this part, profit in the pre-reform period was artificially inflated (exceeding a competitive market return on equity), labor remuneration at the beginning of the economic reform period was below its marginal product value. Elliott Parker (1999) provides some evidence to the effect that wages in the period 1980 through 1992 were below the marginal product value of labor.

[80] Athar Hussain and Nicholas Stern (1995), commenting on the competition hypothesis explored by Gary Jefferson and Thomas Rawski (1995), also suggest that an increase in the share of labor remuneration in value-added may be an alternative explanation for the fall in profitability. The relative rise in labor remuneration appears to be characteristic of all transition economies.

working capital) were measured as the average annual *fixed-quota* working capital; since 1992 as the average annual *total* working capital.[81] In 1992, total working capital was about twice the volume of fixed-quota working capital and approximately equal to net fixed assets.[82]

This chapter re-examines the impact of competition and labor remuneration on industrial SOE profitability in the reform period, especially in the 1990s. Detailed consideration of what constitutes "profitability" suggests that Barry Naughton's and Fan Gang and Wing-Thye Woo's hypotheses are not so much alternative hypotheses as potentially simultaneous explanations. Each of the two causes affects profitability through a different channel. The data show that direct measures of competition and labor remuneration have a simultaneous and significant impact on the ultimate measure of industrial SOE profitability, profit per unit of equity. So do indicators of the two separate channels.

The following section presents the argument for why competition and labor remuneration are not alternative hypotheses but instead are two causes that affect profitability through two separate channels. The third and fourth sections consider each of the two hypotheses separately. When the two arguments are allowed to cooperate (in the fifth section), they explain most of the variation in profitability. The sixth section concludes.

Competition and Excessive Labor Remuneration Are Not Alternative Hypotheses

According to the competition hypothesis, monopoly rents in industrial SOEs are being eroded as the economy is being liberalized and as enterprises under other ownership forms begin to compete with SOEs. In contrast, the

---

[81] A minor discontinuity is that, before 1992, net fixed assets were measured at year-end values and since then at average annual values.

[82] *Statistical Yearbook 1993*, pp. 419 and 430. The statistical break in 1992 does not affect Barry Naughton's conclusions as all his data are pre-1992. Fan Gang and Wing-Thye Woo appear unaware of the statistical break and directly compare the official data of 1989 and 1992. With 1992 data based on an approximately one-third larger denominator, "profit rates" obviously must decline. Fan Gang and Wing-Thye Woo's rejection of the competition hypothesis based on such facts as that in four out of five cases when the SOE market share was unchanged between 1989 and 1992, the "profit rates" were lower in 1992, is thus questionable.

excessive labor remuneration hypothesis claims that profit in SOEs is eroded due to excessive labor remuneration. Yet, the two causes affect the profit rate through two different channels. Each of the two channels can be captured by a different intermediate indicator, an intermediate competition indicator and an intermediate labor remuneration indicator. These two intermediate indicators furthermore reveal that competition and labor remuneration concurrently explain profitability, rather than present alternative hypotheses.

Intermediate Competition Indicator

The intermediate competition indicator is derived as follows. An aggregate industry in a perfectly competitive economy exhibits constant returns to scale. In the absence of significant technological progress, this implies a constant ratio of output to capital. If the industry is not perfectly competitive but enjoys a monopoly position, new entry is likely to erode sales prices. But a decline in sales prices correspondingly reduces sales revenue, while total assets, at least in the short run, remain unchanged or do not fall by as much.[83]

In the long run, firms could respond to a decrease in sales prices towards equalization with minimum average costs by producing the same volume of physical output (at lower sales value) with the same volume of assets. Sales revenue relative to assets falls. Firms could also expand both capacity and output. While the increase in fixed assets (capacity expansion) may occur at newly competitive prices in the producer goods industry, the previously accumulated other fixed assets would, given accounting practices, still be valued at their original price less depreciation, as would most other assets; *all* sales revenue, on the other hand, is valued at current, newly competitive lower prices. Sales revenue relative to assets again falls. Firms could obviously also choose to exit gradually, which is likely to lead to

---

[83] After breaking down the total assets into sub-categories, the value of the following items will not change when product prices change: accumulated inventories (budgeted at past production costs), accumulated accounts receivable, cash and current account deposits, and accumulated fixed assets. Newly incurred accounts receivable may change in accordance with price changes, and additions to inventories and fixed assets may reflect new prices, but accounts receivable and inventories together account for only one-quarter of all assets.

first a reduction in output (apart from the reduction in sales prices), before the disappearance of the assets.

Sales revenue relative to assets can thus serve as an intermediate competition indicator, capturing the channel through which competition affects ultimate profitability (Figure 4.1). As competition intensifies, the ratio of sales revenue to assets is likely to decrease.

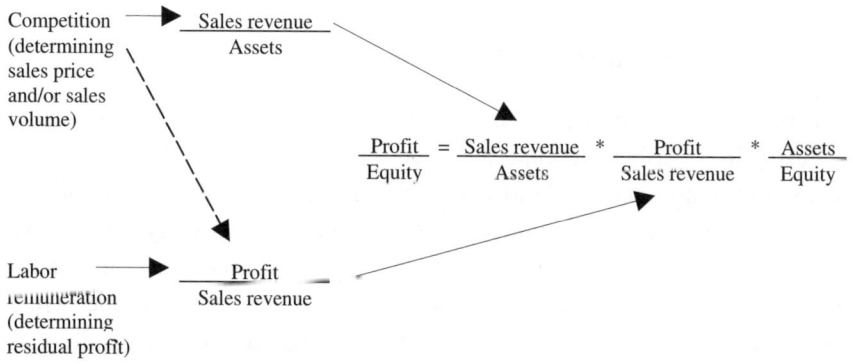

The same causal chain holds using value-added instead of sales revenue.

Figure 4.1   Impact of Competition and Labor Remuneration on Profitability

One potential shortcoming of the ratio of sales revenue to assets as intermediate competition indicator is that it may also be affected by macroeconomic cycles. In periods of recession, sales revenue may fall relative to assets due to a lack of demand. But except for the 1988–1990 period of retrenchment, demand in China has been growing steadily, especially in the period 1993–2000, on which much of the analysis below concentrates. Alternatively, value-added rather than sales revenue may be related to assets. Value-added, in contrast to sales revenue, comprises additions to inventories, and may thus be less responsive to macroeconomic cycles. (Value-added is also net of intermediate inputs, which does not affect the competition argument.)

Fan Gang and Wing-Thye Woo (1996) use the industrial SOE market share as a proxy for competition. Yet, a large industrial SOE market share need not translate into a low degree of competition. An industrial sector or province could have few enterprises with non-state ownership but several thousand industrial SOEs that are competing fiercely with each other. In this case, the industrial SOE market share is high but does not translate into monopolistic pricing power.

While neither the market share nor the intermediate competition indicator of sales revenue or value-added relative to assets is a perfect indicator of competition, the intermediate competition indicator appears to be on logically sounder ground. It furthermore illustrates that competition and labor remuneration explain profitability through two different channels.

Intermediate Labor Remuneration Indicator

The labor remuneration hypothesis, in contrast to the competition hypothesis, involves the issue of distribution. How is the given sales revenue distributed between labor, capital, and intermediate inputs? Fan Gang and Wing-Thye Woo ask this question by relating profit to net output (value-added net of depreciation). How is the given net output distributed between labor and capital? They refer to the fact that operating surplus (which they call and measure as "profit" plus "others"), net taxes on production, and labor remuneration add up to net output. Operating surplus plus net taxes on production, relative to net output value, then is in fact a (inverse) tautology to the ratio of labor remuneration to net output value. If labor remuneration relative to net output value increases, the operating surplus plus net taxes on production (relative to net output value) falls proportionally.

Net output plus depreciation equals value-added. If value-added rather than net output value is used, the direct conflict between labor remuneration and the operating surplus holds as long as depreciation and net production taxes each claim a constant share of value-added. Value-added rather than net output is used here because publication of net output data for industrial SOEs ceased with the 1992 data. Given that changes in the operating surplus per unit of value-added are tautologically related to changes in labor remuneration per unit of value-added — labor remuneration plus operating surplus (plus net taxes on production plus depreciation) equals value-added — operating surplus relative to value-added is an intermediate indicator of distributive issues ("excessive" labor remuneration), rather than the profitability indicator that Fan Gang and Wing-Thye Woo make it out to be.

The fact that Fan Gang and Wing-Thye Woo relate profit rather than operating surplus to net output is problematic because, as seen in the previous chapter, (nationwide) industrial SOE operating surplus is far from identical to profit. But official operating surplus data are not available and cannot be constructed for provinces and industrial sectors. Profit instead of operating surplus is also used here.[84]

One alternative to relating profit to value-added is to relate it to sales revenue. Profit is the residual of sales revenue after deducting sales costs (which include depreciation, intermediate inputs, and most labor remuneration), sales taxes and surcharges, financial and administrative charges, net business profit and a few other items. Labor remuneration and depreciation, apart from intermediate inputs, are likely to account for the bulk of the other items competing with profit (Figure 2.4). Profit relative to sales revenue may thus serve as an alternative intermediate labor remuneration indicator to measure the impact of distributive issues (Figure 4.1).

---

[84] In an earlier article on the issue of competition vs. labor remuneration in explaining industrial SOE profitability, I have referred to both sales revenue (or value-added) relative to assets and profit relative to sales revenue (or value-added) as two intermediate *profitability* indicators, representing competition vs. labor remuneration. While the arguments remain the same, it would seem more appropriate to label the two intermediate indicators as the "intermediate *competition* indicator" and the "intermediate *labor remuneration* indicator," as is done here.

That profit per value-added is not an appropriate measure of profitability can also be seen from the following example. If the rates of return on debt and equity were equal and constant, and the ratio of liabilities to equity increased while total assets (equal to liabilities plus equity) remained constant, then profit per unit of equity would, correctly, remain unchanged. However, profit per value-added declines. The higher volume of interest payments to creditors reduces value-added. And profit (or rather, operating surplus) is the residual of value-added after subtracting labor remuneration, depreciation, and net taxes on production. If all the non-profit items in value-added stayed constant — and there is no reason why they should change in response to a change in the ratio of liabilities to equity — then the residual profit falls exactly by the reduction in value-added, and profit in the numerator falls by relatively more than the denominator value-added (which is the reduced profit plus the sum of all other, unchanged items in value-added). Profit relative to value-added (or sales revenue), because it changes in response to changes in the financing structure, cannot be an appropriate indicator of profitability.

Potential Interaction between Competition and Labor Remuneration

The two hypotheses of competition and excess labor remuneration explain the decline in industrial SOE profitability through two separate channels. Competition directly affects sales revenue (or value-added, or net output) available for distribution. The distributive issue is how to split the sales revenue (or value-added, also below) between labor and equity holders (and the suppliers of intermediate inputs, in the case of sales revenue). The argument that excessive labor remuneration drives down profitability need not rule out the argument that competition reduces monopoly rents by reducing the pie available for distribution in the first place.

However, in as far as items in the profit and loss account, expressed as a share of sales revenue, are affected by changes in the degree of competition, competition may also exert an indirect impact on the intermediate labor remuneration indicator, profit relative to sales revenue. If profit as an approximation to operating surplus is related to value-added, changes in the shares of labor remuneration, depreciation, or net production taxes will affect the intermediate labor remuneration indicator; but those changes could originally be due to competition.

Thus, an increase in competition could force firms to innovate faster than before, which could mean larger write-offs of assets every year. Depreciation relative to sales revenue increases, and the residual profit relative to sales revenue therefore decreases. (But innovation may at the same time lead to more sales revenue and/or lower labor costs per unit of output, which would offset the depreciation effect on residual profit.)

Competition may also matter in that while it reduces the income available for distribution, it may not be possible to reduce the size of some items in sales revenue in correspondence with the reduction in sales revenue. The absolute amount of linearly depreciated fixed assets does not change immediately in response to changes in sales revenue. A decrease in sales revenue (due to increasing competition) relative to (constant) assets then implies an increase in (constant) depreciation per unit of sales revenue. But an increase in depreciation per unit of sales revenue reduces the residual profit per unit of sales revenue. (See the broken arrow in Figure 4.1.)

A similar argument can be made for the case of labor remuneration. A change in sales revenue (due to competition) could affect the distribution of sales revenue, if the quantity of labor employed and pure wages are independent of sales revenue; a reduction in sales revenue while the wage bill remains constant squeezes the residual profit. On the other hand, bonus payments and non-wage labor remuneration could be highly sensitive to sales revenue and thus more than make up for rigid employment and wages.[85] The effect of competition on profitability (profit relative to equity) could thus be obscured if it in part operates through the intermediate indicator of labor remuneration.

But unless the share of depreciation in sales revenue (or value-added) changes significantly, or unless labor remuneration is independent of sales revenue (or value-added), the two channels through which competition and labor remuneration affect profitability are distinct. It is thus possible to trace a decline in profit per unit of equity back to a decline in monopoly rents vs. excessive labor remuneration.

The impact of competition, measured as usually in the literature in the form of the industrial SOE market share, on profitability as well as the relationship between the market share and the intermediate competition indicator are examined in the following section. The section thereafter proceeds similarly for the case of labor remuneration. The two potential causes for the decline in profitability, measured both in the form of the traditional variables (market share vs. wages) as well as in the form of the intermediate indicators, are considered together to explain profitability in the fifth section.

The two intermediate indicators are conveniently related to profit per unit of equity through an identity. Multiplying the intermediate indicators of competition and labor remuneration with each other and adjusting for assets relative to equity yields profit per unit of equity (Figure 4.1). If the variables on the right-hand side were completely independent of each other, then changes in the ultimate profitability indicator — profit relative to equity — could be directly and proportionally attributed to changes in each of the variables on the right-hand side.

---

[85] Since net taxes on production depend on value-added and sales revenue, they will not remain constant in the face of changing sales revenue and value-added.

Competition as a Uni-causal Explanation of Profitability

Barry Naughton (1992) posited that an increase in competition in the sectors where competition was allowed and feasible invariably led to a reduction in profit rates, thus presumably reducing if not eliminating monopoly rents. Yet, an alternative implication of competition could be that it encourages SOEs to improve their performance. Thomas Rawski (1994b), writing about SOE productivity, notes that "the improved performance of Chinese industry is the result of increased competition and growing financial pressures that have accompanied a gradual and still incomplete shift from a planned economy to a market economy" (p. 271).

SOEs may also not have earned monopoly profits to begin with. The traditional planning system did not equate marginal costs to marginal revenue when setting prices, but based its price calculations on average costs and the desired, a priori determined surplus. Profit (surplus) thus was an industry-specific, discretionary variable.[86] The entry of new firms, presumably a sign of an increase in competition, could be the result of industrial liberalization. Industrial liberalization could also lead to a rise in the profitability level of industrial SOEs from possibly artificially depressed to sustainable industry-wide profitability levels.

Competition necessarily increased with the gradual abandonment of external production planning for the existing industrial SOEs and with the entry of new enterprises under other ownership forms. In the pre-reform period, the tendency towards local self-sufficiency, favored by a central planning apparatus that could handle no more than a few major enterprises and products, ensured that SOEs in different localities produced similar products; in the reform period, these SOEs began to compete with each other. By the mid-1980s, the rural collective-owned sector grew rapidly and, by the early 1990s, individual-owned and private enterprises proliferated. Foreign-funded (including Hong Kong, Macao and Taiwanese)

---

[86] See Chu-yuan Cheng (1982), Chapter 8. If average costs were equal to marginal costs, as is the case with a constant returns to scale technology, then a constant surplus relative to the value of output is equal to mark-up pricing. Monopoly pricing can be viewed as mark-up pricing only if the mark-up is a particular function of the elasticity of demand. However, the size of the mark-up in a socialist economy is a political decision; the mark-up could even be negative.

enterprises joined the Chinese market by setting up production sites in China. With import tariffs falling, exports from other countries to China expanded. A far-reaching price liberalization occurred in the early 1990s (Figure 3.3).

In the following, the impact of the market share on profitability is examined first, and then the relationship between the market share and the intermediate indicator of competition, sales revenue (or value-added) per unit of assets. (The impact of the intermediate competition indicator on profitability is examined in the fifth section.) If the intermediate indicator of competition is not only the broader but also the logically sounder measure of competition, then a strong relationship between the market share and the intermediate indicator of competition qualifies the market share as a proxy for competition. Irrespective of the justification of each of the two individual competition indicators, one would want the two indicators to behave similarly if they truly measure similar factors.

Market Share and Profitability

Because equity data are available only since 1993, profitability can be measured as profit relative to equity only since 1993. The statistical break in 1998 implies that data for the years since 1998 need to be handled separately; for the year 1998 itself, no sectoral or provincial industrial SOE data are available. For the years 1986 through 1991, as well as for 1995, loss data for industrial SOEs by sector and province are available, allowing the use of the losses relative to gross profit indicator in these years. Analysis of the impact of competition on profitability, using sectoral and provincial data is thus possible for the years 1986 through 1991 plus 1995 (with severe data limitations), 1993 through 1997, and 1999 through 2000.

Calculation of the industrial SOE market share as an indicator of the degree of competition can be based on sales revenue, value-added, or gross output value. Value-added and gross output value have the disadvantage of including inventories, a disadvantage that matters if the rate of inventory accumulation differs across ownership forms. But data on sales revenue are not always available. Sales revenue furthermore reflects trading activities rather than production activities. Dividing one SOE into two SOEs may lead to a higher aggregate market share of SOEs measured by sales revenue, while the aggregate market share measured by value-added could be unchanged. However, since the different market share measures are very highly correlated, it makes little difference which one is used in the analysis below.[87] Preference in the following is given to the market share measures based on sales revenue or on value-added whenever these data are available. All sales revenue data in this chapter are always net of all sales-related taxes in order to bridge the 1993–94 statistical break in the sales revenue time series.[88]

A further complication is that sales revenue and value-added are available only for the directly reporting industrial enterprises, not for every industrial enterprise in China. The market share of SOEs is thus usually based on a market limited to the directly reporting industrial enterprises. Across provinces only, data on gross output value of (all) industrial enterprises are available until 1997.[89]

The analysis is conducted across sectors as well as across provinces. Following Barry Naughton's hypothesis, one would expect an increase in the SOE market share in a particular sector to decrease SOE profitability in this sector. Across provinces, the argument is weaker. The non-SOE

---

[87] For example, the correlation coefficient between (i) the share of industrial SOE value-added in the value-added of all directly reporting industrial enterprises and (ii) the share of industrial SOE sales revenue in the sales revenue of all directly reporting industrial enterprises, across industrial sectors was 0.9848 in 1993, 0.9842 in 1994, 0.9577 in 1995, 0.9924 in 1996, and 0.9842 in 1997.

[88] Another possible indicator of competition related to the market share, across sectors, is the market share of the largest enterprises in each sector. *China's Industrial Markets Yearbook* (*China Markets Yearbook*) allows the calculation of the market share of up to the ten largest enterprises in the sales revenue of the directly reporting industrial enterprises, or some (unknown) subset thereof, in each industrial sector, for the years 1995, 1996, 1998, and 2000. Any such indicator has to be constructed based on highly dis-aggregated data from approximately 600 sub-sectors, which do not always perfectly add up to the sectoral totals given in the *Statistical Yearbook*. The market share of the largest (or the three largest, or the five largest) enterprises in each industrial sector in 1995 is highly correlated with the industrial SOE share in the sales revenue of all directly reporting industrial enterprises (at the 0.1% significance level). When an indicator of enterprise concentration in each sector is introduced to some of the regressions presented below, the results do not change except that the simultaneously included industrial SOE market share becomes less significant. Since the years for which data on the shares of the largest enterprises are limited, and since their introduction yields no additional insights, this variable is not further reported on.

[89] Data on provincial industrial value-added are also available for all years, but data on the provincial value-added of industrial SOEs are available only since 1993.

economy in one province could expand in sectors that have few or no SOEs, while SOE growth stagnates; consequently, the SOE market share in this province will fall, but since the non-SOEs do not operate in the same sectors as SOEs, SOE profitability need not necessarily be affected. Since data on labor remuneration that are relevant to the two hypotheses are available only by province, not by sector, the competition analysis is also conducted across provinces, despite the potential logical weakness of the market share as a competition measure. In the case of labor remuneration, the analysis across provinces is highly meaningful as one would expect excessive labor remuneration in the SOEs in one province to have an impact on the profitability of SOEs in this province.

The longest time interval for which consistent data are available to explore the impact of a changing market share on profitability is the ten years from 1986 through 1995. Figure 4.2 shows the relationship between the relative change in the industrial SOE market share from 1986 to 1995, and the corresponding relative change in the ratio of losses per unit of gross profit across 26 industrial sectors for which comparable data are available. Figure 4.3 does the same across 29 provinces.[90] For lack of other data, the industrial SOE market share is calculated as the industrial SOE share in the gross output value of the directly reporting industrial enterprises.

Both scattergrams reveal that the larger the relative reduction in the industrial SOE market share, the larger the relative increase in losses relative to gross profit. In other words, as one would expect following Barry Naughton's hypothesis, increasing competition reduces profitability. The correlation coefficient of −0.6106 across sectors is significant at the 1% level, the correlation coefficient of −0.4036 across provinces is significant at the 5% level.

---

[90] Independent data for Hainan Province are available beginning in 1988 only. In comparisons involving 1980s data, Hainan was therefore folded back into Guangdong Province (which it is part of in the 1986 and 1987 data). Similarly, up to 1996, Chongqing Municipality was part of Sichuan Province. Since 1997, the Chongqing data are reported separately in the official statistics. In order to have a consistent time series for the years 1993 through 1997, Chongqing data for 1997 were folded back into Sichuan data whenever data for 1993 through 1997 were used. (In the period 1993 through 1997 as well as 1999-2000, Hainan was retained as a separate observation, and in the years since 1998, Chongqing was retained as a separate observation.)

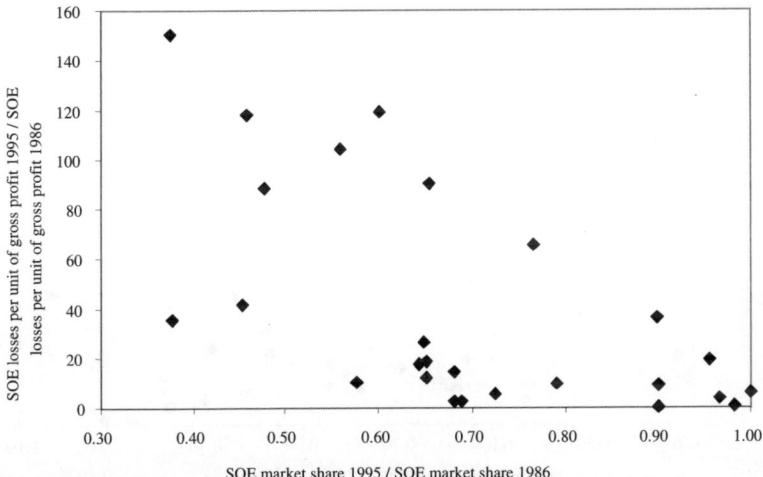

The SOE market share is calculated as the value of the gross output of industrial SOEs divided by the gross output value of all directly reporting industrial enterprises.
Sources: *Statistical Yearbook 1987*, pp. 311, 315, 321, 323; *1996*, p. 414; *Industrial Census 1995*, Vol. 2, pp. 16ff. The 1986 gross output value of both SOEs and all directly reporting industrial enterprises is derived from "profit and taxes per unit of gross output value" and "profit and taxes." The sectoral classification in effect in 1995 was reduced to the one in effect in 1986.

Figure 4.2   Impact of Competition on Industrial SOE Losses per Unit of Gross Profit across Sectors, 1995 vs. 1986

If the period is split into two sub-periods, 1986 vs. 1991, and 1991 vs. 1995, the only significant relationship that remains (using the 10% significance level as cut-off point) is the one across sectors in the more recent period, 1991 vs. 1995, at the 5% significance level. Since it is more meaningful to measure competition by the SOE market share in individual industrial sectors, rather than in individual provinces, this would suggest that competition did exert some influence on industrial SOE profitability at least in the 1990s, after the price liberalization wave of the early 1990s.

Regression analysis using data on all individual years, as far as available, provides a similar picture of a weak relationship between changes in the industrial SOE market share and industrial SOE profitability.[91] Table 4.1

---

[91] In all regression analyses of the years 1993 through 1997, the (in absolute size) very small sector of gas production and supply (see Table 2.3) is omitted due to a missing value-added value for 1996, and not credible values of value-added in other years. This sector would be a far outlier in any analysis involving value-added.

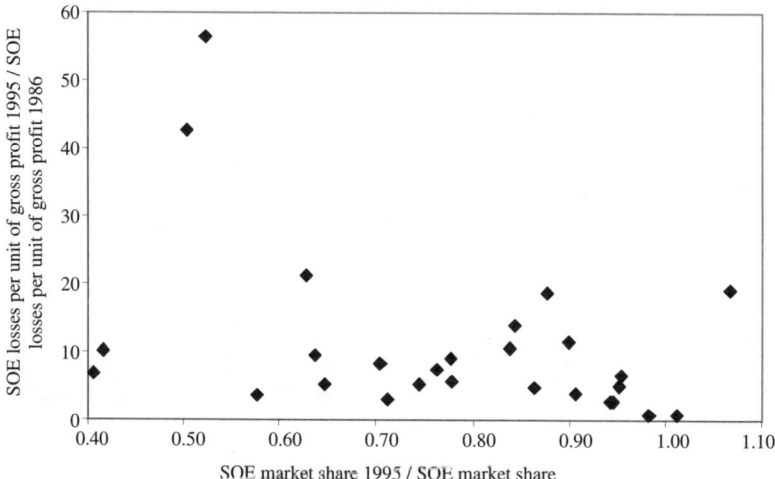

The SOE market share is calculated as the value of the gross output of industrial SOE divided by the gross output value of all directly reporting industrial enterprises.

Sources: *Statistical Yearbook 1987*, pp. 313, 317, 322, 324; *1996*, p. 411; Industrial *Census 1995*, Vol. 3, pp. 412ff. The 1986 gross output value of both SOEs and all directly reporting industrial enterprises is derived from "profit and taxes per unit of gross output value" and "profit and taxes." Hainan Province in both years is part of Guangdong Province.

Figure 4.3 Impact of Competition on Industrial SOE Losses Per Unit of Gross Profit across Provinces, 1995 vs. 1986

reports the results across industrial sectors and across provinces. Across industrial sectors in the late 1980s, the market share of industrial SOEs (based on gross output value) affects profitability (as measured by losses per unit of gross profit) only if the variables are measured in levels, but the sign is not as expected; the larger the market share, the larger are losses relative to gross profit. Across provinces, the market share (based on gross output value) affects profitability with the correct sign if the variables are measured in annual growth rates. (Since sectoral or provincial aggregate industrial SOE profit may be negative, growth rates of profit per unit of equity may not make sense; for sectoral and provincial data in the 1990s therefore the absolute annual change in the indicator is used as a measure of growth.)

Evidence that the market share may have a positive impact on profitability is stronger for the 1990s, especially the years 1993–1997, across sectors when measured both in levels and absolute annual changes, and across provinces when measured in levels (but in growth rates only for one measure of the market share). For the years 1999–2000, the evidence is again rather weak. This suggests that an increase in competition is likely to have led to a reduction in industrial SOE profitability at least throughout the mid-1990s. The two years 1999–2000 constitute a rather short period, with only one set of observations in the case of growth rates. For the 1980s, the evidence is very weak, but the market share can only be poorly measured (based on gross output value).

All regressions were first run with sectoral (provincial) dummies and year dummies. In a second step, if sectoral (provincial) dummies were not jointly significant, they were removed. In a third step, the same procedure was applied to the year dummies. The resulting regression finally was tested for Heteroscedasticity and, if necessary, rerun using White's correction.[92] (The same procedures was applied in all regressions following below.)

The Relationship between the Market Share and the Intermediate Competition Indicator

If competition erodes monopoly profits, then it does so by lowering the prices at which SOEs sell their goods or by lowering the volume of goods sold by SOEs. For a given production capacity, sales revenue (and thereby value-added) falls. Sales revenue (or value-added) relative to assets can thus serve as a broad measure of competition. If this broad measure of competition and the market share both were to measure the same underlying phenomenon (competition), they should be highly correlated.

An annual reduction in the market share between 1993 and 1997 implies a clear reduction in sales revenue (or value-added) per unit of assets, across provinces when measured in levels and growth rates, but across sectors only when measured in levels using value-added (Table 4.2); the market share measures in the sectoral regression with absolute annual changes fall just short of the 10% significance level. Running the regressions with growth

---

[92] The cut-off significance level was the 5% level, using F-tests throughout. Inclusion of dummy variables implies the inclusion, apart from a common intercept, of dummy variables for all sectors (provinces, years) except the first sector (province, year).

Table 4.1 Significance Level of Market Share in Explaining Industrial SOE Profitability (regression results across sectors and across provinces)

	Losses per unit of gross profit 1986-91		Profit per unit of equity			
			1993-97		1999-2000	
	Annual growth rates	Levels	Absolute annual change	Levels	Absolute annual change	Levels
Across sectors: share of SOEs in directly reporting industrial enterprises'						
sales revenue			***+ (N/N/Y)	^+ (Y/N/Y)	insign. (-/-/N)	**+ (Y/N/-)
value-added			**+ (N/N/Y)	^+ (Y/N/Y)	insign. (-/-/Y)	***+ (Y/N/-)
gross output value	insign. (N/Y/N)	**+ (Y/Y/Y)	^+ (N/N/N)	^+ (Y/N/Y)	*- (-/-/N)	***+ (Y/N/-)
Across provinces: share of SOEs in directly reporting industrial enterprises'						
sales revenue			^+ (N/N/N)	^+ (Y/N/Y)	insign. (-/-/N)	insign. (Y/Y/-)
value-added			insign. (N/N/N)	***+ (Y/Y/Y)	insign. (-/-/N)	insign. (Y/Y/-)
gross output value	insign. (N/Y/N)	insign. (Y/Y/Y)	insign. (N/N/N)	**+ (Y/Y/Y)	insign. (-/-/N)	insign. (Y/Y/-)
Across provinces: share of SOEs in all industrial enterprises' (1988-91, 1993-97)'						
gross output value	**- (N/Y/N)	insign. (Y/Y/Y)	insign. (N/N/N)	insign. (Y/Y/Y)		

Significance levels: ^ 0.1%, *** 1%, ** 5%, *** 10%. The information in parentheses refers to whether sectoral (provincial) dummies were included, whether year dummies were included, and whether White's correction for heteroscedasticity was used. N: No, Y: Yes, -: insufficient number of observations.
   Profitability and market share in the upper part of the table both refer to sectors, and in the lower part of the table to provinces. Profitability and market share are measured either both in levels, or both in annual growth rates, or both in absolute annual changes. Sales revenue is always net of all sales-related taxes.
   The original regression equation is: profitability = intercept + coefficient * market share + coefficient * year dummies + coefficient * sectoral (provincial) dummies + error term.
   All regressions were first run with sectoral (provincial) as well as year dummies. Then the redundancy of the sectoral (provincial) dummies was tested (F-test using 5% significance level as cut-off point); if the sectoral dummies turned out to be redundant, the regression was rerun without sectoral (provincial) dummies. In a second step, the same procedure was applied to the year dummies. In a third step, residuals were tested for Heteroscedasticity; if significant at the 5% significance level (F-test), the regression was rerun using White's correction.
Sources: *Statistical Yearbook*; provincial gross output value of industry is obtained from *Seventeen Years of Reform*.

rates rather than with levels appears more meaningful because both the intermediate competition indicator and the market share are likely to be subject to long-term (downward) trends, leading to a potential over-estimation of the

Table 4.2 Impact of Market Share on Industrial SOE Intermediate Competition Indicator

	Across sectors				Across provinces			
	Sales revenue / assets		Value-added / assets		Sales revenue / assets		Value-added / assets	
	1993-97	1999-00	1993-97	1999-00	1993-97	1999-00	1993-97	1999-00
Dependent and independent variables are measured in absolute annual changes								
Industrial SOE market share calculated based on:								
sales revenue	insign. (N/Y/N)	insign. (N/N/Y)			***+ (N/Y/Y)	insign. (N/N/N)		
value-added			insign. (N/Y/Y)	insign (N/N/Y)			^+ (N/Y/N)	insign. (N/N/N)
Dependent and independent variables are measured in levels								
Industrial SOE market share calculated based on:								
sales revenue	insign. (Y/Y/Y)	insign. (Y/Y/-)			^+ (Y/Y/Y)	insign. (Y/Y/-)		
value-added			***+ (Y/Y/Y)	**- (Y/N/-)			***+ (Y/Y/Y)	insign. (Y/Y/-)

Significance levels: ^ 0.1%, *** 1%, ** 5%, *** 10%. The information in parentheses refers to whether sectoral (provincial) dummies were included, whether year dummies were included, and whether White's correction for heteroscedasticity was used. N: No, Y: Yes, -: insufficient number of observations.

The intermediate competition indicators and the market share are measured either both in absolute annual changes, or both in levels.

The SOE share in sales revenue or value-added is the share of SOEs in all directly reporting industrial enterprises. Also see notes to Table 4.1.

Sources: Statistical Yearbook.

strength of the relationship when the regression is run in levels; the inclusion of year dummies may alleviate but not eliminate this problem.

The results for the years 1993–1997 are thus not clear-cut. If the broader intermediate competition measure were the better indicator of competition, the regression results question the reliability of the market share as a proxy for competition (across sectors). In the regressions for 1999–2000, the relationship is predominantly insignificant, but again this is a very short period.

Excessive Labor Remuneration as an Alternative Explanation of Profitability

Fan Gang and Wing-Thye Woo (1996) as well as Jeffrey Sachs and Wing-Thye Woo (1997) propose excessive labor remuneration as an alternative explanation for 'disappearing profits.' Based on survey data from 300 large and medium-sized state enterprises for the years 1984 through 1988, Fan

Gang and Wing-Thye Woo show that, in the aggregate, total income rose faster than did net output value. Their focus, without this being explicit, is on issues of distribution; if the net output value (i.e., value-added net of depreciation) created by the firm is used to pay for excessive labor remuneration, residual profit is reduced.

Fan Gang and Wing-Thye Woo consider income both in the form of direct income (cash income) and indirect income (income in kind):

- direct income: basic wages and various bonuses
- indirect income
    (i)   collective consumption (kindergartens, hospitals, etc.),
    (ii) distribution of private consumer goods at the common level (furniture, clothes, grain, etc.) as well as at the elite level (banquets, travel, cars, etc.), and
    (iii) housing.

Collective consumption is financed out of the welfare fund. The distribution of private consumer goods at the common level is charged to the profit and loss account as material costs and non-production expenditures. Elite consumption is included in net management costs.

Housing is one form of investment in non-productive fixed assets. The inclusion of investment in non-productive fixed assets (housing) in labor remuneration for the purpose of showing the impact on profitability is logically not permissible. Increases in investment in non-productive fixed assets (housing) are not a profit and loss account item and thus cannot reduce profit. Rather, investment is financed *through* profit (or borrowing, or the injection of new capital) and enters the balance sheet as an asset as well as an increase in retained earnings (or in liabilities or newly paid-in capital).

Investment in non-productive fixed assets affects profit indirectly with a small fraction of the initial investment outlays every year. If investment in non-productive fixed assets is financed through liabilities, these liabilities incur additional interest charges, which then in turn enter the cost accounts and thus reduce residual profit. If investment in non-productive fixed assets is financed through accumulated profit, this accumulated profit cannot contribute to future profit as it would, for example, if it were invested in productive projects or earned interest in a bank account. Rental payments by tenants to the enterprise, on the other hand, offset some of the interest charges or opportunity costs.

In the following, the link between the various components of labor remuneration and the intermediate labor remuneration indicator (profit per unit of sales revenue or value-added), as well as the link between the various components of labor remuneration and profitability (profit per unit of equity) are tested using first nationwide and then provincial labor remuneration data.

Analysis Using Nationwide Data

The available nationwide data include wages and salaries and the social insurance and welfare fund. Wages (and salaries) comprise all direct income (official wages and salaries, plus bonuses) as well as some income in kind (what Fan Gang and Wing-Thye Woo term consumption at the common level). Social insurance and welfare funds finance the various uses that Fan Gang and Wing-Thye Woo describe as collective consumption, plus pensions, which by 1997 accounted for the majority of all social and welfare payments. Official data thus cover all of Fan Gang and Wing-Thye Woo's relevant items except "elite consumption," which is hidden in net management costs. The calculations here in addition consider pensions (including social welfare and medical expenses for retired staff and workers). Although investment in non-productive fixed assets does not enter the profit and loss account and can at most affect profit by an amount equivalent to only a small proportion for the investment expenditures, it is also considered.

Table 4.3 presents the correlation coefficients between various measures of industrial SOE labor income per unit of sales revenue and industrial SOE profit per unit of sales revenue for the period 1978 through 2000, using annual data. It also reports the correlation coefficients when all measures are standardized by value-added, and when growth rates are used instead of levels. Some of the correlation coefficients calculated span the 1997–1998 statistical break; these do not differ much from those covering only the period prior to 1998. Significant correlation coefficients carry the expected negative sign throughout.

Fan Gang and Wing-Thye Woo's rate of profit to value-added — which reflects almost solely labor remuneration effects and is thus an intermediate labor remuneration indicator — is, as expected, highly (negatively) correlated with wages and social welfare funds across all periods, including in the four sub-periods that reflect distinct stages in China's economic

Table 4.3 Correlation Coefficients of Individual Components of Labor Remuneration with the Intermediate Labor Remuneration Indicator or Profitability in Industrial SOEs

	1978-97	1978-2000	1978-87	1988-92	1993-97	1998-2000	1993-2000	1993-97	1998-2000	1993-2000
Per sales revenue:			*Profit per unit of sales revenue*					*Profit per unit of equity*		
Wages (and salaries)	^-0.696	*-0.368	***-0.794	-0.344	-0.675	**-0.998	*-0.703	-0.770	***-1.000	-0.513
Social welfare funds	^-0.925	^-0.933	^-0.941	**-0.958	**-0.885	-0.971	**-0.743	**-0.925	-0.983	***-0.913
Wages + social funds	^-0.857	^-0.755	^-0.903	-0.617	-0.759	*-0.995	**-0.775	*-0.841	**-0.999	*-0.643
Non-productive investment	-0.003	-0.003	***-0.839	-0.076						
Housing investment	0.129	0.129	0.033	-0.612						
Wag. + soc. f. + non-prod.	-0.266	-0.106	***-0.853	-0.585						
Per value-added:			*Profit per unit of value-added*					*Profit per unit of equity*		
Wages (and salaries)	^-0.922	^-0.834	***-0.859	*-0.845	*-0.833	*-0.996	**-0.745	**-0.896	*-0.993	-0.603
Social welfare funds	^-0.944	^-0.948	^-0.909	^-0.995	***-0.986	***-1.000	*-0.705	^-0.998	**-1.000	^-0.935
Wages + social funds	^-0.937	^-0.909	^-0.891	**-0.926	**-0.895	**-0.998	**-0.795	**-0.945	*-0.995	**-0.725
Non-productive investment	***-0.614	***-0.614	^-0.958	-0.323						
Housing investment	**-0.572	***-0.572	-0.364	-0.693						
Wag. + soc. f. + non-prod.	^-0.945	^-0.945	^-0.973	**-0.891						
Growth r., per sales rev.:			*Growth rate of profit per unit of sales revenue*					*Growth rate of profit per unit of equity*		
Wages (and salaries)	-0.218	**-0.474	-0.029	-0.819	-0.148	0.082	-0.470	0.236	-0.121	-0.547
Social welfare funds	0.007	-0.321	0.443	-0.862	-0.395	-0.302	-0.497	0.178	-0.488	*-0.674
Wages + social funds	-0.220	**-0.476	0.027	-0.834	-0.211	0.003	-0.480	0.235	-0.198	-0.574
Non-productive investment	0.088	0.088	-0.263	0.107						
Housing investment	-0.281	-0.281	-0.281	-0.246						
Wag. + soc. f. + non-prod.	-0.224	-0.224	-0.280	-0.433						

Table 4.3 (continued)

	1978-97	1978-2000	1978-87	1988-92	1993-97	1998-2000	1993-2000	1993-97	1998-2000	1993-2000
Growth r., per value-a.:	*Growth rate of profit per unit of value-added*							*Growth rate of profit per unit of equity*		
Wages (and salaries)	*-0.410	***-0.549	-0.189	-0.894	-0.488	0.286	-0.536	-0.245	0.179	-0.611
Social welfare funds	-0.086	*-0.368	0.307	**-0.970	-0.743	-0.289	-0.553	-0.760	-0.392	**-0.789
Wages + social funds	*-0.403	***-0.547	-0.152	*-0.919	-0.562	0.204	-0.545	-0.321	0.095	-0.647
Non-productive investment	-0.022	-0.022	-0.552	-0.002						
Housing investment	-0.375	-0.375	-0.379	-0.355						
Wag. + soc. f. + non-prod.	-0.408	-0.408	0.625	-0.669						

Significance levels: ^ 0.1%, *** 1%, ** 5%, *** 10%.
"Wag. + soc. f. + non-prod." denotes wages (and salaries), plus social welfare funds, plus non-productive investment.
Data on non-productive investment and on housing investment are only available for the years 1981 through 1992. Data are available on total investment by all state-owned units, on (only) total investment of industrial SOEs, and on non-productive and housing investment in all state-owned units; it is assumed that the shares of non-productive and housing investment in total investment by industrial SOEs are the same as for all state-owned units.
Sources:
Wages (and salaries), social welfare funds (including for retirees, and including pensions), value-added: see appendices to Chapter 2.
Investment: *Investment Data 1950-1985*, pp. 15, 16, 20; *Statistical Yearbook 1986*, p. 447; *1987*, p. 473; *1992*, p. 150; *1993*, pp. 150f.
Profit and sales revenue: see Table 3.2.

transition (1978–1987, 1988–1992, 1993–1997, 1998–2000). It is also highly (negatively) correlated with non-productive investment and housing investment across the period of 1981 through 1992, the only years for which the latter data are available (reported in the category 1978–1997 or 1978–2000). Once profit is related to sales revenue, investment is no longer significantly correlated with profitability (except non-productive investment in the years 1978–1987), while wages and social welfare funds generally remain significantly correlated except for wages in the years 1988 through 1997.

Wages and social welfare funds also have a direct impact on the profitability indicator of profit per unit of equity in the years since 1993 (the first year for which equity data are available). But significance levels are lower than in the case of the intermediate labor remuneration indicators, and wages may have a clear negative impact on profitability in the most recent years of 1998 through 2000 only.

Although the key variables (wages relative to value-added or sales revenue, social welfare expenditures relative to value-added or sales revenue, and the intermediate labor remuneration indicator profit relative to value-added or sales revenue) are all bound from below by zero and from above by unity, they might still exhibit a trend within this band. Correlation coefficients are therefore also calculated based on the annual growth rates of the various ratios.[93] There is still evidence that wages and social welfare funds matter in the intermediate labor remuneration indicator, but this evidence is weaker than when levels are used. Investment (correctly) no longer matters. The correlation coefficients with profit per unit of equity all turn insignificant except in the case of social welfare funds relative to value-added in the period 1993 through 2000.

In growth rates, the intermediate labor remuneration indicator is much less strongly linked to the two sub-categories of labor remuneration, wages and social welfare funds, than in levels, implying that the other components of sales revenue (or value-added, similarly below) also contribute to the variation in the growth of profit relative to sales revenue. But perhaps the number of nationwide observations is too small to clearly discern the link between wages and social welfare funds on the one hand and the intermediate labor remuneration indicator on the other hand.

---

[93] Using nationwide data, unlike in the case of provincial or sectoral data, growth rates are not problematic since nationwide aggregate industrial SOE profit never turns negative.

Analysis Using Provincial-Level Data

Provincial-level wage data (but no data on other types of labor remuneration) are available to expand the analysis; sectoral data on labor remuneration are not available. In contrast to the case of competition, where analysis across provinces is problematic as the SOE market share in provincial directly reporting industrial enterprises' sales revenue may ignore SOE concentration in certain sectors, relating provincial industrial SOE aggregate wages to provincial industrial SOE aggregate profit is free of such considerations.

The regression results reported in Table 4.4 for the years 1993 through 1997 and in Table 4.5 for the years 1999 and 2000 reveal that the ratio of wages to sales revenue has a strong negative impact on the intermediate labor remuneration indicator, profit relative to sales revenue; the results hold across both time periods, in levels and in absolute annual changes in ratios, using sales revenue or value-added as the denominator. Once the analysis moves beyond nationwide aggregate annual observations to provincial observations (albeit on wages only), the intermediate labor remuneration indicator, profit relative to sales revenue (or value-added), appears to be closely linked to the share of pure wages in sales revenue (or value-added).

But the distributive conflict is not limited to labor remuneration. Depreciation may also play an important role in that operating surplus (as proxied by profit) is the residual of value-added after subtracting labor remuneration, depreciation, and net taxes on production. Lacking depreciation data for all provinces in all years, depreciation is proxied by average annual net fixed assets; this assumes that depreciation rates are constant across provinces, while any variation over time may in part be captured by the year dummies. Including the ratio of average annual net fixed assets to sales revenue in the regression, in levels or in absolute annual changes, in the periods 1993–1997, and 1999–2000, more often than not yields an insignificant coefficient. One exception is the period 1993–1997 with as the dependent variable profit per unit of value-added, when the coefficient is negative and highly significant; it is also somewhat significant (but with the wrong sign) in the 1999–2000 regressions with profit per unit of sales revenue as the dependent variable, both in levels and in absolute

Table 4.4 Impact of Labor Remuneration on the Intermediate Labor Remuneration Indicator for Industrial SOEs across Provinces, 1993–1997

	Absolute annual change in profit per unit of sales revenue			Absolute annual change in profit per unit of value-added		
Number of observations	120	120	120	120	120	120
R^2	0.1720	0.1721	0.2024	0.0678	0.0799	0.1014
Intercept	*0.0142	0.0142	*0.0157	***-0.0175	**-0.0145	**-0.0110
	(1.9408)	(1.5992)	(1.8008)	(-3.2635)	(-2.4453)	(-1.7699)
Absolute annual change in:						
Wages per unit of sales revenue, value-added	^-1.0256	***-1.0280	***-1.0097	***-0.3444	**-0.2581	*-0.2605
	(-3.627)	(-2.9146)	(-2.8904)	(-2.9305)	(-1.8919)	(-1.9233)
Average annual net fixed assets per unit of sales revenue, value-added		0.0015	0.0123		-0.0146	-0.0105
		(0.0323)	(0.2621)		(-1.2366)	(-0.8798)
SOE market share based on: sales revenue, value-added			*0.1495			*0.1797
			(1.6670)			(1.6672)
Provincial dummies	No	No	No	No	No	No
Year dummies	Yes	Yes	Yes	No	No	No
White's correction	No	Yes	Yes	No	No	No

	Profit per unit of sales revenue			Profit per unit of value-added		
Number of observations	150	150	150	150	150	150
R^2	0.7684	0.7582	0.7609	0.8074	0.8273	0.8295
Intercept	^0.1552	^0.1543	*0.1014	^0.4303	^0.4315	^0.3479
	(3.6003)	(6.1373)	(1.7439)	(6.7859)	(7.0868)	(3.9077)
Wages per unit of sales revenue, value-added	**-1.1668	*-0.8300	-0.7736	^-0.7557	**-0.3816	**-0.3845
	(-1.8740)	(-1.7427)	(-1.5307)	(-3.5107)	(-2.3889)	(-2.3976)
Average annual net fixed assets per unit of sales revenue, value-added		-0.0343	-0.0192		^-0.0517	^-0.0447
		(-1.1334)	(-0.6595)		(-5.1434)	(-4.2603)
SOE market share based on sales revenue, value-added			0.0604			0.1228
			(1.1908)			(1.2982)
Provincial dummies	Yes	Yes	Yes	Yes	Yes	Yes
Year dummies	Yes	No	No	Yes	Yes	Yes
White's correction	Yes	Yes	Yes	Yes	Yes	Yes

Significance levels: ^ 0.1%, *** 1%, ** 5%, *** 10%. The numbers in parentheses are t-statistics.
Sources:
Profit, sales revenue, value-added, average annual fixed assets: *Statistical Yearbook*.
Wages: *Statistical Yearbook 1994*, p. 116; *1995*, pp. 94, 118; *1996*, pp. 102, 122; *1997*, pp. 108, 128; *1998*, pp. 138, 164. Wage data are the sum of the wage bills in the three (exhaustive) sub-categories of industry. While for 1993 the wage bill data for each of the three sub-categories are available, for 1994 through 1997 they were obtained by multiplying employment with average wages in the sub-category.

Table 4.5 Impact of Labor Remuneration on the Intermediate Labor Remuneration Indicator for Industrial SOEs across Provinces, 1999–2000

	Absolute annual change in profit per unit of sales revenue			Absolute annual change in profit per unit of value-added		
Number of observations	31	31	31	31	31	31
R^2	0.3842	0.5004	0.5882	0.3997	0.4217	0.4470
Intercept	0.0143	*0.0128	***0.0164	***0.0440	***0.0393	***0.0453
	(1.6740)	(1.9374)	(3.2691)	(3.3912)	(2.8695)	(3.0887)
Absolute annual change in:						
Wages per unit of sales revenue, value-added	*-1.3637	***-2.2704	^-2.2601	^-1.5449	***-1.9595	^-1.9976
	(-2.0235)	(-3.6690)	(-5.3012)	(-4.3943)	(-3.6699)	(-3.7493)
Average annual net fixed assets per unit of sales revenue, value-added		*0.1253	**0.1129		0.0470	0.0465
		(2.0431)	(2.4712)		(1.0308)	(1.0251)
SOE market share based on sales revenue, value-added			**0.4187			0.3687
			(2.4001)			(1.1121)
White's correction	Yes	Yes	No	No	No	No
	Profit per unit of sales revenue			Profit per unit of value-added		
Number of observations	62	62	62	62	62	62
R^2	0.9410	0.9522	0.9605	0.9331	0.9355	0.9384
Intercept	^0.1222	***0.0914	-0.2019	^0.5019	^0.4781	0.2278
	(4.7457)	(3.4512)	(-1.6154)	(5.3788)	(4.9797)	(0.9316)
Wages per unit of sales revenue, value-added	^-1.3652	^-2.2715	^-2.2611	^-1.5443	***-1.9593	^-1.9974
	(-4.2595)	(-4.9301)	(-5.3057)	(-4.3964)	(-3.6725)	(-3.7520)
Average annual net fixed assets per unit of sales revenue, value-added		**0.1252	**0.1129		0.0471	0.0466
		(2.5533)	(2.4716)		(1.0326)	(1.0270)
SOE market share based on sales revenue, value-added			**0.4171			0.3686
			(2.3934)			(1.1125)
Provincial dummies	Yes	Yes	Yes	Yes	Yes	Yes
Year 2000 dummy	Yes	Yes	Yes	Yes	Yes	Yes
White's correction	-	-	-	-	-	-

Significance levels: ^ 0.1%, *** 1%, ** 5%, *** 10%. The numbers in parentheses are t-statistics.
Sources:
Profit, sales revenue, value-added, average annual fixed assets: *Statistical Yearbook*.
Wages: *Statistical Yearbook 2000*, pp. 126, 148; *2001*, pp. 118, 142; *Industrial Yearbook 2001*, p. 119. Wage data are average annual employment (corresponding to the newly defined SOE category), as given in the *Industrial Yearbook*, times average wages calculated based on employment and average wage data in the three sub-categories of industry (in SOEs presumably following the pre-1998 definition), given in the *Statistical Yearbook*.

annual changes.[94] Importantly, the sign and significance of the coefficient of labor remuneration remain unchanged (except for the significance level in the case of the absolute annual change in profit per unit of value-added in 1993–1997). In terms of the distributive fight, thus, labor remuneration always tends to be a significant force.

The possibility finally exists that the share of labor remuneration in sales revenue in turn is determined by competition; competition reduces the sales revenue to be distributed, and if labor remuneration is independent of sales revenue, the decrease in sales revenue together with the constant labor remuneration will, *ceteris paribus*, result in a decrease in profit per unit of sales revenue. But if the market share is explicitly included in the regressions, it almost always has no impact on profit per unit of sales revenue. In the cases when it has an impact, the coefficient sign is correct; labor remuneration continues to have a highly significant (negative) impact on the intermediate labor remuneration indicator.

While the relationship between wages (or social welfare funds) and the profitability indicator, profit per unit of equity, was weak when annual nationwide data were used (Table 4.3), provincial-level data on wages as a sub-category of labor remuneration reveals a usually significant impact on provincial-level profitability. These results are independent of whether wages are standardized by sales revenue or value-added and independent of whether the regression is run in levels or in absolute annual changes in the ratios. (Regressions similar to those in Table 4.4 and Table 4.5 were run, but the results are not reported in a table.) This would suggest that wages by themselves, as a sub-category of total labor remuneration only, across provinces, have a direct impact on profitability. An increase in wages relative to sales revenue reduces industrial SOE profitability.

The next section continues by exploring the joint impact of competition and wages on profitability. This is only possible on a provincial-level basis, which is unlikely to do full justice to the competition argument. It is also

---

[94] The positive sign suggests that the larger the volume of average net fixed assets relative to sales revenue, the larger profit relative to sales revenue. One interpretation would be that a higher capital intensity in the production of the typical product produced by industrial SOEs in a particular province creates savings in other inputs that, despite the higher capital costs, make it more profitable (relative to value-added) than less capital-intensive processes.

only possible using one sub-category of labor remuneration (wages). The alternative is to use the two intermediate competition and labor remuneration indicators to explain profitability.

Explaining Profitability

When competition (in the form of the market share) and labor remuneration (in the form of wages) are allowed to compete across provinces in the explanation of the profitability indicator, profit per unit of equity, the coefficient of wages is highly significant across all variations of the regression (1993–1997 vs. 1999–2000, levels vs. absolute annual changes, standardization using sales revenue or value-added). The coefficient of the SOE market share is significant in five out of the eight regressions, but at lower significance levels. All signs are correct throughout. (See Table 4.6.)

These results suggest that at least throughout the 1990s, both competition and labor remuneration were crucial in explaining profitability. The impact of the SOE market share may be relatively weak because, as elaborated above, the industrial SOE market share in a particular province may not be a good proxy for competition; sectoral wage data, on the other hand, are not available. Competition furthermore may impact on profitability through the labor remuneration measure, as explained in the second section of this chapter; this could weaken the direct effect on profitability.

Switching to the intermediate competition and labor remuneration indicators, namely sales revenue (or value-added) per unit of assets and profit per unit of sales revenue (or value-added), also allows cross-sectoral analysis. The results are unambiguous (Table 4.7). Both intermediate indicators have clear-cut effects on profit per unit of equity throughout the 1990s. Table 4.7, similar to Table 4.6, also suggests that the competition effect is not as strong as the labor remuneration effect, even across sectors.

In a final step, the two intermediate indicators lend themselves as building blocks in the "construction" of profit per unit of equity. Multiplication of the two intermediate indicators and a third term of assets per unit of equity yields (equals) profit per unit of equity (Figure 4.1). If the variables on the right-hand side were completely independent of each other, then changes in profit relative to equity could be directly and proportionally attributed to changes in each of the variables on the right-hand side. Table 4.8 reports

Table 4.6 Impact of Competition and Labor Remuneration on Industrial SOE Profit per Unit of Equity across Provinces, 1993–2000

	1993-97		1999-2000	
	Absolute annual change in profit per unit of equity			
Number of observations	120	120	31	31
R^2	0.1809	0.0891	0.5554	0.4295
Intercept	0.0017	**-0.0094	***0.0194	**0.0190
	(0.3819)	(-2.5741)	(2.8913)	(2.3138)
Absolute annual change in SOE market share (based on):				
sales revenue	^0.3542		**0.5234	
	(4.6771)		(2.2250)	
value-added		0.0814		0.2413
		(1.2451)		(1.2384)
Absolute annual change in wages per unit of:				
sales revenue	***-0.6295		^-2.1196	
	(-2.7381)		(-5.7066)	
value-added		***-0.2168		^-0.9364
		(-2.9904)		(-4.5291)
White's correction	No	No	No	No
	Profit per unit of equity			
Number of observations	150	150	62	62
R^2	0.8098	0.8250	0.9461	0.9309
Intercept	-0.0494	**0.1156	-0.1967	0.0979
	(-1.0061)	(2.4467)	(-1.1597)	(0.6838)
SOE market share (based on):				
sales revenue	^0.3145		**0.5217	
	(6.3338)		(2.2201)	
value-added		**0.1346		0.2411
		(2.1695)		(1.2379)
Wages per unit of:				
sales revenue	***-0.7411		^-2.1205	
	(-2.7178)		(-5.7082)	
value-added		***-0.3300		^-0.9356
		(-3.1012)		(-4.5287)
Provincial dummies	Yes	Yes	Yes	Yes
Year dummies	No	Yes	Yes	Yes
White's correction	Yes	Yes	-	-

Significance levels: ^ 0.1%, *** 1%, ** 5%, *** 10%. The numbers in parentheses are t-statistics.
Sources: *Statistical Yearbook*, Table 4.4, Table 4.5.

the annual contribution of the three factors to the growth rate in profit per unit of equity. Thus, in 1994, using the ratios with respect to sales revenue, the intermediate competition indicator contributed 108.50% of the (negative) growth in profit per unit of equity, while the intermediate labor remuneration indicator contributed 1.60%; the ratio of assets to equity contributed negative 10.10% (implying that it prevented profitability from slipping even more). The ratios with respect to value-added present a qualitatively similar picture; in some years, the quantitatively quite different contribution of competition vs. labor remuneration cautions somewhat against over-interpreting the absolute contributions.

Across the period 1994 through 2000, the impact of competition vs. labor remuneration varies, with competition contributing most to the change in profit per unit of equity in 1994, 1997, and 1998, and labor remuneration contributing most in the years 1995, 1996, 1999, and 2000. Strikingly, the intermediate labor remuneration indicator made a positive contribution to (positive) growth in profit per unit of equity in 1999 and 2000, implying a relative reduction in labor remuneration; this is most likely due to the dismissal of between one quarter and one half of all industrial SOE staff and workers, i.e., due to a reduction in excess labor rather than to a reduction in "excess" wages. (For details on the dismissal of SOE staff and workers, see Chapter 8.) When competition made a significant contribution to profitability, on the other hand, this contribution was always negative.

The time patterns show that competition and labor remuneration not only simultaneously affect profitability, but also repeatedly exchange the role as the driving factor. Identifying distinct roles for competition vs. labor remuneration, however, is only possible if changes in competition do not affect the intermediate labor remuneration indicator and if changes in labor remuneration do not affect the intermediate competition indicator. This is not necessarily the case, but the (sharp) results in Table 4.7 suggest that the interaction effect between the two is likely to be small.

The ratio of assets to equity varies little over time, with a noticeable contribution only in 1998. However, this ignores the fact that increases in assets could be associated with, for example, new bank loans and thus the ratio of profit relative to sales revenue. Technological progress embedded in the new assets may also affect the ratio of sales revenue to assets. Assets relative to equity could still play a significant role in determining

Table 4.7 Impact of Intermediate Competition and Labor Remuneration Indicators on Industrial SOE Profit per Unit of Equity, 1993–2000

	Across sectors				Across provinces			
	1993-97	1999-2000	1993-97	1999-2000	1993-97	1999-2000	1993-97	1999-2000
	Dependent variable: Absolute annual change in profit / equity							
Number of observations	152	37	152	37	120	31	120	31
R^2	0.7558	0.8565	0.7587	0.8967	0.6862	0.9656	0.7709	0.9185
Intercept	-0.0074	-0.0009	**-0.0056	*-0.0105	***-0.0054	**-0.0062	0.0017	**-0.0089
	(-1.1904)	(-0.2039)	(-2.1797)	(-1.7898)	(-2.0359)	(-2.5301)	(0.5325)	(-2.3626)
Absolute annual change in intermediate competition indicator:								
sales revenue per unit of assets	**0.0861	0.0211			*0.0705	^0.1839		
	(1.9775)	(0.4182)			(1.6769)	(3.7822)		
value-added per unit of assets			-0.0167	^0.8088			^0.3111	**0.4225
			(-0.2155)	(4.0201)			(3.7664)	(2.4022)
Absolute annual change in intermediate labor remuneration indicator:								
profit per unit of sales revenue	^1.5333	^1.3946			^1.0042	^1.1962		
	(10.3326)	(13.1395)			(4.3844)	(22.3816)		
profit per unit of value-added			^0.6238	^0.5913			^0.5050	^0.5096
			(18.4522)	(4.8569)			(6.8469)	(6.6094)
Sectoral / Provincial dummies	No	No	Yes	Yes	No	No	Yes	Yes
Year dummies	Yes		Yes		Yes		Yes	
White's correction	Yes	No	Yes	No	Yes	No	Yes	Yes

Table 4.7 (continued)

	Across sectors				Across provinces			
	1993-97	1999-2000	1993-97	1999-2000	1993-97	1999-2000	1993-97	1999-2000
	Dependent variable: Profit / equity							
Number of observations	190	74	190	74	150	62	150	62
R^2	0.9423	0.9736	0.9526	0.9814	0.9317	0.9958	0.9509	0.9901
Intercept	^-0.0572 (-6.2035)	0.0071 (0.3940)	-0.0179 (-1.1926)	^-0.0960 (-3.6917)	^-0.0722 (-4.3802)	^-0.0903 (-3.8099)	^-0.0505 (-7.4675)	***-0.0812 (-3.1416)
Intermediate competition indicator:								
sales revenue per unit of assets	^0.1296 (5.3287)	0.0181 (0.3804)			^0.1935 (4.4364)	^0.1832 (3.7776)		
value-added per unit of assets			0.0821 (1.0450)	^0.7658 (4.6364)			^0.3467 (4.2739)	*0.4217 (2.0417)
Intermediate labor remuneration indicator:								
profit per unit of sales revenue	^1.3705 (12.8405)	^1.3897 (13.6845)			^0.9249 (4.6396)	^1.1964 (22.4204)		
profit per unit of value-added			^0.6103 (15.0015)	^0.5873 (9.1117)			^0.4246 (8.1405)	^0.5097 (12.5753)
Sectoral / Provincial dummies	Yes	Yes	Yes	Yes	Yes	Yes	Yes	Yes
Year dummies	No	No	No	Yes	No	Yes	No	Yes
White's correction	Yes	-	Yes	-	Yes	-	Yes	-

Significance levels: ^ 0.1%, *** 1%, ** 5%, * 10%. The numbers in parentheses are t-statistics.
Sources: see Table 4.2, Table 4.4, and Table 4.5.

Table 4.8 Contribution of Intermediate Competition and Labor Remuneration Indicators to Change in Profitability of Industrial SOEs, 1994–2000

	Profitability chain based on sales revenue				Profitability chain based on value-added			
	Profit / equity	Sal. rev. / assets	Profit / Sal. rev.	Assets / equity	Profit / equity	VA / assets	Profit / VA	Assets / equity
Annual growth rate (in %)								
1994	-13.69	-14.85	-0.22	1.38	-13.69	-8.30	-6.77	1.38
1995	-49.33	-3.99	-38.98	-6.37	-49.33	-16.02	-26.94	-6.37
1996	-60.39	-6.75	-51.62	-2.03	-60.39	-5.45	-52.92	-2.03
1997	-7.01	-8.44	0.69	0.74	-7.01	-6.34	-1.41	0.74
1998	-6.30	-5.24	2.03	-3.10	-6.30	-5.06	1.85	-3.10
1999	50.89	-0.28	57.33	-6.15	50.89	1.95	55.09	-6.15
2000	81.32	11.96	71.84	-2.48	81.32	8.41	75.39	-2.48
Contribution to change in profit / equity (in %)								
1994	100.00	108.50	1.60	-10.10	100.00	60.64	49.46	-10.10
1995	100.00	8.08	79.01	12.92	100.00	32.47	54.61	12.92
1996	100.00	11.17	85.47	3.36	100.00	9.02	87.62	3.36
1997	100.00	120.44	-9.83	-10.61	100.00	90.49	20.12	-10.61
1998	100.00	83.10	-32.21	49.11	100.00	80.26	-29.37	49.11
1999	100.00	-0.56	112.65	-12.09	100.00	3.83	108.26	-12.09
2000	100.00	14.71	88.34	-3.05	100.00	10.34	92.71	-3.05

Sal. rev.: sales revenue net of all sales-related taxes. VA: value-added.
The annual growth rate was obtained by subtracting the natural logarithm of one year's value from the natural logarithm of the next year's value.
Sources: Statistical Yearbook.

profitability, but this impact may in part be achieved through changes in the other two ratios.

The ratio of assets to equity is a measure of leverage. It behaves qualitatively in the same way as the liability-asset ratio (liabilities per unit of assets). The following chapter further examines the impact of the liability-asset ratio on profitability (and vice-versa).

Conclusions

Earlier discussions of whether competition or excessive labor remuneration account for the decline in industrial SOE profitability were marred by a dearth of data and a misinterpretation of profit relative to value-added as a measure of profitability. Competition could well drive down the ultimate profitability indicator, profit relative to equity, and not have any impact on what is in effect an intermediate labor remuneration indicator, profit per unit of value-added.

While no perfect measure of competition exists, at least nationwide industrial SOE labor remuneration can now be pieced together, with data on one sub-category of labor remuneration, namely wages, available (or derivable) across all provinces. The available data indicate that competition, measured in the form of the market share, as well as labor remuneration, measured in the form of wages, are highly likely to exert a simultaneous influence on profit per unit of equity.

The discussion of whether competition or excessive labor remuneration has driven down SOE profitability is fully resolved once it is recognized that the two causes affect profitability primarily through different channels. They are not alternative hypotheses but simultaneous explanations of changes in profitability. Competition affects the price at which a product is sold and/or its sales quantity and thus affects sales revenue (or value-added). Labor remuneration affects the residual profit available out of a given amount of sales revenue (or value-added).

These intermediate indicators can also proxy for the degree of competition (for which no unambiguous concept, let alone indicator, is available) and the extent of labor remuneration (for which no comprehensive sectoral or provincial data are available). The intermediate competition indicator is only weakly related to the market share measure, implying that one of the two, or both, may not be the best measure(s) of competition. The intermediate labor remuneration indicator is closely related to wages and social welfare payments. Once allowed to impact jointly on profitability, these intermediate competition and labor remuneration indicators explain much of the variation in profitability across sectors and regions between 1993 and 2000.

Industrial SOEs are unlikely to see their fortunes improve with respect to competition. In late 1998, the government reverted to direct administrative price determination for selected industrial products in order to prevent what was viewed as "malicious" (*e'xing*) competition. The government interfered in the price determination process in order to prevent the sale of products below production costs and consequently the loss of state assets. The measures were hotly debated even in China. The Economic and Trade

Commission first issued a regulation focusing on price-fixing through sectoral associations. Then the State Development and Planning Commission, members of which first objected to any price-fixing, promoted the primary role of the traditional price administration bureaus.[95] (Chapter 8 provides more details.)

If the original price cuts were pure marketing measures, the temporary respite may yet help. If the original price cuts, however, were triggered by lower production costs in non-state enterprises, the government would have to return to permanent price administration to help industrial SOEs. The measures taken furthermore were highly selective and thus unlikely to make much difference across the aggregate of all industrial SOEs.

While competition has clearly increased during the reform period, driving down industrial SOE profitability, the negative impact of increasing labor remuneration on industrial profitability up through the mid-1990s need not reflect "excessive" labor remuneration in the sense that industrial SOE laborers are increasingly paid a wage above their marginal product value. The typical industrial SOE laborer most likely was originally underpaid when alternative employment opportunities at market rates were not available. "Excessive" labor remuneration until today also reflects underemployment rather than necessarily excessive wages for those productively engaged in an industrial SOE.

---

[95] See, for example, *Xinbao* (10 Sept. 1998, 24 Sept. 1998, 8 Dec. 1998, and 5 August 1999), or *China News Digest* (11 Nov. 1998).

5
The Impact of the Liability-Asset Ratio on Profitability

One frequently cited reason for the decline in industrial SOE profitability is the rise in the SOEs' liability-asset ratio.[96] During the reform period, the liability-asset ratio of industrial SOEs rose from around 11% in 1978 to approximately 68% in 1994. In as many as one-fourth of industrial SOEs, liabilities have even come to exceed assets; these enterprises are de facto insolvent. The World Bank (1996a, 42) suggests that debt restructuring may be necessary for the most heavily indebted enterprises.

The rising liability-asset ratio is viewed with growing concern by the Chinese leadership. The SOE reform decision by the Chinese Communist Party Central Committee (CCPCC) on 22 September 1999 lists as the main problems of SOEs their poor management, over-employment, a low technological level, and a high liability-asset ratio. The high liability-asset ratio is perceived as leading to high interest payments and therefore to low profitability. On the link between a high volume of liabilities and low profitability, the deputy minister of the State Economic and Trade Commission (SETC) states explicitly: "with all the interest to be paid on such a large volume of liabilities, it has already become very difficult for

---

[96] The liability-asset ratio is defined as liabilities divided by (total) assets. Leverage, in contrast, indicates the ratio of liabilities to equity. Since assets are equal to liabilities plus equity, any change in the liability-asset ratio implies a change in leverage with the same sign (and vice versa). Both concepts, the liability-asset ratio and leverage, are equally valid in the profitability analysis. The Chinese practice of using the liability-asset ratio is adopted in the following.

enterprises to still earn money" (Chen Qingtai, 1998, p. 6). Figure 5.1 with 1995 industrial census data across the 37 industrial sectors confirms the negative relationship between the liability-asset ratio and profitability.

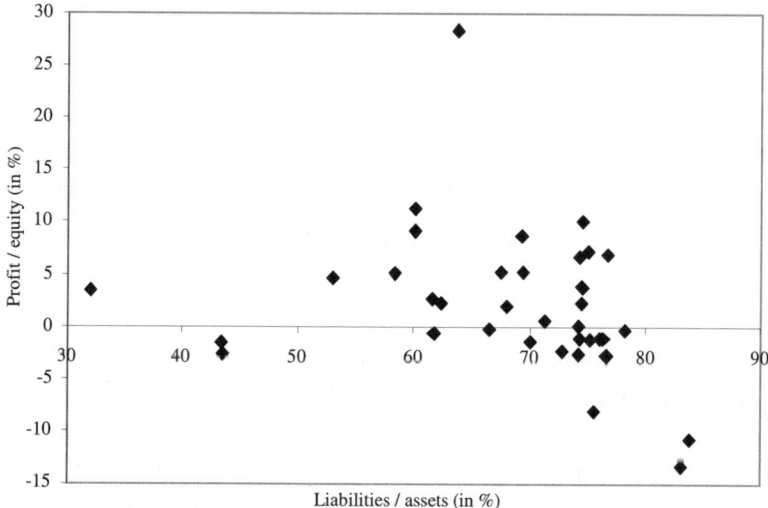

Source: *Industrial Census 1995*, Vol. 2, pp. 16-167.

Figure 5.1   Industrial SOE Liability-Asset Ratios and Profitability across Sectors, 1995

But the liability-asset ratio in industrial SOEs is not increasing continuously. The liability-asset ratio of industrial SOEs rose continuously only throughout the 1980s. This increase is not so much a sign of deterioration as of the economic transition; it was caused by economic reforms that changed the financing mechanisms of SOEs. In the early 1990s, the liability-asset ratio stabilized.

Moreover, a high liability-asset ratio need not even imply low profitability.[97] If two firms are identical except for their liability-asset ratio,

---

[97] Following the Modigliani-Miller theorem, the return on equity cannot be raised by increasing or decreasing the ratio of liabilities to equity (or assets). Yet the Modigliani-Miller theorem is based on a number of assumptions that are virtually never met, perhaps least of all in China. The assumptions are that (i) firms can be identified by "risk class" (or that they have a zero probability of bankruptcy), (ii) individual borrowing can substitute for firm borrowing, (iii) investors have full information about the returns of the firm, and (iv) the tax policy does not treat debt and equity differentially. (See, for example, Joseph Stiglitz, 1988, for further elaboration on the assumptions.)

profit in the firm with the higher liability-asset ratio naturally must be lower than profit in the firm with the lower liability-asset ratio. Profit is the residual of sales revenue after subtracting various costs, *including* interest payments on the liabilities; a high liability-asset ratio entails a large volume of interest payments and therefore a small residual profit. However, a small volume of profit per se is no reason for concern. What matters is the volume of profit *relative* to equity (profitability). If the interest rate paid on debt is the same as the rate of profitability, then the level of the liability-asset ratio has no impact on the rate of profitability.[98]

A high liability-asset ratio may even be conducive to a high level of profitability. For example, if the state-determined, nationwide fixed interest rate on bank loans is low relative to a firm's return on equity, any increase in liabilities relative to equity, *ceteris paribus*, raises the volume of profit relative to equity (profitability). This outcome conflicts with the view held by the CCPCC in its 1999 SOE reform decision.

On the other hand, a high liability-asset ratio could lead to low profitability if banks prefer that SOEs have a certain volume of equity as a pre-condition for extending additional loans. Banks could require equity as security in case the finances of the firm deteriorate. Any potential future losses would first reduce equity rather than directly lead to bankruptcy (which could force banks to forego full recovery of their loans). If a high liability-asset ratio deters banks from lending to a firm, which at the same time faces high administrative barriers in its access to equity and consequently an inability to finance regular production, then enterprise profitability may suffer. A high liability-asset ratio implies low profitability. The total effect of the liability-asset ratio on profitability is not self-evident.

Which of the causalities is correct? Does a high liability-asset ratio indeed imply low profitability and thus justify the concern of Chinese economic policy makers for the level of the liability-asset ratio in SOEs? Or is the

---

[98] For example, assume the residual of sales revenue after subtracting all costs except interest costs was 100 RMB. Firm 1 has a debt of 800 RMB and equity of 200 RMB; Firm 2 has a debt of 300 RMB and equity of 700 RMB. If the interest rate were 10%, Firm 1 would pay 80 RMB interest and earn a profit of 20 RMB on its equity of 200 RMB, i.e., its profit per unit of equity (profitability) equals 10%. Firm 2 would pay 30 RMB interest and earn a profit of 70 RMB on its equity of 700 RMB, i.e., its rate of profitability is also 10%.

perceived link between the liability-asset ratio and the rate of profitability spurious, or perhaps even positive? The necessary detailed nationwide data as well as data across sectors and across provinces to answer these questions are available for the years since 1993. The 1995 industrial census has particularly detailed sectoral data for 1995.

The following section questions the view that the liability-asset ratio in industrial SOEs has deteriorated continuously since the beginning of the economic reforms. In doing so the rise in the liability-asset ratio that has taken place is explained. The third section tests whether a high liability-asset ratio has a negative impact on profitability, as the CCPCC believes. The fourth section concludes.

Explaining the Time Trend of the Industrial SOE Liability-Asset Ratio

The liability-asset ratio of industrial SOEs has increased dramatically during the economic reform period. But this increase is not necessarily negative. Much of the increase simply reflects systemic changes in how the economy operates, breaking free from its socialist past. Since 1994, furthermore, the liability-asset ratio has stabilized. The liability-asset ratio of China's industrial SOEs is not excessive in comparisons on the international level.

The Data

Table 5.1 reports the values of the liability-asset ratio over time. For data up to 1992 the table, in the absence of official data, relies on Nicholas Lardy's liability-asset ratios collected from a large number of dispersed sources.[99] Since 1993, the official time series on assets and liabilities

---

[99] Nicholas Lardy's sources are primarily individual newspaper and journal articles. Not all sources could be located; the data are therefore taken directly from Nicholas Lardy (1998, p. 41). While the general trend, as argued below, is definitely correct, individual data points appear to be of dubious quality. For example, the 1978 ratio for industrial SOEs is in effect the ratio of bank loans (i.e., a sub-category of liabilities) to depreciated fixed capital plus the value of all inventories (the 1995 Industrial Census shows this denominator in 1995 to be equal to 57.50% of total assets.) The 1980 and 1994 ratios for industrial SOEs are based on a sample of 20,000 SOEs (compared to 87,905 SOEs with independent accounting system in 1995); the sampling criteria are not identified in the article.

published in the statistical yearbooks allow the consistent calculation of liability-asset ratios. The liability-asset ratio of industrial SOEs has increased markedly throughout the reform period from perhaps around 10% in the beginning of the reform period to 67% in 1993. Yet, at least since 1994, the liability-asset ratio of both industrial SOEs as well as all industrial enterprises has stabilized.

Table 5.1   Liability-Asset Ratios (in %)

	Nicholas Lardy "Liability-asset ratio"		Statistical Yearbook Industrial SOEs: liabilities[a] /			Directly reporting industrial enterprises: Liabilities[a] / assets
	All SOEs	Industrial SOEs	assets	current + fixed assets[b]	current + net fixed assets[b]	
1978	n.a.	11				
1980	n.a.	19				
1988	n.a.	45				
1989	55	n.a.				
1990	58	n.a.				
1991	61	n.a.				
1992	62	n.a.				
1993	72	68	[c]67.48	71.77	77.80	67.05
1994	75	79	67.84	72.95	80.10	66.66
1995	85	n.a.	65.62	69.97	76.97	64.86
1996			65.06	70.05	77.08	64.73
1997			64.82	70.47	78.45	63.94
1998[d]			63.74	69.92	78.29	63.75
1999[d]			61.51		74.12	61.23
2000[d]			60.34		72.14	60.12

[a]   With total liability data available only for 1995, total liabilities for all years are approximated by the sum of short- and long-term liabilities, thus omitting one very minor item, deferred tax payments. Ratios with liabilities calculated as total assets less equity, possible since 1994, are consistently slightly higher (by up to approximately half a percentage point).

[b]   These two measures do not reflect proper liability-asset ratios but may help in linking up to the earlier data. Total assets less current and fixed assets equals other assets. Other assets include, among others, patents, non-patent technologies, trade marks, copyright, land use rights, and brand name value. Fixed assets less net fixed assets approximately equals unfinished fixed assets. Unfinished fixed assets reflect the current value of realized fixed asset investment in investment projects that have not yet been completed. Once the project has been completed, the value of the investment at the time of completion enters the net fixed assets category.

[c]   Data on assets in 1993 are not available, and thus were approximated by the sum of current and long-term liabilities plus equity. In the case of industrial SOEs, using approximated rather than reported total assets to calculate the liability-asset ratio in 1994 yields a difference in the last (second) decimal only, and in 1995 a difference by one unit in the first decimal. The approximation in 1993 thus appears acceptable; the increase in the ratio between 1993 and 1994 is unlikely to be due to the approximation.

[d]   Ratios for the years since 1998 are not fully comparable to earlier years due to the 1997–1998 statistical break.

Sources: Nicholas Lardy (1998, p. 41); *Statistical Yearbook*; *Industrial Yearbook 2001*, p. 24 (for year-end net fixed assets of industrial SOEs since 1998).

A comparison between the official data for the 1990s and the earlier data could be difficult if the earlier data do not include the value of land use rights, as the official data in the 1990s do. Table 5.1 therefore shows a liability-asset ratio based on liabilities per current and fixed assets. This measure ignores intangible assets, which include, among others, patents, non-patent technologies, trade marks, copyright, *land use rights*, and brand name value. This incorrectly measured liability-asset ratio has stagnated since 1994. Valuation of land use rights or other intangible assets has no impact on the conclusion that the liability-asset ratio has stabilized since 1994.[100]

According to Nicholas Lardy (1998, pp. 40–42), the liability-asset ratio is even higher than reported in the early data because (i) "Chinese sources that analyze enterprise assets and liabilities [...] do not take into account inter-enterprise debt," (ii) "depreciation rates used by Chinese firms are too low," and (iii) "many enterprises hold large inventories of finished goods that they value at full price when in at least some cases the goods may not be saleable."

Yet, there exists no evidence that official statistics on assets and liabilities do not include inter-enterprise debt. Inter-enterprise arrears in the nationwide aggregate balance sheet of industrial SOEs are not consolidated out. The nationwide balance sheet data — reported for all years since 1993 in the statistical yearbooks and used in constructing Table 5.1 — in the year 1995 are equal to those reported in the 1995 nationwide industrial census. The latter source provides detailed sectoral and sub-sectoral data and the liability and asset values add up to the nationwide total. They should not add up to the nationwide value if the nationwide value reflects a consolidated value but the sectoral and sub-sectoral values do not.

---

[100] Nicholas Lardy suggests that the earlier data do not include the value of land use rights; the various sources of his data that could be located do not reveal whether or not land use rights are included. For the definition of total assets and its sub-categories, see *Statistical Yearbook 1998*, p. 490.

In an attempt to find a time series to link up with the dispersed earlier liability-asset ratio data, the ratio of liabilities to current and *net* fixed assets is also included in Table 5.1. Net fixed assets, in contrast to fixed assets, do not include the current value of investment projects that are not yet completed. This ratio has also been stable since 1994.

If any consolidation has taken place, it must have occurred within each individual sub-sector already. But within one sub-sector, not much inter-enterprise arrears should cancel out in the aggregate. Inter-enterprise arrears can also not simply have been omitted since it is unlikely that in each individual sub-sector the accounts payable exactly equal the accounts receivable. If they are not exactly equal and are omitted, the balance sheet no longer balances, but in fact it does for each sub-sector. The accounting regulations furthermore clearly require that all accounts receivable and payable be included (SC Law Office, 1993), and the State Statistical Bureau in its instructions on compiling balance sheets allows no exceptions (NBS 1997).

Fixed assets need not be over-valued. Depreciation rates are centrally determined and often artificially low, thus leading to an upward bias in fixed asset estimates. Yet, at the same time, net fixed assets are calculated by adding the price of each newly acquired fixed asset to the value of previously acquired fixed assets (valued at purchasing price net of depreciation). There is no correction for changes in the price level over time.[101] This leads to a downward bias in fixed asset estimates, potentially offsetting any upward bias introduced by low depreciation rates. The biases were furthermore addressed in the revaluation of SOE assets in the early 1990s (Chapter 3).

Current assets indeed include some stockpiled goods that either cannot be sold at the price at which they are accounted for in the balance sheet, or cannot be sold at all. Inventories at industrial SOEs in 1995 were valued at 14.25% of total assets. This figure is lower than the 16.76% for all industrial enterprises (including SOEs), the 21.52% for individual-owned enterprises, or the 18.39% for foreign-funded enterprises and 18.94% for Hong Kong, Macao, and Taiwanese enterprises. (*Industrial Census 1995*, Vol. 1, p. 48) For comparison, in the U.S. in 1995, inventories of non-financial corporate businesses were equal to 9.60% of total assets (Board of Governors), only

---

[101] Suppose a firm purchases a piece of machinery for 100 RMB. One year later the market price of exactly this type of machinery (if newly bought) is 300 RMB. The actual, second-hand market value of the machine bought the previous year would very likely be "(100 RMB - depreciation) * 3." But the firm accounts only consider the depreciation, not the inflationary factor of three, and thus value this machine at "100 RMB – depreciation."

about one-third lower than in industrial SOEs in China. Furthermore, much of this difference could be due to larger inventories of *material inputs* in Chinese SOEs. To judge from provincial-level data, finished products in Chinese SOEs are likely to account for only one-quarter to one-third of inventories, with the rest consisting of material inputs.[102]

A final, additional argument to the effect that the official liability-asset ratio underestimates the actual liability-asset ratio is that many of the assets of industrial SOEs are non-existent due to asset stripping. A frequently reported figure on asset stripping for all SOEs (not only in the industrial sector) is 50b RMB per year in the early and mid-1990s (Ding Xueliang, 2000; or Russell Smyth, 2000).[103] While this figure by itself may appear large, it is equivalent to only 1.05% of *industrial* SOE assets in 1995. Moreover, while asset stripping may lead to an inflation in reported assets, the inclusion of the value of patents, non-patent technologies, trade marks, copyright, land use rights and brand name rights in the reported assets of industrial SOEs has only just begun. These intangible assets together in 1997 accounted for just 8.01% of total assets, up from 6.22% in 1995.[104] The value of total assets could well be underestimated.

Two conclusions emerge. First, while the liability-asset ratio rose rapidly in the 1980s, it stabilized in the early 1990s. The causes of this particular development are explored in the next section. Second, the various reasons

---

[102] See, for example, the provincial statistical yearbooks *Beijing tongji nianjian 1996*, p. 175, or *Shaanxi tongji nianjian 1996*, p. 299. A breakdown of inventories is not available in the source of the U.S. data.

[103] Wu Tianlin (1993) reports cumulative asset stripping in budgetary industrial SOEs of a total volume of 220b RMB in the seven years 1985 through 1991, and Yu Lixin (1994) reports 300b RMB in (presumably all) SOEs over the "previous five years."

[104] See *Statistical Yearbook 1998*, pp. 440, 454, and *Industrial Census 1995*, Vol. 1, pp. 48f. Intangible assets, current assets plus fixed assets by definition add up to total assets. The intangible asset data reported here are calculated as total assets less current and fixed assets, since the statistics do not report intangible assets directly.

Steven Blayney (1999) reports that in the case of six SOEs in Shanghai that had their assets appraised for their conversion into joint stock companies, approximately 827 million RMB in intangible assets were excluded from the final asset appraisal of 1.688b RMB. In this case intangible assets accounted for one-third of total assets.

advanced on why the liability-asset ratio as calculated based on the official liability and asset data could underestimate the true liability-asset ratio appear either without substance or of insignificant impact.

The Rise in the Liability-Asset Ratio During the Reform Period Reflects the Process of Transition

The increase in the liability-asset ratio throughout the 1980s primarily reflects the phasing out of certain enterprise financing mechanisms employed in the socialist economy. The concept of equity and liabilities did not exist in the pre-reform economy.[105] The Finance Ministry provided regular budget appropriations for both investment and 'fixed-quota working capital' increases. The financial system played at best a supporting role, providing above-quota working capital, with no independent lending decisions. The key turning point was the 1983–1985 tax reform. Enterprises making their own production and investment decisions could no longer surrender all their surplus to the finance ministry to be endowed again with new funds through budget appropriations. As enterprises switched to paying only a portion of their profit as taxes to the state (*ligaishui*), the state withdrew from providing working capital funds as well as investment funds to enterprises, while banks gradually provided more loans (*bogaidai*).

When the economic reforms began in 1978, 62.16% of total investment in fixed assets by *all* state-owned units was financed through budgetary funds, with the rest being provided through the enterprises' own funds as well as some foreign funds; financial institutions accounted for just 1.69% of investment financing.[106] In addition, government working capital appropriations to *all* state-owned units in 1978 were 3.87 times higher than

---

[105] The concept of liabilities and equity did not take hold in official statistics until the early 1990s. The first balance sheet on industrial enterprises to include the two categories was published for the year 1993 (*Statistical Yearbook 1994*). Before, assets were viewed as balanced by state funds, bank funds, and other funds.

[106] See *Investment Yearbook 1950–1995*, p. 23. Industry-specific data are not available. (The bank statistics show loans for investment in fixed assets to begin in 1979 only; see *Financial Statistics 1952–1991*.)

the increase in bank loans outstanding for industrial production.[107] Consequently, the volume of liabilities was close to zero. Given how the economic system functioned, there was no role for debt.

In contrast, by 2000, the government financed only 10.42% of the investment of *all* state-owned unit*s*, with banks providing 25.21% of the funds needed (*Statistical Yearbook 2001*, p. 162); in 1997, the last year for which the data on *industrial* SOEs are available, the government financed only 2.78% of the investment by industrial SOEs, while banks provided the funding for another 31.28%.[108] Similarly, by 1998, *all* government working capital appropriations were equivalent to only 3.27% of the change in bank loans outstanding for industrial production.[109] As the government gradually abandoned its direct financing of industrial activity through the budget, starting in 1978, the liability-asset ratio had nowhere to go but up. Once the transition was virtually complete by the mid-1990s, this force for an increase in the liability-asset ratio disappeared.

---

[107] See *Financial Statistics 1952–1991*, p. 10, and *Statistical Yearbook 1997*, p. 241.

[108] See *Investment Yearbook 1998*, pp. 54, 88f. Data for 1998 in the *Investment Yearbook 1999*, pp. 54, 81f., yield similar ratios (3.63% vs. 32.10%), but the category of industrial SOEs appears to newly exclude state-owned and state-controlled shareholding companies.

[109] See *Statistical Yearbook 2001*, p. 250, and *Financial Yearbook 2001*, p. 374. Year 1998 rather than 1997 and 2000 data are reported for the following reasons. Since 1997, working capital loans to industrial enterprises are likely to include loans to material supply and sales enterprises, and possibly also to urban collective-owned enterprises. As these items in previous years were of a size approximately equal to only one-quarter of loans to industrial enterprises, the impact should be minor except in the first year in which they are likely to have been included in industrial loans (1997). Furthermore, state working capital appropriations may also go to these enterprises, and to SOEs in other sectors of the economy. Working capital loan data specific to industrial SOEs with independent accounting system are no longer available.

Data on government working capital appropriations and bank loans to industry are also available for 2000 (and 1999), but the lending data appear highly unreliable with unexplained changes in lending categories. In 2000, bank loans to industry decreased by 5.18%, presumably largely because of a reclassification of loans. The ratio of the year 2000 total government working capital appropriations (to all enterprises) to *industrial* loans outstanding (definitely excluding loans to industrial township and village enterprises, private enterprises, and foreign-funded enterprises) was 0.42%.

A number of further factors may have contributed to the stabilization of the liability-asset ratio since 1994. First, a serious effort to have banks switch from state-commanded to commercial lending began in 1994–1995. Bankers became reluctant to lend to the worst performing enterprises as they are now supposedly held responsible for their lending decisions. But poorly performing enterprises are those enterprises with low profitability, which therefore have relatively little accumulation of profit to increase equity. If they cannot obtain new bank loans, their liability-asset ratio stagnates; if they can obtain new equity, their liability-asset ratio falls. On the other hand, enterprises that perform well can increase their assets by accumulating profit and may not be interested in additional bank loans, likewise stabilizing if not lowering the liability-asset ratio.

Second, the 1994 tax reform clarified the tax obligations of enterprises and largely ended the practice of handing over most post-tax profit to the superordinate department; the existence of profit then automatically implies an increase in net worth. Third, since the opening of the Shanghai and Shenzhen stock markets in December 1990, more than one thousand, mostly large SOEs have been able to raise new external funds in the form of equity rather than debt, which has a dampening effect on the liability-asset ratio. Fourth, bankrupt SOEs are being closed or sold; if the SOEs that are most likely to have a high liability-asset ratio leave the pool, this lowers the average liability-asset ratio of the remaining SOEs.

Fifth, a final element which may explain some of the reduction in the aggregate industrial SOE liability-asset ratio in 2000 is the debt-equity swap organized by the central government. Six hundred and one mostly large industrial SOEs had 460b RMB of debt swapped into equity. This amount is equivalent to 5.72% of total assets of industrial SOEs at year-end 1999 (but the swap is unlikely to have been implemented in full by year-end 2000).

With the completion of the financial separation of government and enterprises in the early 1990s, the main causal factor for the continuous rise in the liability-asset ratio disappeared. Related banking and enterprise reforms all implied pressures on the liability-asset ratio to stabilize if not fall. By the late 1990s, industrial SOEs appear to have reached a relatively stable ratio of liabilities to assets at around 60%.

The Liability-Asset Ratio of China's Industrial SOEs Is Not Excessive in Domestic and International Comparisons

If Chinese policy makers are concerned about the negative impact of the currently "high" liability-asset ratio of industrial SOEs on their profitability, their concern should equally apply to enterprises under other ownership forms. Industrial SOEs' liability-asset ratio of 65.81% in 1995, the year for which detailed data are available, is clearly below that of collective-owned enterprises (71.67%), and only half a percentage point above the nationwide average (65.31%) (Table 5.2).[110] The centrally owned SOEs have the lowest liability-asset ratio among all SOEs at 59.15%, close to that of the foreign-funded enterprises, which have the lowest ratio overall. Locally owned SOEs, on the other hand, have a relatively high ratio at 69.48%.

Table 5.2   Liability-Asset Ratios of Directly Reporting Industrial Enterprises, 1995

		Liabilities / assets (in %)	Financial charges / sales revenue (in %)
Nationwide total		65.31	4.78
State-owned enterprises		65.81	5.53
Centrally owned	59.15		4.89
Locally owned	69.48		5.89
County-level	73.16		6.81
Collectively owned enterprises		71.67	4.38
Private enterprises		58.61	2.84
Joint enterprises		64.38	3.76
Shareholding enterprises		55.07	4.08
Foreign-funded enterprises		55.72	3.11
Hong Kong, Macao and Taiwanese enterprises		63.35	3.94
Other enterprises		59.97	4.40
Profitable enterprises		61.72	3.95
Loss-making enterprises		76.05	9.02

    Liabilities comprise all liabilities, i.e., short- and long-term liabilities as well as deferred tax payments.
    Financial charges comprise all costs associated with bank loans and other forms of borrowing, whether they are interest rates or fees.
Source: Industrial Census 1995, Vol. 1, pp. 46–53.

---

[110] The Industrial SOEs' liability-asset ratios in Table 5.1 and Table 5.2 are slightly different. With total liability data available only for 1995, total liabilities in Table 5.1 were calculated as the sum of short- and long-term liabilities, thus omitting deferred tax payments. Table 5.2 ratios are based on the actual total liability data. Also see notes to the two tables.

The liability-asset ratio of Chinese industrial SOEs is not even inherently high in international comparisons. The industry category in China comprises (i) mining and quarrying, (ii) manufacturing, and (iii) production and supply of electricity, gas and water, with the first two categories accounting for 85.80% of industrial SOE value-added in 1997 (*Statistical Yearbook 1998*, p. 448). In Germany, a country with (like China) a strong emphasis on banks rather than stock markets, the liability-asset ratios of mining and manufacturing enterprises in 1996 were 93.98% and 76.11%, respectively. If pension liabilities and other provisions are excluded from the liabilities, the German ratios were 83.15% and 49.49%, respectively.[111] The corresponding ratios in China's industrial SOEs, presumably largely free of pension liabilities, in 1996 were 59.98% and 68.92%, with an average of 65.06% for all industry.

The liability-asset ratio in the U.S. non-financial corporate business sector in 1996 was 51.94%.[112] The ratio for all non-financial incorporated enterprises in Japan in 1996 was 53.83%; this includes private enterprises with relative low liability-asset ratios as well as public corporations with very high liability-asset ratios.[113] In Korea, the liability-asset ratio across

---

[111] The year 1996 was chosen as it is the most recent year for which data across several countries are available. In the years 1991, 1981, and 1971 (the first year for which data are available) the ratios for mining (without pension liabilities and other provisions in parentheses) were 94.65% (83.92%), 95.15% (87.85%), and 88.94% (83.19%). For manufacturing, the ratios were 77.06% (51.68%), 76.82% (58.11%), and 70.07% (58.82%). All ratios are based on (West German) enterprises reporting to the central bank. Mining enterprises reporting to the central bank in 1994 accounted for approximately 96.3% of the value-added taxes paid by all mining enterprises; for the manufacturing enterprises, the percentage was 73.1%. Sales of the mining sector in 1994 were 45.0b DM, and of the manufacturing sector 2158.5b DM. (Deutsche Bundesbank, 1999) No data are available on the "production and supply of electricity, gas and water" in Germany.

[112] The liability-asset ratio of non-farm, non-financial corporations in 1994, the most recent year for which these data are available, was 52.28%, up from 49.09% in 1991 and 31.97% in 1981 (Board of Governors, pp. 36f.). For *all* active corporations, the ratio in 1991, the most recent year for which the data are available, was 72.27% (Internal Revenue Service, 1994, p. 33). All active corporations include financial institutions; according to the first source (p. 43), private financial institutions in 1991 had a liability-asset ratio of 92.22%.

[113] In 1997, the ratio was 54.77%; in 1990 43.22%; and in 1985 51.34% (Economic Planning Agency, 1999, pp. 322f.).

industry in 1996 was 77.0%, in mining and quarrying 77.7%, and in manufacturing 76.0%.[114]

In domestic as well as cross-country comparisons, the liability-asset ratio of China's industrial SOEs thus does not appear excessively high. Yet, the ultimate question is whether the liability-asset ratio has a negative impact on profitability, as the Chinese leadership believes. If so, then a relatively high liability-asset ratio may well be undesirable.

Linking the Liability-Asset Ratio to Profitability

Figure 5.1 at first sight suggests that a high liability-asset ratio implies a low rate of profitability. But the figure presents correlations, not a particular causal relationship. Other factors need to be controlled for, and the direction of the causality needs to be further explored.

Accounting Link between the Liability-Asset Ratio and Profitability

The liability-asset ratio is related to profit through financial charges. A high liability-asset ratio implies a large volume of interest payments (financial charges). In a second step, high financial charges, subtracted from sales revenue, reduce the residual profit. (See Figure 5.2.) For example, all loss-making industrial enterprises (regardless of ownership) in 1995, when the data are available, paid financial charges equivalent to 9.02% of their sales revenue (Table 5.2). For profitable enterprises, the percentage was only 3.95%.

The liability-asset ratio links to financial charges through two channels. First, a high liability-asset ratio implies a relatively large volume of loans on which interest has to be paid.[115] Second, the marginal and therefore also average interest rate paid could depend positively on the liability-asset

---

[114] In 1997, the ratio for all industry was 80.9%; in mining and quarrying 89.3%; and in manufacturing 79.8% (National Statistics Office of Korea).

[115] This assumes that the share of interest-free liabilities (such as salaries and taxes due but not yet paid) in total liabilities is constant; if an increase in the liability-asset ratio went hand in hand with an increase in interest-free liabilities, the increase in the liability-asset ratio may not be accompanied by a larger volume of interest payments.

ratio. If banks are reluctant to lend to highly leveraged firms, they may demand a high marginal interest rate. However, interest rates on bank loans are centrally determined and uniformly applied across China; they only vary according to the maturity of the loan. Banks in the most recent years have been given some leeway to vary lending rates, but only on loans to non-state enterprises and only within severe limits.[116] Empirical analysis confirms that there is no correlation between the liability-asset ratio and the rate of interest paid.[117]

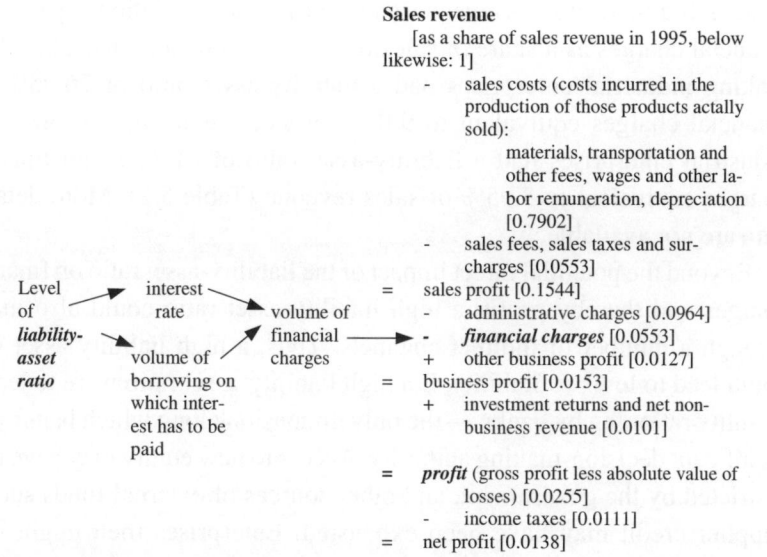

Source: Industrial Census 1995, Vol. 1, pp. 51ff., for shares of individual items in industrial SOE sales revenue. (The original data exhibit very minor data discrepancies.)

Figure 5.2   Linking the Liability-Asset Ratio to Profitability Measures

---

[116] In the case of industrial SOEs, for interest rate variation to potentially matter in the analysis below, borrowing in different sectors and regions would have to be characterized by different maturity structures to yield different average sectoral or regional interest rates.

[117] Plotting the liability-asset ratio against the financial charges per unit of liabilities for the 37 industrial sectors in 1995 does suggest a significant, slightly positive correlation. Once three outliers are removed, the correlation vanishes. In addition, on average, liabilities equal to perhaps 25% of all assets are interest-free liabilities. (See, for example, detailed data available on township- and village-run enterprises in the *Township Enterprise Yearbook 1996*, pp. 254f.) They include such items as inter-enterprise arrears, pre-payments received, and salaries and taxes due but not yet paid. The correlation coefficient for the 37 industrial sectors in the case of SOEs turns insignificant once the estimated interest-free liabilities (equal to 25% of all assets) are removed, even if the three outliers are still included.

The second part of the argument, that high financial charges reduce the residual profit, is only correct if all other factors are held constant. Profit is derived from sales revenue in the profit and loss account by subtracting various expenses, *among them* financial charges (Figure 5.2). But between 1993 and 1997, these other expenses were not constant; the correlation between financial charges and profit was negative, but insignificant.[118]

The 1995 data on loss-making vs. profitable industrial enterprises do suggest a positive relationship between the liability-asset ratio and financial charges as a share of sales revenue, and then a negative relationship between financial charges as a share of sales revenue and profitability. Thus, loss-making industrial enterprises had a liability-asset ratio of 76.05% and financial charges equivalent to 9.04% of sales revenue, and profitable industrial enterprises had a liability-asset ratio of 61.72% and financial charges equivalent to 3.95% of sales revenue (Table 5.2). More detailed data are not available.

Beyond the potential direct impact of the liability-asset ratio on financial charges and thereby profit, a high liability-asset ratio could also matter through a number of indirect channels. Thus, a high liability-asset ratio could lead to low profitability, if a high liability-asset ratio were to lead to quantity rationing by banks — the only dimension along which banks have significant decision-making authority. Access to new equity may have been restricted by the government, and other sources of external funds such as supplier credit may have been exhausted. Enterprises then might have difficulty finding the funds necessary to maintain production and would thus be driven into losses simply due to the lack of funds. In this scenario, a high liability-asset ratio is negatively correlated with profit due to risk considerations of the bank and perhaps systemic restrictions on raising equity.

On the other hand, well-informed bankers could actively support an enterprise with good prospects and thus drive up the liability-asset ratio. Access to new loans in itself, in an economy where access to new equity is quite restricted, could lead to a rise in profitability if profitable investment

---

[118] The correlation coefficient between (annual nationwide industrial SOE) financial charges and profit for the years 1993 through 1997 is negative 0.7331, but this correlation coefficient is not significant (at the 10% level).

projects can be implemented and regular production maintained. Enterprises whose products are in high demand could finance new investment by borrowing (an increase in the liability-asset ratio), raising the absolute value of financial charges, but at the same time the increase in output and sales revenue could more than compensate for the extra cost and yield a larger residual profit. Even if financial charges increased relative to sales revenue, a counter-effect of, for example, efficiency-increasing investment could be that other expenses such as sales costs fall relative to sales revenue. Overall, profit and, given a constant amount of equity, profitability, need not decline. Similarly, if interest rates are below an enterprise's return on equity, any swap that increases liabilities while reducing equity by the same amount immediately leads to a further increase in profitability.

A high liability-asset ratio, finally, should imply a high degree of external control as creditors, concerned about the payment of interest and the repayment of the principal, have incentives to monitor the enterprise. Highly leveraged SOEs thus should be subject to better supervision than those SOEs whose assets are primarily financed through 'free' state equity that comes with little monitoring. A higher degree of supervision could lead to higher profitability. Until the mid-1990s, banks carried little responsibility for their lending practices and had few incentives to monitor enterprises, but this is likely to have changed in recent years.

The impact of a high liability-asset ratio on profit is thus far from clearcut. *Ceteris paribus*, a high liability-asset ratio has a direct negative cost effect on profit, yet other financial factors are not always constant and profit does not equal profitability. A high liability-asset ratio could invite credit rationing creating difficulties for firms to maintain production, leading to a reduction in profit. On the other hand, an increase in the liability-asset ratio could allow profitable investments to be realized and thus imply an increase in profitability. A high liability-asset ratio could also encourage better external supervision with beneficial effects on profitability.

Testing the Link Between the Liability-Asset Ratio and Profitability Measures

The bivariate relationship between the liability-asset ratio and profit per unit of equity pictured in Figure 5.1 does not take into account other variables that might affect profitability. One such variable is the degree of competition, measured as the industrial SOE share in the sales revenue (net of all sales-related taxes) of all directly reporting industrial enterprises.[119] The higher the share of SOE sales revenue, the more likely SOEs are to set monopolistic prices and thus to achieve higher profit. In the extreme, in sectors in which SOEs enjoy a monopoly by government decree, such as in petroleum and natural gas extraction (with the SOE market share of 97.73% in 1995) or tobacco processing (95.90%), prices are likely to be such that production is profitable — profit per unit of equity in the two sectors in 1995 was well above the economy-wide average for SOEs (at 11.35% and 28.32%, respectively, compared with the aggregate average of 4.10%).[120]

A second factor to control for is market demand. The higher the demand at a given price, the higher capacity utilization is likely to be and thus the higher the likelihood for SOEs to be profitable, or less loss-making. A lack of demand is proxied by the volume of inventories relative to value-added.[121]

The regression is run for two different sets of data. The first dataset comprises sub-sectoral data from the 1995 industrial census. Instead of using the 37 industrial sectors as observations, the complete set of their 191 sub-sectors is used. (For some sub-sectors, the data are incomplete and the number of observations in the regressions is therefore slightly lower). This allows inclusion of 37 first-digit sectoral dummies in a fixed effects model.

---

[119] Sales revenue net of all sales-related taxes (for industrial SOEs and for the directly reporting industrial enterprises) is used in order to bridge the 1993-94 statistical break in sales revenue. For regressions involving only the years 1999 and 2000, sales revenue need not be net of sales-related taxes; for the sake of consistency, sales-related taxes are always subtracted from sales revenue and thus sales revenue net of all sales-related taxes are used throughout all years and in all variables involving sales revenue. The impact on the regression results should be negligible.

[120] Competition could also have been measured as sales revenue relative to assets. One reason for using the market share in the following is that it is the standard measure of competition in the literature. Also, as outlined in the previous chapter, if the intermediate competition indicator, the intermediate labor remuneration indicator, plus a measure of the liability-asset ratio are included together in linear regression analysis (in logarithms or growth rates), profit per unit of equity results through an identity. Labor remuneration in the following is excluded to allow analysis across sectors (for which no labor remuneration data are available).

[121] Yuk-shing Cheng and Dic Lo (2002) note the potential impact of demand on industrial SOE profitability but do not explore the demand further in statistical analysis.

The first three columns of Table 5.3 report the regression results for three different profitability indicators on which data are available from the 1995 industrial census. The three profitability indicators are profit per unit of equity, profit plus financial charges per unit of assets, and losses per unit of gross profit. The independent variables are the industrial SOE market share, inventories per unit of value-added, and the liability-asset ratio. The 37 sectoral dummies were included, and their importance is confirmed by an F-test on their joint significance (using the 5% significance level as cut-off point). A subsequent test for heteroscedasticity (White's F-test using the 5% significance level as cut-off point) led to the use of White's correction in all three regressions.

The regression results show that the higher the liability-asset ratio, the lower the profitability in two out of the three regressions, with insignificant results in the third regression. (All coefficient signs in the regression with losses per unit of gross profit as the dependent variable should be opposite to those in the case of profit per unit of equity, as losses per unit of gross profit is a loss rather than a profitability indicator.) The first conclusions drawn from Figure 5.1 thus appear to be confirmed. In addition, as expected, the higher the SOE market share, the higher the profitability. Also, as expected, the larger the volume of inventories relative to value-added, i.e., the lower the demand for industrial SOEs' products, the lower the profitability (except in the case of losses per unit of profit).

The second dataset covers the years 1993 through 1997 as well as 1999 and 2000. Since inventory data are available only for 1995, the inventory per value-added variable is replaced by the current assets (working capital) per valued-added variable. Current assets besides inventories (37.33% of current assets in 1995) comprise such items as cash and bank deposits, accounts receivable, and pre-payments made. Current assets per value-added are thus likely to be an imperfect measure of demand.[122] Data on losses

---

[122] No detailed data on the composition of 1995 industrial SOE current assets beyond the figure on inventories are available. To judge from more detailed data on township and village enterprises (in the *Township Enterprise Yearbook*), cash and bank balances as well as pre-payments made should be very small, while accounts receivable could account for as much as half of the current assets. The implications of demand behavior on accounts receivable should be the same as on inventories. High demand could allow enterprises to demand immediate payment, thus reducing accounts receivable (same sign as in the case of inventories).

Table 5.3 Impact of the Liability-Asset Ratio on Industrial SOE Profitability, 1995

	OLS	OLS	OLS	3SLS	3SLS	3SLS
Number of observations	186	182	179	186	182	179
Equation 1: dependent variable	Profit / equity	Profit + financial charges / assets	Losses / gross profit	Profit / equity	Profit + financial charges / assets	Losses / gross profit
R^2	0.5085	0.4801	0.5339			
Intercept	***0.3269	**0.0365	-4.4549	-1.4374	-0.0847	-14.4288
	(3.3670)	(2.2072)	(-1.2458)	(-1.2366)	(-1.1206)	(-1.0174)
SOE market share	**0.1153	***0.0347	-1.0327	*0.2561	^0.0435	-0.4370
	(2.4877)	(3.0253)	(-1.050)	(1.9580)	(3.7493)	(-0.2268)
Inventories / value-added	*-0.0255	-0.0041	*-2.2912	**-0.0588	***-0.0063	^-2.5820
	(-1.7305)	(-1.4538)	(-1.7765)	(-2.1113)	(-2.7003)	(-6.2248)
Liability-asset ratio	^-0.5605	-0.0353	*10.0553	1.9530	0.1380	24.3939
	(-4.1933)	(-1.5526)	(1.8797)	(1.1895)	(1.3080)	(1.2185)
37 sect. dummies/ White's correction	yes/yes	yes/yes	yes/yes			
Equation 2: dependent variable				Liability-asset ratio	Liability-asset ratio	Liability-asset ratio
Intercept				^0.5841	^0.6012	^0.5967
				(10.2809)	(9.8506)	(6.1130)
Profit per unit of equity				*-0.3752	-1.3514	0.0290
				(-1.8826)	(-1.5157)	(0.8007)
Inventories /value-added				-0.0050	-0.0010	0.0770
				(-0.5044)	(-0.1187)	(0.8882)
Current assets / assets				***0.2371	0.2918	0.06516
				(2.6806)	(3.3392)	(0.2748)
37 sectoral dummies (both eq.)				yes	yes	yes
Significance of liability-asset ratio in each of two independent variations:						
If use Full Information Maximum Likelihood				insign.	near-singular	near-singular
If drop sectoral dummies				insign. (+)	**+	insign. (+)

Significance levels: ^ 0.1%, *** 1%, ** 5%, * 10%. The numbers in parentheses are t-statistics.
For further notes on the OLS regressions, see Table 5.4, and on the 3SLS regressions Table 5.5.
Sources: *Industrial Census 1995*, Vol. 1, pp. 46-197, Vol. 2, pp. 16-167.

and financial costs are not available (except for 1995), reducing the number of available profitability indicators in the joint analysis of several years to only profit per unit of equity, the core profitability indicator. After inspection of the raw data, the 38th sector, gas production and supply, was removed in the years 1993–1997 due to questions about the quality of its value-added data, leaving 190 observations (38 sectors times 5 years).[123] Regressions are again run using a common intercept and then sectoral dummies for all sectors except the first one. Year dummies were also included, except for the earliest year in the series, in order to capture such factors as changes in the interest rate over time (with interest rates applying uniformly across sectors and provinces).[124]

The regressions were run across sectors and provinces, for the years 1993–1997 and for the years 1999 and 2000, in levels and in growth rates. Growth rates are measured in absolute annual changes of the various ratios, since profit is frequently negative. With negative profit, it is impossible to take the first difference of the logarithms, and if growth rates are calculated as percentage changes over the previous year, they cannot properly capture improvements vs. deterioration in profitability when changes from positive to negative (or vice versa) profitability rates are involved.

The independent variables are the industrial SOE market share, current assets (proxying for inventories) per unit of value-added, and the liability-asset ratio. Regressions were first run including sectoral (provincial) dummies as well as year dummies. An F-test (using the 5% significance level as the cut-off point) indicated first whether the sectoral (provincial) dummies should be included; if not, these were removed and the regression was rerun without them. The same procedure was then applied to the year dummies. In a third step, residuals were tested for heteroscedasticity; if significant at the 5% significance level (F-test), the regression was rerun using White's correction.

---

[123] Value-added in this sector in 1994 fell to one-quarter of its 1993 value, then fell by one-half again in 1995; 1996 data on value-added in this sector are not available, and the 1997 value is up again at the 1993 level. (This sector was also dropped in the 1993–1997 sectoral analysis in the previous chapter.)

[124] Lacking data on (total) liabilities for the years 1993 through 2000, total liabilities are calculated as the sum of current and long-term liabilities (except across provinces in 1999 and 2000, when data on total liabilities are available.)

The results are reported in Table 5.4. In all regressions, the liability-asset ratio is insignificant. This suggests that the relationship between the liability-asset ratio and profitability is, after all, not as simple as Figure 5.1 would have it. Only if a limited measure of labor remuneration is included in the provincial analysis (for which wage data are available), does a high liability-asset ratio have a significant effect on profitability, and only in the 1999–2000 regressions (in levels and growth rates). This impact is negative. The fact that it is negative in only 1999-2000 hints at changes in the characteristics of the relationship between the liability-asset ratio and profitability in the most recent years.

The other two variables included in the regression yield no surprises. In the sectoral and provincial analysis in levels and growth rates for the years 1993 through 1997 (four different cases), the market share is significant and carries the correct sign. The demand indicator (current assets relative to value-added) is significant only in the provincial analysis in levels, with the correct sign.

Resolving Potential Endogeneity Problems

The straightforward OLS regression of profitability on the liability-asset ratio and two control variables ignores the fact that the liability-asset ratio is an endogenous variable. The rate of profitability may have an effect on the liability-asset ratio. A high degree of profitability immediately implies that the relative addition to net worth through newly accumulated profit, should it not be paid out to the owners, is large; *ceteris paribus*, the liability-asset ratio decreases.

The liability-asset ratio may depend not only on profitability but also on the demand for SOEs' products. If demand at a given price level is high, inventories relative to value-added tend to be low or are being run down, reducing the need for funding (the amount of funds tied up in these inventories). If inventories were primarily financed through bank loans, then low inventories relative to value-added imply a low liability-asset ratio.

With two equations, one determining profitability, and the other determining the liability-asset ratio, another exogenous variable is needed in the determination of the liability-asset ratio in order for the first equation to be identified. This is the share of current assets in total assets. Since

Table 5.4 Impact of the Liability-Asset Ratio on Industrial SOE Profitability, 1993–2000

	Across sectors				Across provinces			
	Profit / equity		Absolute annual change in profit / equity		Profit / equity		Absolute annual change in profit / equity	
Dependent variable	1993–1997	1999–2000	1993–1997	1999–2000	1993–1997	1999–2000	1993–1997	1999–2000
Number of observations	194	74	154	37	150	62	120	31
R^2	0.7806	0.8413	0.1388	0.1417	0.8224	0.9165	0.1465	0.3110
Intercept	^-0.2971	***0.7677	-0.0061	0.0085	0.0039	0.2337	-0.0015	0.0246
	(-3.4255)	(2.7767)	(-0.3482)	(0.5798)	(0.0524)	(0.7497)	(-0.3567)	(2.9919)
Levels or absolute annual change, as for the dependent variable								
SOE market share	^0.4244	-0.3863	*0.3530	-0.1941	^0.2809	0.2298	^0.3159	0.2315
	(6.8494)	(-1.1185)	(1.7330)	(-0.4184)	(4.8294)	(0.7427)	(3.9298)	(0.9660)
Current assets / value-added	-0.0003	-0.0300	-0.0124	-0.0254	^-0.0394	***-0.0850	-0.0150	-0.0850
	(-0.7091)	(-0.8370)	(-1.0897)	(-0.6832)	(-3.9277)	(-3.2548)	(-1.5682)	(-2.2681)
Liability-asset ratio	-0.0436	-0.6012	-0.0259	-0.5960	0.0159	-0.2860	0.0085	-0.2851
	(-0.3313)	(-1.5268)	(-0.1388)	(-1.4942)	(0.1837)	(-0.8560)	(0.0918)	(-0.5887)
Sectoral / provincial dummies	yes	yes	no	N/A	yes	yes	no	N/A
Year dummies	no	no	yes	N/A	no	yes	no	N/A
White's correction	yes	-	yes	no	yes	-	no	yes
Significance of liability-asset ratio if include SOE wages / sales revenue					insign. (+)	***-	insign. (-)	**-

Significance levels: ^ 0.1%, *** 1%, ** 5%, * 10%. The numbers in parentheses are t-statistics.

The SOE market share is the share of industrial SOEs in the sales revenue (net of all sales-related taxes) of the directly reporting industrial enterprises. (The ratio of wages to sales revenue is also based on sales revenue net of all sales-related taxes in order to avoid a statistical break in the sales revenue series between 1993 and 1994. Wage data are available only across provinces.)

All regressions were first run with sectoral as well as year dummies. Then the redundancy of the sectoral dummies was tested (F-test using 5% significance level as cut-off point); if the sectoral dummies turned out to be redundant, the regression was rerun without sectoral dummies. In a second step, the same procedure was applied to the year dummies. In a third step, residuals were tested for heteroscedasticity; if significant at the 5% significance level (F-test), the regression was rerun using White's correction. (In two cases White's correction should have been implemented but could not due to an insufficient number of observations.)

Sources: Statistical Yearbook.

additions to fixed assets are traditionally financed primarily through the enterprise's own sources of funds (usually around half of all investment funding), while the provision of working capital is traditionally viewed as the banks' task, a high ratio of current assets to total assets should imply a high liability-asset ratio.[125]

The system of two equations to be estimated then is

$$\text{Profitability} = \beta_1 + \beta_2 * \text{SOE market share} \\ + \beta_3 * \text{inventory / value-added} \\ + \beta_4 * \text{liability-asset ratio} + \varepsilon_1, \text{ and}$$

$$\text{Liability-asset ratio} = \beta_5 + \beta_6 * \text{profitability} \\ + \beta_7 * \text{inventory / value-added} \\ + \beta_8 * \text{current assets / assets} + \varepsilon_2.$$

The second set of three columns in Table 5.3 reports the three stage least squares regression results for the 1995 dataset and Table 5.5 reports the results of the same regressions for the 1993–1997 and 1999–2000 dataset. The two datasets and the range of profitability measures are the same as those used previously; sectoral (provincial) and year dummies are included as previously determined in the single equation model.

In the 1995 regressions, the liability-asset ratio in the first equation (determining profitability) is positive but insignificant across the three profitability measures. (The pattern in Figure 5.1 would suggest a positive sign only for the losses per unit of gross profit indicator.) In the 1993 through 1997 regressions, across sectors or provinces, in levels or in growth rates (four cases), the sign of the liability-asset ratio turns significantly positive. In other words, once the endogeneity of the liability-asset ratio is accounted for, the higher the liability-asset ratio, the higher the rate of profitability.

---

[125] The third explanatory variable in the one-equation model explaining profitability, the SOE market share (as a proxy for monopolistic pricing power), should have no direct impact on the liability-asset ratio (second equation) other than through the profitability variable. Similarly, the share of current assets in total assets (second equation) should not have any direct impact on profitability (first equation) other than through the liability-asset ratio. Both equations are then just identified, with each equation containing one exogenous variable not included in the other equation.

These results do not change if the estimation is based on full information maximum likelihood rather than the three stage least squares method. They do not change systematically if all dummy variables are dropped in those equations where they were previously included (as determined in the single-equation regression); only in one case does the coefficient of the liability-asset ratio turn (just) insignificant, while in one other case, a previously insignificant positive coefficient turns significant. If a limited measure of labor remuneration is included in the provincial regressions (in levels and growth rates, 1993–1997), the coefficient of the liability-asset ratio turns just insignificant. (See the bottom rows in Table 5.3 and Table 5.5.)

The industrial SOE market share is significant with the expected sign in the sectoral analysis, but insignificant in the provincial analysis. (As elaborated in the previous chapter, changes in the industrial SOE share in the sales revenue of the directly reporting industrial enterprises of one province may not have a direct impact on profitability, if the industrial SOE market share in those sectors in which industrial SOEs operate does not change much.) The demand indicator is significant only in the provincial analysis in levels, with the expected sign.

The fact that a high liability-asset ratio implies a high level of profitability suggests that contrary to economic theory (the Modigliani-Miller theorem), industrial SOEs in China may indeed be able to achieve leverage effects. The positive impact of the liability-asset ratio on profitability could in part be driven by artificially low government-determined interest rates on loans. If interest rates are below aggregate industrial SOEs' average current return on equity, industrial SOEs can improve their profitability by borrowing more. Profitability is thus a function of access to bank loans.[126]

The results for 1999-2000 differ. Across sectors, the liability-asset ratio has no impact on profitability, but across provinces (in levels or in growth rates) the impact is negative. This suggests a break, at least across provinces, between the period 1993–1997 and 1999–2000. This break coincides with the three-year industrial SOE reform program of 1998–2000. The key

---

[126] Government-subsidized bank lending rates simply reflect a redistribution of economic surplus from the budget through banks to SOEs. Any improvement in profitability due to a rise in the liability-asset ratio thus has to be measured against government subsidies through low interest rates.

Table 5.5 Impact of the Liability-Asset Ratio on Industrial SOE Profitability after Accounting for Endogeneity (3SLS Results), 1993–2000

	Across sectors				Across provinces			
	Profit / equity		Absolute annual change in profit / equity		Profit / equity		Absolute annual change in profit / equity	
	1993–1997	1999–2000	1993–1997	1999–2000	1993–1997	1999–2000	1993–1997	1999–2000
Number of observations	194	74	156	37	150	62	120	31
Equation 1: dependent variable								
Intercept	^-0.7387 (-5.2670)	3.2411 (0.8610)	-0.0061 (-0.4076)	-0.0088 (-0.1330)	*-0.8604 (-1.7381)	**1.0306 (2.4204)	-0.0056 (-0.9397)	0.0003 (0.0142)
Depending on dependent variable, levels or absolute annual change:								
SOE market share	^0.3703 (6.9672)	3.0463 (0.5904)	^0.7413 (3.3578)	2.6290 (0.4901)	-0.0222 (-0.1192)	-0.1134 (-0.3866)	0.0944 (0.5813)	-0.1121 (-0.2701)
Current assets / value-added	0.0009 (0.9148)	0.4457 (0.6265)	-0.0083 (-0.8382)	0.4085 (0.5190)	***-0.0437 (-2.7428)	^-0.1018 (-4.4999)	-0.0160 (-1.2961)	***-0.1019 (-3.1812)
Liability-asset ratio	***0.7574 (3.1343)	-10.7684 (-0.7150)	***1.2987 (2.6639)	-10.0902 (-0.5940)	*1.7680 (1.7852)	**-1.5732 (-2.5614)	*0.8450 (1.7337)	*-1.5740 (-1.8129)
	Liability-asset ratio		Absolute annual change in liability-asset ratio		Liability-asset ratio		Absolute annual change in liability-asset ratio	
Equation 2: dependent variable								
Intercept	^0.4571 (18.4563)	^0.7451 (6.3344)	**-0.0164 (-2.2989)	0.0153 (0.4300)	^0.4934 (7.9737)	0.7911 (1.3746)	0.0074 (1.4099)	0.0126 (0.2539)
Depending on dependent variable, levels or absolute annual change:								
Profit per unit of equity	-0.1771 (-1.6180)	***-0.5228 (-2.7248)	**-0.4276 (-2.2306)	-1.0028 (-0.7195)	0.6528 (1.4929)	-0.9899 (-0.9566)	*0.7521 (1.9572)	-0.9837 (-0.6778)
Current assets / value-added	^-0.0028 (-6.8924)	0.0178 (1.0069)	**-0.0158 (-2.5188)	0.0011 (0.0166)	0.0274 (1.5565)	-0.0837 (-1.4260)	0.0126 (0.9675)	-0.0834 (-1.0130)

Table 5.5 (continued)

	Across sectors				Across provinces			
	1993–1997	1999–2000	1993–1997	1999–2000	1993–1997	1999–2000	1993–1997	1999–2000
Current assets / assets	^0.3926	*-0.4490	^0.4438	-1.0672	-0.0327	-0.2898	0.1263	-0.2856
	(5.6694)	(-1.7447)	(5.0285)	(-0.6145)	(-0.1218)	(-0.3114)	(0.5617)	(-0.2183)
In both equations								
Sectoral / provincial dummies	yes	yes	no	N/A	yes	yes	no	N/A
Year dummies	no	no	yes	N/A	no	yes	no	N/A
Significance of liability-asset ratio in each of three independent variations:								
If use FIML	***+	near-sing.	***+	insign. (-)	^+	near-sing.	*+	insign. (-)
If include wages / sales revenue	***+	insign. (+)	**+	N/A	insign. (+)	^-	insign. (+)	**-
If drop all dummy variables	***+	insign. (+)	**+	N/A	^+	**+	N/A	N/A

Significance levels: ^ 0.1%, *** 1%, ** 5%, * 10%. The numbers in parentheses are t-statistics.

First equation: Profitability = $\beta_1 + \beta_2$ * SOE market share + β_3 * current assets / value-added + β_4 * liability-asset ratio + ε_1.

Second equation: Liability-asset ratio = $\beta_5 + \beta_6$ * profitability + β_7 * current assets / value-added + β_8 * current assets / assets + ε_2.

In one variation, as noted in the table, the ratio of industrial SOE wages per unit of sales revenue (net of all sales-related taxes) is included in the first equation.

FIML: Full information maximum likelihood estimation. (In some cases FIML cannot be used as the matrix is near-singular.)

The SOE market share is the share of industrial SOEs in the sales revenue (net of all sales-related taxes) of the directly reporting industrial enterprises. (The ratio of wages to sales revenue is also based on sales revenue net of all sales-related taxes in order to avoid a statistical break in sales revenue between 1993 and 1994. Wage data are only available across provinces.)

All regressions were run with sectoral (provincial) and year dummies as determined in the single equation with profitability as dependent variable (cases reported in previous table). In a variation, all regressions were also run dropping all sectoral (provincial) and year dummy variables.

Sources: Statistical Yearbook.

objective of the reform program was to turn losses into profit, using various measures ranging from a drastic reduction in industrial SOE employment to the sale of small industrial SOEs. It is likely that this major industrial SOE reform program caused both an improvement in profitability (through factors such as a reduction in employment or the merger of poorly performing SOEs with successful SOEs) and a decline in the liability-asset ratio of industrial SOEs (through government-financed recapitalization or debt-equity swaps). The causal link between the liability-asset ratio and profitability could be weak, if not non-existent, but the regression picks up the omitted reform policy factor in the form of a negative coefficient of the liability-asset ratio in the first regression.

The second equation offers additional implications. In 1995 and in the years 1993–1997, the demand indicator and the indicator of asset financing both carry the expected sign when they are significant, but they are significant only in a few cases. More striking is the sign of profitability in the second equation. A high degree of profitability tends to have a negative impact on the liability-asset ratio when it is significant (with a weakly positive impact only in the provincial regression in growth rates in 1993–1997). This suggests that enterprises with high profitability retain their newly accumulated profit (thus increasing equity) and do not incur a large amount of new loans, if any at all.

Interviews with enterprise managers in 1997 and 1998 revealed that enterprise managers in fact often preferred not to have to deal with banks. Bank loans are frequently viewed as unreliable because they are overwhelmingly short-term and then need to be rolled over. They tend to come with strings attached, such as part of the loan has to be kept as a deposit. In general, dealing with bank officials appears to be an unpleasant experience, perhaps precisely because it leads to some degree of external control. Many enterprise managers thus appear happy not to incur new bank loans as long as their current profitability and liquidity levels allow them to finance ongoing production and investment.

On the other hand, the negative sign of profitability in the second equation also implies that a low rate of profitability concurs with a high liability-asset ratio and that a fall in profitability concurs with an increase in the liability-asset ratio. That low profitability implies a high liability-asset ratio is understandable if banks tend to (or are forced to) lend to low-profitability

SOEs in order to maintain production. In recent years, such loans have taken the form of "closed-circuit" lending (*fengbi daikuan*). Bank loans are to be used for designated purposes only; banks strictly monitor the use of these loans; bank loans must be repaid as soon as the output has been sold; and the loans are repaid preferentially in the case of firm bankruptcy. The economic and trade commission helps to identify production processes that are potentially profitable but lack funding. Thus, low-profitability enterprises end up with a higher liability-asset ratio. The first equation shows that, on average, this high liability-asset ratio, controlling for other factors, indeed implies improved profitability.

The regressions can be run following a number of variations. If the ratio of inventory to value-added in the 1995 regressions across 191 sub-sectors is replaced by the ratio of current assets to value-added (which is used in the regressions for 1993–1997 and 1999–2000 due to a lack of inventory data), the coefficient of the liability-asset ratio in the first equation continues to be insignificant with the same sign. If the ratio of inventories (or current assets) to value-added is dropped in the second equation (in all regressions), because it is perhaps measuring similar effects as current assets per total assets does, the coefficients of the liability-asset ratios and the significance levels are unchanged across regressions in all periods, except in the 1993–1997 provincial regressions (in levels and growth rates) where the coefficients turn insignificant.

Conclusions

The perception of a continuously deteriorating liability-asset ratio in industrial SOEs with, as a consequence, ever larger losses, is doubly wrong. The increase in the liability-asset ratio during the 1980s reflects the transition from a socialist economy to an economy partly financed through financial intermediaries; by the mid-1990s, the ratio has stabilized. Furthermore, Chinese policy makers concerned about the negative impact of a high liability-asset ratio on profitability need to note that once other factors are controlled for, a high liability-asset ratio tends to imply a high rather than a low rate of profitability.

This suggests that current industrial SOE reforms in China that focus on debt alleviation are misguided. Thus, the debt-equity swap implemented across 601 large and medium-sized industrial SOEs is questionable if its objective truly was to improve enterprise profitability. Numerous reports on individual swaps all indicate that the liability-asset ratio consequently fell from a level in the 60% range to a level in the 30% or 40% range. By reducing financial charges, the absolute amount of profit as a residual of sales revenue after subtracting financial charges will necessarily rise. But the regression results show that profitability, namely profit per unit of equity, might well decline.

The debt-equity swap simply implies a financial transfer from the government (which has to buy the debt from the state commercial banks by issuing interest-carrying bonds) to the enterprises (which no longer have to pay as much interest due to the reduction in their debt). The government in return holds additional enterprise equity. In the case when the interest rate on debts and the return on equity in a particular industrial SOE were equal prior to the debt-equity swap, the regression results suggest that the government may be paying more interest on its newly issued bonds than it receives in return on its equity (either as dividends or capital gains). The same objective could have been achieved through a reduction in corporate income tax rates or outright subsidies. Potentially more relevant policy issues such as a general lack of aggregate demand are not addressed by turning debt into equity.

The predominantly positive impact of the liability-asset ratio on profitability raises further questions on the mechanisms through which the causalities operate. What would a survey of bank managers reveal about how banks make their lending decisions? As bank managers are increasingly held responsible for their lending decisions, they will take enterprise profitability into consideration before extending loans. Does the causality from low profitability to a high liability-asset ratio then reflect conscious bank lending decisions to extend a loan despite current low profitability, or external pressure on bank managers to lend? And does a high liability-asset ratio strengthen external control over SOEs and thus improve the governance structure (and thereby in the end profitability), or does the positive impact of a high liability-asset ratio on profitability operate solely through the leverage effect (due to artificially low lending rates)?

Part II
Industrial SOE Profitability in Perspective

The previous part explained the decline in industrial SOE profitability over time. The following three chapters raise three additional questions about industrial SOE profitability.

Chapter 6 compares the profitability of industrial SOEs to the profitability of enterprises under other ownership forms. At first sight, privatization of industrial SOEs may appear to be an immediate solution to any profitability problems in these enterprises. Yet, as the comparison of industrial SOEs and non-SOEs shows, privatization is far from necessary to improve industrial SOEs' profitability.

Chapter 7 examines the characteristics of industrial SOE profitability today by distinguishing among four characteristics of industrial SOEs: their size, ownership level, sectoral classification, and location. In a perfectly competitive market, none of these characteristics should matter. Profit rates, perhaps adjusted for risk, should equalize across these characteristics. But in China, they do not. Some characteristics are more conducive to high profitability than are others. This has implications for industrial SOE reform.

Chapter 8 presents and evaluates the most recent industrial SOE reform measures, in particular the 1998–2000 three-year SOE reform program. While the main reform objectives have been achieved, the process of industrial SOE reform is still incomplete. Furthermore, important questions about the governance structure of industrial SOEs remain unresolved.

6
SOEs versus Non-SOEs

The poor profitability of industrial SOEs has led authors to conclude that SOEs are in urgent need of radical reform. Nicholas Lardy (1998, p. 22) tentatively concluded that "reforms to date have failed in large portions of the state-owned sector and that their ultimate success will depend on the willingness of the Chinese Communist Party to embrace privatization." Jeffrey Sachs (1998) argued: "Now China has reached the stage where it cannot delay the process [of state enterprise reform] any longer because there are too many problems. The losses are too great; the financial loss resulting from the money-losing state-sector is too serious." (p. 13) In the long run, "China must go along the way of privatization" (p. 19).

This chapter first questions the view that non-SOEs by far outperform SOEs. Various industrial SOE profitability indicators indeed all declined over time, but so did the profitability of non-SOEs. The dissimilarity between SOE and non-SOE profitability lies not in the time trend. The dissimilarity lies in a, over time and for most profitability indicators, rather constant gap in favor of non-SOEs.

The relative inferiority of SOEs has been explained with historical and systemic arguments. These arguments say that SOEs are burdened with excessive capital and labor as well as heavy pension and other social welfare obligations and that SOEs face distorted output prices; SOEs' governance structure leads to poor incentives for management and workers and often comes with a soft budget constraint.[127] But the data show that the gap in profitability in the case of industrial enterprises can be explained by just two factors, namely a higher rate of circulation taxes for SOEs and higher SOE capital intensity. Both can be traced to historical and policy factors. While privatization is unlikely to change an enterprise's circulation tax burden, it might lower an enterprise's capital intensity. However, a relative reduction in capital intensity does not require privatization.

The comparison of SOEs and non-SOEs is furthermore biased against SOEs. SOE average performance is poor because the worst SOEs are not allowed to exit in sufficient numbers, while some of the best SOEs prior to 1998 left the SOE category by turning into companies or joint ventures. Private enterprises included in the group of directly reporting industrial enterprises, on the other hand, are likely to constitute only the very best enterprises in their ownership group, namely those that grew to a sufficient size to be included (or, prior to 1998, to be registered at higher administrative levels).

The following section presents profitability time series data on industrial SOEs as well as on non-SOEs. The various selection biases are outlined in the third section. The fourth section explains the gap in profitability between industrial SOEs and non-SOEs. The fifth section concludes.

Profitability Patterns of SOEs versus Non-SOEs

The profitability of SOEs can be compared to the profitability of the aggregate of all other enterprises included in the group of directly reporting industrial enterprises ("non-SOEs"), as well as to the profitability of individual ownership groups within the non-SOEs. Subtracting SOE data

---

[127] Justin Yifu Lin, Cai Fang, and Li Zhou (1998 and 1999) elaborate on the historical disadvantages of SOEs, while Huang Yiping and Ron Duncan (1997a and 1997b) explore a large number of (partly historical) enterprise-specific variables and find several of them significant in explaining profitability. The issues of governance structure and softness of the budget constraint are raised, for example, by Qian Yingyi (1996), Edward Steinfeld (1998), Zhu Tian (1999), On Kit Tam (1999) or also Justin Yifu Lin, Cai Fang, and Li Zhou (1998 and 1999).

from data on the directly reporting industrial enterprises yields the group of non-SOEs. The 1995 industrial census furthermore offers a complete listing of ownership categories that add up to the total of all directly reporting industrial enterprises. For all other years, the list of ownership groups is incomplete and the variable coverage limited.

SOEs versus the Aggregate of Non-SOEs

The time trend of industrial SOE profitability was the subject of Chapter 2. Table 6.1 reproduces the data presented earlier. To compare industrial SOEs and non-SOEs, Table 6.2 covers the same profitability indicators for non-SOEs. Figure 6.1 shows the time trend of non-SOE profitability divided by SOE profitability for four separate profitability indicators. The comparison of industrial SOE vs. non-SOE profitability yields the following results.

(i) The return on equity between 1993 and 1997 declined for both SOEs and non-SOEs by approximately six percentage points. In 1997, non-SOE return on equity was almost four times larger than the SOE return on equity. If circulation taxes are included, SOEs and non-SOEs again experience an identical decline in percentage points, but the gap is narrower than in the case of profit per unit of equity.

Non-SOE losses per unit of gross profit in the early 1980s grew faster than the same ratio for SOEs, with non-SOE losses relative to gross profit even exceeding the SOE value in the mid-1980s. But in the late 1980s, non-SOEs began to outperform SOEs.

Between 1998 and 2000, SOE profitability measured as return on equity, with or without circulation taxes, or measured as losses relative to gross profit, all improved significantly more than the relevant values for non-SOEs, so that by 2000 SOEs had almost pulled equal to non-SOEs.

(ii) The return on assets in non-SOEs always exceeded the return on assets in SOEs in the years for which comparison data are available (1993–2000). The percentage point difference is rather constant at two to three percentage points. The same pattern holds for the social return on assets, except that the gap is always narrower.

Table 6.1 Profitability of Industrial SOEs, 1978–2000

	Losses in 1978 b RMB	Losses / gross profit (%)	Profit / equity (%)	Profit + taxes / equity (%)	Return on assets[a] (%)	Social return on assets[b] (%)	Profit / sales revenue[c] (%)	Profit + taxes / sales revenue[c] (%)
1978	4.21	7.64			16.09	24.70	18.21	28.30
1979	3.58	6.07			16.66	25.31	18.60	28.56
1980	3.36	5.53			16.57	25.35	17.81	27.59
1981	4.50	7.35			15.28	24.15	17.25	27.47
1982	4.66	7.37			14.86	23.89	16.35	26.59
1983	3.15	4.77			15.32	24.12	15.97	25.74
1984	2.58	3.63			16.05	25.44	15.94	26.01
1985	2.89	4.21			14.53	25.17	14.08	25.44
1986	4.67	7.32			12.35	22.38	11.59	22.53
1987	4.85	7.20			12.37	22.12	11.01	21.17
1988	5.66	8.41			12.37	22.64	9.95	19.80
1989	10.50	19.52			10.14	20.13	7.38	17.60
1990	19.53	47.33			5.96	15.19	3.66	14.18
1991	19.35	47.71			5.35	14.29	3.17	13.11
1992	18.23	40.83			5.82	14.57	3.50	12.72
1993	18.02	35.64	7.70	23.13	4.07	9.09	3.89	11.69
1994	16.08	36.79	6.72	23.30	4.85	10.17	3.88	13.47
1995	18.54	49.00	4.10	17.71	4.45	9.10	2.63	11.35
1996	22.28	63.71	2.24	14.87	3.52	7.92	1.57	10.41
1997	23.48	66.01	2.09	14.20	3.02	7.21	1.58	10.74
1998	33.91	68.66	1.96	12.60	2.72	6.52	1.61	10.35
1999	29.19	49.21	3.26	13.34	2.99	6.82	2.86	11.69
2000	20.69	22.63	7.36	17.97	4.33	8.46	5.87	14.32

[a] Return on assets denotes 'profit plus (net) financial charges, per unit of assets,' where assets prior to 1993 comprise only average annual fixed-quota working capital plus year-end net fixed assets. Assets in 1993 are the sum of liabilities and equity. Net financial charges prior to 1993 are approximate. (See explanation with 'sources' below.)
[b] Social return on assets denotes 'profit plus taxes plus (net) financial charges, per unit of assets.' On assets and financial charges, see 'a.'
[c] Sales revenue is net of all sales-related taxes.

Sources:

Losses, profit, and 'profit and taxes:' *Statistical Yearbook 1998*, p. 461; *Industrial Yearbook 2001*, p. 24. Ex-factory price index of industrial products: *Statistical Yearbook 1994*, p. 246; *2001*, p. 297.

Equity and assets: *Statistical Yearbook* (see Table 2.5). Average annual fixed-quota working capital: *Statistical Yearbook 1993*, p. 430; year-end net fixed assets: *Statistical Yearbook 1998*, p. 461.

Financial charges: *Statistical Abstract 1994*, p. 86; *1995*, p. 86; *Industrial Census 1995*, Vol. 1, p. 51; *Statistical Abstract 1997*, p. 106; *1998*, p. 112; *1999*, p. 108; *2000*, p. 113; *2001*, p. 125; *Financial Yearbook* various issues and pages. Except for 1995, data are preliminary data first published in March of the following year. The revised data on financial charges are not published. Data for the years prior to 1993 are approximated as total working capital loans (i.e., loans with less than one year maturity) of state banks to industrial state-owned enterprises (*Financial Statistics 1952-1996*) times the average annual interest rate on working capital loans of six months or less maturity (calculated from various issues of the *Financial Yearbook*); in 1993, the approximated value exceeds the actual value by 4.36%.

Sales revenue, sales taxes and surcharges, and value-added tax: *Seventeen Years of Reform*, p. 146, for years prior to 1991; since 1991: *Statistical Yearbook* (see Table 2.5). Sales-related taxes up through 1993 are obtained as the difference of 'profit and taxes' and profit.

Table 6.2 Profitability of Industrial Non-SOEs, 1978–2000

	Losses in 1978 b RMB	Losses / gross profit (%)	Profit / equity (%)	Profit + taxes / equity (%)	Return on assets[a] (%)	Social return on assets[b] (%)	Profit / sales revenue[c] (%)	Profit + taxes / sales revenue[c] (%)
1978	0.30	3.25						
1979	0.38	4.01					14.46	20.50
1980	0.44	4.04					14.01	20.14
1981	0.74	6.84					11.62	17.84
1982	0.81	7.17					11.39	18.12
1983	0.54	4.02					11.84	18.34
1984	0.73	4.94					10.34	16.52
1985	0.72	3.77					10.64	17.05
1986	1.54	8.71					8.45	14.57
1987	1.88	9.79					7.65	13.31
1988	1.71	7.65					7.57	13.05
1989	3.14	17.32					5.72	11.16
1990	5.88	37.94					3.57	9.22
1991	5.72	31.08					3.80	9.04
1992	4.93	18.59					4.99	9.78
1993	7.41	19.17	14.33	26.81	6.65	10.81	5.32	9.95
1994	9.66	23.05	10.27	21.85	6.66	11.18	4.84	10.31
1995	16.21	36.58	8.61	19.34	6.47	10.27	3.65	8.19
1996	18.05	37.30	8.11	18.16	5.72	9.30	3.53	7.90
1997	21.36	37.21	7.89	17.53	5.34	8.85	3.63	8.07
1998	17.27	38.59	7.35	16.95	5.25	8.85	3.08	7.09
1999	15.00	27.80	9.18	18.66	5.53	9.18	3.83	7.79
2000	12.68	17.87	11.89	21.77	6.40	10.31	4.76	8.72

[a] Return on assets denotes 'profit plus (net) financial charges, per unit of assets.' 1993 assets are the sum of liabilities and equity.
[b] Social return on assets denotes 'profit plus taxes plus (net) financial charges, per unit of assets.'
[c] Sales revenue is net of all sales-related taxes.

Sources for directly reporting industrial enterprises (industrial non-SOEs equals directly reporting industrial enterprises less industrial SOEs; for industrial SOEs, see Table 6.1):

Losses, profit, and 'profit and taxes:' *Industrial Yearbook 1998*, p. 51; *Industrial Yearbook 2001*, p. 23. Ex-factory price index of industrial products: see Table 6.1

Equity and assets: *Statistical Yearbook 1994*, pp. 378, 381; *1995*, pp. 384, 386; *1996*, pp. 410, 412; *1997*, pp. 425f.; *1998*, pp. 445f.; *1999*, pp. 433f.; *2000*, pp. 420f.; *2001*, pp. 411f.

Financial charges: *Statistical Abstract 1994*, p. 85; *1995*, p. 85; *Industrial Census 1995*, Vol. 1, p. 51; *Statistical Abstract 1997*, p. 106; *1998*, p. 112; *1999*, p. 108; *2000*, p. 112; *2001*, p. 124.

Sales revenue, sales taxes and surcharges, and value-added tax: *Seventeen Years of Reform*, p. 146; *Statistical Yearbook 1992*, p. 411; *1993*, p. 417; *1994*, p. 381; *1995*, p. 387; *1996*, p. 413; *1997*, p. 423; *1998*, p. 443; *1999*, p. 435; *2000*, p. 422; *2001*, p. 413. (Sales-related taxes up through 1993 are obtained as the difference of 'profit and taxes' and profit.)

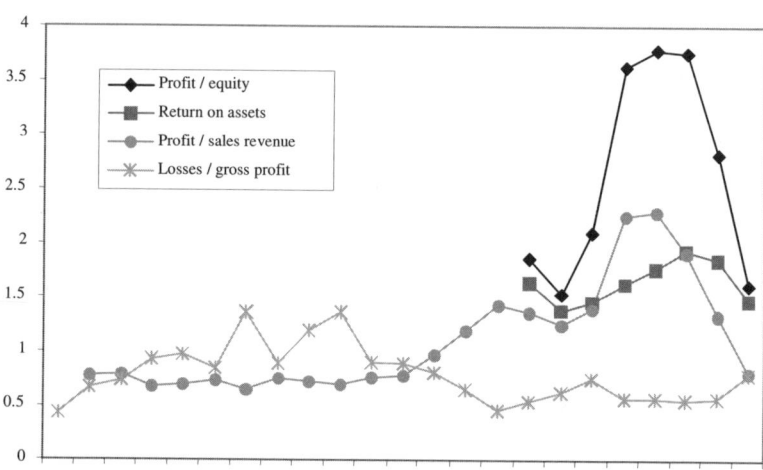

Sources: See Tables 6.1 and 6.2.

Figure 6.1   Non-SOE Profitability Divided by SOE Profitability

(iii) Profit per unit of sales revenue of both SOEs and non-SOEs declined gradually in the early 1980s, but then precipitously between 1985 and 1990. Between 1988 and 1990, SOE profitability declined from 9.95% to 3.66% and non-SOE profitability from 7.57% to 3.57%. Profitability recovered slightly in the following years before falling again, to 1.58% and 3.63%, respectively, in 1997. If circulation taxes are included, the overall decline is much smaller, SOEs consistently outperform non-SOEs, and the 1990s saw almost no decline.

Between 1998 and 2000, SOE profitability improved more significantly than that of non-SOEs (using either indicator), so that by 2000 even SOE profit (excluding circulation taxes) relative to sales revenue exceeded the corresponding non-SOE value.

Four general patterns emerge. First, non-SOE profitability, as a rule, declined and recovered in the same periods as SOE profitability. In particular, non-SOE profitability plummeted between 1988 and 1990, just as SOE profitability did. Second, between 1998 (the first year after the statistical break) and 2000, profitability of both SOEs (including state-controlled enterprises) and non-SOEs improved. But the profitability gap between non-SOEs and SOEs narrowed in absolute percentage terms across all measures. In terms of profit (with or without circulation taxes) relative to sales revenue, SOEs clearly outperformed non-SOEs by 2000.

Third, SOEs fared significantly worse than non-SOEs in terms of profit per unit of equity. If an overall return on assets or a social return on assets is considered, the difference is minor, and it almost disappears in the most recent years (it disappears in 2000) once profit is related to sales revenue. This implies that SOEs utilize a relatively large volume of equity and assets in order to earn a given amount of sales revenue. Fourth, the profitability gap between SOEs and non-SOEs consistently narrows once circulation taxes are included with profit in the numerator. This suggests that SOEs carry a higher tax burden than do non-SOEs. These two issues will be considered in a separate section below.

While the above data combine all non-SOEs into one category, non-SOEs comprise a wide variety of enterprises, ranging from collective-owned enterprises to foreign-funded and private enterprises. The performance of the individual sub-categories may differ widely. Detailed data on all sub-categories are available for the year 1995 from the 1995 industrial census, and limited data on only some sub-categories for other recent years.

Distinguishing among Non-SOEs

Data from the 1995 industrial census at first sight suggest that SOEs perform rather poorly compared to other ownership groups. In 1995, 34% of SOEs were running losses, while the average rate for all enterprises nationwide was only 25% (Table 6.3). Using the same individual profitability indicators as above yields the following findings.

(i) SOE's return on equity in 1995 at 4.10% was low compared with the nationwide average of 5.95%. If profit and circulation taxes together are related to equity, SOEs perform at the nationwide average. The performance of private enterprises in particular is always superior, with a return on equity of 24.58% and a ratio of profit and circulation taxes to equity of 37.24%.

(ii) SOEs are close to the average in terms of return on assets and the social return on assets. Private enterprises clearly outperform SOEs.

(iii) The gap between SOEs and the various other ownership groups is markedly reduced in the case of profit relative to sales revenue, and disappears once circulation taxes are included in the numerator. This is also true for the direct comparison between SOEs and private enterprises.

Except in the case of the profit relative to equity indicator, the performance of the various non-SOE ownership groups does not differ much from that of the SOEs. Collective-owned enterprises and shareholding enterprises perform only marginally better than do SOEs. Foreign-funded enterprises, as well as the enterprises with Hong Kong, Macao or Taiwanese participation (HKMT enterprises), also perform little better than SOEs. Only the private enterprises consistently outperform the SOEs, except in the case of profit and taxes relative to sales revenue, where SOEs and private enterprises are very close.

Collectively owned enterprises may often not differ much in their organization from formal SOEs, while the category of shareholding enterprises is likely to include a fair number of former SOEs. Enterprises with foreign or HKMT investment are likely to enjoy unique transfer pricing opportunities that allow them to locate their profit abroad.

By 2000, the superior performance of private enterprises had waned and collective-owned enterprises, (non-Chinese) foreign-funded enterprises, and HKMT enterprises now achieved results on a par with those of the private enterprises (Table 6.4). The profitability of private enterprises as measured by profit relative to equity dropped drastically in 1997 to 14.01%, down from 24.58% in 1995 and 24.12% in 1996; in the same year, their tax burden relative to equity also rose by three percentage points. The 1998 statistical break is unlikely to have had any strong redefinition effect on the group of private enterprises. The total number of private enterprises changed little between 1997 and 1999 (the next year for which data on private enterprises are available) from 13,188 to 14,601. Private enterprise profitability in 1999 and 2000 was little different from its 1997 level, with profit relative to equity in 2000 at 11.39%.

Table 6.3 Financial Performance of Enterprises with Independent Accounting System at the Township Level and Above (in %), 1995

	Share of loss-making enterprises	Share of value-added	Losses / gross profit	Profit / equity	Profit + taxes / equity	Return on assets[a]	Social return on assets[b]	Profit / sales revenue[c]	Profit + taxes / sales revenue[c]
Nationwide total	25.06	*100.00*	42.30	5.95	18.38	5.26	9.57	*3.15*	9.73
State-owned enterprises	33.75	53.78	49.00	4.10	17.71	4.45	9.10	2.63	11.35
Collective-owned enterprises	21.12	25.03	41.56	9.23	25.54	6.97	11.59	2.66	7.36
Private enterprises	16.69	0.26	10.55	24.58	37.24	13.74	18.98	8.20	12.42
Joint enterprises	28.80	1.01	47.93	5.96	17.81	5.30	9.52	2.53	7.56
Shareholding enterprises	21.66	5.02	9.43	10.27	18.57	7.13	10.86	7.60	13.74
Non-Chinese foreign-funded enterprises	39.34	7.73	36.50	8.54	16.19	6.17	9.55	4.98	9.43
Hong Kong, Macao and Taiwanese ent.	41.59	7.04	47.41	6.19	12.46	5.15	7.45	3.12	6.28
Other enterprises	24.87	0.12	19.04	7.63	13.49	6.20	8.55	4.30	7.61

[a] Return on assets denotes 'profit plus (net) financial charges, per unit of assets.'
[b] Social return on assets denotes 'profit plus taxes plus (net) financial charges, per unit of assets.'
[c] Sales revenue is net of all sales-related taxes.

Source: Industrial Census 1995, Vol. 1, pp. 46–53.

The performance of the collective-owned group first improved in 1998 with the redefinition of the group of directly reporting industrial enterprises. Many of the smallest collective-owned enterprises since 1998 are no longer included; the number of collective-owned enterprises dropped from 319,438 in 1997 to 47,745 in 1998. Profitability then improved further in the following two years to, in the case of profit relative to equity, 13.61% in 2000.

Table 6.4 Financial Performance of SOEs and Other Ownership Groups within the Directly Reporting Industrial Enterprises (in %), 1996–2000

	Share of loss-making enterprises	Share of value-added	Profit / equity	Profit + taxes / equity	Profit / sales revenue[a]	Profit + taxes / sales revenue[a]
1996						
Nationwide total	21.98	100.00	4.70	16.25	2.62	9.06
SOEs, pre-1998 definition	33.57	40.50	2.24	14.81	1.57	10.41
Collective-owned enterprises	17.96	28.64	9.71	25.09	2.77	7.16
Private enterprises	7.76	0.60	24.12	36.71		
Joint enterprises	23.07	1.04	4.98	14.66		
Shareholding companies	20.64	5.28	8.11	15.83	6.37	12.43
Non-Chinese foreign-funded ent.	34.59	8.51	7.43	14.61	4.41	8.66
HKMT enterprises	34.85	7.32	5.97	12.61	3.06	6.48
Residual	17.06	0.10	6.47	14.27		
Note: State-controlled ent.	30.22	9.69	6.56	14.88		
1997						
Nationwide total	23.61	100.00	4.65	15.67	2.74	9.23
SOEs, pre-1998 definition	38.22	46.35	2.09	14.20	1.58	10.74
Collective-owned enterprises	18.91	26.50	9.49	24.61	2.81	7.30
Private enterprises	13.32	1.09	14.01	29.57		
Joint enterprises	24.87	0.83	4.36	14.93		
Shareholding companies	23.78	7.21	8.06	15.42	6.29	12.05
Non-Chinese foreign-funded ent.	38.71	10.05	7.07	14.26	4.15	8.36
HKMT enterprises	34.15	7.80	6.22	12.65	3.30	6.72
Residual	23.67	0.18	4.59	19.41		
Note: State-controlled ent.	34.45	9.18	8.18	16.05	6.40	12.55
1998						
Nationwide total		100.00	3.70	14.00	2.32	8.78
Pure SOEs						
Collective-owned enterprises		17.00	11.03	24.54	3.44	7.65
Private enterprises						
Joint enterprises						
Stock companies		2.95	12.88	27.25	4.25	9.00
Non-Chinese foreign-funded ent.		10.26	4.50	11.73	2.67	6.97
HKMT enterprises		10.62	5.00	11.75	2.73	6.41

Table 6.4 (continued)

	Share of loss-making enterprises	Share of value-added	Profit / equity	Profit + taxes / equity	Profit / sales revenue[a]	Profit + taxes / sales revenue[a]
Residual						
Note: SOEs, post-1997 definition		57.03	1.96	12.60	1.61	10.35
1999						
Nationwide total	27.27	100.00	5.13	15.02	3.34	9.78
Pure SOEs	41.09	38.04	1.98	13.34		
Collective-owned enterprises	17.29	14.70	11.85	24.93	4.00	8.42
Private enterprises	13.57	3.74	13.18	25.75		
Joint enterprises	21.73	1.10	2.79	12.84		
Stock companies	21.83	7.50	8.68	15.48	7.69	13.72
Non-Chinese foreign-funded ent.	30.41	11.69	8.19	15.97	4.52	8.81
HKMT enterprises	30.87	10.80	7.23	13.78	3.89	7.41
Residual	20.96	12.42	3.60	13.01	2.50	9.02
Note: SOEs, post-1997 definition	39.15	56.26	3.26	13.34	2.86	11.69
2000						
Nationwide total	23.26	100.00	8.89	19.25	5.31	11.50
Pure SOEs	36.36	28.41	4.23	16.37		
Collective-owned enterprises	15.93	12.10	13.61	26.86	4.21	8.32
Private enterprises	12.59	5.19	11.39	22.71		
Joint enterprises	19.44	1.00	8.43	18.56		
Stock companies	19.25	14.12	16.55	25.79	12.97	20.20
Non-Chinese foreign-funded ent.	26.43	12.61	12.37	20.91	6.03	10.18
HKMT enterprises	27.14	11.37	10.67	17.71	5.34	8.87
Residual	19.23	15.21	5.51	15.30		
Note: SOEs, post-1997 definition	34.07	54.26	7.36	17.97	5.87	14.32

[a] Sales revenue is net of all sales-related taxes. Data on sales-related taxes are not available for all ownership categories and the relevant profitability indicators thus could not be calculated for all ownership groups in all years.

The directly reporting industrial enterprises prior to 1998 comprised all industrial enterprises with independent accounting system at the township level and above. Since 1998, they comprise all industrial SOEs and all industrial non-SOEs with independent accounting system and annual sales revenue in excess of 5m RMB. (All ownership groups are likely to be affected. The SOE category is affected due to its redefinition.)

The official statistics list state-controlled enterprises (in 1996 and 1997) and "state-owned and state-controlled enterprises" (post-1997 definition SOEs) in addition to and separately from the ownership classification.

Sources:
1996: *Industrial Yearbook 1998*, pp. 76f., 80f.; *Statistical Yearbook 1997*, p. 427.
1997: *Industrial Yearbook 1998*, pp. 76f., 80f.; *Statistical Yearbook 1998*, p. 447.
1998: *Statistical Yearbook 1999*, pp. 432, 434f.
1999: *Industrial Yearbook 2001*, pp. 48f., 52f.; *Statistical Yearbook 2000*, p. 417.
2000: *Industrial Yearbook 2001*, pp. 48f., 52f.; *Statistical Yearbook 2001*, p. 413.

The statistical break had a slightly negative effect on the profitability of (non-Chinese) foreign-funded enterprises and HKMT enterprises. Their profitability then improved sharply in both 1999 and 2000, in terms of profit relative to equity in 2000, to 12.37% and 10.67%, respectively.

Reporting on all shareholding companies (limited liability companies and stock companies) ceased in 1998; instead, only data on stock companies are available since 1998. The performance of stock companies in 1998 through 2000 varied greatly in each year; at the same time, their share in value-added rose rapidly from 2.95% in 1998 to 14.12% in 2000. In 2000, stock companies at 16.55% reported a higher ratio of profit relative to equity than any other ownership category. Most of these companies are likely to be state-controlled (and double-counted in the post-1997 SOE category).

The 1996 and 1997 data also show that state-controlled enterprises, of which only the solely state-owned limited liability companies are included in the (pre-1998 definition) category SOEs, performed significantly better than the SOEs and at a level comparable to that of shareholding companies (which most of them are likely to be). The 1999 and 2000 data then show that the profitability level of the newly defined (post-1997) SOE category, which includes, among others, the state-controlled companies, is about double that of the pure SOEs, with profit relative to equity in 2000 at 7.36%. But the pure SOEs by themselves also improved their profitability level to 4.32 % in 2000.

The fact that state-controlled enterprises in 1996 and 1997 far outperformed the (pre-1998 definition) SOE category suggests that profitability levels of the SOE category prior to 1998 were biased downward through the exclusion of some of the best SOEs (such as the state-controlled companies). The following section further examines the issue of selection bias for both private enterprises and SOEs.

Selection Bias

The stellar performance of private enterprises in 1995 and their still excellent performance in 2000 needs to be seen in perspective. The group of private enterprises included in the directly reporting industrial enterprises constitutes only a small sub-category of all private and individual-owned enterprises (on which no detailed balance sheet and profit and loss account data are available). Thus the private enterprises reporting directly to the statistical bureaus in 1995 accounted for only 0.26% of the value-added of the directly reporting industrial enterprises (Table 6.3), but private and individual-owned industry, for which no value-added data are available, in the same year accounted for 14.55% of the gross output value of all industry. By 1999, the directly reporting private enterprises accounted for 3.74% of the value-added of the directly reporting industrial enterprises (Table 6.4), but private and individual-owned industry in total accounted for 18.18% of the gross output value of all industry (gross output values for 2000 are not available).

The self-employed individuals in industry ("individual-owned enterprises") are by definition not included in the directly reporting industrial enterprises; self-employed individuals in industry turn into a "private" industrial enterprise as soon as they employ more than seven persons and thus reach a certain size. Until 1997, private industrial enterprises were included in the group of directly reporting industrial enterprises only if they were registered at the township level and above, i.e., were located in urban areas. Since 1997, private enterprises are included only if their sales revenue exceeds 5m RMB per year (but all SOEs independent of their sales revenue are included). If it is the case that only those individual-owned units that are profitable tend to grow to a significant size — turn into private enterprises and meet the registration (and since 1998 sales) criterion — then the group of private enterprises included in the detailed statistics reflects the top performers in the individual-owned sector. The comparison between SOEs and private enterprises thus loses some of its significance.

The comparison of SOEs and private enterprises (or all non-SOEs) is, in addition, further biased against SOEs for two reasons. The first reason is the occasional exit between 1993 and 1997 of the potentially best-performing SOEs. The best-performing large and medium-sized SOEs are increasingly being turned into limited liability companies or stock companies. Solely state-owned limited liability companies have always been included in the category "SOEs," but all other state-controlled companies have only been included in the new category "state-owned and state-controlled enterprises" since 1998, as are data on all other enterprises in which the state holds a stake (proportional to the ownership stake).

SOE profitability levels did not immediately improve after the re-categorization in 1998. This, however, does not rule out the possibility that the profitability of SOEs in the pre-1998 definition would have fallen drastically in 1998, had the SOE category not been redefined. A belated and only approximate comparison is possible for 1999. The nationwide 3.26% return on equity of "state-owned and state-controlled enterprises" compares to a 1.98% return on equity for the pure SOEs (which probably account for about 90% of value-added of the pre-1998 definition SOE category) (Table 6.4). The profitability level of the SOE category prior to 1998 thus may be a downward biased measure of the profitability level achieved with all state-controlled assets.

The second reason is that the worst-performing SOEs exit only slowly. Formal SOE bankruptcy procedures are limited to selected large and medium-sized SOEs included in a central bankruptcy plan with a tight limit on the number of SOEs formally allowed to go bankrupt every year. A higher degree of exit among bankrupt SOEs would imply a higher level of profitability for the group of surviving SOEs in the aggregate.[128]

The provincial statistical yearbooks of five provinces contain data on a separately listed group of loss-making directly reporting industrial enterprises as well as a separately listed group of loss-making industrial SOEs, for all three years since 1998. Together with the aggregate data on all directly reporting industrial enterprises and on all industrial SOEs, this allows the calculation of the respective groups of profitable enterprises. Subtracting SOEs from all directly reporting industrial enterprises then

---

[128] Losses are highly concentrated in a relatively small number of SOEs across all sectors. Well-targeted bankruptcies thus could drastically improve aggregate profitability of the remaining SOEs. For details, see Chapter 7. Small SOEs are historically the worst performing enterprises among all SOEs. Many of these SOEs, owned by local governments, have in recent years been privatized or closed, thus possibly reducing the bias against SOE profitability over time. (No detailed data on the privatization of small SOEs are available.) Small SOEs in 1997, the last year for which the data are available, accounted for 15% of SOE value-added.

yields data on profitable non-SOEs and, separately, on loss-making non-SOEs. Table 6.5 reports the results.[129]

If the argument that the SOE category suffers from a severe lack of exit is correct, then the share of loss-making enterprises should always be higher among SOEs than non-SOEs. Table 6.5 confirms that this argument is correct for the five provinces; the share of loss-making enterprises among SOEs tends on average to be one-third higher than the share of loss-making enterprises among non-SOEs. Tables 6.3 and 6.4, using nationwide data, further indicate a higher share of loss-making enterprises among SOEs than among all enterprises (the non-SOE category is not presented separately). The discrepancy is even more severe between SOEs and private enterprises, where the share of loss-making enterprises nationwide tends to be about ten percent, compared with SOEs' thirty to forty percent (Table 6.4). For three out of the five provinces, a comparison based on value-added further shows that loss-making SOEs account for a higher share of SOE value-added than loss-making non-SOEs account for non-SOE value-added. The reverse is true for Heilongjiang, while there is no clear difference in Shandong.

While the prevalence of loss-making enterprises among SOEs, as compared with non-SOEs, is unambiguous, the profitability level of the loss-making enterprises does not differ much across ownership categories. Loss-making SOEs are clearly less profitable than loss-making non-SOEs in Shaanxi in 1998 and 2000, in Inner Mongolia in 2000, and in Heilongjiang and Shandong in 1998 and 1999. (Profit data for loss-making enterprises in Inner Mongolia and equity data for loss-making enterprises in Shaanxi in 1999 are of highly questionable quality, affecting the 1999 data of both loss-making and profitable enterprises, for both SOEs and non-SOEs.) On average, loss-making SOEs thus tend to be less profitable, or more loss-

---

[129] The SOE category in 1998 covers only the pure SOEs except in Shandong and Shaanxi, where it could also reflect the pre-1998 definition SOEs. In 1999 and 2000, the coverage extends to all state-owned and state-controlled enterprises, except in Inner Mongolia and Heilongjiang in 1999, where the coverage is still the pure SOEs. This implies that SOEs account for a greater share of value-added among all directly reporting industrial enterprises over time, rising, depending on province, from approximately half of value-added to three-quarters of value-added (Table 6.5).

making relative to equity, than non-SOEs. The exit of a given number of loss-making SOEs thus might have a larger effect on aggregate SOE profitability than the same measures in the case of loss-making non-SOEs. On the other hand, profitable SOEs are less profitable than non-SOEs, except in Heilongjiang. A lack of exit among loss-making SOEs thus cannot fully account for the difference in aggregate profitability of SOEs and non-SOEs.

The pattern across different profitability indicators is the same as noted before. SOEs always fare better once profit and taxes are considered together, rather than only profit, and if profit or profit and taxes are related to sales revenue rather than equity. This pattern is further examined in the next section.[130]

Explaining the Profitability Gap between Industrial SOEs and Non-SOEs

The comparison of SOEs and non-SOEs or private enterprises using different profitability indicators suggests that two factors may be able to explain the profitability gap, apart from the potential selection bias in enterprise categories. First, the gap is smaller once profit plus taxes is considered rather than profit by itself. With profit by definition including income taxes, the smaller gap implies a higher rate of circulation taxes for SOEs than for non-SOEs. Second, the gap is smaller in the case of profit per unit of sales revenue than in the case of profit per unit of equity, suggesting that equity in the case of SOEs is relatively large, which in turn can be shown to reflect a relatively large volume of assets compared to sales revenue (high capital intensity).

---

[130] In three out of the five provinces in Table 6.5, profit relative to equity of profitable SOEs increased over time, and by more than in the case of profitable non-SOEs. In the same three provinces, losses of loss-making SOEs relative to their equity fell over time, while losses of loss-making non-SOEs relative to their equity actually increased over time. While the improvement in SOE performance could be due to the three-year reform program, the switch from pure SOEs to all state-owned and state-controlled enterprises (see previous note) could also matter in that the better performing SOEs, which earlier left the pool of pre-1998 definition SOEs, are now again included in the newly defined SOE category (of all state-owned and state-controlled enterprises).

Table 6.5 Profitable *vs.* Loss-making Industrial SOEs and Non-SOEs in Five Provinces, 1998-2000 (all values in %)

	Share in value-added of directly reporting ind. ent.			Share in total number of enterprises in this ownership			Share in value-added of enterprises in this ownership			Profit / equity			Profit + tax / equity			Profit / sales revenue[a]		
	1998	1999	2000	1998	1999	2000	1998	1999	2000	1998	1999	2000	1998	1999	2000	1998	1999	2000
Shanxi																		
Profitable SOEs	37.09	50.27	58.26							6.68	5.33	3.95	17.47	12.52	10.90	7.17	7.08	5.18
Profit. non-SOEs	41.66	25.77	24.05							5.88	9.89	10.73	14.31	24.89	24.88	5.41	5.28	5.86
Loss-making SOEs	14.66	18.19	13.49	26.08	29.90	26.80	28.33	26.57	18.81	-9.37	-14.09	-16.14	-3.18	-8.25	-6.20	-14.11	-17.04	-16.73
Loss-m. non-SOEs	6.59	5.76	4.20	20.24	22.25	20.96	13.65	18.27	14.87	-19.78	-21.11	-33.21	-9.32	-2.67	-9.15	-13.17	-9.98	-11.05
Inner Mongolia																		
Profitable SOEs	42.02	36.08	73.13							6.73	3.33	4.34	17.18	12.89	11.83	8.86	4.13	5.35
Profit. non-SOEs	46.43	50.04	17.06							5.12	6.39	10.42	11.96	13.24	24.57	6.09	6.72	5.84
Loss-making SOEs	8.63	10.98	7.48	33.33	29.32	23.65	17.04	23.32	9.28	-19.41	-7.01	-25.88	-12.53	-1.77	-16.85	-15.91	-11.78	-25.84
Loss-m. non-SOEs	2.91	2.91	2.33	20.00	18.56	18.99	5.90	5.49	12.02	-24.50	-133.7	-14.45	-19.02	-123.25	-5.49	-15.21	-77.98	-10.37
Heilongjiang																		
Profitable SOEs	68.90	76.21	82.19							23.60	30.44	47.92	42.58	48.29	64.80	19.97	25.53	42.37
Profit. non-SOEs	14.02	16.64	7.62							8.21	5.57	11.97	18.18	14.25	22.20	5.70	4.73	6.48
Loss-making SOEs	9.54	4.96	8.70	42.41	40.07	38.54	12.16	6.12	9.57	-41.15	-26.72	-15.90	-27.71	-11.67	-1.54	-22.52	-17.05	-10.26
Loss-m. non-SOEs	7.55	2.19	1.50	25.86	23.63	19.85	35.00	11.62	16.44	-12.18	-18.68	-38.45	-6.34	-12.89	-25.65	-12.48	-16.78	-13.58
Shandong																		
Profitable SOEs	38.59	45.94	45.23							5.85	6.81	15.83	18.12	18.28	28.68	4.42	5.01	10.45
Profit. non-SOEs	55.41	48.79	48.58							18.54	19.68	20.59	30.73	31.73	33.42	6.72	6.54	6.53
Loss-making SOEs	2.37	2.54	4.29	32.41	25.78	21.49	5.78	5.25	8.67	-27.46	-25.62	-11.13	-18.47	-16.78	-0.94	-14.25	-15.57	-7.20
Loss-m. non-SOEs	3.64	2.73	1.90	13.06	11.76	9.52	6.17	5.31	3.76	-13.89	-16.30	-19.66	-9.09	-8.90	-9.26	-10.68	-8.97	-8.98
Shaanxi																		
Profitable SOEs	47.00	67.41	70.19							6.86	6.39	12.38	19.91	17.35	22.63	5.55	6.55	10.63
Profit. non-SOEs	33.33	17.51	17.52							13.43	15.85	16.54	22.74	24.95	26.89	8.40	10.87	11.83
Loss-making SOEs	13.64	12.20	9.31	53.58	48.56	44.76	22.49	15.32	11.71	-41.98	-33.89	-37.52	-32.99	-26.08	-22.20	-28.02	-28.60	-30.13
Loss-m. non-SOEs	6.03	2.88	2.98	30.57	24.62	26.09	15.32	14.12	14.53	-12.11	-105.6	-20.15	-5.67	-54.96	-2.70	-19.22	-14.03	-6.57

[a] Sales revenue is net of all sales-related taxes.

Data on non-SOEs are obtained as the difference between all directly reporting industrial enterprises and the SOEs. The SOE category in 1998 covers only the pure SOEs except in Shandong and Shaanxi, where it could also reflect the pre-1998 definition SOEs. In 1999 and 2000 the coverage extends to all state-owned and state-controlled enterprises, except in Inner Mongolia and Heilongjiang in 1999, where the coverage is still the pure SOEs.

Sources: Individual provincial yearbooks of the five provinces of the years 1999, 2000, and 2001.

Difference in the Rate of Circulation Taxes

The narrowing of the gap between SOEs and non-SOEs when switching from a numerator consisting only of profit to one comprising profit and circulation taxes is striking, because one would expect circulation tax rates to be the same across all industrial enterprises. But in fact SOEs pay about twice as much sales-related taxes (circulation taxes) per unit of sales revenue than do non-SOEs (Table 6.6). Since 1994, a breakdown of sales-related taxes into "sales taxes and surcharges" and the widely adopted value-added tax is available. The proper measure to standardize sales taxes and surcharges is sales revenue, and the proper measure to standardize the value-added tax is value-added. Throughout the 1990s, sales taxes and surcharges relative to sales revenue are two to four times higher in SOEs than in non-SOEs; the value-added tax relative to value-added is about one and a half times higher in SOEs than in non-SOEs (Table 6.6).

Across the close to forty industrial sectors, the mean ratio of the value added tax to value-added is significantly higher for SOEs than for non-SOEs at the 0.1% significance level (two-tailed t-test) throughout all years for which sectoral data are available, 1994 through 1997, and 1999 and 2000 (first block of data in Table 6.7).

However, there is no significant difference in the mean ratio of sales taxes and surcharges relative to sales revenue across industrial sectors for SOEs vs. non-SOEs in any of these years (using the 10% significance level as cut-off point). This implies that SOEs' higher aggregate rates of sales taxes and surcharges are due solely to the concentration of SOEs in sectors with high sales taxes and surcharges. Indeed, the higher the rate of sales taxes and surcharges that SOEs face on average in a particular industrial sector, the larger the SOE market share in this industrial sector (where the market share is calculated based on the sales revenue net of all sales-related taxes). On the other hand, the higher the rate of sales taxes and surcharges that non-SOEs face on average in a particular industrial sector, (i) the smaller the non-SOE market share in this industrial sector, and (ii) the smaller the sales revenue of non-SOEs in this particular industrial sector relative to total non-SOE sales revenue. (See the second block of data in Table 6.7 for the significance levels of the correlation coefficients over time and the notes to the table on the range of the calculated correlation coefficients.)

Table 6.6 Sales-related Taxes

	Industrial SOEs			Industrial non-SOEs		
	Sales-related taxes	Sales taxes and surcharges	Value-added tax	Sales-related taxes	Sales taxes and surcharges	Value-added tax
In % of sales revenue[a]						
1980	9.79			6.13		
1985	11.36			6.41		
1990	10.52			5.64		
1993	7.80			4.63		
1994	9.59	3.44	6.14	5.46	1.66	3.80
1995	8.72	3.10	5.62	4.54	1.02	3.42
1996	8.84	3.28	5.56	4.37	1.04	3.33
1997	9.16	3.34	5.81	4.44	0.99	3.45
1998	8.74	3.05	5.69	4.01	0.80	3.21
1999	8.83	3.04	5.79	3.96	0.73	3.23
2000	8.45	2.80	5.65	3.83	0.66	3.17
In % of value-added						
1980	22.04			12.84		
1985	25.88			16.13		
1990	30.11			17.14		
1993	22.49			12.29		
1994	25.90	9.31	16.60	16.05	4.88	11.17
1995	26.58	9.46	17.12	16.91	3.80	12.73
1996	26.59	9.88	16.71	14.36	3.41	10.95
1997	26.97	9.84	17.13	14.64	3.26	11.37
1998	25.69	8.97	16.72	14.59	2.92	11.68
1999	25.40	8.76	16.64	14.13	2.60	11.52
2000	25.19	8.35	16.84	14.19	2.44	11.75

[a] Sales revenue is net of all sales-related taxes.

Sources:
Sales revenue, sales taxes and surcharges, and value-added tax: see Tables 6.1 and 6.2.
Value-added: see appendix to Chapter 2.

In other words, while SOEs have a large market share in the industrial sectors in which they pay the highest sales taxes and surcharges, the reverse is true for non-SOEs. Moreover, non-SOE production activities are allocated primarily to those sectors in which they face the lowest sales taxes and surcharges, while the SOE allocation of industrial production activities across sectors does not depend on sales taxes and surcharges in any way. This suggests historical or governmental policy reasons for the high market share of SOEs in industrial sectors in which they pay high sales taxes and surcharges.

The most extreme example is the tobacco (processing) sector, in which SOEs face a rate of sales taxes and surcharges of more than 65%, compared with a rate of approximately ten to thirty percent for non-SOEs. The SOE

Table 6.7 Circulation Taxes and Capital Intensity of SOEs vs. Non-SOEs across Industrial Sectors (significance levels in %)

	1993	94	95	96	97	99	00
T-tests: comparing SOEs to non-SOEs, the mean ratio of...							
sales-related taxes to sales revenue is higher in SOEs than in non-SOEs	n.a.						
sales taxes and surcharges to sales revenue is higher in SOEs than in non-SOEs	n.a.						
value-added tax to value-added is higher in SOEs than in non-SOEs	n.a.	0.1	0.1	0.1	0.1	0.1	0.1
total assets to sales revenue is higher in SOEs than in non-SOEs	0.1	0.1	0.1	0.1	0.1	0.1	0.1
current assets to sales revenue is higher in SOEs than in non-SOEs	0.1	0.1	0.1	0.1	0.1	0.1	0.1
net fixed assets to sales revenue is higher in SOEs than in non-SOEs	1	1	1	1	1	1	1
Correlation coefficients: the higher the ratio of ...							
sales taxes and surcharges to sales revenue for SOEs, the larger the SOE market share	n.a.	5	5	5	5	5	5
value-added tax to value-added for SOEs, the larger this sector's contribution to total SOE sales revenue	n.a.		1	1	1	10	5
sales taxes and surcharges to sales revenue for non-SOEs, the smaller the non-SOE market share	n.a.	5	1	0.1	0.1	1	1
sales taxes and surcharges to sales rev. for non-SOEs, the smaller this sector's contribution to total non-SOE sales rev.	n.a.		5	5	5	5	5
value-added tax to value-added for non-SOEs, the larger this sector's contribution to total SOE sales revenue	n.a.	5	1	1	5	1	5
current assets to sales revenue for SOEs, the smaller the SOE market share	10	5		10	5	5	10
current assets to sales revenue for SOEs, the smaller this sector's contribution to total SOE sales revenue	5	1	5	1	1	1	0.1
net fixed assets to sales revenue for SOEs, the larger the SOE market share	1	1	1	5	10	1	5
net fixed assets to sales revenue for SOEs, the smaller this sector's contribution to total non-SOE sales revenue	5	5	5	5	5	1	1
net fixed assets to sales revenue for non-SOEs, the smaller the non-SOE market share	5	5	5	5	1	0.1	1
net fixed assets to sales revenue for non-SOEs, the larger this sector's contribution to total SOE sales revenue		5	10	5	1	1	5

Table 6.7 (continued)

An empty field implies the t-value or correlation coefficient is not significant at the 10% level. Sales revenue is net of all sales-related taxes.

Correlation coefficient results were calculated between, on the one hand: (i) sales taxes and surcharges relative to sales revenue, (ii) value-added tax relative to value-added, (iii) current assets relative to sales revenue, and (iv) net fixed assets relative to sales revenue, all four for (A) SOEs and (B) non-SOEs, and, on the other hand, (i) the market share of SOEs based on sales revenue (the correlation coefficient for the market share of non-SOEs is identical but with the opposite sign), (ii) SOE sales revenue in a particular sector relative to total SOE sales revenue, and (iii) non-SOE sales revenue in a particular sector relative to total non-SOE sales revenue; this yields 24 correlation coefficients per year. Correlation coefficients which are insignificant across all years are omitted from the table. The following significant correlation coefficients are not included in the table because they are only significant in one or two years: (i) the higher the ratio of value-added tax to value-added for SOEs, the smaller the SOE market share (10% significance level in 1995); (ii) the higher the ratio of value-added tax to value-added for non-SOEs, the smaller the non-SOE market share (5% level in 1994 and 1999); (iii) the higher the ratio of current assets to sales revenue for non-SOEs, the smaller the non-SOE market share (1% level in 1999, and 10% level in 2000); (iv) the higher the ratio of net fixed assets to sales revenue for non-SOEs, the smaller this sector's contribution to total non-SOE sales revenue (10% level in 1999). The signs of significant correlation coefficients were always the same across all years.

Data limitations: The industrial sector "gas production and supply" was omitted in the years 1993 through 1997 as the values for value-added were of highly dubious quality. 1993 through 1997 correlation coefficients then are based on 38 industrial sectors; 1999 and 2000 correlation coefficients are based on 37 industrial sectors (data on two small sectors "others" are no longer published). SOE data by industrial sector for 1998 are not available.

Sources: Numerous pages of the industry section of the *Statistical Yearbook 1994* through *2001*. (See Table 2.5.)

market share in the tobacco processing sector was 98.17% in 1993 and 99.13% in 2000. The SOE rate of sales taxes and surcharges in the tobacco processing sector is more than six times higher than in the sector with the second-highest rate for SOEs, and the value of sales taxes and surcharges in the tobacco processing sector consistently accounts for almost half of total SOE sales taxes and surcharges. (Omitting the tobacco processing sector does not systematically change the results reported in Table 6.7.)

Another example is the resource tax, which as a component of sales taxes and surcharges is levied on the production of seven different resources, such as petroleum, natural gas and coal (PRC FM Tax Office, 1996, pp. 59ff and 129ff.). Across these industries, state ownership dominates.

The consistent positive correlation between the SOE rate of sales taxes and surcharges and the SOE market share across industrial sectors suggests that the government may purposefully impose high tax rates on state monopoly sectors (such as the tobacco processing sector) or sectors in which a few, often centrally owned and large SOEs dominate. The government can effectively collect taxes from these highly controlled enterprises, while it has difficulty in collecting taxes from other enterprises such as locally owned, often small SOEs or non-SOEs. Whether a lowering of the rate of sales taxes and surcharges would increase profit and thereby benefit aggregate SOE profit depends on whether product prices are state-determined and fixed, in which case the answer is positive, or on whether product prices are the result of market forces, in which case the answer depends on the elasticity of demand and supply. It would seem that in as far as prices in the sectors tobacco processing, petroleum (and natural gas) extraction, petroleum processing (and coking), production and supply of electricity (as well as of steam and hot water), and coal mining (and dressing), the five major sectors with a large SOE market share, are determined by the state, a lowering of sales taxes and surcharges in these sectors would immediately improve profit.[131]

---

[131] A high market share does not necessarily translate into high levels of profitability. In 2000, the SOE return on equity in the ten industrial sectors in which SOEs had a market share above 60% (compared with the economy-wide average SOE market share of 49.63% based on tax-adjusted sales revenue) was above the economy-wide SOE average return on equity of 7.36% in only two sectors (petroleum extraction and tobacco processing at 45.85% and 13.54%).

The case of the value-added tax is different. Across all industrial sectors, the mean ratio of the value-added tax to value-added is significantly higher for SOEs than for non-SOEs; furthermore, much of aggregate SOE sales revenue is created in sectors in which the value-added tax rate is high (Table 6.7). The difference in mean ratios is perhaps in part explained by three regulatory peculiarities. The general value-added tax rate in China is 17%, with several hundred products subject to a lower rate of 13%; SOEs thus may have a large market share in the 17% value-added tax rate sectors. Second, "small" tax payers face only a value-added tax rate of 6%, where "small" in the case of production units is defined as having taxable sales revenue of 1m RMB or less. The consistently lower value-added tax rate paid by non-SOEs may thus in large part be due to the fact that many of these enterprises are quite small.[132] If an identical product offered by SOEs and non-SOEs sells for the same price in the market (a price that includes all sales-related taxes), then, after paying sales-related taxes, SOEs end up with less residual profit for the identical product than do non-SOEs just because of the higher value-added tax rate they face. Third, a value-added tax rate of zero applies to exports, perhaps over-proportionally benefiting foreign-funded enterprises, which may predominantly produce for export.[133]

In as far as SOEs are predominantly located in high-tax industrial sectors for historical or policy reasons, or in as far as SOEs face higher tax rates due solely to their size, any profitability comparison between SOEs and non-SOEs should take into account this tax discrimination against SOEs. The comparison then should be based on a profitability measure that includes circulation taxes in the numerator. In 1997, SOE profit plus circulation taxes relative to equity stood at 14.20%, compared with non-SOEs' only

---

[132] In 1993, *average* sales revenue per SOE was 26.07m RMB, compared to 4.00m RMB for non-SOEs. In 2000, the difference (for the newly defined directly reporting industrial enterprises and the SOE category) was only 76.75m RMB vs. 38.09m RMB, but the group of non-SOEs for which the average value has been calculated is now limited to those enterprises with annual sales revenue in excess of 5m RMB. On the value-added tax regulation, see Wang Zheng and Yang Wenli (1997), pp. 8 and 19f. (For the list of products subject to a 13% value-added tax rate, see pp. 21–27; the list is too long and detailed to try to reach a conclusion on whether these products are predominantly produced by SOEs or by non-SOEs.)

[133] Non-SOEs may also be more adept than SOEs at avoiding payment of the value-added tax.

slightly higher 17.53%. In other years, the gap was of similar size (Tables 6.1 and 6.2).

Difference in Capital Intensity

The fact that the gap between SOEs and non-SOEs is smaller when profit relative to sales revenue is considered — rather than profit relative to equity — shows that equity in the case of SOEs is relatively large. Equity relative to sales revenue in 1993 was 1.36 times larger in SOEs than in non-SOEs, rising to a multiple of 1.64 times in 1997 and 2.06 in 2000 (for the newly defined SOE category). With the liability-asset ratio approximately the same for both SOEs and non-SOEs over time, assets and liabilities in SOEs are also larger by a similar amount in SOEs than in non-SOEs. (See Table 6.8.) SOEs thus employ a correspondingly larger volume of assets to produce a given amount of sales revenue than do non-SOEs, i.e., SOEs have a higher capital intensity.

Costs of a High Level of Capital Intensity

SOEs are hurt twice by the higher ratio of equity (or assets or liabilities) to sales revenue. First, for a given amount of sales revenue, their residual profit is lower. They incur higher financial charges (because they have more liabilities) as well as larger depreciation charges (with the larger volume of assets comes a larger volume of net fixed assets). Financial charges and depreciation are subtracted from sales revenue and thus decrease the residual profit. Second, for a given amount of profit, the ratio of profit to equity is lower because the volume of equity is larger.

Considering only the second factor, the equity factor, had SOEs had the same ratio of equity to sales revenue as non-SOEs had, SOEs' profit per unit of equity in 1993 would have been approximately 10.47% (7.70% * 1.36), compared with non-SOEs' 14.33%. In 1997, SOEs' profit per unit of equity would have been 3.43% (2.09% * 1.64) compared with non-SOEs' 7.89%, and in 2000 14.65% (7.36% * 1.99) compared with non-SOEs' 11.89%. (See Tables 6.1, 6.2, and 6.8.) In terms of profit plus circulation taxes relative to equity, SOEs would have outperformed non-SOEs at 31.45% (23.13% * 1.36) vs. 26.81% in 1993, 23.29% vs. 17.53% in 1997, and 35.76% vs. 21.77% in 2000.

Table 6.8 Capital Intensity

	SOE ratio / non-SOE ratio				Liabilities / assets		Net fixed assets / assets	
	Equity / sales rev.	Assets / sales rev.	Current assets / sales rev.	Net fixed assets / sales rev.	SOEs	Non-SOEs	SOEs	Non-SOEs
1980				1.94				
1985				2.15				
1990				1.79				
1993	1.36	1.39	1.08	1.82	0.67	0.67	0.41	0.31
1994	1.23	1.49	1.23	1.84	0.68	0.65	0.41	0.33
1995	1.51	1.57	1.22	2.05	0.66	0.64	0.45	0.34
1996	1.61	1.64	1.27	2.10	0.65	0.64	0.45	0.35
1997	1.64	1.73	1.35	2.11	0.65	0.63	0.44	0.36
1998	1.96	2.06	1.62	2.20	0.64	0.62	0.43	0.40
1999	2.10	2.13	1.61	2.39	0.62	0.61	0.42	0.38
2000	2.06	2.02	1.53	2.51	0.60	0.60	0.44	0.35

Sources:
Equity: *Statistical Yearbook 1994*, p. 381; *1995*, p. 391; *1996*, p. 416; *1997*, p. 426; *1998*, p. 446; *1999*, p. 434; *2000*, p. 416; *2001*, p. 412.
Sales revenue (net of sales-related taxes): see Tables 6.1 and 6.2.
Assets: *Statistical Yearbook 1994*, pp. 380f.; *1995*, p. 384; *1996*, p. 415; *1997*, p. 425; *1998*, p. 445; *1999*, p. 433; *2000*, p. 415; *2001*, p. 411. 1993 data are the sum of liabilities and equity.
Current assets: *Statistical Yearbook 1994*, p. 379; *1995*, p. 389; *1996*, p. 415; *1997*, p. 425; *1998*, p. 445; *1999*, p. 433; *2000*, p. 415; *2001*, p. 411.
Net fixed assets: *Industrial Yearbook 1998*, p. 51; *Statistical Yearbook 1998*, p. 461; *1999*, p. 433; *2000*, p. 415; *2001*, p. 44. Data since 1998 are average annual net fixed assets, all other data are year-end data.
Liabilities: *Statistical Yearbook 1994*, pp. 380f.; *1995*, pp. 390f.; *1996*, p. 416; *1997*, p. 426; *1998*, p. 446; *1999*, p. 434; *2000*, p. 416; *2001*, p. 412.

Once financial charges and depreciation are also considered, the balance tilts clearly in favor of SOEs. Suppose SOEs had had the same capital intensity (assets relative to sales revenue) in 1993 as non-SOEs had. Due to the similar liability-asset ratio (Table 6.8), this is the same as assuming that SOEs had the same ratio of liabilities (or equity) to sales revenue as non-SOEs had. This implies that SOEs had the same rates of financial charges and depreciation relative to sales revenue as non-SOEs. Since the SOE ratio of net fixed assets to total assets is very similar to that of non-SOEs (Table 6.8), the SOEs' ratio is taken to be the same as that of non-SOEs, which avoids complications in adjusting for SOE depreciation. (This simplification works to the detriment of SOE profitability.) SOE profit relative to equity in 1993 would then at 16.65% have exceeded non-SOE profit relative to equity at 14.33%. SOEs clearly outperformed non-SOEs in terms of profit plus circulation taxes per unit of equity at 37.92%

compared with 26.81%. (See bottom lines of Table 6.9.) For 1997, the differences are even more striking at 14.85% compared with 7.89% (profit relative to equity) and 34.86% compared with 17.53% (profit plus taxes relative to equity). In 2000 the differences are larger still at 28.49% compared with 11.89% and 50.25% compared with 21.77%.

These 1993 values are obtained in two steps as follows. (For the detailed data and derivation for all years, see Table 6.9). First, if SOE financial charges and depreciation as a percentage of sales revenue had been the same as in non-SOEs, SOE profit per unit of sales revenue would have risen by the difference between the SOE and non-SOE rates of financial charges and depreciation (relative to sales revenue) since profit is the residual of sales revenue after subtracting, among others, financial charges and depreciation. In 1993, SOE profit per unit of sales revenue would have been 6.16%, which is equal to 3.89% in original profit (relative to sales revenue) plus (2.44-2.08)%, the difference in financial charges (relative to sales revenue), plus (4.29-2.38)%, the difference in depreciation (relative to sales revenue).

Second, adjusted SOE profit per unit of sales revenue still needs to be translated into adjusted profit per unit of *adjusted equity*. SOE equity is adjusted such that the ratio of equity to sales revenue in SOEs is the same as in non-SOEs. This implies the multiplication of adjusted SOE profit relative to sales revenue with non-SOE sales revenue relative to equity to yield 16.65%, which equals 6.16% multiplied by one over 0.37.[134]

For the profit plus taxes relative to equity indicator, payment of circulation taxes can be calculated as the difference between profit plus circulation taxes relative to equity and profit relative to equity. Equity still needs to be adjusted as above when only the equity factor was considered.

Similar calculations can be made in the comparison of SOEs with private enterprises in 1995, the only year for which sufficient data on private

---

[134] A round-about second step would be first to translate SOE adjusted profit relative to sales revenue into SOE adjusted profit relative to *un*adjusted equity. To obtain SOE adjusted profit relative to *un*adjusted equity, multiply SOE adjusted profit per unit of sales revenue by SOE sales revenue per unit of equity (6.16% * 1 / 0.51). SOE equity is then adjusted by further multiplying this term with the ratio of SOE equity to sales revenue and dividing by the ratio of non-SOE equity to sales revenue (altogether 6.16% * 1 / 0.51 * 0.51 / 0.37, or, in short, 6.16% / 0.37).

Table 6.9 Adjusting SOE Profitability to Match Non-SOEs' Capital Intensity and Circulation Tax Rates (all data in %, unless otherwise noted)

	1993 SOEs	1993 Non-SOEs	1994 SOEs	1994 Non-SOEs	1995 SOEs	1995 Non-SOEs	1996 SOEs	1996 Non-SOEs	1997 SOEs	1997 Non-SOEs	1998 SOEs	1998 Non-SOEs	1999 SOEs	1999 Non-SOEs	2000 SOEs	2000 Non-SOEs
Profit / sales revenue	3.89	5.32	3.88	4.84	2.63	3.65	1.57	3.53	1.58	3.63	1.61	3.08	2.86	3.83	5.87	4.76
Financial charges/ sales revenue	2.44	2.08	4.86	3.19	5.71	4.08	5.48	3.46	5.01	3.10	4.64	2.80	4.03	2.16	3.00	1.66
Depreciation / sales revenue	4.29	2.38	6.17	3.54	6.25	3.39	6.42	3.09	6.42	3.08	6.59	2.72	6.09	2.63	6.34	2.44
Equity / sales rev. (share, not %)	0.51	0.37	0.58	0.47	0.64	0.42	0.70	0.44	0.76	0.46	0.82	0.42	0.88	0.42	0.80	0.39
Profit / equity	7.70	14.33	6.72	10.27	4.10	8.61	2.24	8.11	2.09	7.89	1.96	7.35	3.26	9.18	7.36	11.89
Profit + taxes / equity	23.13	26.81	23.3	21.85	17.71	19.34	14.87	18.16	14.20	17.53	12.6	16.95	13.34	18.66	17.97	21.77
Taxes / equity	15.43	12.48	16.58	11.58	13.61	10.73	12.63	10.05	12.11	9.64	10.64	9.60	10.08	9.48	10.61	9.88
Taxes / adjusted equity	21.27		20.46		20.74		20.09		20.01		20.77		21.12		21.76	

1. *SOE profit adjusted for financial charges and depreciation, relative to sales revenue* = SOE profit / sales revenue + (SOE financial charges / sales revenue - non-SOE financial charges / sales revenue) + (SOE depreciation / sales revenue - non-SOE depreciation / sales revenue)
Example 1993: 6.16 = 3.89 + (2.44-2.08) + (4.29-2.38)

	6.16		8.18		7.12		6.92		6.83		7.32		8.19		11.11	

2.a. *SOE adjusted profit relative to SOE adjusted equity* = (SOE adjusted profit / sales revenue) / (non-SOE equity /sales revenue)
Example 1993: 16.65 = 6.16 / 0.37

	16.65		17.40		16.95		15.73		14.85		17.43		19.50		28.49	
Compare: non-SOE profit / equity		14.33		10.27		8.61		8.11		7.89		7.35		9.18		11.89

2.b. *SOE taxes and adjusted profit relative to SOE adjusted equity* = SOE adjusted profit / adjusted equity + SOE taxes / adjusted equity
Example 1993: 37.92 = 16.65 + 21.27 [where 21.72 = 15.43 * 0.51 / 0.37]

	37.92		37.86		37.69		35.82		34.86		38.20		40.62		50.25	
Compare: non-SOE taxes+profit / equity		26.81		21.85		19.34		18.16		17.53		16.95		18.66		21.77

Sales revenue is net of sales-related taxes.
Sources (non-SOE data are obtained as the difference between all directly reporting industrial enterprises and SOEs):
Profit / sales revenue, profit / equity, profit + taxes / equity: see Tables 6.1 and 6.2.
SOE financial charges / sales revenue, SOE depreciation / sales revenue: see Table 3.2.
Equity: *Statistical Yearbook 1994*, pp. 381; *1995*, pp. 381; *1996*, p. 391; *1997*, p. 416; *1998*, p. 426; *1999*, p. 446; *2000*, p. 434; *2001*, p. 412.
Directly reporting industrial enterprises: Financial charges: *Statistical Abstract 1994*, p. 86; *1995*, p. 86; *Industrial Census 1995*, Vol. 1, p. 51; *Statistical Abstract 1997*, 106; *1998*, p. 112; *1999*, p. 108; *2000*, p. 113; *2001*, pp. 124. Average annual net fixed assets: *Statistical Yearbook 1994*, p. 379; *1995*, p. 390; *1996*, p. 415; *1997*, p. 425; *1998*, p. 445; *1999*, p. 433; *2000*, p. 415; *2001*, p. 411. The non-SOE depreciation rate was assumed to be the same as the one of SOEs.

enterprises are available. In 1995, profit per unit of equity in SOEs stood at 4.10%, compared with the six-fold higher level of 24.58% in private enterprises (Table 6.3). Adjusting the equity of SOEs such that the ratio of equity to sales revenue in SOEs is the same as in private enterprises leads to a return on equity of 7.72% in SOEs compared with 24.58% in private enterprises; the ratio of profit and circulation taxes relative to adjusted equity in SOEs in 1995 was 33.34% compared with 37.24% in private enterprises. If one considers all implications of imposing the same capital intensity on SOEs as private enterprises enjoy, i.e., if one also considers adjustments to financial charges and depreciation, adjusted SOE profit relative to equity in 1995 at 24.82% was equal to that of private enterprises (24.58%); SOE profit plus circulation taxes relative to equity in 1995 stood at 45.56% compared with that of private enterprises at 37.24%.[135]

In other words, once SOE profitability is adjusted to take into account SOEs' higher capital intensity, private enterprises no longer outperform SOEs. By 2000, the original twenty percentage point gap between private enterprise and SOE profit relative to equity had shrunk to just seven percentage points (unadjusted, Table 6.4). The adjusted SOE profitability is thus likely to exceed by far private enterprises' profitability level in 2000, a year for which not enough data on private enterprises are available to repeat the calculations.

Causes of High SOE Capital Intensity

With the profitability gap between SOEs and non-SOEs or private enterprises more than accounted for solely by SOEs' higher capital intensity, the issue of capital intensity in turn requires further examination. The data

---

[135] The calculation procedure is exactly the same as previously for non-SOEs. The ratio of SOEs' vs. private enterprises' equity relative to sales revenue in 1995 was 1.88. SOEs' liability-asset ratio was assumed to equal that of the private enterprises (SOEs' actual ratio was 0.6581; that of private enterprises 0.5861). SOEs' ratio of net fixed assets to assets was also assumed to equal that of the private enterprises (SOEs' actual ratio was 0.4500; that of private enterprises 0.3040); given the discrepancy in actual data, this assumption works to the detriment of adjusted SOE profitability. For the data, see *Industrial Census 1995*, Vol. 1, pp. 46–53.

reveal that SOEs are more capital intensive than are non-SOEs on an industry-by-industry basis. Across the close to forty industrial sectors in China, the mean ratio of assets to sales revenue is significantly higher for SOEs than for non-SOEs at the 0.1% significance level throughout all years for which the data are available, 1993 through 1997, and 1999 and 2000 (Table 6.7). Assets can be further broken down into current assets and net fixed assets. The SOE mean ratio of current assets to sales revenue is also significantly higher than the non-SOE mean ratio of current assets to sales revenue, and the same is true for the ratio of net fixed assets to sales revenue.

As regards current assets, SOEs are not "punished" twice by having a higher average ratio of current assets to sales revenue than non-SOEs and then being predominantly located in the sectors with the highest ratios. A high ratio of SOE current assets to sales revenue in a particular industrial sector implies that the SOE market share in the particular industrial sector is small; it also means that the contribution of SOE sales revenue in the particular industrial sector to aggregate SOE sales revenue is small (Table 6.7). These outcomes suggest that SOE exhibit market-oriented behavior.

In terms of net fixed assets relative to sales revenue, however, the higher the SOE ratio of net fixed assets to sales revenue, the larger the SOE market share; the higher the non-SOE ratio, the smaller the non-SOE market share. Non-SOEs thus appear to stay clear of those industrial sectors in which a large volume of fixed assets is required relative to sales revenue, while SOEs dominate in those industrial sectors. This points to a historical interpretation. The SOE market share may have become eroded by new entrants in the sectors in which the fixed asset requirement is low. SOEs, predominantly a mature group of enterprises with no or very few new entrants, continue to provide the bulk of industrial output in fixed asset intensive industrial sectors in which non-SOEs do not wish to, are unable to, or are prohibited to tread.[136]

---

[136] The correlation coefficients for relationships involving the total assets of SOEs are far more ambiguous in terms of significance levels and years in which the correlation coefficients are significant, presumably due to the different patterns of relationships of current vs. net fixed assets (both relative to sales revenue) with the market share or the contribution to aggregate SOE sales revenue. Since nothing is gained by presenting the correlation coefficients involving total assets of SOEs, they are not reported in Table 6.7.

What causes the higher capital intensity in SOEs? If the larger volume of current assets relative to sales revenue in SOEs reflects a relatively large volume of financial investments, then these current assets may lead to non-business revenue. If the return on these financial assets is lower than the return on productive activities, the overall return on equity for SOEs is lowered. But current assets related to *productive* activities are also relatively high in SOEs. Thus, in 1997, net accounts receivable for SOEs were equivalent to 20.61% of (unadjusted) sales revenue, compared to 16.37% for non-SOEs; in 2000 the two percentages were still different at 19.27% compared with 15.50% (*Statistical Abstract 1998*, p. 112; *2001*, pp. 24f.). The higher net accounts receivable imply higher financial charges if accounts receivable are financed through bank loans, thus reducing profit. It seems that customers of SOEs, perhaps primarily the state commercial system, have a particularly poor payment history. Similarly, inventories relative to sales revenue are larger for SOEs than for non-SOEs.[137]

If the larger volume of net fixed assets relative to sales revenue simply reflects the prevalence of excessive fixed assets and thus a low degree of capacity utilization (perhaps due to poor planning in previous years), the current limitations on the disposition of fixed assets may be too restrictive.[138] On the other hand, management may have incentives to prefer the accumulation of fixed assets over the creation of profit. Second, the larger volume of fixed assets could also reflect under-depreciated fixed assets and thus represent a historical burden that needs to be written off. A third consideration is that a relatively large share of SOEs' fixed assets are non-productive. In 1985, 34.57% of fixed asset investment by *all* state-owned units across the economy was in non-productive fixed assets,

---

[137] In 1997, inventories of materials, semi-finished goods and finished products as a share of (unadjusted) sales revenue were 27.37% in SOEs compared with 22.51% in non-SOEs; inventories of finished products alone stood at 10.19% compared with 9.66% (*Statistical Abstract 1998*, p. 112). In 2000, inventories of finished products were roughly equal at 8.16% compared with 8.25% (*Statistical Abstract 2001*, pp. 124f.; data on all inventories are not available).

[138] Data on capacity utilization in SOEs compared with non-SOEs are not available. It is thus impossible to determine whether capacity utilization is consistently lower in SOEs than in non-SOEs. SOEs' and non-SOEs' capacity utilization clearly moves in step. The ratio of net fixed assets to sales revenue for both groups rose in 1989–1990, fell in the early 1990s, and rose again in the mid-1990s.

compared with 24.72% in collective-owned units; in 1992, the last year for which such data are available, the two percentages were 30.06% and 16.16%.[139] Half of this non-productive fixed asset investment was in housing. In other words, some of industrial SOEs' fixed assets reflect employee welfare and housing benefits for the use of which employees are unlikely to pay market prices (if they pay at all). If these assets were sold off at market prices and the corresponding amount of liabilities repaid, SOE profitability would immediately improve.

In as far as the higher capital intensity of SOEs is due to policy factors, the hypothetical adjustments to SOE profitability undertaken above are necessary to achieve a fair comparison of SOE and non-SOE profitability. Once the higher capital intensity is accounted for, SOE profitability exceeds that of non-SOEs. Similarly, in as far as non-SOEs do not choose to venture into industrial sectors that have a high fixed asset requirement relative to sales revenue, SOEs may simply be operating in these sectors for historical reasons, with government decisions on industrial structure and product pricing possibly taking precedence over profitability-oriented production decisions by SOEs.[140]

---

[139] See *Statistical Yearbook 1993*, pp. 150, 200. Apart from data on fixed asset investment by state-owned and collective-owned units, only economy-wide data are available. Percentages for the economy-wide data are slightly above those of state-owned units, but appear inappropriate for comparison since they include the real estate sector and housing investment by farmers.

Some provincial statistical yearbooks occasionally carry data on industrial SOEs' productive vs. non-productive fixed assets (measured in original values). Thus, in 1992, non-productive fixed assets accounted for 20.89% of all net fixed assets of industrial SOEs across four provinces, with the percentage obtained as the arithmetic mean across the four provinces. In 1993, the percentage was 27.89% (6 provinces); in 1994, 27.92% (5); in 1995, 22.09% (5); in 1996, 28.01% (5); in 1997, 23.54% (5); in 1998, 19.85% (4); in 1999, 15.15% (3); and in 2000, 28.74% (4).

[140] In 2000, the SOE ratio of net fixed assets to sales revenue is not significantly correlated across the 37 industrial sectors with the SOE return on equity (at the 10% significance level), nor is the market share if the monopoly sector of petroleum extraction is omitted due to its extremely high return on equity. If low SOE profitability in capital-intensive sectors with a high SOE market share were not due to government policy decisions, such as on product pricing, fierce competition among SOEs could be driving prices and thereby profitability down. Non-SOEs may not wish to enter these excess capacity sectors, while SOEs are limited in their possibility to exit the sector and may find no market in which to sell any excessive assets.

Conclusions

Privatization is often regarded as a cure for the many ailments of SOEs. Yet time series data reveal that, in China, non-SOEs fared little better over time than did SOEs. Non-SOEs' profitability deteriorated as drastically as SOE profitability, following the same cyclical patterns. What distinguishes non-SOEs from SOEs is a rather constant profitability gap in favor of non-SOEs across all years. For private enterprises, the gap is particularly large in 1995 but it narrows significantly in the following years.

Time series data furthermore reveal that the gap is smaller when the numerator of profitability consists of profit plus taxes, rather than profit alone. The gap is also smaller when sales revenue rather than equity is used in the denominator. SOEs outperform non-SOEs when profit plus taxes relative to sales revenue are considered. Circulation taxes and capital intensity more than explain the profitability gap between SOEs and non-SOEs (as well as, separately, between SOEs and private enterprises). The high capital intensity implies that a given amount of sales revenue needs to pay for twice as much borrowing and depreciation (reducing profit directly) and that the residual accounting profit constitutes the return on twice as much equity (reducing the ratio of profit per unit of equity).

SOEs do not appear to pursue a high degree of capital intensity as objective in itself. The higher the ratio of current assets to sales revenue in a particular industrial sector, the smaller the SOE market share in that sector, and the smaller the contribution of this sector to the sales revenue of all industrial SOE. Current assets are relatively large in SOEs for such reasons as a high ratio of net accounts receivable to sales revenue; customers of SOEs have an especially poor payment history.

The higher the ratio of net fixed assets to sales revenue in a particular industrial sector, the larger the SOE market share in that sector. SOEs could have a large volume of net fixed assets due to policy reasons, such as governments and their planners issuing accumulation targets to enterprise managers. But perhaps one-third of these net fixed assets are non-productive, a share that is much higher than in non-SOEs; non-productive assets such as employee housing may not earn a return that is comparable to the return that would be achieved in the market.[141]

In as far as high circulation taxes and the high capital intensity are historical legacies or the result of enduring SOE-specific policies, SOEs cannot be blamed for the profitability gap. If SOE capital intensity were the same as that in non-SOEs, SOE profit relative to equity would exceed non-SOE profitability in all years. SOE profitability would match the profitability of private enterprises in 1995, the year in which private enterprises performed particularly well. Once the SOEs' higher tax burden is considered, SOEs by far outperform non-SOEs.

SOEs are further exonerated by three selection biases. The group of private enterprises is likely to comprise only the best performing private enterprises, since only the healthiest ones are likely to grow from individual-owned enterprises (less than eight employees) into private enterprises, and then since 1998 to a sufficiently large size for them to be included in the detailed statistics. Aggregate SOE profitability, on the other hand, is relatively low in part due to the fact that the worst SOEs do not necessarily exit (for policy reasons), while the best SOEs between 1993 and 1997 all too often turned into companies or joint ventures that were no longer counted as SOEs. (Since 1998, the latter factor has been redressed.)

Deducing the need for privatization from low SOE profitability is not justified. The bias in circulation tax rates against SOEs, reflecting historical factors and governmental policy decisions, does not point towards privatization as a solution to low SOE profitability. Neither does SOEs' higher capital intensity if it is due, again, to historical legacies and policy factors. The consistent selection bias against SOEs further questions the meaning of low profitability in SOEs compared to profitability in enterprises under other ownership forms.

---

[141] A positive sign is that real growth in investment in fixed assets by SOEs has been close to zero since 1993, while the industry-wide average is around ten percent. If the investment that is taking place leads to technological updating and innovation rather than further capacity expansion, SOEs could yet reduce the amount of fixed assets needed to produce a given amount of output.

Circulation taxes, in particular the value-added tax, do not automatically fall if an SOE turns into a private enterprise. A reduction in capital intensity may possibly be encouraged by privatization, but privatization is not a necessary condition (if even a sufficient one). Privatization furthermore appears a gamble. China's industrial SOEs currently operate in a historically created institutional and political framework. They constitute the core of China's industrial sector. In 2001, private enterprises, i.e., individual-owned enterprises with more than seven employees and with annual sales revenue in excess of 5m RMB, accounted for just 5.19% of the value-added of all industrial enterprises with annual sales revenue in excess of 5m RMB, compared with the 54.26% of the state-owned and state-controlled enterprises. Across-the-board privatization would mean the creation of utterly new privately controlled and often large enterprises for which there is virtually no precedent in China today.

7
Profitability across Industrial SOEs

In contrast to the causes of the decline in industrial SOE profitability over time, the patterns or characteristics of profitability across different industrial SOEs have received little attention. Cao Yuanzheng, Qian Yingyi, and Barry Weingast (1999) as well as Robert Ash and He Liping (1998) have noted that large industrial SOEs tend to be more profitable than medium-sized ("medium") or small SOEs are. Similarly, centrally owned ("central") SOEs have a higher profit rate than do locally owned ("local") SOEs (Robert Ash and He Liping, 1998). Song Qun et al. (1992) tried to identify qualitatively the loss patterns in 1987 through price changes, size, sectoral, and regional characteristics. Systematic, including quantitative analysis, however, is still lacking.

The available data on industrial SOEs allow identification of profitability patterns according to (i) industrial sector, (ii) location, (iii) size, and (iv) ownership level. In a perfectly competitive economy, none of these factors should matter for enterprise profitability. The industrial SOE profit rate, adjusted for risk (such as different levels of risk associated with investments in different sectors), should equalize across the various dimensions. But China's economy is not a perfectly competitive economy.

Each of these four dimensions thus may have a specific impact on profitability. Different industries may face different government policies, such as restrictions on entry. Different provinces could be endowed with different regional characteristics, such as a particular quality of the labor force or different degrees of government interference in the economy. Large enterprise size could imply larger returns to scale or preferred treatment by planners. Central rather than local ownership may come with a particular administrative rank and thereby particular access to resources. Understanding the profitability patterns among industrial SOEs along these four dimensions matters in policy discussions. Patterns of low profitability may immediately suggest potential reform policies.

This chapter uses data at the nationwide as well as at the provincial level to identify any patterns along these four dimensions (sector, location, size, and ownership level). Much of the analysis focuses on the years since 1993 when the current accounting system with data on equity and value-added was introduced. The data are from various issues of the *Statistical Yearbook*, the 1995 industrial census, and provincial statistical yearbooks. Table 7.1 provides an overview of the data sources and their coverage. In the analysis based on data from provincial statistical yearbooks, only those "selected" provinces are included for which data along the two dimensions size and ownership level are available.

The 1998 statistical break in nationwide aggregate data on industrial SOEs is implemented in different provincial statistical yearbooks with a different time lag, with some provincial yearbooks not even clearly specifying their coverage of industrial SOEs, especially in 1998. (Table 2.4 provides summary statistics on the time lag.) This renders meaningful separate analysis of the years 1998 through 2000 based on provincial-level SOE data difficult. In regression analysis, the years 1998 through 2000 are combined with the 1993–1997 data and dummy variables are included to account for the different SOE coverage in the different provinces in the years 1998 through 2000. Summary data on the selected provinces are, where relevant, reported for the individual years 1998 through 2000; these need to be treated with special caution as the different SOE coverage in different provinces throughout these years is not controlled for.

The following section examines each dimension in turn, providing a theoretical argument on why the particular dimension could matter and some basic data to test the hypotheses individually. The third section uses multivariate analysis to incorporate all four dimensions simultaneously. Sector-specific characteristics are further explored in the fourth section. The fifth section concludes.

Table 7.1 Availability of Data on Industrial SOE Profitability

	Statistical Yearbook		Industrial Census 1995 (national volumes)[a]		Provincial statistical yearbooks 1993-2000[b]	
	Losses / gross profit, only 1986–1991	Profit / equity, 1993–1997, 1998–2000	Losses / gross profit	Profit / equity	Losses/ gross profit	Profit / equity
Nationwide	√	√	√	√	—	—
Sectors[c]						
Nationwide	30 sectors	39 sectors	37 sectors	37 sectors	—	—
Provincial-level	—	—	—	—	40 sectors	40 sectors
Provinces[d]	√	√	√	√	√	√
Size						
Nationwide	—	√	√	√	—	—
Provincial-level	—	—	—	—	√	√
Ownership						
Nationwide	—	—	√	√	—	—
Provincial-level	—	—	—	—	√	√

[a] Only the volumes issued for all of China were consulted; the province-specific volumes were not consulted.
[b] Only those provinces are included for which data both according to size and ownership level are available. Hainan in the year 1994 would meet this criterion but is such an outlier that it was ignored. (The ten central SOEs, of which half were loss-making, had aggregate profit equivalent to -92.74% of equity.) This leaves the following provincial observations for profit per unit of equity. (Those provinces for which data on losses per unit of gross profit are available are marked with a *.)
   1993: Beijing*, Shanxi*, Liaoning, Jiangxi*, Shandong;
   1994: Beijing*, Shanxi*, Liaoning*, Heilongjiang*, Fujian*, Jiangxi*, Shandong, Shaanxi*;
   1995: Beijing, Shanxi, Liaoning, Heilongjiang, Anhui, Jiangxi, Shandong, Shaanxi*;
   1996 and 1997: Beijing*, Shanxi (* 1997 only), Liaoning, Heilongjiang*, Anhui, Fujian*, Jiangxi*, Shandong*, Guizhou*, Xinjiang*, Shaanxi*.
   1998 and 1999: Beijing*, Shanxi*, Neimenggu, Liaoning, Shanghai, Anhui, Fujian (* only), Jiangxi*, Shandong*, Hunan, Hainan* (1998 only), Guizhou*, Shaanxi*, Xinjiang*.
   2000: Beijing*, Shanxi*, Neimenggu, Liaoning, Jiangxi*, Shandong*, Shaanxi*, Gansu, Xinjiang*.
   Coastal provinces include Liaoning, Shanghai, Fujian, Shandong, and Hainan; Beijing, although not located at the coast, is also included. (No size and ownership level data are ever available for the coastal provinces Tianjin, Hebei, Jiangsu, Zhejiang, Guangdong and Guangxi.) Central provinces include Shanxi, Neimenggu, Heilongjiang, Anhui, Jiangxi, and Hunan. (No size and ownership level data are ever available for Jilin, Henan, and Hubei.) Western provinces include Guizhou, Shaanxi, Gansu, and Xinjiang. (No size and ownership data are ever available for Sichuan, Yunnan, Tibet, Qinghai and Ningxia.) Central and Western provinces together constitute the 'interior' provinces.
[c] On the changes in the number of industrial sectors over time and their coverage of all industry, see Chapter 2. Some provincial statistical yearbooks provide data on the, in the *Statistical Yearbook* missing, sector "weapons and ammunition."
[d] In 1988, Hainan was newly included in the reported statistics as a separate province, raising the number of provinces to 30. Chongqing first appeared as a separate province in the reported statistics on 1997, raising the total number of provinces to 31. In the following, Hainan is folded back into Guangdong in all analyses covering the years 1986–1991, and Chongqing is folded back into Sichuan in all analyses covering the years 1993–1997.

Individual Profitability Patterns

In the following, a theoretical argument is presented on each of the four dimensions on why it might matter to industrial SOE profitability. Some univariate and bivariate statistics are included to provide summary measures and to show basic correlations. Once all four dimensions have been explored, individually, the next section proceeds with multivariate analysis of their joint importance in explaining differences in provincial-level industrial SOE profitability and differences in sectoral industrial SOE profitability within provinces.

Industrial sectors

The rate of industrial SOE profitability may not be equal across industrial sectors for a number of reasons. Remnants of the planned economy could lead to continuing distortions across sectors, and recent government industrial policy measures may continue to favor some sectors at the expense of others. The spectrum of distortions ranges from guaranteed inputs at fixed prices to output quotas with fixed prices, general price controls on all or parts of the output, and restrictions on entry to a specific industrial sector. Production and price controls may be accompanied by a concentration of production in very few enterprises, which may all be subordinate to a central line ministry. Petroleum and natural gas extraction, and also the tobacco industry, are prime examples of central state monopolies, except that prices are set administratively and need not reflect the profit-maximizing rule of marginal cost equals marginal revenue. Electricity prices are determined by the government at the provincial level (and approved at the central level). Other sectors, such as the furniture industry, have been largely liberalized with prices determined in close to perfectly competitive markets.

Table 7.2 shows the variation in the profit rates across different sectors for all years since 1986 as far as the data are available in the *Statistical Yearbook*. First, the arithmetic mean of the sectoral profitability of industrial SOEs is always below aggregate nationwide industrial SOE profitability, which indicates that profitability in small sectors is lower than that in large sectors. (A sector is judged to be small or large depending on gross profit or equity, the two denominators of losses per unit of gross profit and profit per unit of equity.) Sectoral distortions, if any, appear to advance the profitability levels of sectors in which a large share of industrial SOEs (in terms of gross profit or equity) are located. SOEs could also have over time expanded more in those sectors that are most profitable.

Second, while industrial SOE profit rates across sectors converged relative to the (arithmetic) mean in the late 1980s, they drifted further apart (relative to the mean) in the 1990s. Between 1986 and 1991, across sectors, the coefficient of variation of industrial SOE profitability, measured as losses relative to gross profit, fell by half. This implies a relative reduction in the distortion of profit rates across industrial sectors (relative to the mean across sectors); in other words, a gradual equalization of profit rates across industrial sectors occurred. However, the mean value of losses relative to gross profit across sectors quadrupled. The standard deviation thus rose between 1986 and 1991, but not as much as the mean. The range of profit rates across sectors also doubled in the same period. The rising standard deviation and range of values are a sign of increasing *absolute* differences in profit rates across sectors. In absolute terms, there has been no equalization of profit rates in the late 1980s.

For the in terms of price liberalization crucial years 1991 through 1993 no consistent measure of profitability is available. In 1993 through 1997, the range and standard deviation of profitability remained remarkably stable. A particular degree of liberalization might have been achieved in 1993 and was then held constant over the following years. However, because the mean sectoral industrial SOE profitability decreased over the period, while the range and standard deviation did not, dispersion relative to the mean increased. (Because of the negative mean profit rates across sectors in 1996 and 1997, and the rather low positive values in the other years, the meaning of a particular value of the coefficient of variation is unclear and the coefficients of variation for the 1990s are therefore not reported in the table.) For 1999 and 2000, the picture is highly ambiguous. In 1999, absolute variation decreased compared with 1997, but in 2000 absolute variation increased while relative variation decreased. (Below, more light will be shed on the dispersion patterns of the 1990s.)

If profitability of industrial SOEs varies across sectors due to historical or policy reasons, the effect of government interference in a particular sector on the profitability of industrial SOEs in this sector could be either positive or negative. Lacking an accurate indicator of state control across sectors, two approximations are the share of SOEs in the sales revenue of all directly reporting industrial enterprises and the share of the top three enterprises in each individual sector by sales revenue.

Table 7.2   Industrial SOE Profitability across Sectors and Provinces, 1986–2000

	Losses per unit of gross profit						
	1986	1987	1988	1989	1990	1991	1992
Nationwide aggregate	0.0732	0.0720	0.0841	0.1952	0.4733	0.4771	0.4083
Sectors							
Mean across sectors	0.1615	0.1632	0.1858	0.3877	0.7843	0.8138	
Standard deviation	0.4880	0.5147	0.4686	0.7913	1.2495	1.1794	
Coefficient of variation	3.0210	3.1530	2.5215	2.0412	1.5931	1.4493	
Range	2.6479	2.8857	2.4737	3.7419	6.6242	5.7925	
Provinces							
Mean across provinces	0.1502	0.1174	0.1167	0.2096	0.5007	0.5518	
Standard deviation	0.2482	0.1109	0.0817	0.1072	0.2121	0.2633	
Coefficient of variation	1.6518	0.9445	0.7002	0.5115	0.4237	0.4771	
Range	1.4087	0.5881	0.4177	0.4848	0.8036	1.0578	
	Profit per unit of equity						
	1993	1994	1995	1996	1997	1999	2000
Nationwide aggregate	0.0770	0.0672	0.0410	0.0224	0.0209	0.0326	0.0736
Sectors							
Mean across sectors	0.0534	0.0220	0.0185	-0.0106	-0.0126	0.0168	0.0404
Standard deviation	0.0737	0.0823	0.0688	0.0769	0.0750	0.0506	0.0872
Range	0.3415	0.5372	0.4167	0.4459	0.3867	0.2618	0.6209
Provinces							
Mean across provinces	0.0705	0.0581	0.0312	0.0111	0.0109	0.0211	0.0587
Standard deviation	0.0540	0.0578	0.0539	0.0506	0.0497	0.0400	0.0640
Range	0.2454	0.2716	0.3093	0.2641	0.2228	0.2073	0.3545

Range denotes the maximum value less the minimum value.

Not available are loss data across sectors and provinces for the years since 1992, equity data for the years prior to 1993, and sectoral and provincial data for the year 1998.

Sources: Statistical Yearbook 1987 through *Statistical Yearbook 2001.*

Table 7.3 Degree of Monopolistic Pricing Power and Industrial SOE Profitability (%)

		1995			2000	
		Profit / equity	Market share	Top 3	Profit / equity	Market share
Nationwide industrial SOE average		4.41	48.80		7.36	49.63
1	Coal Mining and Dressing	2.62	78.72	9.69	-0.59	82.74
2	Petroleum and Natural Gas Extraction	11.35	97.73	52.76	45.85	97.43
3	Ferrous Metals Mining and Dressing	-1.53	46.50	16.32	0.32	39.26
4	Nonferrous Metals Mining and Dressing	8.70	58.67	18.78	8.06	46.27
5	Non-metal Minerals Mining and Dressing	-0.73	32.06	3.47	-0.01	35.82
6	Other Minerals Mining and Dressing	4.04	40.00	21.21	n.a.	n.a.
7	Logging and Transport of Timber and Bamboo	5.22	96.58	5.73	0.89	99.37
8	Food Processing	-0.39	52.22	2.99	0.30	35.86
9	Food Production	-1.14	39.17	5.77	6.72	29.64
10	Beverages	5.99	51.86	4.52	10.96	49.22
11	Tobacco (Processing)	28.32	95.90	26.02	13.55	97.45
12	Textiles	-13.36	40.74	1.37	4.68	33.42
13	Garments and Other Fiber Products	-2.29	6.76	2.11	2.89	6.34
14	Leather, Fur, Down and Related Products	-11.91	8.94	2.23	-16.24	3.59
15	Timber, Bamboo, Cane, Palm Fiber & Straw Pr.	-8.09	19.28	3.95	-1.95	15.03
16	Furniture	-1.31	9.84	3.94	2.44	6.40
17	Paper	3.86	38.55	2.35	4.15	28.28
18	Printing and Record Media	2.22	40.95	2.56	7.84	38.79
19	Cultural, Educational and Sports Goods	2.15	11.69	5.01	3.56	6.34
20	Petroleum Processing and Coking	9.18	88.62	21.41	-0.75	91.27
21	Chemical Raw Materials and Products	5.26	57.34	7.12	2.39	50.73
22	Medical and Pharmaceutical Products	6.76	52.38	4.67	9.73	52.46
23	Chemical Fibers	3.74	35.96	1.40	6.05	55.34
24	Rubber	-1.10	41.07	9.33	-3.99	32.92
25	Plastics	-1.13	13.03	1.89	4.64	12.40
26	Non-metal Mineral Products	-0.15	33.66	0.98	0.83	31.45
27	Ferrous Metals Smelting and Pressing	5.14	71.39	17.24	3.26	75.24
28	Nonferrous Metals Smelting and Pressing	10.05	56.46	7.05	4.99	53.57
29	Metal Products	-2.76	14.85	2.33	1.34	12.65
30	Ordinary Machinery	0.62	41.63	2.95	0.93	39.46
31	Special Purpose Equipment	-1.43	52.92	3.62	-0.54	42.81
32	Communication and Transport Equipment	1.99	52.51	13.76	5.43	68.15
33	Electric Equipment and Machinery	0.03	23.33	4.95	3.74	20.04
34	Electronic and Telecommunications Equipment	6.94	25.72	9.05	11.35	37.67
35	Instruments, Meters, Cultural and Office Mach.	-2.57	34.11	5.36	1.99	23.56
36	Other Manufacturing	-7.41	10.53	3.82	n.a.	n.a.
37	Electricity, Steam and Hot Water Prod./Supply	4.60	82.55	12.03	5.75	90.94
38	Gas Production and Supply	-2.69	86.39	25.76	-1.65	78.46
39	Tap Water Production and Supply	3.45	84.72	17.72	0.58	87.64
40	Weapons and ammunition	n.a.	n.a.	n.a.	n.a.	n.a.

"Market share" is the share of SOEs in the sales revenue (net of all sales-related taxes) of the directly reporting industrial enterprises. "Top 3" denotes the share of the three largest companies (in terms of sales revenue, due to data limitations not net of sales taxes and surcharges), independent of ownership, in the sales revenue of the directly reporting industrial enterprises in this sector; data on the fourth industrial sector are highly incomplete, covering only approximately half of this sector.
Sources: *Statistical Yearbook 1994* through *2001*, *China's Industrial Markets Yearbook 1997*.

In Chapter 4, these two shares were used as approximations for competition across industrial sectors. As it turned out, the greater the competition, the lower the industrial profitability. Table 7.3 presents data for 1995 and 2000. The correlation coefficients here reflect the earlier findings across several years. In 1995, industrial SOE profit per unit of equity was positively correlated with the industrial SOE market share (SOE share in sales revenue, net of all sales-related taxes, of all directly reporting industrial enterprises) at the 0.1% significance level; the same significance level applies to the correlation coefficient between industrial SOE profit per unit of equity and the market share of the top three enterprises (in the sales revenue of all directly reporting industrial enterprises in this sector). In 2000, the positive correlation coefficient between industrial SOE profitability and the industrial SOE market share was significant at the 5% level. This suggests that government control or monopolistic market power translates into high profitability.

Two extreme cases both in 1995 and 2000 are the petroleum and natural gas extraction and the tobacco processing sectors. These two sectors in both years had the highest levels of industrial SOE profitability across sectors, and at the same time the two largest market shares (above 95%). If these two sector are omitted, the correlation coefficient in 1995 is still significant at the 0.1% level, but the significance of the correlation coefficient in 2000 disappears. One explanation could be that the industrial SOE market share by 2000 in the remaining sectors no longer reflects a certain degree of state control or monopolistic power; even if the aggregate industrial SOE market share in a particular sector is large, competition *among SOEs* could be fierce.

Provinces

Industrial SOE profitability levels may differ between coastal and interior provinces. Interior provinces tend to be less developed and more firmly anchored in the traditional planning system. This could imply a higher degree of government control over the economy and thus government-determined, relatively high profitability levels. Government control would ensure that, in the case of tradeables, these profitability levels are protected from interprovincial trade through restrictions on market access. In contrast, competition in a more market-oriented environment could drive down profit margins in coastal provinces.[142]

On the other hand, governments in interior provinces could be willing to keep loss-making SOEs alive simply to avoid sharp rises in unemployment when one of their few firms goes bankrupt; a situation of low, perhaps even negative, profitability could then prevail over a long period of time. Furthermore, due to the lower level of economic development, interior provincial governments are likely to be more strapped for revenues than the governments of coastal provinces would be. They could attempt to make up for the shortfall by levying fees and profit remittance obligations on their SOEs. SOEs then may have few incentives to strive for profit, again leading to lower profitability levels in interior provinces.

As in the sectoral analysis, average industrial SOE profitability across provinces is always below nationwide aggregate industrial SOE profitability, which implies that industrial SOEs in small provinces (in terms of gross profit or equity) are on average less profitable than those in large provinces (Table 7.2), or that industrial SOEs have over time expanded more in those provinces where they are more profitable. Throughout all years, the dispersion across provinces is much smaller than across sectors, which suggests that sectoral differences may be more important than provincial differences in explaining aggregate industrial SOE profitability.

Between 1986 and 1988, profitability levels drew closer across provinces both in absolute and relative terms (both the standard deviation and the coefficient of variation fell). But between 1988 and 1991, the absolute differences increased again while the relative differences continued to decline further (similar to the sectoral case). In the 1990s, the absolute differences remained constant, while the relative differences increased due to the falling mean, except in 1999 and 2000, when the mean rose again (also similar to the sectoral case). In other words, while there may have been a trend towards equalization of profit rates in the second half of the 1980s, profit rates across provinces did not converge further in the 1990s.

---

[142] Martin Raiser (1997b), based on a survey of 372 enterprises in 1995 (distributed over 34 industrial sectors), notes, among others, a significantly higher degree of administrative restrictions in the labor market in the interior sample, compared with the coastal sample, and concludes that locational differences outweigh ownership differences in the determinants of enterprises' financial performance.

Explaining differences in provincial profitability by their coastal vs. interior (central and Western) location appears not well justified. For example, in 1997 the three provinces with the highest level of profitability were Heilongjiang, Yunnan, and Fujian; the three provinces with the lowest level of profitability were Jilin, Guangxi, and Shaanxi. Only one of the high-profitability provinces is a coastal province (Fujian); none of the low-profitability provinces is. Analysis of variance shows that the industrial SOE provincial profitability levels in each of the three regions (coastal, central, and Western) do not differ significantly in any of the years 1993 through 1997 (at the 10% significance level).

The provincial analysis can be combined with the sectoral analysis. Profitability data from the selected provinces — the provinces for which both size and ownership-level data are available — allow a significance test on whether or not provinces are performing consistently well across sectors (using data on industrial SOE profitability in the different industrial sectors in each of the selected provinces). Applying a Friedman test to the 1997 data shows that provinces differ in their average profitability ranking across sectors (at the 1% significance level).[143] Thus, for the "typical" industrial sector, Shandong tends to achieve a higher level of profitability than do Shanxi and Guizhou; these two have a higher level than does Jiangxi, which is followed by Anhui, Liaoning, Heilongjiang, Xinjiang and Shaanxi.

Similarly, sectors also differ in their profitability levels for the typical province, at an even higher significance level (0.1%). In other words, the pattern of differential sectoral profitability holds across provinces. The higher significance level in the sectoral case again suggests that the sectoral factor may be stronger than the provincial factor in explaining industrial SOE profitability.

---

[143] The Friedman test takes one sector at a time and compares the profitability of this sector across the provinces. The province with the highest profitability level in this sector receives the highest rank, the province with the second-highest profitability level in this particular sector the second-highest rank, and so on. This is repeated for all sectors. The ranks a particular province achieves in the various sectors are added up to yield an overall provincial rank. The Friedman test compares these overall provincial ranks.

Size

Industrial enterprises come in three sizes: large, medium and small. Some provincial-level statistical yearbooks, especially in recent years, report on an expanded range of six sizes — extra-large, large(1st), large(2nd), medium(1st), medium(2nd), and small — which can then be reduced to the three standard sizes.

In the early reform period, the enterprise size classification followed the capital construction (investment) categorization of 1978. A product-specific enterprise size classification scheme was adopted in 1988 and then revised in 1992. Size categories were established for each industrial sector (or sub-sector) separately, in most cases focusing on the original value of fixed assets or the physical production volume (SEC, 5 April 1988 and 8 July 1988). In 1999, the Chinese press reported as imminent a new classification system based on sales volume, as in international practice (*China Infobank*, 19 April 1999). Yet by late 2002, the new classification system was still "forthcoming," while the old classification remained in effect.[144]

Being classified as a large or medium industrial SOE comes with a number of privileges. Some large joint enterprises in 1987 were granted extra-plan status under the central plan (i.e., separate listing within the central plan). Large and medium enterprises were the first candidates for import-export licenses in 1992. They were the main beneficiaries of attempts to resolve the triangular debt problem in the early 1990s and enjoyed preferential low interest rates on working capital loans. Two special support measures in 1991 and 1995 embraced numerous items of preferential treatment. In 1997, large and medium enterprises were listed as the main recipients of medium-term working capital loans and syndicated loans. Bad loans of large and medium enterprises heading for bankruptcy were

---

[144] The delay in the introduction of the new, sales-based classification system suggests that enterprises currently classified as large or medium, which would potentially lose their status if the new classification system were applied, are objecting to the transition. Shandong Province appears the first to have broken rank in mid-2002 when it drew up a new list of large enterprises independent of ownership and based only on the sales revenue criterion (*China Infobank*, 15 July 2002).

preferentially written off between 1998 and 2000. In 2000 and 2001, 601 mostly large, centrally owned enterprises had 460b RMB of their debt swapped into equity, thus reducing their interest burdens (but not necessarily improving their profitability since the transaction increased both profit and equity at the same time).[145]

Overall, these privileges enjoyed by large and medium SOEs should boost their profitability. Furthermore, if large size facilitates access to restricted sectors, or if government policy on restricted sectors comes with a government preference for large enterprises, and if prices in the restricted sectors are state-determined and high, then large size immediately implies high levels of profitability. Small SOEs, in contrast, may be producing technologically simple goods similar to those often produced by small non-SOEs, and could thus be subject to more competition from outside the state sector. If a large size facilitates access to rationed funding, then a large size could also imply the ability to maintain regular production and to achieve economies of scale or scope through the choice of optimal size.

On the other hand, if size is the result of overinvestment due to the traditional socialist "quantity drive" with its focus on increasing production capacity, then a large size may imply low profitability. The ever helping hand of the state may also lead to moral hazard problems. Enterprise managers, aware that the state will always come to their rescue, do not need to be concerned with the profitability of their enterprises.

The data suggest that size and profitability are positively related. The 1995 industrial census shows that large SOEs outperform all other SOEs in a number of respects. The share of loss-making enterprises is smallest in the category of large SOEs at 28.20%, compared with 34.87% and 33.94% for medium and small SOEs (Table 7.4). The distinction is even sharper for the two profitability indicators, losses per unit of gross profit and profit per unit of equity. Losses among large SOEs are equivalent to only one-quarter of the gross profit of large SOEs, but losses among medium and small SOEs exceed the gross profit in their respective categories. This implies that the 4,685 large SOEs, accounting for two-thirds of SOE value-added,

---

[145] See SPC (2 April 1987), SC (26 March 1990, 16 May 1991, 11 May 1992, 6 March 1995), PBC (18 April 1990, 6 Oct. 1997, 7 Oct. 1997), and *China Infobank* (17 Jan. 2001).

are the only SOEs that yield an overall positive profit in 1995; the aggregate profit in the 72,237 small SOEs and the 10,983 medium SOEs is negative. Similarly, in large SOEs profit per unit of equity stood at 6.42% in 1995, compared with a small negative return on equity in medium and small enterprises.

The pattern of profit per unit of equity across size categories is the same for the years 1993, 1994, 1996, and 1997, the only other years for which data according to the size classification are available for industrial SOEs. (Loss data are not available.) Large industrial SOEs in the aggregate are more profitable than medium industrial SOEs, which in turn are more profitable than small industrial SOEs, except in 1993 when small industrial SOEs slightly outperformed medium industrial SOEs.

Table 7.4 Profitability across Size and Ownership Level of Industrial SOEs, 1995

	Total	Large	Medium	Small	Central	Local
Enterprise number and output						
Number of industrial SOEs	87,905	4,685	10,983	72,237	4,738	83,167
Share in total ind. SOE value-added	1.0000	0.6885	0.1688	0.1427	0.4612	0.5387
Profitability						
Share of loss-making ind. SOEs	0.3375	0.2820	0.3487	0.3394	0.3255	0.3382
Losses per unit of gross profit	0.4900	0.2550	1.1023	1.2464	0.2432	0.7248
Profit per unit of equity	0.0410	0.0642	-0.0067	-0.0170	0.0700	0.0197
Profit or loss per enterprise, m RMB						
Losses per loss-making ind. SOE	2.1558	18.7260	5.0410	0.8122	10.0331	1.7239
Gross profit per profitable ind. SOE	2.2412	28.8424	2.4486	0.3348	19.9068	1.2154
Profit per industrial SOE	0.7572	15.4299	-0.1632	-0.0545	10.1627	0.2214

Sources: *Industrial Census 1995*, Vol. 2, pp. 16f., 20, 22.

Ownership

Industrial SOEs belong either to the central government or to a local government (provincial, municipal/prefectural, or county government). Industrial SOEs owned by the central government ("central SOEs") are directly subordinate to either a central line ministry or the State Council itself. Some of the largest central industrial SOEs report to the CCPCC Enterprise Work Committee (*zhongyang qiye gongwei*), since 1998 headed by Wu Bangguo, a Politburo member and Vice-Premier. The central government is the sole recipient of central SOEs' income taxes and profit remittances.[146]

In a large-scale decentralization of economic authority between 1970 and 1973, many enterprises previously controlled by central ministries were transferred to local governments. On 12 April 1978, in a reversal of this policy, the CCPCC recentralized key enterprises of importance for the national economy. These enterprises came under dual central-local leadership, with the main leadership exerted by the central government (*yi zhongyang bumen wei zhu*). At the beginning of the industrial reforms in 1984, authority over numerous SOEs was again transferred to local governments, but this time the transfer appears to have been more piecemeal and industry- if not enterprise-specific.[147]

Central ownership could matter for industrial SOE profitability in that the direct subordination to a central line ministry or the central government, as well as the direct link to the CCPCC, may be of advantage in overcoming physical and financial constraints. In the planned economy, a central SOE's input requirements took precedence over those of local SOEs; in the reform period, the number of materials under central control have dwindled but central control has not yet disappeared altogether. Central SOEs are more likely to be well connected to the most capable (central) research institutes relevant in their sectors. With the banking system under central control, central SOEs are likely to have easier access to external funding than would local SOEs. In general, preferential access to resources is likely to advance profitability.

---

[146] See SC (15 Dec. 1993), and FM (11 Feb. 1995).

[147] On the 1970s, see Carl Riskin (1991, pp. 197f., 343) and Wu Guoheng (1994, p. 88). On the dual leadership structure, see Thomas Lyons (1990). Systematic data on the decentralization since the mid-1980s are not available. Xiang Zhi (1995) mentions decentralization of 67 central SOEs originally subordinate to the central machinery ministry in 1984. The only evidence of a change in subordination that could be found in *China Infobank*, which includes a database on Chinese laws and regulations, concerns engineering design units in 2001 — presumably these are not part of industry (SC, 10 Jan. 2001).

On the other hand, as central SOEs lose much of their previous supply of planned, cheap inputs in the course of economic reforms, costs rise and profitability may fall. Unrestricted access to bank funds may allow SOEs to neglect cash flow and profit.[148] The fact that all central SOEs must be located in some locality and that this always requires some form of cooperation with the local government, which may only add complications to enterprise management, could also negatively affect SOE profitability.

Data from the 1995 industrial census suggest that SOE ownership by the central government has a positive effect on the SOE's profitability (Table 7.4; at the national level, ownership data are available only for 1995). In 1995, the 4,738 central industrial SOEs accounted for 46.12% of industrial SOE value-added (Table 7.4). A very similar share of enterprises in both ownership categories — 32.55% of the central SOEs and 33.82% of the local SOEs — was loss-making. But the discrepancy in profitability is striking. In central SOEs, losses were equivalent to only one-quarter of gross profit, while in local SOEs this ratio was three-fourths. Central SOEs earned a 7.00% return on equity, while local SOEs managed only 1.97%.

That both central industrial SOEs as well as large industrial SOEs tend to have high levels of profitability, compared with local industrial SOEs and medium or small industrial SOEs, appears plausible. Many central SOEs are likely to be large SOEs. (A cross-tabulation is not available.) Across the selected provinces — the provinces for which both size and ownership data are available — profit per unit of equity of central SOEs is highly correlated with profit per unit of equity of large SOEs in each of the years 1993 through 1997. The profitability level of local SOEs, on the other hand, is highly correlated with that of medium or small SOEs (Table 7.5). In the years 1998 through 2000, this pattern is not as clear-cut as in the previous years, but it still persists. For losses per unit of gross profit, the results are less sharp, both in the period 1993–1997 and in the period 1998–2000, but overall they still follow the same pattern.

---

[148] Edward Steinfeld (1998) notes the exceptional arrangements for Shougang (Capital Iron and Steel Company) which for many years faced a hard budget constraint in exchange for management autonomy. In these years, profit was used to finance investment and thereby rapid growth. Profitability and expansion collapsed once the hard budget constraint disappeared.

Table 7.5 Correlation Coefficients of Industrial SOE Profitability across Ownership and Size, Selected Provinces 1993–2000

	Number of observations	Correlation coefficient across selected provinces between aggregate industrial SOE profitability in a particular ownership category vs. size category					
		Central vs.			Local vs.		
	(Provinces)	Large	Medium	Small	Large	Medium	Small
Profit per unit of equity							
1993	5	***0.9866	*0.8751	0.5700	0.6336	0.7546	**0.8911
1994	8	***0.9163	-0.1063	-0.3968	-0.2597	***0.8367	**0.8321
1995	8	^0.9667	-0.0985	0.0277	-0.0884	**0.8215	**0.7483
1996	11	^0.9318	0.1178	0.2224	0.2156	^0.8873	0.3318
1997	11	^0.9518	0.1042	0.2286	-0.0624	^0.9028	0.5052
1998	13	*0.4873	-0.1512	0.4139	**0.5655	0.3799	**0.6530
1999	12	0.0676	**0.6113	0.1055	0.1721	0.4704	**0.6400
2000	9	^0.9574	0.4845	0.3837	***0.8463	**0.7056	**0.7329
Losses per unit of gross profit							
1993	3	^1.0000	*0.9942	*0.9930	0.9782	*0.9944	0.9430
1994	7	***0.9129	0.0143	-0.2947	0.0666	***0.8846	***0.8613
1995	1	n.a.	n.a.	n.a.	n.a.	n.a.	n.a.
1996	8	*0.6286	*0.6655	0.4300	*0.6609	0.5585	*0.6371
1997	9	*0.6628	0.2547	0.5489	0.5217	**0.6720	***0.8398
1998	9	0.0852	0.1246	*0.5920	0.5553	0.1959	***0.8215
1999	8	0.4232	***0.8899	**0.7226	0.5669	**0.7116	***0.8666
2000	6	^0.9963	**0.8834	0.6662	***0.9359	**0.9031	**0.8778

Significance levels: ^ 0.1%, *** 1%, ** 5%, * 10%.
For details on the provinces included, see notes to Table 7.1.
Data for the years 1998 through 2000 do not consistently cover the same group of enterprises in one year across all provinces. Some provinces report on SOEs in the post-1997 definition (state-owned and state-controlled enterprises), some on pure SOEs, and others on SOEs in the pre-1998 definition; for some provinces, the SOE coverage is not clear.
Sources: Provincial statistical yearbooks.

Multivariate Analysis

Multivariate analysis is possible in two variations. First, provincial-level aggregate industrial SOE profitability can be regressed on measures of the four dimensions (sector, location, size, ownership level). Second, industrial SOE profitability in a particular sector within a particular province can be regressed on measures of three of the four dimensions. (Ownership-level data are not available for provincial-level sectoral industrial SOE aggregates.)

Provincial-Level Industrial SOE Profitability

If all four dimensions, sector, province, size, and ownership are analyzed together, some of the results of the univariate analysis disappear. Table 7.6 and Table 7.7 report the results when provincial-level industrial SOE profitability (for the selected provinces) is regressed on the share of *large* SOEs in provincial industrial SOE value-added, the share of *central* SOEs in provincial industrial SOE value-added, *provincial* dummies, the SOE value-added produced in a particular *group of sectors* as a share of total provincial industrial SOE value-added, year dummies, and dummies for the type of enterprises included in the "SOE" category (needed to somewhat control for the statistical break between 1997 and 1998). The sectoral variables are aggregated into groups of sectors due to, depending on the regression, the otherwise small or even insufficient number of degrees of freedom. Tables 7.6 and 7.7 report the regression results for the dependent variables profit per unit of equity and losses per unit of gross profit as the respective dependent variables. (In the case of losses per unit of gross profit, one would expect the coefficients to have the reverse sign, compared with the case of profit per unit of equity, because it is a loss rather than a profitability indicator).

The first regression reported in each table started out with all the variables listed above, but groups of variables were then eliminated following tests for the joint significance of all variables included in a particular group of variables. Tests for redundancy were conducted in the following order, with the regression rerun if a group of variables turned out to be redundant (and was then omitted): year dummies, SOE type dummies, provincial dummies, sector shares. In the end, White's correction for heteroscedasticity was applied if needed (and if the number of observations was large enough to test for heteroscedasticity in the first place). The second regression in each table first removes the provincial dummies, then proceeds with the same tests. The third regression in each table first removes the sectoral value-added shares, then proceeds with the same tests.

Table 7.6 Patterns of Province-wide Industrial SOE Profit per Unit of Equity, 1993–2000

	Dependent variable: provincial industrial SOE profit per unit of equity		
Number of observations	63	63	73
R^2	0.9596	0.7356	0.9033
Intercept	-0.1159	**-0.2339	^-0.1367
	(-0.9191)	(-2.5822)	(-4.3385)
Share of large SOEs in provincial industrial SOE value-added	-0.0020	***0.2890	***0.1570
	(-0.0228)	(3.5330)	(3.2701)
Share of central SOEs in provincial industrial SOE value-added	0.0147	-0.0953	0.0754
	(0.2311)	(-1.4795)	(1.3698)
Provincial dummies (13; a 14th dummy for Shanxi is omitted)	^+Beijing *-Inner Mong. ^+Fujian **+Hunan **+Guizhou ***-Xinjiang		***+Beijing ^-Liaoning ^+Heilongjiang ^+Fujian *+Jiangxi ^-Shaanxi ***-Xinjiang
SOE value-added produced in a particular group of sectors as share of total provincial industrial SOE value added	**+ 1-6 **+ 8-10	*+ 8-10 ***- 12-14 ** +37-39	
Dummy variables for (i) pure SOEs, (ii) state-owned and state-controlled enterprises, and (iii) pure SOEs or SOEs according to pre-1998 definition (unclear which one)			***+ state-owned and state-controlled enterprises
Year dummies (except for 1997)	**+1993 ^+1994 *+1995 **-1998 ^+2000	***+1993 ^+1994 *+1995 ^-1998 **-1999	^+1993 ^+1994 **+1995 ***-1998 **-1999
White's correction	-	Yes	Yes

Significance levels: ^ 0.1%, *** 1%, ** 5%, *** 10%. The numbers in parentheses are t-statistics.
    In the first regression reported, all variables were first considered together. Testing for the redundancy of (in the following order) the year dummies, the SOE type dummies, the provincial dummies, and the sector shares, only the SOE type dummies turned out to be redundant and were removed (before testing for the redundancy of the remaining groups of variables). In the second regression, the provincial dummies were removed in a first step (without any test), and the same tests were then applied as in the first regression (as far as relevant). In the third regression, the sectoral group shares were removed in a first step, before testing for the joint significance of each of the groups of variables.
    Each regression was finally tested for heteroscedasticity, and White's correction was applied unless heteroscedasticity was rejected by an F-test at the 5% level; "-" implies that not enough observations were available to test for heteroscedasticity.
    The 14 provinces are Beijing, Shanxi, Inner Mongolia, Liaoning, Heilongjiang, Anhui, Fujian, Jiangxi, Shandong, Hunan, Hainan, Guizhou, Shaanxi, and Xinjiang. The eleven sectoral groups comprise the sectors 1–6, 8–10, 11, 12–14, 15 and 16, 17–19, 20–25, 26–29, 30–32, 33–35, and 37–39. Sectors 26–29 were omitted to avoid singularity; the two very small sectors 7 and 36 were also omitted, as was sector 40 on which data are only available for a few provinces. (On the individual sector names, see Table 7.3.)
Sources: Provincial statistical yearbooks.

Table 7.7 Patterns of Province-wide Industrial SOE Losses per Unit of Gross Profit, 1993–2000

	Dependent variable: provincial industrial SOE losses per unit of gross profit		
Number of observations	46	52	73
R^2	0.9285	0.2039	0.8972
Intercept	1.3450	***1.4997	^2.7595
	(0.6265)	(2.9063)	(6.4594)
Share of large SOEs in provincial industrial SOE value-added	-1.5593	***-2.4654	**-1.9924
	(-0.7812)	(-3.4462)	(-2.7214)
Share of central SOEs in provincial industrial SOE value-added	**-2.8002	***2.0993	**-1.5259
	(-2.4128)	(3.1767)	(-2.2787)
Provincial dummies (8; a 9th dummy for Shanxi was omitted)	***+Heilongjiang ^-Fujian **-Jiangxi ^-Guizhou ^+Xinjiang		*-Beijing *+Liaoning **+Heilongjiang ^-Fujian ^+Shaanxi ^+Xinjiang
SOE value-added produced in a particular group of sectors as share of total provincial industrial SOE value-added	^+ 11 *- 12-14 **+ 30-32		
Dummy variables for (i) pure SOEs, (ii) state-owned and state-controlled ent., and (iii) pure SOEs *or* SOEs according to pre-1998 definition (unclear which one)	***- pure SOEs or SOEs according to pre-1998 definition		
Year dummies (except for 1997)			***-1994 **+1998
White's correction	-	Yes	No

Significance levels: ^ 0.1%, *** 1%, ** 5%, *** 10%. The numbers in parentheses are t-statistics.

In the first regression reported, all variables were first considered together. Testing for the redundancy of (in the following order) the year dummies, the SOE type dummies, the provincial dummies, and the sector shares, only the year dummies turned out to be redundant and were removed (before testing for the redundancy of the remaining groups of variables). In the second regression, the provincial dummies were removed in a first step (without any test), and the same tests were then applied as in the first regression (as far as relevant). In the third regression, the sectoral group shares were removed in a first step, before testing for the joint significance of each of the groups of variables.

Each regression was finally tested for heteroscedasticity, and White's correction was applied unless heteroscedasticity was rejected by an F-test at the 5% level; "-" implies that not enough observations were available to test for heteroscedasticity.

The ten provinces are Beijing, Shanxi, Liaoning, Heilongjiang, Fujian, Jiangxi, Shandong, Guizhou, Shaanxi, and Xinjiang. The eleven sectoral groups are the same as in the previous table.

Sources: Provincial statistical yearbooks.

The univariate statistics suggested that the group of large industrial SOEs is significantly more profitable than medium and small industrial SOEs. This also holds in the multivariate analysis. If the share of large industrial SOEs in provincial industrial SOE value-added is replaced by the share of large and medium industrial SOEs together, the coefficient tends to be slightly less significant but with the same sign. However, if the share of large industrial SOEs in provincial industrial SOE value-added is replaced by the share of small industrial SOEs, the coefficient tends to change its sign (the larger the share of small SOEs in provincial industrial SOE value-added, the lower provincial-level industrial SOE profitability). One interpretation of this result is that the various privileges granted to large and medium industrial SOEs are indeed effective in raising the profitability of these SOEs.

Another interpretation would be that privileges may have no significant effect on profitability and large and medium SOEs enjoy higher profitability due to other advantages, such as economies of scale and scope. This appears particularly plausible because a continuous size indicator "value-added per enterprise" to replace the official size categories tends to have an equally positive and significant coefficient. But if economies of scale and scope show up in the regression coefficients of large enterprises, this suggests that other enterprises are unable to realize economies of scale and scope. In other words, restrictions such as bureaucratic constraints to entry and expansion, or financial constraints, are likely to currently be binding for small industrial SOEs.

A third interpretation of the positive and significant coefficient of large (and medium) SOEs size could be that large (and medium) SOEs are predominantly located in sectors that are strictly state-controlled and highly profitable due to the government's pricing policies. The government could choose to organize production in these sectors in a small number of enterprises in order to facilitate bureaucratic oversight. No accurate measure of state control across sectors is available. In as far as the industrial SOE market share can proxy for state control, this interpretation is justified. The share of large SOEs in a province's industrial SOE value-added across the selected provinces and the years 1993–2000 is positively correlated (at the 0.1% significance level) with the share of industrial SOEs in total provincial industrial value-added (at the 5% significance level in the case of large and medium SOEs). In other words, the more industrial SOE value-added is accounted for by large SOEs, the larger is the market share of industrial SOEs in their aggregate.

Size is a potentially endogenous variable in that the highly profitable enterprises may be the ones that expand production. Yet, a separate regression (not reported in the table) reveals that lagged provincial-level industrial SOE profitability (profit per unit of equity) has no impact on the share of large SOEs in provincial industrial SOE value-added, or on the absolute annual change therein, even after controlling for years, type of SOE, province, and sectoral shares. Size thus does not depend on profitability.

Across the regressions with profit per unit of equity as the dependent variable, central ownership does not matter. In two of the regressions with losses per unit of gross profit as the dependent variable, the larger the share of central SOEs in provincial industrial SOE value-added, the smaller the provincial-level industrial SOE losses relative to gross profit. However, in the second regression with losses per unit of gross profit as the dependent variable (the one where provincial dummy variables were omitted and all other groups of variables are then tested for redundancy and removed if found redundant), a large share of central SOEs in the provincial industrial SOE value-added implies relatively large losses. In this regression, size and ownership compete directly in explaining provincial industrial SOE profitability since each of the other groups of variables turned out to be redundant; the fact that 1993-2000 data are all thrown together without controlling for years and SOE types makes this result somewhat dubious.

The insignificance of ownership in the first set of regressions and the ambiguous sign in the second set suggest that ownership may not be such an important characteristic after all. Central SOEs' potentially privileged access to resources may not be a clear blessing. For example, a hard budget constraint could have a positive effect on profitability.

Due to the historical development of SOE subordination, ownership cannot be an endogenous variable. Today's distribution of SOEs as centrally or locally owned was determined in 1978 based on the choice of products then perceived to be of national importance. These decisions were made under a completely different economic regime in which the profitability indicator measured as profit per unit of equity did not exist and could not be calculated. No major adjustment to the pattern of subordination occurred during the reform period.

The signs of the significant provincial dummy variables are almost entirely consistent across the different regressions. Only for Heilongjiang do the signs differ depending on the regression. The expected coastal vs. interior pattern does not emerge even in the multivariate analysis. (Nor does a coastal vs. central vs. Western distinction yield three groups of provinces with distinct patterns of profitability.) Coastal Beijing and Fujian have higher profitability levels than the omitted central Shanxi, but coastal Liaoning has a lower profitability level. Similarly, interior Hunan, Jiangxi, and Guizhou fare better than Shanxi, but Inner Mongolia, Shaanxi, and Xinjiang fare worse. These results suggest either that province-specific characteristics such as provincial industrial policies affect industrial SOE profitability and such characteristics do not easily follow the central-interior divide, or that provincial profitability reflects other factors which are included in the regression, such as sectoral characteristics, but the small number of observations does not allow enough distinction between sectors.

One variable that could to some degree capture the provincial government's influence on the economy is the degree of price liberalization within a province. The third regression reported in Tables 7.6 and 7.7 was rerun including three separate indicators of price liberalization, namely the shares of (i) retail sales, (ii) agricultural procurement, and (iii) producer goods purchases in a particular province in a particular year at market prices. (These data are available until 1999; the observations for 2000 were thus omitted).

In the regression with profit per unit of equity as the dependent variable, only retail sales matter, and only at the 10% significance level. The sign implies that the larger the volume of retail sales at market prices, the higher the industrial SOE profitability in the province. In the regression with losses per unit of gross profit as the dependent variable, retail sales as well as producer goods purchases matter (at the 10% and 5% significance levels). The larger the volume of retail sales at market prices, the higher the industrial SOE profitability in the province (the lower the losses relative to gross profit), but the larger the volume of producer goods purchased at market prices, the lower the industrial SOE profitability in this province.[149] Inclusion of the price liberalization measures does not yield major changes in the significance levels of the provincial dummies and there is no switch in signs. If the degree of price liberalization were a good proxy for the interference of local governments in the economy, then the fact that the provincial dummies remain significant even after the price liberalization indicators are included implies that non-government factors, such as sectoral characteristics, are likely to account for much of the differences in industrial SOE profitability levels across provinces.

The impact of different sectors on aggregate provincial-level industrial SOE profitability was measured by including the share of different groups of sectors in provincial industrial SOE value-added. The larger the share of high-profitability sectors in provincial industrial SOE value-added, the higher should be provincial-level industrial SOE profitability. The 40 sectors were aggregated into eleven groups in order to preserve degrees of freedom. Sectors were grouped according to the similarity of their products. One of the eleven groups, the one comprising the sectors processing metals and non-metal minerals (26 through 29), was omitted to avoid singularity; two extremely small sectors (7 and 36) were also omitted, as was the weapons and ammunition sector (sector 40) on which data are available only for a few provinces. (For the names of the individual sectors, see Table 7.3.) Across the four relevant regressions, only a few groups of sectors exert a significant impact on provincial-level industrial SOE profitability that is different from the omitted sectors, and the choice of significant groups differs somewhat from regression to regression. It would thus appear that the sectoral factor does not matter that much in explaining differences in profitability among industrial SOEs. However, the small number of observations could obscure differences between sectors. The sectoral share in an individual province's industrial SOE value-added may also not be the best measure of the sectoral impact on industrial SOE profitability. This

---

[149] The fact that industrial SOEs benefit from market determined prices for their retail sales, but are hurt by market determined prices of producer goods could be interpreted as implying that plan prices for both retail goods *sold* by industrial SOEs and producer goods *purchased* by industrial SOEs tend to be lower than market prices.

share could be due to historical reasons rather than reflecting the sectoral potential in contributing to provincial-level industrial SOE profitability.

Across the regressions with profit per unit of equity as the dependent variable, year dummies for all years except 1997 are always included and always follow the same pattern. The years 1993 through 1995 are associated with higher levels of profitability than 1997; the year 1998 and sometimes the year 1999 with lower profitability; and the year 2000 in the first regression with higher profitability. This pattern matches the industrial SOE time trend discussed in Chapter 3. In the regressions with losses per unit of gross profit as the dependent variable, year dummies turned out to be redundant in the first two regressions, but were included in the third one with significant coefficients (and with the expected signs) for 1994 and 1998. Dummy variables included to account for the changing coverage of SOEs in 1998 through 2000 are significant in only two regressions. In each regression, only one of the three dummy variables is significant, which somewhat justifies the combination of pre-1998 and post-1997 data for the purpose of the regressions.

Within-Province Sectoral Industrial SOE Profitability

The fact that the ownership level of industrial SOEs has no impact on their profit relative to equity (and an ambiguous impact on their losses relative to gross profit), suggests that the ownership variable could be dropped. But once the ownership variable is dropped, a new range of regressions becomes possible. Some provincial statistical yearbooks offer data on the aggregate of industrial SOEs in individual industrial sectors within the province, but not on the ownership distribution (or size distribution) within provincial-level sectors. The lack of such ownership data appears acceptable in light of the regression results reported above. Size, on the other hand, can be approximated by value-added per enterprise. In the previous regressions, replacing the share of large SOEs in provincial industrial SOE value-added by the value-added per industrial SOE did not change the regression results, and this approximation of the size variable thus appears justified. Value-added per enterprise may, in addition, reflect economies of scale.

Table 7.8 reports the regression results for profit per unit of equity as well as losses per unit of gross profit. The profitability indicator is regressed on an intercept, the size variable "value-added per enterprise," provincial dummies, sectoral dummies, dummies for different SOE categories since 1998, and year dummies. The individual observation is one industrial sector within one of the "selected provinces" (those for which the original size and ownership variables are available) in one year.[150]

The regression results for both regressions show that size, province, and sector all matter. This implies that meaningful reform policies could target small industrial SOEs, individual provinces, and individual sectors. It also implies that, for example, sectoral characteristics cannot explain (all) provincial differences. Industrial SOEs in coastal provinces tend to fare better than industrial SOEs in interior provinces, but the divide is not perfectly clear-cut. A large number of industrial sectors differ significantly from the omitted sectors 26–29, with either better or worse performance and with almost perfectly consistent signs across the two regressions. The patterns across different sectors warrant further examination.

Sectoral Profitability Patterns

The pattern of industrial SOE profitability across sectors in the following is explored in five respects. First, what is the pattern of industrial SOE profitability in different sectors over time? Second, how important are the best-performing and the worst-performing sectors for aggregate industrial SOE profitability (polarization across sectors)? Third, what are the implications of the distribution of industrial SOE profitability across sectors for provincial-level aggregate industrial SOE profitability? Fourth, how uniform is industrial SOE performance within each industrial sector (polarization within sectors)? Fifth, are industrial SOEs in low-profitability sectors and low-profitability industrial SOEs across all sectors being reformed over time?

---

[150] Retaining the set of "selected provinces" even though the size and ownership variables are not used in the new regressions means that the results reported in Table 7.8 are comparable to those reported in Tables 7.6 and 7.7.

Table 7.8 Patterns of Within-Province Industrial SOE Profitability, 1993-2000

	Profit per unit of equity	Losses per unit of gross profit
Number of observations	2200	1681
R^2	0.2229	0.1378
Intercept	***-0.0374 (-2.7973)	^+7.0946 (5.0598)
Value-added per enterprise (in 10,000 RMB per enterprise)	*1.41E-7 (1.8772)	**2.52E-6 (2.0043)
Provincial dummies (dummy for Shanxi is omitted)	^+Beijing, *-Liaoning ^-Heilongjiang, ***-Anhui ^+Shandong, *-Hunan **-Guizhou, ^-Shaanxi ^-Xinjiang	^-Fujian **-Jiangxi ^-Shandong *+Shaanxi
Sectoral dummies (dummies for sectors 26-29 are omitted)	**+ 2, ***+ 4, ***+ 6, ^+ 7, ^- 8, ^- 9, *+ 10, ^+ 11, ^- 12, **- 14, ***- 15, ***- 17, ^+ 18, **+ 20, **+ 30, ***- 36, ^- 37, ^+ 38, ^+ 40	^- 2, ***- 6, ^- 7, *- 9, ^- 11, ***+ 12, *+ 14, **+ 17, ^- 18, **- 22, **- 34, **+ 37, ^- 38, **+ 39
Dummy variables for (i) pure SOEs, (ii) state-owned and state-controlled ent., and (iii) pure SOEs or SOEs according to pre-1998 definition (unclear which one)	**+ pure SOEs or SOEs according to pre-1998 definition	*- state-owned and state-controlled enterprises
Year dummies (except for 1997)	***+1993, *+1994 ***+1995	^-1993 *-1994
White's correction	Yes	Yes

Significance levels: ^ 0.1%, *** 1%, ** 5%, *** 10%. The numbers in parentheses are t-statistics.
In neither of the two regressions is any individual group of variables redundant (based on an F-test), where groups of variables comprise the year dummies, the SOE type dummies, the provincial dummies, and the sector dummies.

In the first regression, two types of observations were removed. First, if a sector within a province has negative equity, the profitability indicator profit per unit of equity does not measure what it is meant to represent. (For example, negative equity and negative profit lead to a positive profit rate.) All observations with negative equity were therefore removed. Second, when equity is very close to zero, the profit rate reaches a very large value, which is likely to distort the regression results. Therefore, all observations (approximately 50) in which the absolute value of the ratio of profit to equity exceeded unity (100%) were removed. In the second regression, if gross profit is very small, this profitability indicator becomes very large and a few such observations easily determine the regression results. Therefore, all observations (approximately 50) in which losses exceeded gross profit by more than 100 times were removed. If these far outliers (in both regressions) are not removed, virtually all of the approximately 60 independent variables are highly insignificant. The rules on which observations to remove were obtained by a visual inspection of the data; no other rules were explored.

In the first regression, the provinces on which relevant sectoral data for at least one year are available are Beijing, Inner Mongolia, Liaoning, Heilongjiang, Anhui, Jiangxi, Shandong, Hunan, Hainan, Guizhou, Shaanxi, Xinjiang. Loss data are available for the same provinces, except for Inner Mongolia, Liaoning, Anhui, and Hunan. The sectoral dummies for the sectors 26 through 29 were omitted. In the second regression, the dummy variable for "pure SOEs or SOEs according to pre-1998 definition" was also excluded to avoid singularity.
Sources: Provincial statistical yearbooks.

Sectoral Profitablity Trends

A cluster analysis of SOE sectoral profitability across the years 1993 through 1997 identifies which sectors share a common profitability pattern over time. Table 7.9 presents the different groups and identifies each group by its profitability pattern. Nationwide sectoral data on industrial SOEs would also have been available for the years 1999 and 2000, but only for the newly defined SOE category, with no possibility to control for the statistical break between 1997 and 1998. Year 1999 and 2000 data are therefore not included.

Between 1993 and 1997, the performance of industrial SOEs in different sectors can be summarized as following nine different patterns, where two patterns suffice to describe the development of more than two-thirds of all sectors. Thus, half of all sectors were on a low, sometimes negative, but relatively stable profitability level. Another one-third experienced a gradual decline.

An additional six sectors, apart from a residual sector, each followed its own distinct path: (i) petroleum and natural gas extraction saw a gradual improvement from a negative to a highly positive profitability level; (ii) the tobacco industry enjoyed high profitability throughout; (iii and iv) profitability in the food processing industry deteriorated rapidly, and profitability in the leather, fur, down and related products industry deteriorated gradually, both to a highly negative level; (v) the textile industry was unprofitable in all years, and increasingly so; and (vi) the non-metal mineral products industry saw a rapid drop in profitability to a moderately negative level.

Profitability in the first two of these six sectors, petroleum and natural gas extraction and tobacco processing, is clearly the outcome of state-determined prices. Although no sector-specific data are available on the extent to which prices are state-determined, the *Price Yearbook* each year contains a number of regulations on pricing in the petroleum and tobacco industries.

Following the wide-ranging price liberalization in the early 1990s, prices in the other four sectors should be largely market determined. The exact extent to which prices in a particular sector are market determined, however, is not known.[151] Price liberalization is likely to be accompanied by increasing competition, either because new non-state enterprises enter the sector (with price liberalization proxying for a general opening up of the particular sector), or because industrial SOEs increasingly compete among themselves (as the transportation and distribution system improve and profit-maximizing SOEs explore new markets and products).

Industrial SOEs in these four sectors experienced a rapid fall in their individual sectoral market share by 25–60 percentage points between 1993 and 1997 — compared to a 18 percentage point drop across the aggregate of all sectors. By 1997, industrial SOEs numbered 8057 in the food processing industry, 595 in the leather, fur, down and related products industry, 3,391 in the textile industry, and 6,529 in the non-metal mineral products industry; these numbers compare to an average across all sectors of 1,904 SOEs. In the highly profitable (and price-regulated) petroleum and natural gas extraction sector, in contrast, SOEs numbered only 52, and, similarly, in tobacco processing only 289.[152]

The instances petroleum and natural gas extraction and tobacco processing show that if the state wishes to maintain high profitability levels in sectors in which it still controls prices, it can easily do so.[153] On the other hand, it appears that as soon as prices are liberalized and the output planning system has been dismantled, profitability quickly deteriorates. SOEs in some sectors clearly fare worse than in others. The textile sector is one example. But textile enterprises under other ownership forms also fare poorly, worse than the nationwide average of all enterprises under other ownership forms.[154]

---

[151] Enterprises in many sectors still suffer from numerous minor price administration measures. One example is the paper industry, where the price of paper sold to central news organizations is centrally determined; central news organizations presumably purchase from state-determined suppliers.

[152] The number of industrial SOEs in 1997 is negatively correlated with industrial SOE profitability (profit per unit of equity) across sectors at the 10% significance level.

[153] Creating SOE profit through government pricing policies is a reversal from the 1980s, when government pricing policies meant losses rather than profit. (See, for example, Dic Lo, 1999.)

[154] The match between SOE and non-SOE sectoral profitability does not necessarily hold across all sectors. For example, in 1997 and 2000, sectoral profitability of SOEs was significantly and positively correlated with sectoral profitability of non-SOEs at the 1% and 0.1% significance level. But if the top profitability sector in each ownership form, namely petroleum and natural gas extraction, is omitted, the correlation coefficient of profit per unit of equity between SOEs and non-SOEs is only significant at the 10% level in 1997, and not significant at all in 2000.

Table 7.9   Industrial SOE Sectoral Profitability Clusters, 1993 through 1997

Cluster 1: low and stable level of profitability (positive or negative)
coal mining and dressing; ferrous metals mining and dressing; non-metal minerals mining and dressing; other minerals mining and dressing; foods; garments and other fiber products; timber, bamboo, cane, palm fiber and straw products; furniture; paper; cultural, educational and sports goods; raw chemical materials and chemicals; chemical fibers; rubber; plastics; metal products; ordinary machinery; special purpose equipment; electric equipment and machinery; instruments, meters, cultural and office machinery; gas production and supply.

Cluster 2: gradual improvement from negative to high positive level
petroleum and natural gas extraction.

Cluster 3: low-level profitability with gradual decrease
nonferrous metals mining and dressing; logging and transport of timber and bamboo; beverages; printing and record media; petroleum processing and coking; medical and pharmaceutical products; smelting and pressing of ferrous metals; smelting and pressing of nonferrous metals; communication and transport equipment; electronic and telecommunications equipment; electricity, steam and hot water production and supply; tap water production and supply.

Cluster 4: rapid deterioration to high negative level
food processing.

Cluster 5: high profitability throughout
tobacco (processing).

Cluster 6: gradual decrease in always negative profitability
textiles.

Cluster 7: gradual decrease in always very negative profitability
leather, fur, down and related products.

Cluster 8: rapid decrease from high profitability to medium negative level
non-metal mineral products.

Cluster 9: gradual decrease to high negative level, with short-lived recovery in 1994 only
other manufacturing.

The number of clusters was determined in a visual inspection of the dendogram of sectoral profitability (profit per unit of equity) across time. The choice of the number of clusters was made such that a decrease in the number of clusters would not be accompanied by merging two clusters with a large "distance," i.e., merging clusters would end before two groups with relatively different levels of profitability or relatively different profitability trends were merged. (Sectors were number-coded and the number of clusters thus not influenced by any knowledge of which sectors were being merged at any one point of time.) After the number of clusters had been determined, the characteristics of each cluster were ascertained by looking at the profitability data of all members of a cluster.
Sources: Statistical Yearbook 1994 through 1998.

Polarization Across Sectors

Industrial SOEs in some sectors consistently outperform those in other sectors. Table 7.10 distinguishes between the five and ten best-performing sectors and the five and ten worst-performing sectors out of the total of 39 sectors in the years 1993 though 1997 and 37 sectors in 1999 and 2000. The implications of the data on the ten best- or worst-performing sectors are similar to those of the data on the five best- or worst-performing sectors; the focus in the following is therefore only on the five best- or worst-performing sectors.

Profitability in the worst-performing sectors declined drastically between 1993 and 1996–1997. Whereas the five sectors with the lowest profitability levels as measured by profit per unit of equity in 1993 accumulated losses

Table 7.10 Sectors with Highest and Lowest Industrial SOE Profitability, 1993–2000

	Five sectors with highest (lowest) profitability			Ten sectors with highest (lowest) profitability		
	Share in SOE profit (in %)	Share in SOE value-added (in %)	Share in SOE employment (in %)	Share in SOE profit (in %)	Share in SOE value-added (in %)	Share in SOE employment (in %)
Sectors with highest level of industrial SOE profit per unit of equity						
1993	65.08	31.44	n.a.	75.68	42.92	n.a.
1994	79.68	38.99	n.a.	90.02	49.42	n.a.
1995	52.81	27.13	8.40	68.58	40.43	23.71
1996	121.49	35.86	11.82	145.11	50.99	24.52
1997	88.23	26.89	9.03	152.77	53.84	29.05
1999	66.58	29.08	10.52	96.13	47.17	20.24
2000	64.82	31.75	9.32	83.73	49.82	20.85
Sectors with lowest level of industrial SOE profit per unit of equity						
1993	-5.55	7.31	n.a.	-10.14	20.46	n.a.
1994	-4.41	8.26	n.a.	-6.33	12.91	n.a.
1995	-10.84	5.17	12.82	-13.45	8.90	20.32
1996	-40.02	7.68	14.56	-54.76	13.34	25.68
1997	-30.78	7.19	13.63	-45.42	12.55	24.44
1999	-7.21	6.86	12.82	-11.88	13.87	30.44
2000	-1.09	6.06	3.75	-1.48	14.13	23.94

In 1995 through 1997, the very small sector "other manufacturing" (accounting for about 0.1% of industrial SOE value-added) was among the least profitable sectors; no employment data are available for this sector. Since 1999, this sector as well as "other minerals mining and dressing" (accounting for less than 0.01% of industrial SOE value-added), for which employment data are also not available, are excluded from the official statistics altogether. No employment data are available for any sector in 1993 and 1994. Nationwide sectoral data for 1998 are not available.

Sources: *Statistical Yearbook 1994* through *2000*. Employment data are from *Industrial Census 1995*, Vol. 2, pp. 172ff.; *Industrial Yearbook 1998*, p. 89; *Industrial Yearbook 2001*, p. 61.

equivalent to only 5.55% of the aggregate industrial SOE profit, by 1996 that share had risen to 40.02% and by 1997 still stood at 30.78%. The contribution of these five sectors to aggregate value-added was stable throughout at approximately 7%.

This means that if enterprises in these five out of the thirty-nine sectors (i.e., 12.82% of all sectors) had been closed in 1997, aggregate SOE profit would have risen by more than 30%, while aggregate SOE value-added would only have fallen by about 7%. It is in terms of employment that closing SOEs in these sectors appears most difficult; the share in total industrial SOE employment at around 14% is double the output share. Within the five worst-performing sectors, two sectors, food processing and textiles, with profitability levels in 1997 of negative 18.47% and negative 15.40%, respectively, accounted for the bulk of all losses (equal to 28.36% of total profit), 6.63% of value-added, and 12.66% of total employees in industrial SOEs. (For sector-specific data on the three best and the two worst performing sectors in the years 1993 through 2000, see Table 7.11. For the data on all individual sectors in 1997 and 2000, see Table 7.12.)

In contrast, the five sectors with the highest profitability levels in 1997 contributed 88.23% of aggregate industrial SOE profit and 26.89% of aggregate industrial SOE value-added, but employed only about 9% of all industrial SOE laborers. Among these five sectors, two sectors stand out, namely petroleum and natural gas extraction and tobacco processing, with profitability levels of 13.28% and 18.16%, respectively. Together, they accounted for 69.77% of total profit and 20.85% of value-added, but for less than 4% of total employees of industrial SOEs. As noted earlier, these two sectors are state monopolies with state-determined prices.

A third sector, electricity, steam and hot water production and supply (in the following abbreviated as the "electricity sector" or "electricity production and supply") has a lower profit rate at 4.71% and is not among the five best-performing sectors, but accounts for another 41.30% of total industrial SOE profit, 13% of industrial SOE value-added, and close to 5% of industrial SOE employment.[155] Prices in this sector are determined at the provincial level (and approved at the central level).

---

[155] Apart from the three sectors of petroleum and natural gas extraction, tobacco processing, and electricity production and supply, only one other sector contributed more than 10% of aggregate industrial SOE profit in 1997. That was petroleum processing and coking at 10.18%.

Table 7.11 Performance of Industrial SOEs in Selected Sectors

	1993	1994	1995	1996	1997	1999	2000
Industrial SOEs nationwide:							
Profit per unit of equity (in %)	7.70	6.72	4.10	2.24	2.09	3.26	7.36
Petroleum and natural gas extraction							
Profit per unit of equity (in %)	-2.76	13.68	11.35	11.44	13.28	12.21	45.85
Share in SOE profit (in %)	-2.87	16.66	17.48	31.75	40.97	29.75	45.95
Share in SOE value-added (in %)	7.75	9.50	10.70	10.91	12.09	11.84	14.86
Share in SOE employment (in %)	n.a.	n.a.	3.29	2.83	3.06	3.25	1.92
Tobacco (processing)							
Profit per unit of equity (in %)	12.31	28.83	28.32	21.36	18.16	13.15	13.55
Share in SOE profit (in %)	4.34	11.19	19.02	28.53	28.80	12.62	5.91
Share in SOE value-added (in %)	5.69	6.85	7.23	8.50	8.76	7.26	6.73
Share in SOE employment (in %)	n.a.	n.a.	0.69	0.69	0.74	0.78	0.82
Electricity, steam and hot water production and supply							
Profit per unit of equity (in %)	7.68	8.01	4.60	7.10	4.71	4.49	5.75
Share in SOE profit (in %)	15.99	22.14	19.57	5.28	41.30	26.38	15.72
Share in SOE value-added (in %)	7.69	8.43	11.84	11.52	13.07	15.71	14.71
Share in SOE employment (in %)	n.a.	n.a.	4.04	4.20	4.73	6.05	7.21
Food processing							
Profit per unit of equity (in %)	2.71	3.93	-0.39	-17.26	-18.47	-13.03	0.30
Share in SOE profit (in %)	0.77	1.24	-0.22	-14.46	-13.04	-4.08	0.04
Share in SOE value-added (in %)	4.37	4.31	2.77	3.29	2.93	2.47	2.12
Share in SOE employment (in %)	n.a.	n.a.	3.55	3.61	3.52	3.07	2.77
Textiles							
Profit per unit of equity (in %)	-8.96	-5.02	-13.36	-23.23	-15.40	-3.55	4.68
Share in SOE profit (in %)	-3.81	-2.05	-9.19	-23.17	-15.32	-2.16	1.33
Share in SOE value-added (in %)	5.37	5.81	3.93	3.75	3.70	3.44	3.24
Share in SOE employment (in %)	n.a.	n.a.	10.32	9.92	9.14	8.02	7.68

Sources: see Table 7.10.

Table 7.12 Sector-specific Industrial SOE Performance, 1997 and 2000

	Profit / equity (in %)		Share in SOE profit (in %)		Share in SOE value-added (in %)		Share in SOE employment (in %)	
	1997	2000	1997	2000	1997	2000	1997	2000
Nationwide industrial SOE average	2.09	7.36						
1 Coal Mining and Dressing	2.90	-0.59	8.14	-0.30	6.07	3.62	10.98	11.53
2 Petroleum and Natural Gas Extract.	13.28	45.85	40.97	45.95	12.09	14.86	3.06	1.92
3 Ferrous Metals Mining and Dressing	-0.20	0.32	-0.06	0.02	0.25	0.21	0.40	0.47
4 Nonferrous Metals Mining and Dr.	5.58	8.06	1.87	0.47	0.75	0.55	1.15	1.11
5 Non-metal Minerals Mining and Dr.	-1.47	-0.01	-0.44	0.00	0.56	0.40	1.16	1.12
6 Other Minerals Mining and Dressing	-2.44		0.00		0.00			
7 Logg./ Transp. of Timber, Bamboo	0.46	0.89	0.15	0.05	0.91	0.44	2.70	2.46
8 Food Processing	-18.47	0.30	-13.04	0.04	2.93	2.12	3.52	2.77
9 Food Production	-2.13	6.72	-0.71	0.64	0.89	0.92	1.60	1.25
10 Beverages	10.51	10.96	8.89	2.94	2.95	2.45	2.09	2.05
11 Tobacco (Processing)	18.16	13.55	28.80	5.91	8.76	6.73	0.74	0.82
12 Textiles	-15.40	4.68	-15.32	1.33	3.70	3.24	9.14	7.68
13 Garments and Other Fiber Products	-3.39	2.89	-0.32	0.09	0.27	0.30	0.53	0.67
14 Leather, Fur, Down, Related Prod.	-20.51	-16.24	-1.03	-0.10	0.19	0.10	0.44	0.26
15 Timber, Bamboo, Cane, Palm, Straw	-8.13	-1.95	-0.93	-0.06	0.23	0.20	0.53	0.45
16 Furniture	-3.29	2.44	-0.11	0.02	0.06	0.05	0.12	0.10
17 Paper	-4.44	4.15	-1.59	0.62	0.95	0.88	1.57	1.44
18 Printing and Record Media	3.76	7.84	1.30	0.71	0.83	0.66	1.21	1.06
19 Cultural, Educat. and Sports Goods	-1.65	3.56	-0.06	0.06	0.11	0.09	0.22	0.16
20 Petroleum Processing and Coking	4.71	-0.75	10.91	-0.43	5.35	5.04	1.45	1.59
21 Chemical Raw Materials and Prod.	-0.48	2.39	-1.47	2.06	5.68	5.12	7.07	7.42
22 Medical and Pharmaceutical Prod.	4.33	9.73	2.89	2.82	1.64	2.33	1.66	2.03
23 Chemical Fibers	-2.58	6.05	-0.83	1.37	0.45	1.24	0.66	0.90
24 Rubber	-0.34	-3.99	-0.07	-0.28	0.67	0.52	0.89	0.93
25 Plastics	-2.81	4.64	-0.49	0.32	0.35	0.40	0.64	0.56
26 Non-metal Mineral Products	-5.47	0.83	-9.57	0.34	3.02	2.64	6.25	5.49
27 Ferrous Metals Smelting and Press.	0.59	3.26	3.75	4.88	8.37	7.49	6.42	6.83
28 Nonferrous Metals Smelting and Pr.	-0.95	4.99	-0.96	1.47	1.86	2.14	2.01	2.35
29 Metal Products	-6.22	1.34	-1.63	0.09	0.67	0.58	1.32	1.09
30 Ordinary Machinery	-2.43	0.93	-3.70	0.37	2.92	2.43	5.53	5.10
31 Special Purpose Equipment	-3.10	-0.54	-3.72	-0.14	2.44	1.73	4.90	4.30
32 Communication and Transport Eq.	0.88	5.43	2.64	5.23	4.88	6.45	6.36	7.07
33 Electric Equipment and Machinery	-1.61	3.74	-1.15	1.02	1.65	1.91	2.45	2.65
34 Electronic and Telecomm. Equipm.	7.36	11.35	7.71	7.20	2.34	5.38	1.99	2.50
35 Instrum., Meters, Office Mach.	-6.56	1.99	-1.52	0.12	0.46	0.42	1.15	0.91
36 Other Manufacturing	-11.53		-0.46		0.13			
37 Electricity, Steam, Hot Water Pr./S.	4.71	5.75	41.30	15.72	13.07	14.71	4.73	7.21
38 Gas Production and Supply	-2.60	-1.65	-1.32	-0.22	0.07	0.20	0.50	0.52
39 Tap Water Production and Supply	1.82	0.58	2.55	0.20	1.05	0.99	1.02	1.44
Mean	-1.26	4.04	2.60	2.72	2.55	2.69	2.65	2.65
Standard deviation	7.50	8.72	11.30	7.91	3.27	3.59	2.69	2.75
Mean without sectors 2, 11	-2.18	2.57	0.85	1.39	2.13	2.23	2.70	2.73
Standard deviation without sectors 2, 11	6.49	4.91	8.47	3.03	2.74	2.93	2.75	2.81

Sources: Statistical Yearbook *1998* and *2001*.

The data suggest a classification of industrial SOEs in 1997 by sectors into three categories. Three fully state-controlled sectors, of which two are highly profitable, account for the bulk of aggregate industrial SOE profit, a fair share of value-added, but a relatively small share of employment. The state is dependent on these three sectors to support aggregate SOE profit and may well have chosen prices in these sectors correspondingly. Petroleum and natural gas prices affect virtually all other industrial sectors; tobacco prices directly affect many consumers; and electricity prices affect all other industrial sectors as well as all consumers. If the state in 1997 had ridded itself of all industrial SOEs except those in the three sectors of petroleum and natural gas extraction, tobacco processing, and electricity production and supply, the aggregate profit of industrial SOEs would have been 11.07% higher, while value-added and employment would have been reduced by 66.08% and 91.47%.

Two highly unprofitable sectors in 1997 accounted for a severe amount of losses (equivalent to one-third of profit), an average share of value-added, but a relatively large share of employment. These two sectors, food processing and textiles, would be prime candidates for enterprise closures were it not for the employment problem.

Apart from the two best-performing sectors (in terms of profit per unit of equity) or the three largest profit accumulators, and the two worst-performing sectors, no other sectors stand out. Aggregate profit of the residual thirty-four sectors divided by their aggregate equity in 1997 yielded a meager 0.58% return. Although sectoral profitability levels in this group of thirty-four residual sectors still differ, there are no easy targets for reform that would immediately improve aggregate profit.

For example, the sector "other manufacturing" in 1997 had a profitability level of negative 11.53%, but its contribution to profit and value-added was below half a percentage point (employment data are not available). Similar cases are the four sectors of (i) leather, fur, down and related products, (ii) timber, bamboo, cane, palm fiber and straw products, (iii) metal products, and (iv) instruments, meters, cultural and office machinery. Only one other sector, non-metal mineral products, had a below-average profitability level (of negative 5.47%) together with a relatively large contribution to aggregate profit (of negative 9.57%); its share in value-added was 3.02%, and in employment 6.25% (Table 7.12).

The 1997 sectoral pattern of profitability and profit suggests two reform strategies. First, the food processing and textile sectors (and perhaps the non-metal mineral products industry) should be handled as special reform cases. Turning the food processing and textile sectors into zero-profit sectors would immediately improve aggregate industrial SOE profit by 28.36%. Second, with no other easy reform target in view, all other sectors, even the relatively well performing ones, need to raise their profitability levels.

The 1999 and 2000 data show that the Chinese government has adopted exactly these two reform strategies. By 2000, the two sectors of food processing and textiles had been turned around. The absolute changes in sectoral profitability levels in these two sectors were by far the largest of all sectors, with the exception of petroleum and natural gas extraction, which experienced an even larger improvement. (See Table 7.12.) At the same time, industrial SOE profitability in all sectors (excluding petroleum and natural gas extraction, tobacco processing, and electricity production and supply) rose to an aggregate level of 3.53%.

The five worst-performing sectors by 2000 accounted for just negative 1.09% of aggregate industrial SOE profit, 6.06% of aggregate industrial SOE value-added, and, perhaps most importantly, only 3.75% of aggregate industrial SOE employment. The five best-performing sectors, in contrast, still managed to account for 64.82% of aggregate industrial SOE profit, a figure that is comparable to the 88.23% in 1997 when the volume of aggregate industrial SOE profit was pulled down by a large amount of losses. The two sectors of petroleum and natural gas extraction and electricity production and supply alone accounted for 61.67% of aggregate industrial SOE profit in 2000.

It appears that the situation in 1997 could have been much worse. In 1997, sectoral profitability across the thirty-four residual sectors was positively correlated with the sectoral share in aggregate industrial SOE profit (at the 0.1% significance level) and with the sectoral share in aggregate industrial SOE value-added (1%), but not with employment. (For all thirty-nine sectors, the same two correlation coefficients are significant at the 0.1% and the 5% significance level.) In other words, relatively profitable sectors tend to be large both in terms of profit as well as value-added. Low-profitability sectors, on the other hand, contribute much to losses but not much to value-added. Employment exhibits no pattern with regard to profitability. The situation would have been worse if relatively profitable sectors had come with a relatively small volume of profit. It would also have been worse if relatively profitable sectors had been small in terms of value-added and employment, and if the sectors with the lowest profitability levels had been large in these respects.

By 2000, these beneficial patterns had vanished. Excluding the two top profitability sectors (petroleum and natural gas extraction and tobacco processing) from the analysis shows that profitability across the remaining then 35 sectors was no longer correlated with profit or value-added (or employment). These results further hold if the electricity production and supply sector is also dropped. (If the two top profitability sectors are included, profitability is positively correlated with profit only, at the 0.1% significance level.)

The disappearance of the beneficial pattern could be due to less government price manipulation. Prices in those sectors in which SOEs have a large volume of equity and value added, relative to SOEs in other sectors, may no longer be set such that profitability in the prior is artificially high. No further evidence to explore this possibility is available.

The disappearance of the beneficial pattern could also be due to competition among SOEs in those sectors that contribute much to aggregate industrial SOE value-added and equity. The number of industrial SOEs in each sector is positively correlated with this sector's share in aggregate industrial SOE value-added in both years at the 1% significance level, as long as the two sectors of petroleum and natural gas extraction and tobacco processing are excluded. (If they are included, the significance disappears.) In other words, the number of SOEs in those sectors in which much of industrial SOE value-added is produced is large, reflecting a potential for strong competition among SOEs. Competition among SOEs could have increased between 1997 and 2000 due to such factors as price liberalization, improvements in market access with a reduction in provincial protectionism, and greater decision-making authority in enterprises.

If one is willing to treat the two sectors of petroleum and natural gas extraction and tobacco processing as special cases due to their highly monopolistic character, with direct central government control and price determination, then the earlier conclusion on the absence of a convergence of profitability across sectors in the late 1990s must be revised. The last two rows of Table 7.12 show that if these two sectors are excluded, profitability converged across sectors between 1997 and 2000 (compare Table 7.2). The relative dispersion, with a coefficient of variation of about two in 2000, is still large, but mean profitability across sectors was quite low in 2000; the absolute standard deviation in 2000 was 4.91%, compared to 6.49% in 1997.

Implications of Sectoral Industrial SOE Profitability for Provincial-Level Aggregate Industrial SOE Profitability

The sectoral profitability pattern inherent in the nationwide industrial SOE data have implications for provincial-level aggregate industrial SOE profitability if sectoral production activities, differing in their rates of profitability, are not equally distributed across provinces. Examining the selected provinces (the provinces for which data on industrial SOEs by size and ownership level are available) regarding their sectoral patterns yields the following insights.

In provinces with SOEs in the petroleum and natural gas extraction sector, the bulk of industrial SOE profit can be attributed to this sector. For example, in Heilongjiang, petroleum and natural gas extraction consistently accounted for more than 100% of provincial-level aggregate industrial SOE profit in the years 1994-1997. The same is true for Xinjiang, except that, in Xinjiang, petroleum and natural gas extraction strongly alleviates the aggregate losses. Provincial fortunes also change dramatically when a province initiates exploitation of its petroleum reserves. Thus, in Shaanxi, petroleum and natural gas extraction in terms of value-added rose five-fold between 1998 and 1999, and by another one-half in 2000. Profit in this sector in 1999 accounted for negative 108.13% of the aggregate negative profit in 1999 (i.e., made a positive contribution to profit), and for 93.96% of aggregate (positive) profit in 2000.

Tobacco processing contributed 98.92% of provincial-level aggregate industrial SOE profit in Yunnan in 1997 and 95.84% in 2000.[156] In Hunan,

---

[156] Yunnan is not part of the selected provinces as no data according to both size and ownership level are available, but sectoral data are available and they were consulted in this case because Yunnan is a major producer of tobacco (accounting for one-third of the value-added in nationwide aggregate industrial SOE tobacco processing in 2000).

in 1999, it was the largest negative contributor to negative aggregate industrial SOE profit (i.e., the largest positive contributor to profit across all sectors). In Shanghai, tobacco processing in 1999 reached 58.74% of aggregate industrial SOE profit, up from 35.90% in 1998. Similarly, Jiangxi, which had virtually no tobacco processing industry in 1995, derived 182.39% of aggregate industrial SOE profit by 2000 from tobacco processing.

In many provinces, the electricity production and supply sector has in recent years become the main contributor to provincial-level aggregate industrial SOE profitability. In Shanxi, this sector accounted for more than 60% of provincial-level aggregate industrial SOE profit in 1996, 1997, 1999, and 2000, and for negative 240.27% of the aggregate negative profit in 1998 (as the largest positive contributor to profit). Similar percentages apply to Liaoning in 1999, Anhui in 1997 and 1999, Fujian in 1994 and 1996–99, and Guizhou in 1996 through 1999.[157]

However, in some provinces, the contribution of industrial SOEs in the electricity production and supply sector to provincial-level aggregate industrial SOE profit is consistently close to zero over several years. This is the case, for example, in Shaanxi and Xinjiang. This suggests that some provinces purposefully "tax" the various industrial sectors through high electricity prices, while others do not. In the latter two provinces, industrial SOE profitability across all sectors is rather low (except in petroleum and natural gas extraction); higher electricity prices might have pushed even more sectors into the red.

The performance of the electricity production and supply sector is intricately linked to the existence and performance of a petroleum and natural gas extraction industry. Relying only on data from 2000, and switching to *all* provinces for which sectoral data are available (i.e., not limited to the selected provinces on which size and ownership data are available), shows that a large contribution of the petroleum and natural gas extraction sector to aggregate industrial SOE profit in a particular province is associated with a small contribution by the electricity production and

---

[157] The fact that only a few years are listed does not imply that similar percentages do not hold for other years. Sectoral data may not have been examined because in a particular year no size and ownership data were available and the province thus was not selected, or because profit data on electricity production and supply are missing in a particular year.

supply sector to aggregate industrial SOE profit (at the 0.1% significance level).[158] It appears that provinces which are unfortunate and do not possess any petroleum and natural gas reserves rely on the electricity production and supply sector to bolster their aggregate industrial SOE profit figures. This would make sense if provincial governments face profit targets for the aggregate of all industrial SOEs. It also makes sense from a provincial government's revenue point of view. The provincial government collects corporate income taxes on profit in its SOEs. It also collects a share of the resource tax levied on petroleum and natural gas extraction (PRC FM Tax Office, 1996, p. 131). If electricity production were concentrated in provincial SOEs, the provincial government may further be able to collect a share of profit beyond the corporate income tax.[159]

The contribution of the electricity production and supply sector to provincial-level aggregate industrial SOE profit is also somewhat correlated, negatively, with the industrial SOE market share in a province (at the 5% significance level).[160] A province appears thus to charge electricity prices based on the share of the non-state economy in the province — the larger the non-state economy, the higher the electricity prices.

---

[158] The correlation coefficient is negative 0.8245. The contribution of electricity production and supply to provincial-level aggregate industrial SOE profit varies from negative 102.75% in Qinghai to positive 78.93% in Shanghai. Sectoral data are available for 24 out of the 31 provinces, but only twelve provinces report production in petroleum and natural gas extraction; data on this sector in Xinjiang in 2000 are missing. If the remaining eleven provinces were included with a zero value for profit contribution, the correlation coefficient is still significantly negative at the same significance level.

[159] Even though electricity prices are set by the province — as the regular requests by provincial price bureaus to the State Planning Commission for approval of their new price schemes, documented across numerous issues of the *Price Yearbook*, attest — the central government was responsible for 72.25% of all *investment* in electricity production and supply in 1998 (*Investment Yearbook 1999*, p. 68), the latest year for which these data are available, up from 69.35% in 1996 (*Investment Yearbook 1997*, p. 64), the first year for which they are available. One reason for this large central share could be the Three Gorges project, but no further details are given in the statistics. The fact that provinces set electricity prices, on the other hand, suggests that electricity *production* occurs in SOEs under provincial control.

[160] The market share is calculated as the industrial SOE share in sales revenue of all directly reporting industrial enterprises in a particular province. (Data on sales-related taxes are not available for all provinces; these have therefore not been subtracted out.)

Switching back to the selected provinces over the period 1993–2000, the food processing and textile sectors which, nationwide, until 1999, were among the five worst performers, invariably have a negative effect on provincial-level aggregate industrial SOE profit across all provinces. However, these two sectors rarely have a negative effect on profit on a similar scale as the positive effect of the three high-profit sectors.

The contribution of individual sectors to provincial-level aggregate industrial SOE profit in a particular province tends to vary over the years. Some of this variation could be due to the introduction of new production processes in a particular sector or to the exit of loss-making enterprises. However, it may also reflect government pricing policies, which immediately change the profitability of individual sectors and, in the longer run through their impact on the incentive structure, affect investment plans.

One example is the petroleum and natural gas extraction sector, which was not particularly profitable in any of the selected provinces in 1993, but then became a top contributor to provincial-level aggregate industrial SOE profit in 1994. The change in the volume of profit between 1993 and 1994 coincided with an approximate doubling of ex-factory prices for raw petroleum and petroleum end-products (such as gasoline) in April 1994.[161]

The continued importance of the three sectors of petroleum and natural gas extraction, tobacco processing, and electricity production and supply for aggregate industrial SOE profit is conspicuous. These three sectors in 2000 still accounted for 67.58% of nationwide aggregate industrial SOE profit. In all three sectors, prices are state-determined (at the central level for the first two, and the provincial level for the third) and in all three sectors SOEs had a market share above 90%, suggesting restrictions on market access. (See Tables 7.12 and 7.3.) To the extent that a province

---

[161] The *Price Yearbook*, where the new prices are announced, does not offer a direct comparison of previous to new prices. For a list of petroleum end product prices in 1993, see State Price Bureau (27 March 1993); for the corresponding list in 1994, see SPC (27 April 1994). The 1994 prices across the whole range of products are close to double the 1993 prices. For raw petroleum, no 1993 price could be found; the "general" price (*pingjia*) of raw petroleum in 1991 was 205 RMB per ton (*Price Yearbook 1992*, p. 34); in 1994, it was set at 700 RMB (SC, 23 April 1994).

enjoys petroleum and natural gas reserves, or manages to set up tobacco processing facilities, aggregate industrial SOE profit in this province is high. Similarly, to the extent that a province manipulates electricity prices, it can control provincial-level aggregate industrial SOE profit.

Polarization Within Sectors

Profitability differs not only between sectors, but also between individual enterprises within one sector. Nationwide sectoral data from the 1995 industrial census show that losses in a particular sector are positively correlated with gross profit in the same sector, at the 5% significance level. (The same pattern holds across provinces, at the 1% significance level.) In other words, sectors with a relatively large volume of gross profit at the same time incurred relatively large losses; sectors with a relatively small volume of profit also had relatively small losses.[162]

The same pattern holds across sectors in the selected provinces for most years. Proceeding year by year in the period 1993-2000 and using data on all sectors in the selected provinces, gross profit in a particular sector is positively correlated with losses in this sector in 1994 (at the 0.1% significance level), 1995 (0.1%), 1996 (0.1%), 1997 (0.1%), 1998 (5%), 1999 (0.1%), and 2000 (1%).[163] This polarization within each sector suggests a severe lack of exit. If loss-making enterprises were allowed to exit freely, all correlation would disappear as the loss-making enterprises closed.

---

[162] In the sectoral case the two sectors of petroleum and natural gas extraction and tobacco processing were omitted; if they were included, the positive correlation would be even more significant. In the provincial case, one outlier, Yunnan, was removed; if it were included, the correlation coefficient would change its sign.

The same pattern also holds per enterprise (at the 5% significance level across sectors and the 1% level across provinces). The higher the losses per loss-making SOE in a particular sector (province), the higher the (gross) profit per profitable SOE.

[163] The number of observations varies from year to year, depending on the number of selected provinces (those provinces for which size and ownership data are available) and on the number of sectors in each province on which profit and loss data are available, but it is usually around two hundred. Gross profit per profitable enterprise is positively correlated with losses per loss-making enterprise in 1995 (0.1%), 1996 (0.1%), 1997 (10%), and 1998 (10%).

Performance and Exit

The fact that across many industrial sectors highly profitable and highly loss-making enterprises co-exist suggests a lack of enterprise exit. Yet, a lack of exit does not imply the absence of any form of exit. The nationwide data that are available for the years 1993–1997 and 1999–2000 suggest that, perhaps since 1996, loss-making enterprises are indeed systematically closed. Without data on individual enterprises, one hypothesis is the following. In the sectors or provinces with the lowest profitability levels, the worst performing enterprises should close. Their closure should then reduce the share of this sector's (province's) SOE value-added in the nationwide aggregate industrial SOE value-added, and the number of SOEs in the particular sector (province) itself.[164]

The aggregate industrial SOE profitability level in a particular sector in 1996 is, as expected, positively correlated with the relative change in that sector's share of economy-wide industrial SOE value-added as well as that sector's number of SOEs in 1997 over 1996 (at the 1% and 5% significance level). The same results across sectors are obtained for year 1999 profitability with the changes in the two indicators in 2000 over 1999 (at the 5% significance level for both indicators); 1998 sectoral or provincial industrial SOE data are not available. In no other year is there any significant correlation, and across provinces only the 1993 profitability level is significantly (positively) correlated with the 1994 over 1993 relative change in the market share.

The significant correlation coefficients for the recent years show that highly loss-making industrial SOEs are closed at some point in time, although not necessarily in a very timely manner. Provincial-level data on five provinces that report separate data on profitable vs. loss-making industrial SOEs for 1998 through 2000 allow further conclusions on the exit of loss-making industrial SOEs. Table 7.13 shows that profit and value-added per profitable industrial SOE increased significantly between 1998 and 2000 in all five provinces. Losses per loss-making industrial SOE, on the other hand, tended to stagnate; with value-added per loss-making

---

[164] A counterargument would be that profitable SOEs in a sector or province could expand production, or that new SOEs could be established.

enterprise increasing in all provinces, losses per unit of value-added in loss-making enterprises fell. It appears that loss-making enterprises unsuccessfully attempted to reduce their losses by increasing their output (losses per enterprise remained stable). But at least losses per unit of value-added did not increase; in two provinces, Heilongjiang and Shandong, losses even fell relative to value-added.

In three provinces (Shanxi, Inner Mongolia, and Shaanxi) losses per unit of value-added in loss-making enterprises were significantly higher than profit per unit of value-added in profitable enterprises, while profit or losses per laborer were approximately the same in absolute values. These enterprises should be prime candidates for reform, but reform may be difficult due to the relatively large number of employees in loss-making enterprises (relative to value-added).

Conclusions

In a perfectly competitive economy, factors such as ownership level, size, location, and industrial sector should not determine enterprise profitability. But China's economy is not a perfectly competitive economy. While univariate analysis suggests that each of these factors matters for industrial SOE profitability, the multivariate analysis shows that the ownership level has either no, or an ambiguous impact on profitability. Size, location, and industrial sector, however, matter.

The fact that being categorized as a 'large' industrial SOE implies relatively high profitability could have several explanations. Large industrial SOEs may enjoy numerous privileges in comparison to small industrial SOEs. Small industrial SOEs may be unable to realize economies of scale and scope, perhaps due to the lack of well-functioning capital markets. Or large industrial SOEs could be predominantly located in sectors where prices tend to be state-controlled at a level that yields a high rate of profitability. (SOEs could be large in order to facilitate government control.) While the regression results at first sight justify the Chinese government's attempt to form numerous large conglomerates, if size implies profitability due solely to administrative decisions such as on prices or entry rules, the rationale for forming conglomerates will disappear as (if) the economy is liberalized further.

Table 7.13 Profitable vs. Loss-making Industrial SOEs, Selected Provinces 1998–2000

	Profitable industrial SOEs			Loss-making industrial SOEs		
	1998	1999	2000	1998	1999	2000
Per industrial SOE						
Shanxi						
Profit (m RMB)	1.35	2.60	2.52	-4.81	-5.35	-4.24
Value-added (m RMB)	10.38	15.51	19.19	11.64	13.16	12.14
Laborers	n.a.	n.a.	703	n.a.	n.a.	872
Inner Mongolia						
Profit (m RMB)	2.09	1.37	4.59	-6.07	-3.94	-8.43
Value-added (m RMB)	15.70	16.26	35.37	6.45	11.92	11.69
Laborers	n.a.	n.a.	n.a.	n.a.	n.a.	n.a.
Heilongjiang						
Profit (m RMB)	11.06	21.60	61.47	-6.25	-4.43	-7.46
Value-added (m RMB)	44.58	70.62	102.15	8.38	6.88	17.24
Laborers	672	961	964	1041	888	1152
Shandong						
Profit (m RMB)	4.56	5.82	15.12	-3.65	-4.65	-4.28
Value-added (m RMB)	38.23	42.60	52.94	4.89	6.79	18.37
Laborers	1033	970	918	545	616	750
Shaanxi						
Profit (m RMB)	2.38	3.88	8.47	-4.88	-4.93	-4.30
Value-added (m RMB)	17.44	26.20	31.98	4.38	5.02	5.23
Laborers	646	715	740	641	625	523
Reference ratios						
Shanxi						
Profit / value-added (in %)	13.04	16.76	13.11	-41.31	-40.69	-34.90
Profit / laborer (th. RMB)			3.58			-4.86
Value-added / laborer (th. RMB)			27.29			13.93
Inner Mongolia						
Profit / value-added (in %)	13.31	8.41	12.97	-94.17	-33.05	-72.16
Profit / laborer (th. RMB)						
Value-added / laborer (th. RMB)						
Heilongjiang						
Profit / value-added (in %)	24.80	30.59	60.18	-74.61	-64.41	-43.25
Profit / laborer (th. RMB)	16.45	22.48	63.74	-6.01	-4.99	-6.47
Value-added / laborer (th. RMB)	66.34	73.50	105.93	8.05	7.75	14.96
Shandong						
Profit / value-added (in %)	11.93	13.66	28.57	-74.73	-68.43	-23.32
Profit / laborer (th. RMB)	4.42	6.00	16.47	-6.70	-7.55	-5.71
Value-added / laborer (th. RMB)	37.01	43.90	57.66	8.97	11.03	24.48
Shaanxi						
Profit / value-added (in %)	13.62	14.82	26.49	-111.23	-98.16	-82.24
Profit / laborer (th. RMB)	3.68	5.43	11.45	-7.61	-7.89	-8.23
Value-added / laborer (th. RMB)	27.01	36.64	43.24	6.84	8.04	10.00

The selected five provinces are the only provinces for which separate data on profitable vs. loss-making industrial SOEs are available for each of the three years.
Sources: Provincial statistical yearbooks.

Industrial SOEs located in coastal provinces have a tendency to be more profitable than industrial SOEs located in interior provinces, but the distinction is not clear-cut. The detailed sectoral analysis suggests that in many provinces the level of aggregate industrial SOE profit in recent years is directly a function of the accumulation of profit in three specific sectors, namely petroleum and natural gas extraction, tobacco processing, and electricity production and supply. For example, Heilongjiang's high level of profitability is due solely to the formidable size of its petroleum and natural gas extraction industry.

Petroleum and natural gas extraction, tobacco processing, and electricity production and supply are high-profit (and the first two also high-profitability) sectors thanks to government pricing policies.[165] This reflects a clever government choice. High prices in the petroleum and natural gas extraction industry affect all industrial sectors; high prices in the tobacco industry affect a large number of consumers. This indirect 'tax' on the economy is collected by a very few SOEs, in the sectors petroleum and natural gas extraction and tobacco processing mostly under central government control. All SOEs pay corporate income taxes on their profit, SOEs in the petroleum and natural gas extraction sector, furthermore, pay a resource tax to the central as well as the local governments, and SOEs in the tobacco processing sector pay a consumption tax to the central government (PRC FM Tax Office, 1996, pp. 72, 131). The government thereby secured a stable source of income. Thanks to the concentration of production in very few enterprises, the potential for leakage is minimal.

High electricity prices affect all productive activities as well as all consumers. Price determination in the electricity sector is a matter of the provinces and the data show that provincial governments use this authority flexibly; provinces without a sizeable petroleum and natural gas extraction industry tend to accumulate a large volume of profit in the electricity sector, while those with a sizeable petroleum and natural gas extraction industry

---

[165] In earlier years prices in petroleum and natural gas extraction and in tobacco processing were set such that profitability was negative. In 1992, coal mining and dressing had the largest negative contribution to aggregate industrial SOE profit, equivalent to negative 10.94% of profit. This sector was followed by petroleum and natural gas extraction at a negative 9.99% contribution to profit. Tobacco processing ranked sixth, with a negative 0.11% contribution. (*Statistical Yearbook 1993*, p. 427).

(accounting for a fair share of provincial-level aggregate industrial SOE profit) appear to not use their electricity pricing power to accumulate profit in the electricity industry. Electricity prices appear also to be higher, the higher the non-SOE market share in a particular province.

In contrast to these three high-profit sectors, food processing and the textile industry are largely liberalized sectors with abysmal profitability records throughout the 1990s. Since 1998, the central government in its three-year SOE reform program indeed focused on the textile industry, and the data show that layoffs and output reductions have allowed both sectors, but in particular the highly labor-intensive state-owned textile industry, to turn the corner. While there may be further scope for sector-specific measures in a number of other low-profitability sectors, no other sector contributes significantly to aggregate SOE losses.

The 1998–2000 SOE reform program has also affected the spread of profitability rates. Profitability in absolute terms converged across sectors between 1997 and 2000, but only if the two sectors of petroleum and natural gas extraction and tobacco processing are excluded. The decline in the standard deviation of profit per unit of equity across sectors (excluding the two sectors of petroleum and natural gas extraction and tobacco) suggests that the degree of market distortions has fallen in the past few years. Further improvements in aggregate industrial SOE profitability will have to come from reforms across all sectors. Two types of reform measures are plausible.

First, highly loss-making industrial SOEs continue to co-exist with highly profitable industrial SOEs in virtually every sector. These worst-performing SOEs could simply be closed. It appears that well-targeted industrial SOEs are already closed down, but the pace of exit could be accelerated.

Second, aggregate industrial SOE profitability in a large number of industrial sectors continues to be close to zero. Exit of the worst-performing enterprises is likely to help in most of these sectors, but this may not be enough. Reforms may have to be very broad and apply to a wide variety of factors that impact on the performance of industrial SOEs in general. The 1998 through 2000 reform program, for example, has made some limited progress in liberalizing industrial SOE employment practices, but may not have gone far enough. The next chapter examines and evaluates these recent SOE reform policies and their successes in greater detail.

8
Recent Industrial SOE Reform Policies

Industrial SOE profitability is intricately linked to government policies. In the pre-reform economy, the government "taxed" agriculture through mandatory agricultural procurement at low prices. Low food prices allowed low wages in urban industry. With the prices of industrial products set relatively high, the result was a large volume of profit in state industry. This profit was passed on to the government; it constituted the main source of government revenues. Virtually all SOE investment and the largest part of SOE working capital in return were appropriated through the government budget. Industrial production was organized in SOEs located in urban areas; the SOEs provided extensive employment opportunities and a cradle-to-grave social security system to their workers.

After twenty years of economic reforms, prices are largely market determined, transfers between enterprises and governments are mostly in the form of clearly specified taxes, and banks and the stock market have replaced the government as the main source of external funding. Yet, SOEs by the late 1990s in many ways still operated along similar lines as in the pre-reform period, with an iron rice bowl for staff and workers, an enterprise-based social security system, and government control over management appointment and enterprise operations. The three-year industrial SOE reform program of 1998–2000 was meant to change some of these practices and to move industrial SOEs further towards market-oriented behavior.

This chapter discusses the most recent innovations in industrial SOE reform with a focus on their impact on industrial SOE profitability. The following section reports on and evaluates the 1998–2000 three-year industrial SOE reform program. The section thereafter concentrates on one long-term transition goal, the improvement of enterprise management. A brief final section provides an outlook on the industrial SOE reform direction in the coming years.

The 1998–2000 Industrial SOE Reform Program

The First Plenum of the 15th Chinese Communist Party Central Committee (CCPCC) at its meeting on 19 September 1997 initiated a three-year reform program (1998–2000) for SOEs that focused on, but was not limited to, industrial SOEs. The overall reform slogan promoted by Party Secretary Jiang Zemin was "seize the big ones and let go of the small ones" (*zhuada fangxiao*). For large and medium(-sized) industrial SOEs, the reform program consisted of two major objectives. First, most large and medium SOEs were to adopt the modern enterprise system. Second, most loss-making large and medium SOEs were to "escape their difficulties" (*tuokun*).[166] Small industrial SOEs were to be "enlivened" (*gaohuo*) by any means necessary to improve their finances. Since most small industrial SOEs are owned by local governments, the central government left it up to the latter to develop specific policies. The government bureaucracy on all levels subsequently promulgated individual reform measures. On 22 September 1999, the Fourth Plenum of the 15th CCPCC confirmed the various central government reform measures with a comprehensive SOE reform decision.

A further slogan that became prominent at the beginning of the three-year reform program was "three reforms and one enhancement" (*sangai yi jiaqiang*), namely reducing employment in SOEs while trying to create re-employment opportunities, increasing the equity of SOEs relative to debt, letting some SOEs go bankrupt or merging them with other enterprises, and enhancing enterprise management (SETC, 28 Nov. 1997). The measures, which aimed to reform large and medium industrial SOEs, to enliven small

---

[166] See SETC (28 Nov. 1997). In a visit to Liaoning Province on 18–24 July 1997, Zhu Rongji may have been the first to set the three-year deadline (Academy of Social Sciences, 2000, p. 933). A singular document explicitly listing all specific targets of the three-year reform program does not exist. Specific targets are scattered across numerous government and ministerial circulars.

industrial SOEs, and to implement the three reforms, are described and evaluated in this section. Enhancing enterprise management is discussed in the section thereafter.

The Modern Enterprise System

The focus on large and medium industrial SOEs in the promotion of the modern enterprise system is not astonishing. In 1997, the 14,923 large and medium industrial SOEs accounted for only 20.06% of all industrial SOEs, but for 85.43% of industrial SOE value-added and 74.68% of average annual employment in industrial SOEs; the 4,800 large industrial SOEs alone accounted for 70.08% of value-added and 51.01% of employment.[167] Thus, a focus on a relatively small number of industrial SOEs promised to cover a large share of production while offering clear target enterprises that could be dealt with individually.

The modern enterprise system encompasses four elements, "clearly allocated property rights, clear rights and responsibilities, separation of government and enterprise, and scientific management."[168] The State Economic and Trade Commission (SETC) published a long document outlining the various aspects of the modern enterprise system on 28 September 2000. Key to the establishment of the modern enterprise system is the gradual switch to the company system (with further details explored in a separate section below.) But no concise three-year targets for the transformation of SOEs into formal companies were issued.

By late 2000, altogether 2,919 SOEs had been selected to become formal companies; this includes the 100 industrial SOEs originally chosen by the State Council as trial enterprises, the 514 state key industrial SOEs, and numerous enterprises of importance to provincial economies. Of these 2,919 enterprises, 2,005 had become formal companies, including 440 of the 514

---

[167] See *Statistical Yearbook 1998*, p. 448; *Industrial Yearbook 1998*, p. 89. The 'SOE Escape Difficulties Research Group' (1999) offers a number of 16,879 large and medium industrial SOEs in 1997, rather than of 14,923 as the *Statistical Yearbook* does.

[168] See, for example, SETC (28 Nov. 1997) or CCPCC (22 Sept. 1999). The "modern enterprise system" appears to have been first mentioned and defined by the CCPCC on 14 November 1993.

state key enterprises, by the end of 2000.[169] The approximately 12,000 large and medium industrial SOEs which have not yet turned into companies presumably still did not have a formal separation of owners, management, and employees, or a separate supervisory board at the start of 2001.

Turning Around Large and Medium Industrial SOEs

The second overall objective, to make most loss-making large and medium SOEs "escape their difficulties," may have been at least partly achieved, if "escaping difficulties" is taken to imply turning losses into profit. In 1997, China had 6,599 large and medium loss-making industrial SOEs, accounting for 44.22% of all large and medium industrial SOEs or 8.87% of all industrial SOEs, with losses of 66.59b RMB, accounting for 80.13% of the losses of all industrial SOEs. By the end of 2000, the number of loss-making industrial SOEs had been reduced by 4,799.[170] A further 301 SOEs had stopped production.[171]

This, however, does not imply that the number of loss-making large and medium industrial SOEs had by end-2000 fallen to 1,499 (6,599 less 4,799 less 301). Some formerly profitable SOEs had in the meantime turned loss-making, so that, by the end of 2000, altogether 3,634 large and medium industrial SOEs were running losses of 41.76b RMB, accounting for 59.29% of the losses of all industrial SOEs. The number of large and medium loss-making industrial SOEs as well as the absolute volume of losses were thus reduced by only about 40% between the end of 1997 and the end of 2000. Over the same period, however, gross profit, i.e., the profit of profitable

---

[169] See *China Infobank* (25 June 2001a). An earlier article reported that 430 of the 514 key SOEs had been turned into companies, but of these 430, only 282 had become limited liability companies or stock companies (*China Infobank*, 8 Jan. 2001). The remaining 148 key SOEs that were turned into companies may have been turned into solely state-owned limited liability companies, with the authors perhaps not recognizing these as full-fledged companies that are distinct from SOEs.

[170] See *China Infobank* (25 June 2001b). On the number of industrial SOEs and aggregate industrial SOE losses, see *Statistical Yearbook 1998*, p. 448, and *Industrial Yearbook 2001*, p. 24.

[171] See Yu Xiaoyun (2001). This source claims a reduction in the number of large and medium loss-making industrial SOEs of 4,800 rather than 4,799.

enterprises, also increased, from 125.883b RMB in 1997 (and 167.584b RMB in 1998) to 311.260b RMB in 2000.[172]

Furthermore, much of the improvement might have been due to reasons external to industrial SOEs. According to an SETC research report, 70% of the rise in profit across all industrial SOEs was due to improvements in the macroeconomic environment and state policies, rather than to better performance originating in the enterprises (*China Infobank*, 25 June 2001b). Indeed, similar efforts to turn losses into profit had failed in 1996, even though responsibility for achieving concise targets had been assigned to the administrative (government) leadership in charge of each industrial SOE, with target fulfillment becoming part of the cadre evaluation. SOE management and employees were promised bonuses and threatened with penalties (SETC, 24 July 1996). (Also see Chapter 3.)

Enlivening Small Industrial Enterprises

While the central government concentrated its industrial SOE reform efforts on large and medium SOEs, reform of small SOEs — predominantly owned by local governments and in 1997 accounting for barely 15% of industrial SOE value-added — was left to local governments. Governments across China began to experiment with a host of reform measures for small industrial SOEs. These included the sale of small SOEs to their employees (adoption of the "stock cooperative" system), the merger of two or more SOEs, the take-over of one or more small SOEs by a larger SOE, the transfer of profitable production processes into new SOEs while letting the old ones go bankrupt, the leasing of complete SOEs or some of their assets, privatization, the creation of joint ventures with foreign enterprises, and bankruptcy.[173] Some localities began to privatize with such fervor that on 11 February 1999 the SETC issued strict guidelines on privatization.

---

[172] For the data on gross profit, see *Statistical Yearbook 1998*, p. 461, and *Industrial Yearbook 2001*, p. 24. The volume of profit for 1997 is different in the two sources; the lower value, offered in the *Statistical Yearbook 1998* (as well as in the *Industrial Yearbook 1998*, p. 52), has been adopted here since balance sheet and profit and loss account data are available to match the lower but not the higher figure.

[173] For details see, for example, Fan Hengshan (1997). Yi-min Lin and Zhu Tian (2001) provide some statistical analyses of the early stages of SOE ownership restructuring. They do not report information on the size classification of the enterprises, but presumably most, if not all, of the enterprises in their survey were small SOEs.

Economy-wide data on industrial SOEs according to size are not available for the years 1998 through 2000. But with the number of large and medium industrial SOEs in the three-year period reduced at most by 1,415 (see the discussion of industrial SOE bankruptcy below), the number of small industrial SOEs must have fallen by one-third between 1997 and 2000. In 2000, the remaining small industrial SOEs achieved a small aggregate profit of 4.81b RMB (compared to the total profit of all industrial SOEs of 240.833b RMB), which was the first aggregate profit of small industrial SOEs after six years of losses (Zhang Tai, 2001).

More recent data on small industrial SOEs are available at the provincial level. Table 8.1 reports on small industrial SOEs in those 17 provinces for which 1997 as well as 2000 data on small industrial SOEs are available. While the 1997 data across all provinces cover SOEs under the pre-1998 definition (i.e., pure SOEs, solely state-owned limited liability companies, and SOE-SOE joint operations), the 2000 data in most provinces cover the larger group of "state-owned and state-controlled enterprises," but, in a few other provinces, either the pure SOEs or the pre-1998 definition SOEs (see notes to the table). The data from 1997 and 2000 are thus not perfectly comparable in that the 2000 group comprises a potentially larger set of enterprises. However, given the lack of data on small SOEs, and given the fact that few small SOEs are likely to have adopted the formal company form, the definitional inconsistencies are ignored in the following paragraphs.

Across the 17 provinces, the number of small industrial SOEs fell from a provincial arithmetic mean of 2,233 to a provincial average of 1,457, a reduction by 34.75%. With most industrial SOEs being of small size, the average provincial number of all industrial SOEs also fell by 31.59%. The average provincial number of large and medium industrial SOEs, in contrast, fell by only 18.96% (not reported in the table, but obtainable by taking the difference between the number of all industrial SOEs and the number of small industrial SOEs). The average provincial share of small industrial SOEs in all industrial SOEs fell by only 3.76 percentage points to 76.86%, and their share in provincial industrial SOE value-added by only 1.46 percentage points to 15.90%. While the overall number of small industrial SOEs fell by one-third, their share in all industrial SOEs, either in enterprise numbers, or in value-added, thus was almost unchanged.

The average provincial number of loss-making small industrial SOEs fell by only 30.06%, slightly less than the total number of small industrial SOEs. The average provincial share of loss-making small industrial SOEs among all small industrial SOEs thus rose (from 35.17% to 37.19%). Either local governments dispensed of more profitable small SOEs than they did of loss-making small SOEs, or previously profitable small SOEs became loss-making even while loss-making small SOEs were closed. The average provincial share of loss-making small industrial SOEs in all loss-making industrial SOEs fell by only 1.02 percentage points, from 82.18% to 81.16%, while the average provincial share of small industrial SOEs in the amount of losses of all loss-making industrial SOEs even increased by half a percentage point, from 32.85% to 33.34%. Small industrial SOEs thus continued to account for a share in industrial SOE losses that is twice as large as their share in industrial SOE value-added.

Average provincial profitability of small industrial SOEs improved, but remained poor. Average provincial profit per unit of equity of small industrial SOEs rose by 4.10 percentage points, but, in 2000, it was still negative 1.88%.[174] In contrast, average provincial profitability of medium industrial SOEs improved by 7.78 percentage points to 1.81%, and that of large industrial SOEs by 1.87 percentage points to 4.30%. Despite the far-reaching scope for enlivening small industrial SOEs, the remaining small industrial SOEs continue to perform poorer than large and medium industrial SOEs.

Dismissal of Industrial SOE Staff and Workers

Although the dismissal of industrial SOE staff and workers was a cornerstone of the three-year industrial SOE reform program, an overall target for the reduction in industrial SOE employment over the three years appears to never have been issued. The one target issued, for 1998, was 2m workers. The textile sector as one of the chief loss-making sectors became the key

---

[174] The table also reports losses relative to gross profit. Losses per unit of gross profit between 1997 and 2000 fell by 22.70 percentage points to 64.82%. This implies a positive profit, contrary to the negative profitability indicator of profit per unit of equity. The different conclusions are due to slightly different groups of provincial observations, which in turn is due to differing data availability for profit, equity, and losses.

Table 8.1 Small Industrial SOEs across Provinces, 1997 vs. 2000

	Number of Industrial SOEs		Number of small industrial SOEs		Share of small SOEs in the number of ind. SOEs (in %)		Share of small SOEs in industrial SOE value-added (in %)	
	1997	2000	1997	2000	1997	2000	1997	2000
Beijing	3381	1981	3013	1696	89.12	85.61	23.10	10.69
Shanxi	2465	1791	2118	1470	85.92	82.08	19.70	18.07
Liaoning	4045	2454	3129	1992	77.35	81.17	6.31	14.06
Shanghai	2946	1278	2317	966	78.65	75.59	n.a.	6.90
Jiangsu	3452	1880	2388	1321	69.18	70.27	14.35	n.a.
Anhui	1688	1128	1256	719	74.41	63.74	12.22	11.56
Fujian	1935	1367	1745	1160	90.18	84.86	35.52	32.03
Jiangxi	3596	2387	3184	2038	88.54	85.38	n.a.	21.25
Shandong	3877	2774	2437	1442	62.86	51.98	8.45	10.42
Henan	3133	3177	2295	2375	73.25	74.76	n.a.	n.a.
Hubei	3611	2965	2966	2284	82.14	77.03	21.17	18.60
Guangdong	4757	3320	3890	2520	81.77	75.90	23.47	12.44
Chongqing	1191	931	903	636	75.82	68.31	16.38	14.49
Guizhou	1673	1397	1452	1182	86.79	84.61	18.14	26.07
Yunnan	1733	1144	1470	923	84.82	80.68	9.24	10.89
Shaanxi	2418	1633	1972	1243	81.56	76.12	24.26	11.62
Xinjiang	1608	900	1418	796	88.18	88.44	10.79	35.23
Mean	2795	1912	2233	1457	80.62	76.86	17.36	15.90

	Number of loss-making small industrial SOEs		Share of loss-making SOEs in the number of small ind. SOEs (in %)		Share of small SOEs in the number of loss-making ind. SOEs (in %)		Share of small SOEs in industrial SOE losses (in %)	
	1997	2000	1997	2000	1997	2000	1997	2000
Beijing	590	468	19.58	27.59	87.41	91.41	28.95	35.18
Shanxi	496	387	23.42	26.33	79.61	80.63	21.13	41.45
Liaoning	n.a.	n.a.	n.a.	n.a.	n.a.	n.a.	n.a.	n.a.
Shanghai	n.a.	n.a.	n.a.	n.a.	n.a.	n.a.	n.a.	n.a.
Jiangsu	n.a.	n.a.	n.a.	n.a.	n.a.	n.a.	n.a.	n.a.
Anhui	n.a.	n.a.	n.a.	n.a.	n.a.	n.a.	n.a.	n.a.
Fujian	590	n.a.	33.81	n.a.	92.19	n.a.	60.47	n.a.
Jiangxi	1060	859	33.29	42.15	85.83	83.80	37.82	33.52
Shandong	719	405	29.50	28.09	66.95	67.95	22.55	30.25
Henan	n.a.	n.a.	n.a.	n.a.	n.a.	n.a.	n.a.	n.a.
Hubei	1132	827	38.17	36.21	77.91	77.58	32.05	21.30
Guangdong	1589	675	40.85	26.79	79.33	74.42	30.31	35.23
Chongqing	n.a.	n.a.	n.a.	n.a.	n.a.	n.a.	n.a.	n.a.
Guizhou	552	n.a.	38.02	n.a.	84.15	n.a.	24.23	n.a.
Yunnan	621	460	42.24	49.84	85.77	85.03	n.a.	n.a.
Shaanxi	908	590	46.04	47.47	79.79	80.71	30.54	35.50
Xinjiang	594	400	41.89	50.25	85.10	88.89	40.43	34.29
Mean	805	563	35.17	37.19	82.18	81.16	32.85	33.34

Table 8.1 (continued)

	Profit per unit of equity (in %) in industrial						Small industrial SOEs: losses / gross profit (in %)	
	large SOEs		medium SOEs		small SOEs			
	1997	2000	1997	2000	1997	2000	1997	2000
Beijing	1.69	1.80	1.14	8.75	8.20	1.29	40.68	30.79
Shanxi	3.29	2.40	0.42	-0.96	-0.20	-2.11	56.97	61.67
Liaoning	0.73	5.64	-8.54	1.78	-15.54	0.60	n.a.	n.a.
Shanghai	n.a.	1.52	n.a.	1.25	n.a.	-8.17	n.a.	n.a.
Jiangsu	4.44	4.19	-2.24	2.73	-4.21	0.37	n.a.	n.a.
Anhui	3.03	3.30	-1.01	0.99	-16.75	-0.48	n.a.	n.a.
Fujian	n.a.	n.a.	n.a.	n.a.	n.a.	n.a.	20.88	n.a.
Jiangxi	3.68	1.40	-5.89	2.79	-9.60	-5.17	128.50	85.83
Shandong	4.85	15.39	2.77	5.41	0.56	0.59	31.53	7.75
Henan	2.54	5.57	1.78	4.42	-5.55	0.30	n.a.	33.13
Hubei	n.a.	n.a.	n.a.	n.a.	n.a.	n.a.	90.60	41.57
Guangdong	8.02	10.66	-3.29	6.48	-2.45	4.15	60.48	13.64
Chongqing	-4.15	1.72	-17.34	-1.04	-12.76	-3.08	n.a.	n.a.
Guizhou	3.09	n.a.	-12.99	n.a.	-1.81	n.a.	103.34	n.a.
Yunnan	n.a.	n.a.	n.a.	n.a.	n.a.	n.a.	n.a.	n.a.
Shaanxi	-2.52	8.63	-16.21	4.83	-10.78	-5.33	227.04	41.18
Xinjiang	2.95	-6.36	-16.18	-13.86	-6.83	-7.40	115.20	267.78
Mean	2.43	4.30	-5.97	1.81	-5.98	-1.88	87.52	64.82

Year 1997 industrial SOE data cover industrial SOEs according to the pre-1998 definition. Year 2000 industrial SOE data cover industrial SOEs according to the new, post-1997 definition, with the following exceptions: data on Yunnan cover SOEs according to the pre-1998 definition, data on Xinjiang cover the pure SOEs only, and data on Beijing, Shanghai, Jiangsu, and Jiangxi cover either only pure SOEs, or SOEs according to the pre-1998 definition (no unambiguous definition is provided). For all provinces not listed here, no data according to the size classification are available for both years (1997 and 2000).
Sources: Provincial statistical yearbooks.

reform sector in 1998. Employment was to be cut by 600,000, and 4.8m "backward" cotton spindles were to be taken out of production (out of a total of approximately 40m). Similar efforts since 1991 had largely failed. But by the end of 1999, SOEs in the textile sector had completed the reform process with a total reduction in staff and workers of 1.2m and a reduction in spindles by 10m.[175]

Employment in industrial SOEs following the pre-1998 definition of SOEs (focusing only on the pure SOEs, solely state-owned limited liability companies, and SOE-SOE joint operations) fell by half between 1997 and 2000, from 40.40m in 1997 to 27.21m in 1998, to 24.12m in 1999, and to 20.96m in 2000 (*Statistical Yearbook 2001*, p. 402). However, these data are of only limited use for two reasons. First, the definition of employment changed in 1998 to include only those staff and workers actually in their posts, i.e., the staff and workers still employed by the enterprise but no longer working in the enterprise are newly excluded. No data are available on how many staff and workers were not "in their post" in the years prior to 1998 — perhaps none. Second, some of the reduction could be due to SOEs turning into state-controlled limited liability companies or stock companies. Since the employment data in the *Statistical Yearbook* are based on the pre-1998 definition of SOEs, employees of SOEs which have turned into companies are no longer counted as SOE employees.

Average annual employment in the newly defined (post-1997) industrial SOE category fell from 33.95m in 1999 to 29.95m in 2000 (*Industrial Yearbook 2001*, p. 61). This reduction by 4m employees between 1999 and 2000 is similar to the 3.16m reduction in the number of employees in the group of pre-1998 definition SOEs (above), which suggests that the above

---

[175] See *China Infobank* (8 Jan. 1998) and China Textile Association (5 March 1998). In 1991, China had 41.92m cotton spindles, of which about 10m were "backward." Beginning in 1992, the government issued a special plan to update spindle technology and to take 5m backward spindles out of production. In 1994, provinces were reminded of this 5m spindle reduction target and a new target of a reduction by 10m spindles to be achieved by 1998 was issued. Between 1992 and 1996, only 4.65m spindles were taken out of production, with a further 1.06m expected to have been taken out of production by the end of 1998. But in the same period (presumably between 1992 and 1996), 4.44m new spindles were added, so that the total by the end of 1996 was 41.71m spindles.

data for 1998 through 2000 on industrial SOE employment following the pre-1998 definition with an approximately one-quarter (6.25m) reduction between 1998 and 2000 are likely to be representative of all industrial SOEs. A deputy head of the SETC reported a 10m person reduction in industrial SOE employment by mid-2000 (probably since the end of 1997; *Xinbao*, 30 Aug. 2000, p. 9), a figure which presumably is not encumbered with the difference in how staff and workers no longer "in their post" are accounted for since 1998. Employment in *all* SOEs (i.e., not only in industrial SOEs) fell by 25.5m between 1998 and 2001 (SC, April 2002, p. 41).[176]

The large-scale dismissal of SOE laborers and thus the surge in urban unemployment required drastic measures to create re-employment opportunities and to support the long-term unemployed. The CCPCC on 9 June 1998 stressed that dismissed regular (originally permanent) workers of SOEs enjoy "two guarantees" (*liangge quebao*). The first guarantee concerns the remuneration of working age laborers. These are to enter a "re-employment service center" (*zai jiuye fuwu zhongxin*), usually located within the SOE, for a period of three years. During the three years, the center helps find re-employment and, during the period of unemployment, it pays a "basic living allowance" (*jiben shenghuo fei*) as well as laid-off workers' pension contributions, medical insurance and unemployment insurance. If the dismissed worker cannot find re-employment within the three years, the relationship with the SOE is severed and the former worker receives regular unemployment insurance payments for a maximum of two years. The third safeguard is the standard, local minimum living allowance beginning in the sixth year after dismissal. The second guarantee concerns the remuneration of retired workers; a sufficient pension is to be paid in a timely manner.

During the time in the re-employment service center, dismissed workers also undertake retraining sessions. In the period 1998 through 2000, altogether 13m dismissed SOE workers (not limited to industrial SOEs) received retraining, and 60% of them found employment within half a year

---

[176] *Xinbao* (18 Sept. 2002, p. 1) reports a similar reduction in SOE employment between 1998 and "today" from 75m to 50m. On the difficulty of ascertaining accurate figures on the dismissal of SOE staff and workers, see also Dorothy Solinger (2001).

of the training sessions. Another three-year program to retrain 10m dismissed SOE workers began in 2001.[177]

The three-year SOE reform program was in part preceded and in part accompanied by a complete overhaul of the social security system. Traditionally, all social security tasks were concentrated within an SOE. These tasks now had to be shifted to an external institution so that industrial SOE reform, including enterprise bankruptcy, could proceed unhampered. A provincial-level pension system was established in 1997, a new urban medical insurance system in 1998, and a municipal-level unemployment insurance system in 1999. But the implementation of these social security reforms has not been fully satisfactory.

Despite the elaborate arrangements on pension payments and the basic living allowance for laid-off workers of SOEs, in practice many retirees and laid-off workers appear not to receive what they have been promised. A State Council circular of 28 May 2000 urged local governments to make up any shortfall in funding for these two purposes through additional budget allocations (SC, 28 May 2000). But at the same time the circular created a major moral hazard problem in that it promised financial help for "central and Western regions and the old industrial bases if they are truly in fiscal difficulties." Local governments thus may prefer to delay appropriations for social security purposes in the hope that the central government will be forced to step in by reports of large shortfalls in local government budgets or of impending social unrest due to unpaid pensions and basic living allowances. SOEs may also have few incentives to pay into social security funds if the local or central government can be forced to contribute a larger share by the enterprise successfully pretending to be too weak financially to fulfill its obligations.

---

[177] On details regarding the two guarantees and the re-employment service centers, see SC (April 2002), in particular p. 40f. The services offered to dismissed SOE workers are to be gradually folded into the unemployment insurance system. The reported data on retraining include double-counting in that a dismissed worker who finds a job only to lose it again and to join yet another training session is counted twice. The re-employment data are beset by the same problem.

For example, by late 1999, enterprises nationwide owed the pension insurance system 38.3b RMB, equivalent to 15.82% of all nationwide 1999 pensions payments (presumably including those not actually made but only promised).[178] The social security system in Liaoning Province, an old industrial base, in 2001 appeared badly underfunded, despite central government injections of 120m RMB. SOEs were reported to hold back from dismissing even more workers due to the lack of funding for basic living allowances, while banks were pressured to extend loans to some SOEs simply to keep them alive.[179]

In January 2001, the State Council established a national Social Security Fund (*shehui baozhang jijin*) to hold and invest the central government's contributions to the social security system. These contributions were to primarily consist of funds obtained through the sale of state shares in listed companies, supplemented by budget appropriations (SC, 2 Jan. 2002).[180] The sale of state shares in listed companies began in June 2001 (SC, 6 June 2001), but after a sharp drop in the domestic stock market, the sale of state shares in (domestically) listed enterprises was halted in October 2001 and, as of end-2002, has not been resumed. The Social Security Fund thus continues to be financed primarily through government budget appropriations. Most of the Fund's spending, as determined by the Finance Ministry together with the Labor and Social Security Ministry, is currently on pensions.[181]

---

[178] See Labor and Social Security Ministry (25 Nov. 1999) and *Statistical Yearbook 2000*, p. 765.

[179] On Liaoning Province, see the *Asian Wall Street Journal* of 6 Nov. 2001, p. 1.

[180] A further regulation (SC, 13 Dec. 2001) established clear guidelines for investments by the Social Security Fund. *China Infobank* (31 May 2002) reports on the relative size of the different types of investment, which range from equity investments to bank deposits. The Social Security Fund is a national institution only, organized in the form of an administrative unit directly under the State Council. It employs 50 staff members (SC, 2 Jan. 2002).

[181] China's pension system is a dual track system, with each employee paying into a personal account, and the employer paying both into the employee's personal account as well as into a state-run common pension fund. With this new pension system only established in 1997, the funds in the common pension fund are insufficient to pay the pensions of the currently retired, most of whom never made any contribution to a pension fund. (Prior to 1997, pensions were paid by enterprises out of their current income.) On the complications and innovative variations in Liaoning Province, see Zhao Xiaojian *et al.* (2002).

SOE Equity and Liabilities

One effect of the economic reforms was the increasing indebtedness of SOEs as the state budget no longer provided investment funds and working capital. (Government funding constitutes equity.) By the mid-1990s, industrial SOEs' average liability-asset ratio had reached about 65%. The CCPCC in its SOE reform decision of 22 Sept. 1999 perceived this ratio as too high. In as far as a reduction in debt leads to smaller interest payments, a lower liability-asset ratio implies a larger volume of residual profit. The reform decision elaborated on a number of measures to reduce the indebtedness of SOEs. These included raising equity through land sales, through listing on the stock market, or by turning loans into equity. Debt relative to equity was also to be reduced by banks writing off some loans of merged or bankrupt enterprises, and by keeping interest rates on loans low. Large SOEs could diversify their debt by issuing bonds. By 2000, the liability-asset ratio of (the newly defined and most comprehensive group of) industrial SOEs had fallen back to close to 60%.

The as yet most incisive measure was the debt-equity swap for 601 predominantly large, centrally owned industrial SOEs announced in 2000 (but most likely only implemented in 2001 and 2002, and thus not reflected in the data available at this point of time). This swap at 460b RMB is equivalent to more than five percent of total industrial SOE assets in 2000, and thus must immediately reduce the liability-asset ratio by approximately five percentage points once it has been implemented. In addition, assuming a loan interest rate of 8%, the debt-equity swap yields a reduction in interest payments and thus an automatic increase in profit of 36.8b RMB in every year after it is implemented; this is equivalent to more than one-quarter of the increase in industrial SOE profit in 2000 over the previous year.

The debt-equity swap formed part of a larger transfer of bank loans to "financial asset management companies," in fact resolution trust companies (RTCs). Each of the four state commercial banks set up a RTC in 1999 to which it subsequently transferred some of its bad loans at face value.[182] Each of the RTCs received 10b RMB of government start-up capital as

---

[182] The four RTCs are the Xinda (Cinda) RTC (to take over the bad loans of the Construction Bank of China), the Dongfang RTC (for the Bank of China), the Changcheng RTC (for the Agricultural Bank of China), and the Huarong RTC (for the Industrial and Commercial Bank of China).

well as an unknown volume of refinancing from the People's Bank of China, but otherwise relied on bonds guaranteed by the Finance Ministry and issued primarily to the state commercial banks to finance the purchase in 2000 of 930b RMB of bad loans from the four state commercial banks.[183] (This figure excludes the 460b RMB debt-equity swap.)

In contrast to the bad loan write-offs, the debt-equity swap targeted viable enterprises which the central government wanted to strengthen for future growth. Five basic requirements for enterprises to take part in the debt-equity swap included such criteria as "sales potential" for the enterprises' products and a strong management team. The industrial SOEs that took part in the debt-equity swap were "recommended" to the RTCs by the SETC. The RTCs were then to conduct their own evaluation before deciding on whether or not to acquire the bad loans and to turn them into equity. If the RTC agreed to the debt-equity swap, the SETC as well as the Finance Ministry and the People's Bank of China conducted one further audit before recommending the debt-equity swap to the State Council for approval.

The debt-equity swap announced in 2000 and the writing off of bad loans in 2000 were both one-time measures. But the central government has been financing bad loan write-offs at least since 1997 in order to allow bankrupt industrial SOEs to exit without destroying the state banks' net worth. Thus, the central government set aside more than 30b RMB of budgetary funds in 1997 to write off the bad debts of SOEs, presumably old capital construction (fixed-asset) loans (*China News Digest*, 17 Oct. 1997). In 1998, the government financed another 40b RMB in bad debt write-off as well as a conversion of 57.7b RMB of outstanding loans into

---

[183] The bad loans acquired by the RTCs from the four state commercial banks fall into three categories: (i) loans extended before 1995, which by the end of 1998 had been overdue for more than one year; (ii) all loan losses as of September 1999; and (iii) loans issued after 1995 that "need" to be turned into equity, with approval of the State Council; in addition, some bad loans of the State Development Bank were also acquired by the RTCs (*Financial Yearbook 2000*, pp. 15-6; SC, 20 Nov. 2000). The bad loan transfer out of the bank balance sheets probably happened only after 2000. The bad loan transfer is unlikely to yield a significant reduction in industrial SOE interest payments as these had probably already been suspended earlier.

state equity, without specifying the types of loans covered.[184] In 1999, budgetary funds paid for another bad loan write-off of 50b RMB and, in 2001, of more than 55b RMB.[185]

While a reduction in debt, *ceteris paribus*, can only improve industrial SOE profit, profitability is an altogether different issue. Chapter 5 elaborated in detail why a reduction in debt may not affect profitability, and the quantitative analysis confirmed that a high liability-asset ratio does not necessarily lead to low profitability.

SOE Bankruptcy

According to the 1986 (Trial) Bankruptcy Law, an SOE can be declared bankrupt if it cannot repay its debt (NPC, 2 Dec. 1986, Art. 3). However, many insolvent SOEs are being kept alive because creditors (mainly the state banks) do not initiate bankruptcy proceedings, or because the government invokes an escape clause contained in article 3 of the Bankruptcy Law. According to this clause, bankruptcy cannot be declared — even if the creditor desires it — if the SOE is of utmost importance to the national economy and if the relevant government departments support it financially or take other measures to help clear the debts that are due.

China currently has three distinct enterprise bankruptcy procedures. First, the 1986 Bankruptcy Law, in effect since 1 November 1988, applies to SOEs. Second, bankruptcies of enterprises under all other ownership forms are covered by the Civil Litigation Law of 9 April 1991. Third, following two State Council regulations of 1994 and 1997, first selected

---

[184] See *TCFA Update*, no. 7 (Dec. 1998). The National People's Congress Standing Committee in 1998 also recapitalized the four state commercial banks to help them meet the 8% risk-weighted equity-asset ratio specified in the Commercial Bank Law of 1995 (and recommended by the Bank for International Settlements). After the minimum reserve requirement was lowered, the four state commercial banks, on 18 August 1998, used their now excess reserves in the People's Bank of China to purchase 270 billion RMB of special 30-year interest-bearing bonds. The Finance Ministry then recapitalized the banks by returning the 270 billion RMB. Although the recapitalization was undertaken to meet international capital requirement standards, it also increased the banks' net worth and thus provided a cushion for writing off bad debts.

[185] See *China Infobank* (13 March 1998) and *China News Digest* (15 March 2002).

SOEs and then only selected *industrial* SOEs in a few locations enjoy special bankruptcy treatment (SC, 25 Oct. 1994 and 2 March 1997); these cases are dubbed "policy bankruptcies." The Supreme People's Court in 1991 clarified the bankruptcy proceedings for enterprises covered by the bankruptcy law, and in 2002 issued a more detailed regulation that covers bankruptcies both under the Bankruptcy Law and the Civil Litigation Law. A new bankruptcy law to cover all enterprises independent of ownership has been in the making since 1994, but has reportedly been delayed indefinitely due to fears about a flood of bankruptcies and its social implications (Shi Dong, 2002).

Most industrial SOE bankruptcies appear to fall into the "policy bankruptcy" category. In 1997, the State Council established a "national leading group for SOE mergers and bankruptcies and staff and worker re-employment" to be in charge of all policy bankruptcies.[186] Similar leading groups were established on the provincial level and in 111 cities designated for the "perfection of the capital structure" (*youhua ziben jiegou*); the State Council first designated 18 such cities in 1994, with the number later increased to 56, and then to 111 in 1997. The leading groups identify the local candidates for bankruptcy (or merger) in an annual bankruptcy plan; candidates comprise industrial SOEs subordinate to central, provincial, and municipal governments. Each leading group examines the bankruptcy plan of the lower-level leading groups, with final approval for the nationwide annual bankruptcy plan, which incorporates all local plans, by the State Council.

The number of bankruptcies each year is limited by the size of banks' reserves against bad loans and by additional financial support from the government. The State Council each year determines the amount of bank reserves to be allocated to writing off bad loans of bankrupt industrial SOEs. The State Council then further apportions budgetary funds for the same purpose. The national leading group allocates this amount to central industrial SOEs and the individual provinces and cities.

---

[186] The leading group comprises members from the SETC (which provides the head of the leading group), the State System Reform Commission, the Finance Ministry, the (then) Labor Ministry, the People's Bank of China, the Land Bureau, and the National State Asset Administration Bureau; additional members are invited from the National People's Congress Legislative Committee and the Supreme People's Court. The leading group's office is at the SETC. For details on policy bankruptcies see, in particular, SC (2 March 1997).

A second key concern is securing funding for the laid-off workers and retirees of bankrupt enterprises. The re-employment service centers are to receive funding equivalent to three years' worth of average wages, and special arrangements are to be made to guarantee future pension payments. Bankrupt industrial SOEs included in the nationwide annual bankruptcy plan are allowed to sell their (usually administratively allocated) land use rights on the secondary market (*churang*) in order to secure sufficient funds for labor. If the receipts from land use rights are insufficient to cover all labor costs (from the re-employment service centers to pension payments and retirees' medical insurance), receipts from the sale of other assets, and even of mortgaged assets if need be, are to support labor. In the final instance, the local government is asked to fill any remaining holes.

The national leading group between 1996 and 2000 approved (planned) the merger or bankruptcy of 5,335 industrial SOEs, which required writing off 208.64b RMB in bank loans (principal and interest due). Of these, 2,334 mergers or bankruptcies occurred in the three-year SOE reform period (with 148.66b RMB in bank loans written off). Of the 6,599 large and medium loss-making industrial SOEs in 1997, 1,415 were merged, had entered bankruptcy proceedings, or were closed by 2000.[187]

The leading group each year adopts a specific sectoral focus. In 1999, it favored industrial SOE bankruptcies in the textile, coal, non-ferrous metals, metallurgy, and military sectors. In 2000, it favored the non-ferrous metals, sugar production, textile, and a number of iron and steel sectors as well as military industry. Between 1998 and 2000, the textile industry accounted for 24.1% of the written off bank loans in this period, while China's Northeast (the three provinces of Liaoning, Heilongjiang, and Jilin) accounted for 16.5%.[188]

---

[187] See *China Infobank* (25 June 2001a) and *Fiscal Yearbook 2001*, p. 109. Up through 1991, perhaps no more than two industrial SOEs had been allowed to go bankrupt. Gao Shangquan (1992) reports that, according to incomplete statistics on 26 provinces, 1,097 "budgetary" (*yusuannei*) industrial enterprises had undergone some form of ownership transformation by 1991. Of these, two went bankrupt, 39 were closed, 417 stopped all or part of production, 229 transferred their ownership rights, and 410 merged.

[188] See *China Infobank* (25 June 2001a).

Implications

The three-year SOE reform program with its various accompanying measures clearly improved aggregate SOE finances. Yet, SOE reform appears far from complete. The 2001 as well as the 2002 annual economic and social development plans talk of "further deepening SOE reform" with measures very much the same as before (NPC, 15 March 2001 and 6 March 2002).

That fewer than one-quarter of all large and medium industrial SOEs have been turned into formal companies suggests that property rights in most large and medium industrial SOEs may still only be vaguely defined, with perhaps little distinction between ownership and management, and without a formal supervisory institution. The fact that the number of large and medium loss-making industrial SOEs and their losses have only fallen by about 40% between 1998 and 2000 implies that many SOEs are still not economically viable.

The textile sector, after half a decade of unsuccessful reforms, in 1998 and 1999 turned into a model success story. But this success came at a significant cost to the government. For every reduction of 10,000 spindles, the government paid a subsidy of 3m RMB (half borne by the central government and half borne by local governments). The 3m RMB government subsidy for each reduction of 10,000 spindles amounts to a 3b RMB subsidy for the overall reduction of 10m spindles. This one-time subsidy of 3b RMB is comparable to the total profit of all textile SOEs of 3.194b RMB in 2000 (*Statistical Yearbook 2001*, p. 423).

In addition, for every reduction of 10,000 spindles, banks were to make available 2m RMB in five- to seven-year bank loans with interest payments subsidized by the local government. (These funds were to be used for the development of new products, the development of tertiary sector activities, and for payments to laid-off employees.) Textile SOEs became prime candidates for inclusion in the bankruptcy plan with its government-approved bank write-offs of bad loans; they were allowed to sell their administratively allocated land use rights; and they received a special 11% tax rebate on exports. (SC, 27 Feb. 1998)

Perhaps the aggregate losses of industrial SOEs would have fallen further if enterprises had been able to shed more labor. In late 2000, a deputy head of the SETC, based on the 10m person reduction in employment achieved by mid-2000, felt that SOEs were still overstaffed by as much as one-third of their work force (*Xinbao*, 30 Aug. 2000, p. 9). But the dismissal of excess staff and workers was limited by the ability to find re-employment for laid-off workers and by the financial health of the social security system. Exhortations to find re-employment for at least half of all currently laid-off workers suggests a success rate below 50% (CCPCC, 9 June 1998). Reports from different localities suggest that the social security system was stressed to the breaking-point by 2001. On the other hand, some of the shortfalls in finances could well reflect continued bargaining between the central government, local governments, and enterprises. The latter two, after all, have incentives to underfulfill their social security obligations, given that the central government has in the past been willing to make up shortfalls in social security funding.

As in the case of the textile sector reform, social security reform appears dominated by shifting financial burdens from enterprises to government budgets. Industrial SOEs would have had smaller losses, had they been able to dismiss more workers. They would have been able to dismiss more workers, had the government made a larger contribution to the social security system. The same principle is at work in the debt-equity swaps and the bankruptcy plan. Enterprises are freed of some of the recurrent interest burden by shifting non-performing loans and interest due to the RTCs (and thus in the long run to the central government). Bankruptcy proceedings are in part limited by the amount of central government appropriations to write off bad loans. State commercial banks may further write off non-performing loans and interest due using their own profit, but only within limits determined by the State Council; had they not had to write off the bad loans, or had they not been disadvantaged vis-à-vis labor in the bankruptcy proceedings, no further appropriations from the government would have been necessary, and their net worth (the government's stake in the banks) would have been larger. Bankrupt industrial SOEs are also allowed to sell their land use rights on the secondary land market in order to fund their pension liabilities and the re-employment centers; had this land been returned to the government, the government budget would have profited from the sale.

Shifting financial obligations and bad loans to the government implies an increasing burden on government finances. By guaranteeing the bonds issued by the RTCs, the Finance Ministry has accepted responsibility for the bad loans transferred to the RTCs, which constitute perhaps close to half of all bad loans in the banking system. If RTCs were able to recover approximately 25% of their loan portfolio (and had no operating costs and no interest to pay on the bonds they issued), then the central government would immediately have to cover a financial deficit in the RTCs of 657.5b RMB, an amount equivalent to 49.08% of total budget revenues in 2000, or equivalent to 7.35% of GDP.[189] If the state commercial banks were unable to write off their remaining stock of an equal amount of bad loans over the next few years, the burden on the government budget would double.

Similarly, total pension payments to retired staff and workers in 2000 amounted to 273.33b RMB, equivalent to 20.41% of government revenues or 3.06% of GDP; over the past decade, pension payments have been growing at a rate of 21.30% per year, compared with nominal GDP growth of 17.03% per year (*Statistical Yearbook 2001*, pp. 49, 245, 770). The government may have to shoulder an increasing share of this growing burden. Health insurance, basic living allowances for laid-off SOE staff and workers, and unemployment insurance are not even yet considered, let alone any future rural social security measures.

Even so, the cloud also has a silver lining. To the extent that the government had to rely on bonds to finance the various measures taken during the three-year SOE reform program, it was able to issue long-term debt at a rather low interest rate of two to three percent. Second, government revenues as a share of GDP have been rising continuously from a low of 10.67% in 1995 to 14.98% in 2000. Since the minimum income level to be eligible for income taxes is fixed at a nominal 800 RMB per month, an increasing number of individuals is beginning to pay income taxes; as paying

---

[189] The amount of 657.5b RMB is obtained as (1390b RMB loan transfer to RTCs less 460b RMB debt-equity swap) * 0.75 - 40b RTC start-up capital. For government revenues and GDP data, see *Statistical Yearbook 2001*, pp. 49, 245. A recovery rate of 25% is suggested by the first results of RTCs in collecting debts and selling SOE equity (*Xinbao*, 30 Nov. 2001, p. 4; 6 Dec. 2001, p. 7); if the RTCs are handling their most promising assets first, this recovery rate will fall in the future.

income taxes gradually develops into a widespread practice, a new and reliable source of government revenues is being established. Third, the central government has been able to claim an increasing share of total government revenues, rising from a low of 20 to 30% prior to 1994 to 55.7% in 1994, then falling back several percentage points to 48.9% in 1997, but rising again to 52.2% in 2000 (*Statistical Yearbook 2001*, p. 257). Being able to claim an increasing share of total government revenues allows redistribution to the neediest localities, such as those where much employment is concentrated in quasi-bankrupt SOEs.

At the bankruptcy front, the picture at first also appears bleak. Thus a survey of 121 bankrupt SOEs in 1999, organized by government departments, revealed an average liability-asset ratio of 195%, with an average period of continuous losses of 58 months.[190] It appears that the bankruptcy of industrial SOEs included in the bankruptcy plan is long overdue. In the industrial city Shenyang in Liaoning, 125 enterprises went bankrupt in the past 15 years; yet it still had 162 enterprises "waiting" for approval to enter bankruptcy proceedings.[191] This approval presumably hinges on the availability of funds to write off bad loans and to finance labor benefits. The delay in bankruptcies, however, also has a positive side. The quasi-bankrupt enterprises are likely to have partly or even completely stopped production, and staff and workers may well already be leaving the enterprise on their own accounts. By the time the enterprise enters bankruptcy proceedings, the labor burden may be significantly reduced. The price of immediate action in SOE reform may be prohibitively high. The current gradual and partial reforms may be affordable because they spread the burden widely and stretch it over several years.

Enhancing Enterprise Management

Enhancing enterprise management as a final element of the 1998–2000 SOE reform program falls under the larger heading of improving corporate

---

[190] The bankruptcies are presumably all policy bankruptcies. See *China Infobank* (25 June 2001a).

[191] See Shi Dong (2002, p. 27). The text does not make explicit if these are all SOEs, or even industrial SOEs.

governance. Corporate governance, or the principal-agent problem, refers to how one can ensure that managers of the firm act in the interests of the "owners" (the shareholders), or, following the "multiple principal agent theory," in the interests of all stakeholders (Joseph Stiglitz, 1999).[192]

Property Rights Reform versus the Modern Enterprise System

Privatization is often viewed as a simple method to align the interests of enterprise managers with those of the owners. Yet, while the establishment of non-state enterprises has over the past decade become increasingly accepted, privatization of industrial SOEs has remained highly restricted.

The 1982 Constitution of the People's Republic of China referred to the self-employed individuals (*getihu*; "individual-owned enterprises") as a "supplement" (*buchong*) to the socialist public-owned economy (NPC, 4 Dec. 1982, Art. 11). By 1993 the (amended) Constitution explicitly allowed the existence and development of both individual-owned enterprises (employing no more than seven workers) and private enterprises (*siying jingji*, employing more than seven workers); both were viewed as a "supplement" to the socialist public-owned economy (NPC, 29 March 1993, Art. 11). In the again amended Constitution in 1999, the individual-owned and private enterprises as well as other forms of non-public enterprises had become an "important constituent part" (*zhongyao zucheng bufen*) of the socialist market economy (NPC, 15 March 1999, Art. 16). Governments on all levels have in recent years issued circulars promoting the development of the non-state economy. By 1999, individual-owned and private enterprises

---

[192] On Kit Tam (1999) provides numerous competing definitions of corporate governance, including corporate governance as understood by Chinese authors. On Kit Tam's favored interpretation is a broad definition as "the processes and mechanisms for ensuring that a company performs in a responsible, responsive and pro-active way in the interests of its stakeholders" (p. 18). Qian Yingyi (1994, p. 235) defines corporate governance as a "set of institutional arrangements governing the relationship among several groups of stakeholders (investors, both shareholder and creditor; managers; and workers) in order to realize economic gains from such a coalition. The structure of corporate governance concerns (a) how control rights are allocated and exercised; (b) how boards of directors, managers, and workers are monitored and evaluated; and (c) how incentives are designed and enforced."

accounted for 18.18% of the Gross Output Value of Industry, while private enterprises together with other non-state, non-collective industrial enterprises accounted for another 26.14% of the Gross Output Value of Industry.[193] Yet, the vast majority of these non-state (and non-collective) enterprises consists of newly established individual-owned or private enterprises, rather than privatized former SOEs.

Privatization, after some initial, quickly stalled attempts in the late 1980s, again became an issue in the three-year industrial SOE reform program. General Secretary of the Chinese Communist Party, Jiang Zemin, in his speech to the 15th Party Congress on 12 September 1997 when listing the many ways through which *small* SOEs could be "enlivened" included outright sale and the transformation into stock cooperatives (employee-owned enterprises). Privatization of large and medium industrial SOEs was not on the agenda.

The sale of small SOEs did not proceed smoothly. On 11 February 1999, the SETC complained about the erosion of state assets, bank debt, and tax obligations. In detailed instructions it elaborated on the procedures to be followed in the sale of small SOEs, allocating all approval authority to municipal or higher-level governments. The instructions further laid down strict guidelines for the evaluation of enterprise assets and the treatment of labor and social security liabilities. But it also stressed that this did not mean that small SOEs could no longer be sold; it only meant that the sale of small SOEs was not the main method to reform small SOEs. Despite the SETC measure cautioning against over-enthusiastic and irregular privatization, the CCPCC's SOE reform decision of 22 September 1999 reiterated the same range of reform options for small SOEs as Jiang Zemin did in 1997, including their sale.

---

[193] See *Statistical Yearbook 2000*, p. 409. The source offers Gross Output Value of Industry as well as the gross output value of the exhaustive four sub-categories, namely state-owned and state-controlled industry (28.21%), collective-owned industry (35.37%), individual-owned and private industry (18.18%), and industry under other ownership forms (26.14%). The sum of the four sub-categories exceeds the total due to some double-counting of the state share in companies and other enterprises. (For details on the double-counting, see Carsten Holz and Yi-min Lin, 2001a.) Similar data for 2000 are not available. Nor is a breakdown of economy-wide industrial *value-added* by ownership categories available.

The scale of privatization remained small, if not negligible. Small industrial SOEs in 1997, prior to the privatization measures, accounted for barely 15% of industrial SOE value-added. As the provincial-level data in Table 8.1 show, the number of small industrial SOEs across the provinces for which data on small industrial SOEs in 1997 and 2000 are available fell by one-third between 1997 and 2000, but their average share in provincial industrial SOE value-added remained almost constant (with the aggregate value-added of industrial SOEs rising across all provinces). The absolute value of industrial value-added produced by small SOEs between 1997 and 2000 (a non-inflationary period) fell in only three of the provinces for which data on small industrial SOEs are available for 1997 and 2000, remained approximately constant in one, and increased significantly in nine (not reported in the table). Thus, even in the case of small industrial SOEs, for which privatization became an explicit option in 1997, privatization appears not to have proceeded very far. The OECD (2000) suggests that some small SOEs may have been privatized informally.[194] But even if, in terms of value-added, half of all small industrial SOEs had been de facto privatized, the value-added of the newly privatized former SOEs is still likely to be equivalent to less than 10% of the value-added of the remaining industrial SOEs.

For large and medium SOEs, privatization is not an option. Instead, they are to adopt the "modern enterprise system," characterized by "clearly allocated property rights, clear rights and responsibilities, separation of government and enterprise, and scientific management." (As noted earlier, by the end of 2000, less than one-quarter of the large and medium industrial SOEs had been turned into companies.) On 28 September 2000, the SETC belatedly drew up a 69-point list for industrial SOEs, similarly applicable to other SOEs, outlining in great detail the various aspects of the modern enterprise system. The first, main section focuses on the separation of

---

[194] The OECD (2000, p. 58) study claims that local governments underreport the extent of their divestiture from small SOEs. The central government drive in May 2000 to reregister all state assets might be a response to informal privatization of small SOEs by local governments. The reregistration campaign was largely complete by late 2000, and the provincial data on small industrial SOEs at the end of 2000 may thus be quite reliable (*Fiscal Yearbook 2001*, p. 110).

government and enterprises with the incorporatization of SOEs and the management of state ownership rights.

The incorporatization of industrial SOEs follows the 1993 (revised in 1999) Company Law (NPC, 25 Dec. 1999), which established a regulatory framework for limited liability companies, with the sub-category of solely state-owned limited liability companies, and stock companies. In both types of companies, shareholders elect a board of directors and a supervisory board.[195] The board of directors in turn appoints the manager, who may be a member of the board of directors. Neither members of the board of directors nor the manager may at the same time be members of the supervisory board. In the solely state-owned limited liability company, both the board of directors and the supervisory board are appointed by the investing state unit; the board of directors also fulfills the tasks of the shareholders' meeting.

While incorporatization may achieve the first goal of clearly allocating property rights (necessary to become registered as a company), it is less effective in clearly allocating rights and responsibilities, and perhaps least effective in separating government and enterprises.[196] The Company Law lays out in some detail the tasks of the manager and of each of the three institutions (shareholders' meeting, board of directors, supervisory board), but in practice the boundaries appear rather permeable. The Company Law's unambiguous separation of board of directors and supervisory board appears to have little meaning when in the solely state-owned limited liability companies one investing state unit appoints both; the manager, board of directors, and supervisory board may reflect no more than a reshuffling of former SOE managers, Party committee members, labor representatives,

---

[195] If a limited liability company has two or more state entities as owners, then "democratically elected" labor representatives should be included in the board of directors; labor representatives are definitely included in the supervisory board. The same arrangements apply to all solely state-owned limited liability companies. In the stock company, labor representatives are to be invited to participate in the board of directors' meetings if these are related to labor matters; labor representatives are regularly included in the supervisory board.
[196] The World Bank (1997, p. 39) questions if property rights are indeed clearly allocated. One example is that the state's liability for companies is in practice greater than its formal or legal shareholding. But if this wide interpretation of property rights is used, few large enterprises in supposedly market economies have clearly allocated property rights.

and staff of the superordinate government department. In practice, furthermore, the manager is often pre-selected by the dominant or controlling shareholder (usually a state unit), despite the statutory requirement that the manager be appointed by the board of directors.[197]

Companies are supposed to be shielded from direct government influence through the establishment of a system of state asset management companies. In Shanghai, for example, a state asset committee run by the mayor appoints directors to numerous state asset management companies (in the form of state asset operating companies, which tend to be holding companies, and state asset group companies, which tend to be former line bureaus). These companies control a large number of operating entities (SOEs or formal companies). The operating entities are only indirectly linked to the government through the state asset management companies. These organizational innovations again have yielded little change in substance, however. SOEs are reported to see no difference between the asset management companies and the former line ministries, except a change in name.[198]

While the attempts at clarifying the allocation of rights and responsibilities and at separating the government from enterprises appear a step in the right direction, SOEs, including state-owned or state-controlled companies, differ from privately owned enterprises in two respects. They differ in their objective(s) and they differ in the degree to which poor management is identified and penalized.

According to the Company Law (NPC, 25 Dec. 1999, Art. 5), the objectives of companies are to increase their "economic results" (*jingji*

---

[197] See OECD (2000), p. 71, or CCPCC Organization Department Research Office (2001), p. 457. A 1996 report on the corporate development in Shanghai referred to by On Kit Tam (1999, p. 51f.) also raises severe doubts about the clear allocation of rights and responsibilities as originally envisaged in the Company Law.

[198] See World Bank (1999, Chapter 3). For other examples, see OECD (2000). The state asset management companies are also under the administrative leadership of the local government's state asset management office and the professional leadership of the higher-level government's state asset management office. The state asset management office at the national level, namely the National State Asset Administration Bureau, was abolished in 1998. Its supervisory task was transferred to the SETC and its regulatory task to the Finance Ministry. (SC, 4 July 1998)

xiaoyi) and labor productivity and to maintain or increase their asset value. The SOE Law of 1988 (NPC, 13 April 1988, Art. 3) lists as core tasks of pure SOEs to, in accordance with the state plan and market demand, develop commodity production, create wealth (*chuangzao caifu*), increase accumulation, and satisfy the daily increasing material and cultural needs of society. SOEs not only lack an unambiguous profit objective (or the objective to maximize their market value), but they are further burdened with numerous tasks assigned by state asset management companies or superordinate government departments. One very obvious non-market objective in recent years has been the creation of employment opportunities for excessive labor within the enterprise, when the objective of profit maximization would have demanded a further reduction in the number of employees.

A complement to the ambiguity in objectives is the absence of unambiguous mechanisms to identify poor management. If the objective is profit maximization, the criterion for evaluating management is readily available and easily applied. But if the objectives are not clear, no unambiguous criterion for the evaluation of management exist. Management evaluation is further complicated if effective external controls are not in place.

The following section provides an example of how management behavior that would in the long run not be feasible in a private enterprise can thrive in SOEs; it also shows the extent to which government departments continue to be deeply involved in core SOE management matters. The section thereafter delves deeper into management appointment and supervision mechanisms.

Price Competition

A prime example of the lack of disciplinary mechanisms for SOE managers, as well as of the degree of continued government involvement in SOE matters, is the intense price competition that developed in 1998 in several markets which had reached saturation. A number of enterprises, invariably SOEs, were reported to sell their products below production costs, in what became known as "low-price dumping" (*dijia qingxiao*). Other industrial SOEs complained and asked for government action to suppress such behavior. The SETC responded with a regulation asking sectoral associations to determine dumping prices for products under their authority and to issue "self-discipline" prices (*zilu jia*) among their members (SETC, 17 Aug. 1998).[199] At least one association, the one for agricultural machinery, went as far as levying penalties on individual enterprises for reportedly selling their products at below cost.[200]

The State Development and Planning Commission (SDPC), which comprises the Price Bureau, issued the first regulation prohibiting the sale of industrial goods at below production costs on 16 November 1998, followed by a second regulation approximately one year later (SDPC, 16 Nov. 1998 and 3 Aug. 1999). The later regulation implicitly revoked some of the powers of local price bureaus to intervene in the price determination process, provided clear guidelines for investigations and supervision, and expanded the range of products from industrial products to all products.

On 16 January 1999, the SDPC identified four key products for which low-price dumping appeared rampant and action was called for (SDPC, 16 Jan. 1999). These were glass sheets, steel products, color TV sets, and sugar. A host of regulations on the first three of these products followed.[201] Invariably, the sectoral association was to determine the average production costs across the sector, while the Price Bureau in cooperation with the sectoral association established a lower margin below the average production costs. The Price Bureau was to examine the accounts of enterprises that sold at a price below the lower margin. If their low prices were not justified by low production costs, a sequence of penalties ranging from warnings to

---

[199] The relevant government bureaus (*guojia ju*) were also to be involved in determining the products to which self-discipline prices should apply, and these bureaus together with the local economic and trade commission were to guide the implementation of the self-discipline prices and help resolve any disagreements between the associations and individual enterprises. Financial institutions were asked not to lend to enterprises undercutting the self-discipline price.

[200] See *China Infobank* (8 Dec. 1998) for a detailed case description.

[201] For some of the SDPC regulations, often issued together with the relevant government department, see the *China Infobank* database on laws and regulations on 15 June 1998 (glass), 9 Sept. 1998 (glass), 1 Oct. 1998 (steel products), 24 Dec. 1998 (steel products), 15 March 1999 (color TV sets), and 2 March 1999 (40 industrial products in the machinery industry). Some localities also took action on their own. For example, Fujian Province officially issued a self-discipline price for beer (*China Infobank*, 21 Sept. 1998).

cancellation of their business licenses would follow. In the case of the agricultural machinery association an investigation by the SDPC revealed that the enterprises selling at low prices indeed had low production costs and that they thus did not fall into the "low-price dumping" category (SDPC, 15 Nov. 1998).[202] The SDPC on this occasion also clarified that penalties could only be enacted by the Price Bureau, not by individual associations.[203]

The SDPC appears to have been less than enthusiastic in promoting price controls. The head of the Price Bureau openly welcomed price competition, elaborating on the benefits for consumers, the pressure on enterprises to lower costs and to improve the quality of their products, and the need for sectoral adjustments (i.e., the exit of some enterprises). Consequently, little concrete action beyond regular investigations and perhaps some warnings were taken. There is no evidence that the Price Bureau took drastic measures against individual enterprises. A report in a mainland newspaper published in Hong Kong in August 1999 quoted an unnamed SDPC official as saying that the "self-discipline" prices never worked properly. The SDPC may well have been afraid of encouraging price collusion through the sectoral average cost determination and "self-discipline" prices; price collusion is explicitly prohibited by the PRC Price Law. Guidance prices and state plan prices furthermore are only allowed for a few products, with specific approval of the State Council; all other prices are by law market prices.[204]

The head of the Price Bureau placed the blame for the intense price competition squarely on the lack of "self-constraint" (*ziwo yueshu*) in SOEs. While the Chinese press did not elaborate further, "self-constraint" represents a crucial deficiency of SOEs. Industrial SOEs that are unable to sell at a profit and are in danger of having to close down production may

---

[202] One of the penalized enterprises showed a more than 50% drop in production (for reasons not explained but with the reduction implicitly linked to the action of the association). Being a highly competitive enterprise thus implied direct financial penalties plus presumably lower profit due to foregone production. (*China Infobank*, 8 Dec. 1998)

[203] In a separate document (SDPC, 18 Jan. 1999), the SDPC also reasserted that individual enterprises in their pricing policy are not bound by the average sectoral price or the lower margin price, as long as their production costs are below their sales prices.

[204] See *China Infobank* (8 Dec. 1998, 24 May 1999, and 16 Aug. 1999).

well sell at a price below production costs in order to, for example, be able to pay wages to their staff and workers. The government in the end will bear the difference in sales price and production costs, manifested, for example, in a reduction in the value of fixed assets without the accumulation of offsetting depreciation funds. The government also bears the costs of low-price dumping in the form of lower value-added taxes and the absence of corporate income taxes (when there is no profit).

While the various regulations on low-price dumping remain in place and are occasionally referred to in regulations of the years 2000 through 2002, the fight against low-price dumping has lost momentum. This could reflect the wide-spread use of self-discipline prices, a reduction in excess capacity in highly saturated markets (an endeavor vigorously pursued by the SETC), or simply a broad acceptance of price competition with occasional warnings from the Price Bureau in individual cases where prices indeed fall significantly below production costs. In as far as the use of self-discipline prices (or price collusion) increases industrial SOE profit, rather than simply prevents a decline in profit, self-discipline prices may have contributed to the improvement in industrial SOE profitability in recent years.

Supervision and Personnel Appointment

The low-price dumping episode illustrates potential deficiencies in the management of Chinese SOEs, despite the fact that China's industrial SOEs are subject to complex supervision and personnel appointment procedures. These involve efforts to evaluate enterprise leaders, supervision mechanisms, and ultimately Party control over the appointment processes if not enterprise management.

The development of a formal enterprise management evaluation process began on 15 August 1995 with a set of suggestions issued by the CCPCC Organization Department. It targeted the "leadership teams" (*lingdao banzi*) in large and medium enterprises, with at first a focus on the 100 enterprises chosen by the State Council as trial enterprises for the modern enterprise system. The leadership team of each enterprise was to be evaluated (*kaohe*) with respect to six performance criteria, ranging from the implementation of the Party's policies to the conservation of enterprise assets. Organization departments at all levels were to take the lead in the evaluation.

A circular issued in 1997 provided further details (CCPCC Organization Department, 3 March 1997). The leadership team was taken to consist of the factory manager and the deputy managers, the (enterprise's) Party committee general secretary and deputy secretaries, and the chairman of the board of directors and all deputy-chairmen. The list of evaluation criteria increased from the original six to approximately twenty items, most of which were not operational criteria. The evaluation process involved the enterprises' financial reports; various reports by the leadership team to the relevant superordinate departments, owners and employees; statements by the leadership team; and external evaluations by the superordinate department, the Party disciplinary committee, the supervision departments, the auditing departments, the tax departments, the state asset departments, and the banks. The evaluation would be organized by central and provincial offices established to strengthen the SOE leadership teams.

These instructions of the Organization Department are vague and do not ask for regular, such as annual, evaluation. The Finance Ministry, on the government side, in 1999 followed up with extremely detailed instructions on how to evaluate the achievements (*xiaoji pingjia*) of enterprises (FM, 1 June 1999). Enterprise achievements were to be evaluated with respect to four categories, namely financial results, assets, ability to repay liabilities, and development capabilities; each category had three sets of indicators (basic indicators, secondary indicators, and appraisal indicators). For example, one basic indicator of financial results was the return on assets, a secondary indicator of financial results was the change in net worth, and an appraisal indicator of financial results was the "basic quality" (*jiben suzhi*) of the leadership team. Each indicator carried a specified weight, with all basic and secondary indicators across the four categories accounting for 80% of the overall grade. The overall numerical grade, based on forty different indicators, was then translated into a letter grade. The achievement was reported to (i) the local government, (ii) the departments in charge of the leadership team in order to form the basis for appointment and dismissal decisions and to be added to the leaders' files, (iii) the leadership team itself in order to encourage improvements, and (iv) other government departments as relevant.

This 1999 regulation only stipulated the details on the evaluation content and process, without specifying what degree of a particular indicator would be regarded as satisfactory for a specific enterprise. This was the task of those who organize the evaluation. A regulation from 2000 indicated that the government that owned the SOE would initiate the evaluation of the enterprises that it felt needed to be evaluated, depending on its local economic development strategies; the local finance department, economic and trade department, Chinese Communist Party enterprise work committee, organization and personnel departments, and labor and social security department would then organize the evaluation (FM, 26 April 2000). In early 2001, after two years of trial runs, the Finance Ministry finally asked for the implementation of the evaluation system by governments on all levels for at least their key enterprises; provincial finance departments were to report on their evaluation schemes to the Finance Ministry by the end of March 2001 (FM, 23 March 2001).[205]

Parallel to the increasingly sophisticated evaluation process, a complex supervisory system emerged. The origin of today's supervisory system for SOEs is a 1994 State Council regulation on "property supervision" (*caichan jiandu*) (SC, 24 July 1994), whereby the State Council determines the "supervisory institution" for each central SOE (or conglomerate), usually the superordinate government department, which then formally supervises the SOE; this includes the establishment of a supervisory board. The supervisors, holding concurrent positions in their original departments as well as on the supervisory board, comprise staff delegated from the supervisory institution, from the Finance Ministry, the SETC, the National State Asset Administration Bureau, the banks, specialists hired by the supervisory institution, the enterprise leaders appointed by the supervisory institution, and labor representatives. The broadly defined tasks of the supervisory board include examination of the enterprise's financial reports, management performance (*jingying xiaoyi*), and the conservation or increase of enterprise assets (*caichan baozhi zengzhi*). Should the supervisory board find any misconduct, such as "improper management, losses in more than two years, and losses that are increasing," the supervisory institution has

---

[205] Management evaluation took on particular urgency in loss-making enterprises. The SETC and Personnel Ministry issued a separate regulation on the leadership team in loss-making enterprises on 9 August 1999.

the authority to dismiss, demote, or penalize the manager or any other directly responsible personnel. Provincial governments are to proceed similarly with provincial-level SOEs.[206]

In 1997, the Finance Ministry, concerned about the insufficient financial supervision of SOEs, twice asked the finance departments at all levels to send supervisors to their SOEs and, jointly with other government departments, to begin to supervise (SC, 27 Feb. 1997; FM, 21 Oct. 1997). SOEs that still did not have a supervisory board were nevertheless subject to external financial supervision directly through the finance departments. Ten items of management misconduct are given special attention. For one, enterprise funds may not be misused for consumption and excessive wage payments and after-tax profit must first be used to increase the profit reserves (with the contribution accounting for at least 10% of the after-tax profit), before an amount no larger than the increase in profit reserves may be used to fund social welfare facilities within the SOE.

In 2000, the State Council replaced its 1994 regulation on supervision with a new regulation explicitly on the establishment of supervisory boards (SC, 22 March 2000).[207] Much of the focus of this new regulation is on key large SOEs (*guoyou zhongdian daxing qiye*). The State Council itself appoints the supervisory board and expects a formal report after the annual (or twice annual) inspection of the enterprises; the report requires approval by the State Council before it is passed on to the SETC and the Finance

---

[206] This first regulation triggered numerous provincial-level regulations, such as in Shandong (Shangdong Government, 7 Jan. 1995), as well as regulations by individual government departments, such as the Finance Ministry, the SETC, and the National State Asset Administration Bureau on the dispatch of their supervisors to the supervisory boards (FM, 17 July 1995; SETC, 13 July 1995; National State Asset Administration Bureau, 1 June 1995). A 1995 regulation by the SETC and the National State Asset Administration Bureau then sketched out further details (SETC, 18 April 1995). The SETC together with the Labor Ministry also established an SOE asset management responsibility system, whereby an enterprise would sign a contract with its superordinate government department guaranteeing the conservation if not the increase of the enterprise's assets. Economic and trade commissions at all levels were to make the necessary arrangements. (SETC, 5 April 1995)

[207] While the SETC in 1995 stated that the supervisory boards would be separate from the formal supervisory boards required by the Company Law (SETC, 18 April 1995), the State Council did not make this distinction in 2000.

Ministry. (In 1998, the National State Asset Administration Bureau was folded into the SETC and the Finance Ministry.) The head of the supervisory board, a full-time position, must have the rank of a deputy-minister, while other full-time supervisors must have the rank of a division head (one rank below that of a minister). The supervisory board also includes representatives from labor who are "democratically elected" by the enterprise's staff and worker representative congress. The supervisory board of key large SOEs has clearly defined rights and can, if need be, through the State Council ask the State Audit Bureau to undertake the complete audit of an enterprise. The supervisory board's overarching task is to supervise the conservation and increase in state assets. In more detail, it examines if the enterprise adheres to the relevant laws, rules and regulations; it examines the financial and accounting reports of the enterprise and attests their correctness; it examines the enterprises' economic performance, profit distribution, the use of state assets and changes in their value; it examines the management behavior of the enterprise's responsible persons (*fuzeren*); and it proposes rewards and punishments, appointments and dismissals. In the case of those SOEs to which the State Council does not appoint a supervisory board, provincial governments are asked to decide if they would establish a supervisory board.

A third level of control beyond management evaluation procedures and supervisory boards is the special inspectorate (*jicha tepaiyuan*) established by the State Council in 1998 (SC, 7 May 1998 and 9 July 1998). The State Council regulations again focus on key large SOEs, but in contrast to the supervisory boards, the special inspectorate was not established by the superordinate government department but was initially integrated into the Personnel Ministry. One full-time special inspector at the rank of a minister or deputy-minister, appointed by the State Council, together with four full-time division-rank assistants appointed by the Personnel Ministry, examines five enterprises, each enterprise twice a year. Their report is first verified by the SETC or other relevant departments before it is submitted by the Personnel Ministry to the State Council for final approval. The tasks of the special inspectorate are virtually identical to those of the supervisory board. Consequently, SOEs to which a special inspector has been dispatched do not need to establish a supervisory board. The dispatch of special inspectors is less wide-spread than the establishment of supervisory boards, with provinces not establishing their own special inspectorates. The number of special inspectors is unknown, but presumably on the order of several dozen (not in the hundreds or thousands). In 1998, the special inspectorate office of the Personnel Ministry had thirty (administrative?) staff (SC, 17 July 1998). In late 1999, the special inspectorate was moved from the Personnel Ministry to the newly established CCPCC Enterprise Work Committee; this committee now also approves the special inspectors, who are then appointed by the State Council, and it directly appoints the assistants.[208]

On the fourth level of control are the auditing departments at all government levels. The superordinate government departments of those enterprises without special inspectors are to have the enterprise management evaluated by the corresponding government's auditing department at the end of an appointment period (CCPCC General Office, 29 June 1999). The items to be audited are largely of financial nature, such as the balance sheet and the profit and loss account.

The final guarantor against improper management behavior is the Chinese Communist Party. The Finance Ministry's 1997 drive to eradicate management misbehavior occurred at the same time as the CCPCC laid down "standards" against corruption by Party cadres, which includes government officials and SOE leaders who are Party members.[209] The standards took the form of a detailed list of inappropriate behavior. The SETC, referring to these standards, then drew up its own list of unacceptable behavior for SOE leadership teams in 1999 (SETC, 26 April 1999).[210]

The Chinese Communist Party furthermore is directly involved in the leadership appointment of SOEs at all levels. On 1 December 1999, the CCPCC Enterprise Work Committee took over the administration of 163

---

[208] This new committee replaces the former CCPCC Large Enterprise Work Committee. (CCPCC, 1 Dec. 1999)

[209] In the case of SOEs, the standards apply to Party members in the mid-level administration and above of large SOEs and to those leaders of medium SOEs who are Party members. (CCPCC, 17 April 1997).

[210] Other institutions also played their role in trying to contain corruption in SOEs. The Supreme People's Procuratorate, for example, elaborated on preventive measures against corruption in SOEs on 18 July 2001.

SOEs formerly under the State Council. Of these 163 SOEs, the leadership teams of 39 "backbone" (*gugan*) SOEs is approved by the committee and then appointed by the State Council; in the case of the other backbone SOEs (among the 163), the committee also approves the leadership team, which is then subsequently appointed by the Personnel Ministry. A newly established CCPCC Enterprise Work Commission for Discipline Inspection, · reporting to both the CCPCC Commission for Discipline Inspection and the CCPCC Enterprise Work Committee, supervises the implementation of Party policies as well as of State Council and CCPCC Commission for Discipline Inspection instructions in these SOEs.[211]

Across all SOEs, the Chinese Communist Party insists on its continued political leadership (CCPCC, 24 Jan. 1997). This implies that SOEs have to follow Party policies and state laws, rules, and regulations, and that the Party is in charge of cadre administration (*dang guan ganbu*). In practice, the Party organization in an SOE participates in all major decisions, such as on long-term development plans and annual plans, financial planning, asset restructuring, and the selection of all mid-level and higher-level cadres. The manager and board of directors must ask the SOE's Party committee for its opinion before making major decisions, and the implementation of any decision should later be reported to the Party committee. If the Party committee discovers major problems and these are not redressed, it reports to the relevant government departments and the higher level Party organization.

The Party committee recommends mid- and high-level cadres to the manager or board of directors for appointment and runs checks on anyone who might be appointed to such positions. All mid- and high-level cadres must be cleared by the organization department and the personnel department, and their appointments must be discussed by the Party and administrative leaders (*dangzheng lingdao*) in the SOE before appointment by the manager.

---

[211] See also the CCPCC Commission for Discipline Inspection's 29 June 2000 instructions on the administration of the discipline commission within the selected group of by then 42 (originally 39) backbone SOEs.

In formal companies, the Party secretary may at the same time hold the position of the chairman of the board of directors. If the Party secretary and the chairman of the board of directors are two different persons, then the chairman of the board of directors, if a Party member, can also take up the position of deputy-secretary of the Party committee, while the Party secretary also functions as deputy-chairman of the board of directors. Members of the Party committee may enter the board of directors, the supervisory board, and the management team. In medium and small SOEs, the Party secretary may at the same time function as the manager.

The secondary literature interprets these CCPCC instructions in favor of even greater Party participation in SOE matters. Thus Qi Yu, Hu Linhui, and Miao Qingwang (2002) stress that suitable members of the SOE Party committee should be recommended to become members of the board of directors so that members of the SOE Party committee make up a "proper" (*yiding*) share of the members of the board of directors. Members of the SOE Party committee can enter the board of directors both as representatives of the public (the state) or of the employees. These Party committee members on the board of directors are then the conduit through which to channel Party committee decisions into the board of directors; but the Party committee can also formally inform the board of directors of its decision, just as the board of directors is to report on all major decision-making to the Party committee.[212]

Actual practices vary from locality to locality. One province for which further details are available is Shanxi (Li Chun and Chen Yongqi, 1999). The SOE leadership team in provincial SOEs in Shanxi is appointed either directly by the provincial Party committee, by the provincial Party committee in cooperation with the relevant government departments, or by the provincial organization department as entrusted by the provincial Party committee. At the municipal level, the organization department may sometimes appoint the leadership team, while at other times this task may rest with the economic and trade commission. In everyday operations, the Party cell of a municipal

---

[212] The Party influence, however, has its limitations when members of the board of directors vote on a decision. At this point, members of the board of directors who are at the same time members of the Party committee are supposed to be free to vote as they choose.

SOE reports to the (county-level) city Party committee of the city in which the enterprise is located, but when it comes to the year-end evaluation of the enterprise's leadership, the Party reports to the municipal organization department.[213]

Implications

With privatization not an option for large and medium SOEs, two key questions for these enterprises are what are their objectives, and what are the mechanisms to ensure that these objectives are being pursued and achieved? As it turns out, these SOEs do not have an unambiguous objective of profit maximization. The CCPCC in 1995 and 1997 suggested a number of vague objectives, and the Finance Ministry in 1999 then issued a total of forty categories of objectives, some more operational than others, including unambiguous financial variables. But the Finance Ministry could not determine the degree to which a particular variable should be achieved; this remains the prerogative of the direct owner of the SOE (the corresponding government or one of its departments).

The mechanisms to ensure that SOEs seek to achieve their objectives, whatever they may be (in practice they might often come close to profit maximization), appear weak. The enterprise evaluation process as well as the supervisory boards for all SOEs except the key large SOEs are far too cumbersome to be of any practical use. In both cases, the superordinate department of an SOE has to take the lead and initiate the evaluation process or establish the supervisory board. The evaluation or supervision then involves numerous other government departments. Even if these processes were followed only in the case of the large and medium industrial SOEs,

---

[213] Li Chun and Chen Yongqi (1999) also stress that supervision is too dispersed among the superordinate government department, the auditing department, the tax office, the discipline department, the enterprise-internal Party organization, the trade union, and employees to be effective. The supervisory board is not effectively supervising the board of directors. The supervisory board may send an external accountant to an enterprise, who within a few days is co-opted by the enterprise. (Li Chun and Chen Yongqi are members of the CCPCC Shanxi committee policy research office.)

there would still be around 15,000 evaluation committees and supervisory boards, with delegates from the various government departments. Superordinate government departments may also have no interest in allowing other government departments to meddle with their enterprises.

Not astonishingly, the Finance Ministry in 1997 asked the local finance departments simply to go ahead with the supervision process on their own. But the local finance departments were unlikely to have enough staff to conduct meaningful supervision of all local industrial SOEs. The local auditing department, similarly, would be able to audit only a few SOEs, and it would do so only upon request by the SOE's superordinate government department. Furthermore, none of these evaluation/supervision/audit processes involves any form of control that is truly external to the SOE. From the superordinate government department to the representatives of labor on the supervisory boards and the various local government departments, all are in some significant way linked to the SOE.

The only instance where the supervision process may work as envisaged are the key large central SOEs to which the State Council — since 1999 the CCPCC Enterprise Work Committee — dispatches special inspectors or to which the State Council appoints supervisory boards. While the number of these SOEs, often state-owned conglomerates, may be small, their aggregate value-added may account for a fair share of industrial value-added. (As mentioned above, the 4,800 large industrial SOEs accounted for 70.08% of the value-added of all industrial SOEs in 1997.)

The special inspectors may truly be independent of the enterprise. Given their rank, they are likely to have the necessary authority to gain access to all relevant information and to question the quality of information if necessary. The detailed institutional arrangements of their inspection are all reasonable. The fact that they are attached to the CCPCC Enterprise Work Committee (previously to the Personnel Ministry) implies that their findings carry weight. Similarly, the high rank of the members of the supervisory boards established by the State Council for key large SOEs suggests that these institutions are to be taken seriously.

Apart from the key large SOEs or backbone SOEs, a second group of enterprises should theoretically be subject to proper supervision. This is the group of SOEs that have adopted the formal company system. The formal company system in principle establishes powerful mechanisms to discipline management. The board of directors serves as a first instance to safeguard against incompetent management, and the supervisory board as a second instance. But in practice, the original intent of the formal company system has been undermined by the dominating role of the Party committee within the enterprise. If the Party committee provides most members of the board of directors and the supervisory board, as well as the manager, and if important decisions are made in the Party committee, then the formal company system, with its checks and balances, is no more than a new veneer on old practices. (Ironically, the Company Law does not once mention a Party committee.)

Much hope has been pinned on ownership diversification through listing on the stock market. External control through shareholders is expected to improve industrial SOE profitability. But if the formal company system has in practice been hollowed out, then becoming a company and listing on the stock market makes no difference. Neither does the exact ownership structure of listed companies, as long as the state retains a majority, as it does for virtually all listed SOEs. Perhaps more rigorous publication requirements and the increased exposure to the media can force listed SOEs to operate more responsibly, but the originally envisaged final control through independent shareholders may not exist.

Xu Xiaonian and Wang Yan (1997), in an early study, found that the performance of firms listed on the Shanghai and Shenzhen stock markets was positively correlated with the fraction of legal person shares, suggesting that legal persons may exert a positive influence on performance through effective monitoring of enterprise management. The fraction of state shares had an ambiguous or negative effect on performance, while ownership concentration had a positive effect. Wang Xiaozu, Xu Lixing, and Zhu Tian (2001), in a study including more recent data, did not look at the impact of legal persons' shares, but found that ownership concentration did not significantly affect performance. Neither did the fraction of state shares. While these findings do not necessarily reject the hypothesis that partial privatization via the stock market may be beneficial to enterprise performance, the fact that the fraction of state shares has no impact on performance suggests that the elaborate construct of the shareholders' meeting, the supervisory board, the board of directors and the manager may not work as it is supposed to work.

Overall, China's SOEs lack a reliable mechanism to identify and purge poor management in a timely and reliable fashion. The formal mechanisms appear hollowed out by the pervasive role of the Party. In the case of SOEs listed on the stock market, independent shareholders with sufficient clout (in terms of volume of shares) do not exist thanks to the state majority in listed SOEs; hostile takeovers are as yet unknown. Creditors of SOEs, mostly the state banks, rarely act against their fellow brethren in the circle of state institutions. (SOE bankruptcies happen by plan.)

The "low-price dumping" episode provides a clear instance of the continuing imperfections in China's SOE management administration. It is an example of the potentially severe consequences when management does not have to bear responsibility for its actions. But it also reveals to what extent government departments are still willing and able to interfere in SOEs, despite the often-pronounced separation of government and SOEs. The apparatus for government interference immediately resurfaced once the various SDPC regulations had been issued. Long-abolished industrial line ministries are still fully operational, only now with the title "office" (*ju*) or "association" (*xiehui*). When they call meetings to determine self-discipline prices and sectoral average costs, industrial SOEs attend and listen. The episode also highlighted the conflicts managers face in trying to obey different government departments. The SETC enthusiastically embraced the concept of self-discipline prices, and at least one industrial association went as far as penalizing highly competitive enterprises. It was only when the SDPC interfered through the investigations of its Price Bureau, and when State Council leaders sided with the SDPC, that the anti-competitive fervor became more restrained.

Outlook

The preliminary data for 2001 show that industrial SOEs were almost able to maintain their 2000 performance levels. Industrial SOE profit fell slightly from 240.83b RMB in 2000 to 233.03b RMB in 2001. Losses fell from 70.43b RMB to 68.86b RMB, while gross profit fell from 311.26b RMB to 301.89b RMB. Profitability decreased from 7.36% in 2000 to 6.57% in 2001. The liability-asset ratio fell from 60.34% to 59.46%. The share of loss-making industrial SOEs in all industrial SOEs rose from 34.07% to

35.87%, but the absolute number of loss-making industrial SOEs fell from 18,223 to 17,072. The total number of industrial SOEs fell from 53,489 to 47,593, while sales revenue, at a time of stable prices, increased by 4.96%.[214] The Chinese government appears to have opted for a level of continuing SOE reform that maintains a minimally acceptable profit and profitability level, while not imposing excessive pain on surplus labor.

The 10th Five-Year Plan (2001–2010) delineates the future scope of state ownership in industry (SETC, Oct. 2001). The plan distinguishes between five groups of industrial sectors. (i) Military industry remains overwhelmingly state controlled. (ii) In public goods industries and services as well as in natural monopolies, the state should hold a controlling stake. (iii) In industries of great economic importance for the "strength of the nation," such as the petroleum, car production, telecommunications, machine building, and high technology industries, state backbone enterprises should continue to hold a dominant position. (iv) In key high technology areas, the state should adopt a driving function; it needs not control production, but provides financing and supports basic and applied research. (v) In "ordinary," competitive sectors, the existing SOEs should focus on improving efficiency, with large enterprises adopting the company system and small and medium enterprises undertaking various property rights reforms; domestic enterprises not owned by the state as well as foreign enterprises are invited to participate in the SOE restructuring.[215] The government thus intends to continue to dominate a wide swathe of industrial sectors.[216]

---

[214] See *Statistical Yearbook 2001*, pp. 410-3; *Industrial Yearbook 2001*, pp. 24, 56; *Statistical Abstract 2002*, p. 121.

[215] In 1999, Vice Premier Wu Bangguo listed "three sectors and two types" of enterprises to describe the instances where the state economy should maintain a controlling position. The three sectors are military, natural monopolies, and important public goods and services. The two types of enterprises are important backbone enterprises in "pillar" industries (*zhizhu chanye*) and high-tech industries.

[216] Except for public services, the industrial sectors in which state ownership should dominate are also sectors with high capital intensity. The choice of sectors in which SOEs are to continue to play a major role thus appears rather pragmatic from the point of view of ensuring continued smooth operation of China's economy.

A second aspect of future industrial SOE reform is reform of the administration of SOE management. On 23 June 2000, the CCPCC General Office, in an outline for reform of the cadre system, listed numerous innovations. Positions for SOE managers are to be publicly advertised and the most suitable candidate is to be selected in a competitive manner. Management is to be evaluated annually as well as over the contract period. Files are to be kept on management performance, with poor managers not to be reappointed by the same SOE or appointed by other SOEs. Incentive mechanisms for management are to be improved and may include remuneration in the form of stocks or stock options.

The Labor and Social Security Ministry on 6 November 2000 and then the SETC on 13 March 2001 took the cue: administrative positions in SOEs are to be advertised publicly, and the hiring process to be organized competitively; remuneration within SOEs is to be determined by the particular job position, rather than by age, and remuneration practices for technical personnel and management may take many different forms; the administrative ranking of SOE management was terminated, which should make the interchange of government and enterprise personnel more difficult and thus encourage professional SOE management.

The innovations in the administration of SOE management reflect the last of the four defining principles of the modern enterprise system, "scientific management." Presumably, the "scientific-ness" of a particular manager can be evaluated, such as through the 40-point evaluation list promulgated by the Finance Ministry on 1 June 1999. Databases on managers, controlled by organization and personnel departments, then allow the optimal allocation of managers in traditional central planning fashion, only now of managers instead of production.

But the obstacles to achieving "scientific management" are formidable. The CCPCC Organization Department Research Office (2001, pp. 454–465) reports on changes in the administration of SOE managers that were implemented on a trial basis in eight major cities. In its recommendations for further reform, it rails against the mechanistic application of the principle that the Party administers the cadres; it promotes the creation of a labor market for SOE managers and other qualified personnel. The organization or personnel departments may establish clearing centers for the evaluation and recommendation of higher-level SOE cadres. But the obstacles are numerous, ranging from "work unit protectionism," i.e., the unwillingness of work units to allow qualified staff to leave, to the household registration system that prevents mobility.

A third aspect of future industrial SOE reform is a concentration of the central government's control over SOEs on a small number of very large enterprises. As early as 1991, the State Council decided to choose 100 large SOEs and state-owned conglomerates (*jituan*) and to endow these enterprises with special decision-making authority. These large state-owned conglomerates have come to play a major role in the separation of government from enterprises. In as far as conglomerates are holding companies with numerous subordinate production units (SOEs), the production units are free from *direct* government interference; the government supervises the conglomerates through special inspectors or supervisory boards. Since most central line ministries have been formally abolished, presumably almost all centrally owned SOEs are by now part of some company or conglomerate.

Jiang Zemin in his speech to the 16th Party Congress on 8 November 2002 further stressed the importance of effective control over state assets. Central and local control over state assets is to be clearly separated, and each of the two levels of government then to be fully responsible for the state assets under its control. Thus, the central government will be responsible for large SOEs in the areas of state security, infrastructure, important natural resources, and SOEs in "lifeblood" (*mingmai*) sectors of the national economy. Provincial governments will be responsible for all other assets. Stricter, and clearly delineated control over state assets does not preclude pushing SOEs further towards adopting the shareholding system, developing the mixed-ownership economy, and introducing competition in monopoly sectors. But the state is to hold a controlling share in "important" enterprises and to exercise effective control over these state assets. The following chapter, in the second half, further investigates the issue of effective control over state assets.

9
Conclusions

This final chapter begins with a review of the main findings of the book. The second section examines the implications of these findings for the issue of privatization of industrial SOEs. The third section concludes on the driving factors behind the industrial SOE reforms and evaluates the importance of the obstacles to proper industrial SOE operations commonly noted in the literature. The last section briefly recapitulates the main points of the book.

Main Findings

The question dominating the first part of this book was why industrial SOE profitability declined so drastically throughout the reform period. The overall response is that profitability could not but decline due to changes in the economic system. The economic system prior to the reform period was designed to accumulate an economy-wide surplus in the industrial sector. Once this systemic feature was abandoned, industrial SOE profitability adjusted to, in most sectors, market determined or close to market determined levels.

The adjustment was not spread evenly over the reform period. Reform shocks led to plummeting industrial SOE profitability in the late 1980s and prevented a recovery through the early 1990s. The reform shocks consisted primarily of an administratively ordained economic downturn and then large-scale price reform. The adoption in 1993 of a new accounting system yielded a more meaningful, but also more narrowly defined, measure of profit (and thus a smaller volume of profit).

Industries were opened to new entrants and competition increased throughout the reform period, but perhaps with the largest effects in the 1990s, exerting downward pressure on industrial SOE profitability. Increases in labor remuneration simultaneously reduced the residual profit for a given amount of sales revenue. The discussion of whether competition or excessive labor remuneration reduced industrial SOE profitability over time is resolved once it is recognized that the two are not alternative hypotheses but two separate, simultaneous explanations. The data show that competition as well as labor remuneration played an important role in reducing industrial SOE profitability.

A further factor that may in the course of the economic reforms have reduced industrial SOE profitability is the increase in the liability-asset ratio of industrial SOEs from the early 1980s through the mid-1990s. Yet, a high liability-asset ratio does not necessarily imply low *profitability*. The data show that once other factors are controlled for, a high liability-asset ratio tends to imply a high rather than a low rate of profitability.

Having clarified the reasons for the decline in industrial SOE profitability over time, the second part of this book further explores the characteristics of industrial SOE profitability today. Thus, with the drastic decline in industrial SOE profitability over time, do non-SOEs constitute a preferable alternative to organize industrial production? The time series data show that this is not necessarily the case. The profitability of industrial non-SOEs deteriorated as drastically as that of industrial SOEs, following the same patterns over time. What distinguishes SOEs from non-SOEs is a rather constant profitability gap in favor of non-SOEs across all years. But this gap can be more than explained by just two factors, namely higher circulation taxes and a higher capital intensity in industrial SOEs.

Industrial SOEs face higher circulation taxes because industrial SOEs have a large market share in industrial sectors in which they pay the highest sales taxes and surcharges; the reverse is true for non-SOEs. Within the group of non-SOEs, furthermore, production activities are allocated primarily to those sectors in which they face the lowest sales taxes and surcharges, while the SOE allocation of industrial production activities across sectors does not depend on the rate of sales taxes and surcharges. Industrial SOEs also face a higher average rate of value-added tax than do non-SOEs, in part because small enterprises (mostly non-SOEs) face lower value-added tax rates. In as far as SOEs are predominantly located in high-tax industrial sectors for historical or policy reasons, or in as far as SOEs face higher tax rates due solely to their size, any profitability comparison between SOEs and non-SOEs must take into account this tax discrimination against SOEs.

A similar argument applies to the issue of capital intensity. SOEs are more capital intensive than are non-SOEs industry by industry. The data show that industrial SOEs are trying to avoid production in sectors in which the ratio of current assets to sales revenue is high (in part due to a relatively large volume of accounts receivable). But SOEs are unable to avoid production in sectors with a high ratio of net fixed assets to sales revenue, in contrast to non-SOEs. SOEs are further burdened by a higher share of non-productive fixed assets (an aspect of the social burden). Again, in as far as industrial SOEs' high capital intensity is a historical legacy or the result of enduring SOE-specific policies (such as a lack of market determined exit, or the prevalence of government industrial policies), industrial SOEs cannot be blamed for the profitability gap.

If the capital intensity of SOEs were the same as that in non-SOEs, then industrial SOE profitability, measured as profit relative to equity, would exceed non-SOE profitability in all years. SOE profitability would match the profitability of private enterprises in 1995, the year in which private enterprises performed particularly well. Once the SOEs' higher tax burden is considered, SOEs by far outperform non-SOEs (or the sub-category of private enterprises). These conclusions hold even before three severe selection biases leading to over-estimation of the profitability gap in favor of non-SOEs are considered.

A further chapter in the second part explores the patterns of profitability among industrial SOEs in the mid- and late 1990s. In a perfectly competitive economy, factors such as ownership level, size, location, and industrial sector should not be able to determine enterprise profitability. Yet, China's economy is not a perfectly competitive economy. Multivariate analysis shows that size, location, and industrial sector matter. First, the larger the industrial SOE, the higher its level of profitability. This could be due to such factors as economies of scale, but it could also be due to preferential treatment.

The location of industrial SOEs also matters for their profitability, but the pattern does not unambiguously fit an expected coastal-interior division. Some of the provincial significance is in fact due to differential profitability rates across sectors. For example, Heilongjiang's high level of profitability is due solely to the formidable size of its petroleum and natural gas extraction industry.

The third factor that matters in explaining industrial SOE profitability today is the sector of the SOE. Petroleum and natural gas extraction, tobacco processing, and electricity production and supply are high-profit (and the first two also high-profitability) sectors thanks to government pricing policies. This reflects a clever government choice. High prices in the petroleum and natural gas extraction industry affect all industrial sectors; high prices in the tobacco industry affect a large number of consumers. This indirect 'tax' on the economy is collected by a very few SOEs mostly under central government control. Thanks to the concentration of production in very few enterprises, the potential for leakage is minimal. Much of the profit subsequently finds its way into the government's coffers through corporate income taxes, a special resource tax on petroleum extraction, and a special consumption tax on tobacco products. The case of electricity prices is similar, except that these prices are manipulated by the individual provinces, which make flexible use of this authority to increase provincial aggregate industrial SOE profit (and their own provincial government revenues) when no other high-profitability sectors are available.

In contrast to these three high-profit sectors, the food processing and textile sectors are largely liberalized sectors that had an abysmal profitability record throughout the 1990s. During the three-year SOE reform program, the central government focused on the textile industry, and the data show that layoffs and output reductions have allowed both sectors, but in particular the in 1997 highly labor-intensive state-owned textile industry, to turn the corner. While there may be further scope for sector-specific measures in a number of other low-profitability sectors, no other sector contributes significantly to aggregate SOE losses. However, aggregate industrial SOE profitability in a large number of industrial sectors hovers just above the zero point.

Moving beyond size, location, and sector to individual industrial SOEs reveals that highly loss-making industrial SOEs continue to co-exist with highly profitable industrial SOEs in virtually all sectors. If these worst-performing individual enterprises were closed, aggregate industrial SOE profitability would immediately improve.

But as the previous chapter investigating recent industrial SOE reform policies shows, allowing more industrial SOEs to go bankrupt may not be an option. The government has, during the implementation of the 1998-2000 SOE reform program, paid dearly for turning around the textile sector, establishing a social security network for laid-off workers, transferring a share of SOEs' bad loans from the state banks to resolution trust companies (with much of the price for bad loans in the end to be borne by the government), and providing special appropriations to write off the bad loans of the bankrupt SOEs so that these SOEs can enter bankruptcy proceedings without endangering the stability of the banking system. The government may have chosen to avoid further bankruptcies in order to prevent government debt from increasing even more than it currently does, apart from exacerbating the problem of large-scale unemployment. The gradual reform process also has the advantage that it lowers expectations of workers yet to be laid off and triggers an automatic solution when, for example, more elderly workers reach the retirement age and others look for new jobs on their own account.

The success of the 1998-2000 industrial SOE reform program appears in part due to the shifting of selected financial burdens to the current or future government budget, rather than to improvements in how industrial SOEs operate. Nevertheless, a largely enterprise-financed urban social security system has by now been established, which should allow the continued shedding of excess labor. The mechanisms for further policy bankruptcies are in place, which should continue to remove the worst industrial SOEs every year. Capacity in the textile industry, one of the worst loss-making sectors in 1997, has been reduced, which should limit the continuous destruction of state assets at least in the textile sector; other sectors, such as the coal sector, have also been forced to reduce capacity.

While small SOEs are open to any of a dozen reform measures, including privatization, large and medium SOEs remain under closely controlled state ownership. In 1997, the latest year for which the data are available, large and medium industrial SOEs accounted for approximately 85% of industrial SOE value-added. The state is thus far from abandoning its participation in industrial production. Yet, state ownership raises two questions, namely, what are the objectives of these large and medium industrial SOEs and what are the mechanisms to ensure that these objectives are being pursued and achieved? SOEs do not have an unambiguous profit motive, nor are all except a few subject to potentially well-functioning supervision mechanisms. Almost all large and medium SOEs lack reliable mechanisms to identify and purge poor management in a timely and reliable fashion.

Most of the findings of this book hinge on the quality of the measure of profitability. The key profitability measure throughout is profit relative to equity. This is in contrast to other indicators, namely profit (with or without taxes) relative to net fixed assets or to some other asset measure, indicators that dominate the literature, but bear no unambiguous relationship to the core meaning of profitability, namely the return on equity. The quality of this profitability indicator, profit relative to equity, depends primarily on the quality of the profit measure.[217]

The profit measure used throughout this book is accounting profit. This profit measure is far from perfect as it has been repeatedly redefined through the various revisions to the industrial enterprise accounting system. Furthermore, industrial SOEs faced varying incentives throughout the reform period to misreport profit, with perhaps incentives to overreport in the 1980s, but incentives to underreport in the late 1990s. Yet, accounting profit is still the best measure of profit available. It is perfectly valid for analysis at a particular point of time, while, in time series analysis, the redefinitions need to be kept in mind. The years since 1993 appear a relatively safe period. The alternative measure, operating surplus, based on the income accounts in industry, confirms the time trend of accounting profit. Accounting profit, in contrast to operating surplus, has the further advantage of ready data availability at national, provincial, and sectoral levels, including data that allow tracing the derivation of profit from sales revenue.

---

[217] Equity data are as reliable as the asset data are. Equity is obtained by subtracting liabilities, a usually highly concise measure, from assets. Except for the value of net fixed assets, which account for less than half of total assets, the asset data are likely to also be highly accurate.

Implications for Privatization

The explanations of the decline in industrial SOE profitability and then the examination of the gap between industrial SOE and non-SOE profitability carry direct implications for the ongoing debate on industrial SOE privatization. In as far as the economic transition has run its course and most of China's industrial SOEs now operate in a market environment, enterprises will not be subject to further reform shocks that adversely affect their profitability levels.

The profitability of industrial non-SOEs' declined following a similar time trend as that of industrial SOEs. The over time rather constant gap in the profitability levels of industrial SOEs vs. non-SOEs can be explained by just two factors. Circulation taxes will not automatically fall if an SOE turns into a private enterprise. Neither will SOEs' higher capital intensity, if due to reasons such as historical legacies and policy factors. A reduction in capital intensity may possibly be encouraged by privatization, but privatization is not a necessary condition (if even a sufficient one). The consistent selection bias against SOEs further raises questions on the meaning of low profitability in SOEs compared with the profitability of enterprises under other ownership forms.[218]

The implications are that neither time series data nor present-day comparisons of SOE and non-SOEs provide significant evidence in favor of privatization of the average industrial SOE. This is true not only for non-SOEs in general, which include a wide range of enterprises from collective-owned to foreign-funded enterprises, but also specifically for the sub-category of private enterprises, the best-performing group of enterprises. At the current stage of economic transition with its particular institutional arrangements and economic environment, privatization of industrial SOEs can simply not be expected to lead to immediate improvements in the aggregate profitability of industrial enterprises.

---

[218] On the other hand, SOEs have historically been subject to preferential treatment, which may offset the selection bias against SOEs. Since these effects cannot be quantified, a final comparison is not possible; preferential treatment is likely to have become rarer in recent years.

The Issue of Privatization in the Literature

The position in the literature on privatization is mixed. Nicholas Lardy, quoted in the introduction, after examining the problems in SOEs and in the state banking system, opted for privatization as the only means to successfully reform the state-owned sector. Jeffrey Sachs, also quoted in the introduction, argues that history in China is moving in the direction of privatization. Zhang Weiying (1999), based on what he perceives as the serious governance problems in SOEs, concludes that "privatization is the only way out" (p. 35). In contrast, Thomas Rawski (1999) cautions that "privatization is no magic potion for prosperity. It is only one among many policy alternatives that deserve realistic analyses of costs as well as benefits." (p. 155)

The World Bank in its *World Development Report 1996* outlined three challenges for countries in economic transition (World Bank, 1996b): (i) liberalization, stabilization, and growth; (ii) property rights and enterprise reform; and (iii) social policies that address the ill effects of transition on particular groups. China scores highly on liberalization, stabilization, and growth, the core of the reform package. China has also improved its social policies in recent years. But the progress of enterprise and property rights reform has been slow, in large and medium SOEs focusing on the establishment of a "modern enterprise system," rather than on privatization. For the World Bank, privatization is ultimately a question of whether it improves the performance of the privatized enterprise. The experience in other countries would suggest that it does. Yet "the need to privatize is not equally urgent in all settings. Slower privatization is viable (although not necessarily optimal) if the government, or workers themselves, are strong enough to assert control over enterprises and prevent managers from stealing assets, and if saving and growth in the nonstate sector are high" (p. 50). Saving and growth in China's non-state sector would probably qualify as "high," but Chapter 8 showed that supervision of SOE managers all too often is rather weak.

Other authors are equally cautious in their conclusions on the need for China to privatize its industrial SOEs. Gary Jefferson (1998) argues that SOEs as "public goods" pose three externality problems. These are: (i) since SOEs are owned by all the people, workers, managers, and public officials all extract value in excess of what they put in (the non-excludability problem); (ii) one person's overconsumption need not seriously constrain the ability of others to extract value from the firm (the nondiminishability problem); and (iii) tight money and debt financing divert investment funds and employment-generating opportunities away from the non-state sector. Applying the Coase theorem, externality problems can be resolved without threat to efficiency if costless negotiation is possible, rights are well specified, and redistribution does not affect marginal values. But by lacking functional property rights markets, China is far from meeting these requirements. Gary Jefferson therefore concludes that "privatization and hardening of budget constraints are both elements of a Coasian remedy to public enterprises' externality problem. Although possibly the most effective method, privatization is neither a necessary nor a sufficient condition. Hardening budget constraints is a necessary but not a sufficient condition for eliminating the public-enterprise externality. For smaller enterprises, a hard budget constraint may create the incentive to make a clear and effective assignment of property rights, thus satisfying the second condition of the Coase theorem." (p. 430)

Derek Morris (1995) argues that privatization may be the best solution, but perhaps impractical in the short run. He proposes the establishment of state-owned financial institutions that act as intermediate investment companies for the government. Implementation of such a scheme "will not, of course, be as efficient as private ownership, but we do not take this as a drawback because the whole purpose of the exercise is to improve enterprise governance in those cases where privatization will not be pursued" (p. 67). The state asset management companies (or holding companies) established in recent years should qualify as the "intermediate investment companies" proposed by Derik Morris.

Others find that competition (an outcome of liberalization) is more important than privatization. John McMillan and Barry Naughton (1992) a decade ago maintained that "privatization is not crucial, competition is" (p. 132). For Joseph Stiglitz (1999), "the contrasting experiences of China and Russia suggest that, if one has to make a choice, competition may be more important than private property, especially the form of ersatz privatizations that actually occurred. It is competition that provides the driving force for greater efficiency and lower prices. But competition is also an important part of corporate governance: It is the absence of competition that creates rents that so often get diverted to inefficient uses." (p. 10) As seen in the chapters above, in most industrial sectors China has had no lack of competition.

Peter Nolan (1996, 2001) and Peter Nolan and Wang Xiaoqiang (1999) are perhaps the most positive in their evaluation of China's industrial SOEs. They contest the prevalent view that the small-scale non-state sector has been the main agent of economic growth and argue that private ownership cannot create the large enterprises that form the pillar of China's industrial structure. Privatization of China's large enterprises would only dissipate leadership and control. Drawing parallels to large, sometimes state-owned firms in market economies, Peter Nolan and Wang Xiaoqiang argue that the state has an important role to play in the development of the large enterprises that form the core of a country's industrial base. The need for large enterprises is apparent from the advantages that come with size, such as economies of scale and scope, ability to handle products that require large investments or wide-spread services, or superior R&D. Similarly, Dwight Perkins (1993) argues that, in sectors where economies of scale are large and capital requirements are beyond the financial capacity of local or small-scale firms, there is a role for state agencies. Peter Nolan and Wang Xiaoqiang (1998) ask if perhaps decision-making autonomy for a small group of individuals is not more important than the question of ownership.

The evidence from privatization in other countries is ambiguous. William Megginson and Jeffrey Netter (2001) conclude their survey of empirical studies on privatization with the finding that "research now supports the proposition that privately owned firms are more efficient and more profitable than otherwise-comparable state-owned firms" (p. 380). But they then qualify this finding by pointing out that three aspects of privatization need to be understood much better for public policy reasons; these are the sequencing and staging of privatization, the labor economics of privatization, and the role of privatization in equipping enterprises to meet the challenges posed by major economic forces such as globalization.

Kathryn Dewenter and Paul Malatesta (2001), examining privatization of SOEs among the world's largest non-financial firms, for the case of large firms come to a more differentiated conclusion as to the effects of privatization on firm performance. They conclude that "even though government firms are less profitable than private firms we do not find much evidence that privatization itself increases firm profitability. In our sample, privatization is associated with improved profitability. The improvement, however, largely occurs during the three years just before privatization. The evidence of further privatization is not very robust." (p. 333) Governments appear to restructure their SOEs before the sale in order to achieve a higher sales price, or perhaps manipulate accounting data before selling shares to investors. The authors also suspect that the rationale for privatization may not be to achieve improved performance, but to perpetuate improved performance in the face of changing political circumstances.

Specifically in the case of formerly socialist countries, privatization has been far from an unambiguous success. Bernard Black, Reinier Kraakman, and Anna Tarassova (2000) argue that, in the case of Russia, mass privatization led to massive self-dealing by managers and controlling shareholders. The profit incentives of the newly privatized enterprises were weak in the face of a punitive tax system, official corruption, organized crime, and an unfriendly bureaucracy. The unsuccessful privatization furthermore discredited other reforms and thus undermined longer-term economic reforms.

Simeon Djankov and Peter Murrell (2002) in a quantitative meta-analysis of the literature on enterprise restructuring in transition economies find that the privatization effect on enterprise restructuring (indicators of enterprise performance) in the Commonwealth of Independent States is statistically insignificant. In contrast, state ownership within partially privatized firms is surprisingly effective in promoting enterprise restructuring; competition and hardened budget constraints also matter. These findings augur well for China, where large industrial SOEs are gradually turned into stock companies and listed on the stock market, small industrial SOEs are turned into stock cooperatives, mixed ownership of industrial enterprises is increasingly encouraged (such as by Jiang Zemin at the 16th Party Congress in November 2002), competition in many sectors appears fierce, and budget constraints have hardened over the years.

The Arguments Against Privatization of Large and Medium Industrial SOEs in China

The literature shows that the case for privatization is weaker than the strong statements in favor of privatization by a few prominent authors suggest. China could easily complete the process of economic transition to a largely market-oriented economy by privatizing its SOEs and perhaps, at the same time, its state banks. But the success of such all-out privatization of industrial SOEs would be questionable for a number of reasons.

First, a fair share of China's core industrial enterprises would be unlikely to find a buyer except if the government were to first inject a large amount of funds to restructure their debts. If the government does not pay up, many industrial SOEs will enter bankruptcy proceedings, with numerous, mainly forward linkages causing disruptions across the economy. Courts would not be ready to deal with the onslaught of bankruptcies. The social security system might not be able to handle the wave of the newly unemployed. In the case of East Germany, for example, the German Treuhandanstalt was able to privatize (or liquidate) its 8500 state enterprises relatively quickly, but at an enormous cost in terms of both skilled personnel and explicit or implicit subsidies to buyers (World Bank, 1996b, p. 54). The Chinese leadership may not deem it politically (if not economically) feasible to raise the funds necessary to pay for privatization. As seen in Chapter 8, writing off the bad loans in the state banking system, which would have to go hand in hand with industrial SOE privatization, alone would exceed China's annual budget revenues.

Second, most industrial SOE value-added is produced in large enterprises with relatively high capital intensity. Chapter 7 showed that non-SOEs have so far focused on the least capital-intensive sectors.[219] Private entrepreneurs may not have access to the funds needed to take over capital-intensive SOEs, and the government might be reluctant to sell to foreigners. Even if China's state banks were to truly become commercial banks, bank managers

---

[219] The correlation obviously does not imply a particular causality. The focus of non-SOEs on the least capital-intensive sectors could be their own choice, or it could be due to external constraints such as government policies limiting access to the more capital-intensive sectors.

may not immediately be sufficiently qualified (or bold enough) to reach lending decisions on purely market-based principles. Far-reaching reforms of the financial system, such as interest rate liberalization and an end to credit plans, would have to proceed at the same pace as privatization.

Third, the institutions relevant to privatized industrial enterprises must be in place. Apart from reform of the financial markets, these also include the legal, regulatory and accounting framework, the social security system, the housing system, land markets, and markets for skilled labor.[220] Chapter 8 showed that while work has begun if not advanced well on some of these institutions, it is still incomplete. The new institutions do not yet have a history of firmly established and well functioning practices.

Fourth, given the still imperfect accounting and asset evaluation system in China as well as ambiguous land values (Chapters 3 and 5), an all-out sale of industrial SOEs would be accompanied by large uncertainties on the value of these SOEs. This is particularly true for large and medium industrial SOEs. The current state of SOE finances may also not reflect their future viability and growth opportunities; their growth prospects in part depend on the degree of future government involvement in the economy through such practices as industrial policies and various approval procedures. The government's word that it will in the future abstain from frequent policy changes and from the most interventionary policies would have to be taken on faith as the current economic environment is still heavy with government involvement.

Fifth, a sufficient reservoir of private entrepreneurs would have to stand ready and be qualified to run large-scale production activities that involve hundreds of thousands of employees. Employees would have to be ready for their enterprises to be taken over by private capital even if it would mean that their jobs would be cut. As seen in Chapter 6, private enterprises, i.e., individual-owned enterprises with more than seven employees and with annual sales revenue in excess of 5m RMB, accounted for just 5.19% of the value-added of all industrial enterprises with independent accounting

---

[220] Dwight Perkins (1993, p. 150) includes a brief list of the reforms in the external environment of industrial SOEs that need to occur at the same time as SOE reforms.

system and with annual sales revenue in excess of 5m RMB in 2000, compared with the 54.26% share of the state-owned and state-controlled enterprises. Across-the-board privatization would mean the creation of utterly new privately controlled and often large enterprises for which there is virtually no precedent in China today.[221]

Sixth, the development of China's industrial SOEs matches well-accepted development patterns, with the central government providing a big push in core industries that have numerous forward (and sometimes backward) linkages. Profit opportunities in upstream and downstream industries are then taken up by smaller, local SOEs, or enterprises under other ownership forms. Many industrial SOEs furthermore have large positive externalities through research and development, learning by doing, and their impact on the development of the local infrastructure.[222] Private entrepreneurs focusing on profitability might choose to eschew these industries if they cannot internalize a significant share of the positive externalities; otherwise they might try to reduce the extent to which positive externalities are produced. Technological progress furthermore is traditionally passed on from large, central SOEs to smaller SOEs subordinate to localities. With SOEs increasingly competing against each other and with the line ministries' (now companies') tasks of facilitating this transfer being gradually eroded, these transfers are diminished. But technological progress is still concentrated in large, central SOEs and such progress still benefits other enterprises if not through outright transfer then through the exchange of

---

[221] In terms of sales revenue, the largest private enterprise in China in 2001, Lianxiang konggu youxian gongsi, had annual sales revenue of 32.8b RMB, which made it a rather large enterprise. But the second-largest private enterprise had annual sales revenue of "only" 8.6b RMB and it is unclear how fast sales revenue drop off for the next private enterprises in the size list. In 2001, 1,247 private enterprises had sales revenue in excess of 120m RMB. The *average* industrial SOE, in contrast, including all small industrial SOEs (altogether 53,489 industrial SOEs), in 2000 had annual sales revenue of 79m RMB. (*Xinbao*, 28 Oct. 2002, p. 18; *Statistical Yearbook 2001*, pp. 420, 423)

[222] For example, of the 520 state key industrial enterprises (of which 514 are state key SOEs), 423 had established a formal "technology development center" (*jishu kaifa zhongxin*) by late 2000. The enterprises are expected to expend an amount equivalent to 3-5% of their sales revenue on research and development. (SETC, 1 Sept. 2000) Many township and village enterprises and other non-state enterprises, in contrast, rely on employees of SOEs for advice in setting up and maintaining their production lines.

personnel, and it benefits consumers through competitive pressure in the product markets.[223]

Privatization, finally, would have to be politically feasible. But privatization is not a cornerstone of socialist ideology. At the National Party Congress November 2002, General Party Secretary Jiang Zemin stressed the importance of public (i.e., state or collective) ownership as the foundation of the socialist economic system. The about-face that privatization of industrial SOEs would imply might endanger the justification of the political system itself.

Today's market economies had their fair number of SOEs in their earlier phases of development; the successful newly industrialized countries in Asia caught up through major state ownership across the economy. In the case of China, it is only now, after two decades of reform and development and declining catching-up effects, that the developmental role of the Chinese government may be receding, or shifting domestically from the more-developed coastal regions to less-developed central and Western China. This is a gradual process.

Perhaps the story told by the data earlier in this book remains the strongest argument cautioning against hasty privatization. Over the first 22 years of economic reform, the profitability of industrial non-SOEs declined similarly to that of industrial SOEs. The consistent profitability gap in favor of industrial non-SOEs (or the narrower group of private industrial enterprises within the non-SOEs) can be explained by just two factors, namely the higher rate of circulation taxes faced by SOEs, and the higher capital intensity of SOEs. Privatization cannot change the rate of circulation taxes, and it may also not significantly change the degree of capital intensity. The comparative data thus imply that, given the current economic environment and institutional context, a drastic switch in ownership is unlikely to lead

---

[223] Albert Hu (2001) examines the link between R&D and productivity in Chinese industry based on a survey of all high-tech firms in the Haidian District of Beijing in 1996 (with 1995 data). Of the 813 firms, only five firms were private firms; these were omitted from the further analysis due to their small number. SOEs accounted for 38.87% of all enterprise and collective-owned enterprises for another 26.45%. The R&D intensity (R&D/sales) in SOEs was average, compared with enterprises under other ownership forms, while the technician-labor ratio in SOEs was the highest.

to large improvements in profitability. It furthermore carries the risk of severely interrupting the proper functioning of the core of China's industrial structure in the short to medium term.

Cao Yuanzheng, Qian Yingyi, and Barry Weingast (1999) argued that "part of the reason we project that the central government will eventually privatize some of the largest SOEs is that it too faces the same financial incentives as local governments: Once the central government gives up its monopoly in the key industries, maintaining inefficient enterprises is too expensive" (p. 125). They thus implicitly recognize that local governments are making rational decisions. Rational decisions in the case of large and medium industrial SOEs, by the central government, may well imply continued reform of these industrial enterprises under continued state ownership. The government continues to respond to the challenges of industrial SOE reform as they arise, with the direction of further reform developed in the process of resolving real-world problems.

Key Issues in Industrial SOE Reform

With all-out privatization not a likely reform measure in China in the near future and clearly not a preferred reform option of the current Chinese leadership, maintaining industrial SOE profitability at the levels of 2000 or even raising it further will require continued reform in the future.

The Driving Factors Behind Industrial SOE Reform

In the past 24 years, China has been engaged in moving from one economic system, the planned economy, to a new economic system, a largely market-oriented economy. Both systems, once in place, represent stable modes of operation. But each needs its own set of institutions. The difficult part is finding a viable and sustainable path from one system with its appropriate institutions to another system with its appropriate institutions, and then to pursue this path at the appropriate speed. China may not even have embarked on the journey with a clear view of the path in front, but rather proceeded by trial and error.

Gary Jefferson and Thomas Rawski (1999) describe the transition procedure of the first two reform decades as one where endogenous mechanisms propelled industrial SOE reform. Reform eroded market segmentation, thereby lowering barriers to technology and resources. These reforms intensified competition in markets for industrial products. Competition eroded profits and curtailed the growth of fiscal revenues. Enterprises reacted to market pressure by beginning to search for financial gains; governments extended enterprise autonomy, increased market exposure, and hardened budget constraints. Feedback mechanisms evolved, such as greater autonomy leading to more discretionary wage payments, which in turn encouraged productivity growth, which then further intensified competition. Partial reform also won over former advocates of central planning because the first successful reforms showed managers the benefits they would gain from reform.

In broader terms, three factors appear to have been crucial in the process of industrial SOE reform. First, industrial reforms came with clear gains, and these gains have been widely distributed. Thus, the end of provincial self-sufficiency allowed new economies of scale, price reform led to a better allocation of resources, material incentives for workers led to increases in labor productivity (and higher incomes of laborers), and the adoption of new technologies (from other domestic sources or abroad) improved the productivity of capital. The increase in labor remuneration within industrial SOEs shows that labor benefited. Government bureaucrats benefited in their function as managers of industrial SOEs and, more recently, with the transition of line ministries into holding companies (or state asset management companies), as the leaders of these companies. The first key factor is thus that a large foundation of support for industrial SOE reform has been built up over the years when most SOE employees and relevant government bureaucrats benefited from the reforms.

But any increase in labor's benefits potentially reduces the residual profit; other factors, such as competition, also have a negative effect on profit. This forces the government to act on two fronts. A decline in industrial SOE profit undermines the funding base of an enterprise; the importance of bank funding grows, and/or new sources of equity funding are needed. The subsequent growth in bank lending relative to enterprise assets increases pressure on the state banking system to think twice about the quality of its loans. Once the bad loan problem became a significant issue in the late 1990s, the government was forced to move the state banks further towards market-oriented lending decisions. At the same time, the government increased direct access of industrial SOEs to the capital markets, year by year.

A decline in industrial SOE profit also implies a decline in corporate income taxes. Losses furthermore imply a decline in the value of the state's equity in SOEs, i.e., the annihilation of state assets. The government's industrial SOE measures in the early 1990s and then, in particular, the 1998–2000 SOE reform program, show that the government is willing and able to respond. The recent industrial SOE reforms, although not drastic by big bang standards, have led to a clear, new industrial SOE strategy, outlined at the end of the previous chapter, whereby the government focuses on certain industrial sectors and certain enterprises within these sectors. The originally worst performing small industrial SOEs have or are being cut loose. Localities are even going further and experimenting freely with all types of industrial SOE reforms, including, at the extreme, ownership changes in public utilities.[224] The second key factor is thus that the government has always responded to the challenges that industrial SOEs posed and has inevitably moved forward with further market-oriented reforms. It has little other choice, given that it bears the final financial responsibility for industrial SOEs and state banks. The one period when reforms stalled, in 1989–1991, led to such dreadful results in terms of industrial SOE profitability that this period may have come to serve as a lesson for what happens if the government is not responsive.

The reduction in (total) SOE employment by one-third between 1998 and 2000 is a case in point for the determination of the government. This employment reduction is almost of the size of the total labor force of one of

---

[224] For example, Shenzhen is ready to privatize partially five major enterprises, namely the Shenzhen Energy Conglomerate, the Water Conglomerate, the Fuel and Gas Conglomerate, the Public Transportation Conglomerate, and the General Foods Company. Domestic and international investors have been invited to take a (in total) minority stake in the first four companies; the state retains a majority share as it still exercises price control over these conglomerates' output. A 70% stake of the General Foods Company is to be sold to two foreign partners. Domestic or international auditors, law firms, and asset evaluation institutions, all using international standards, are to be hired to implement the sale. (*Xinbao*, 29 Aug. 2002, p. 12)

the larger European countries. The absence of large-scale labor unrest either implies wide acceptance of the need for industrial SOE reform, or reveals the power and the willingness of the Chinese leadership to enforce reforms that it regards as necessary. The by-and-large successful 1998–2000 SOE reform program set the stage for continuing industrial SOE reform measures in the future.

When Kathryn Dewenter and Paul Malatesta (2001) interpreted their findings that privatization in their sample of the world's largest companies did not lead to improved performance (but performance improved in the three years prior to privatization), they suggested that privatization served to lock in the gains achieved in the previous years. In China, it is the momentum for industrial SOE reform that appears to have been locked in. This is the third important factor in industrial SOE reform in China.

One way the momentum for industrial SOE reform has been locked in is through the unleashing of non-state enterprises. By 2000, industrial SOEs in their broadest definition, including all, even minor state shares in industrial enterprises under other ownership forms, accounted for just 34.82% of economy-wide industrial value-added in China (industry's contribution to GDP). Collective-owned enterprises, foreign-funded enterprises (including those funded by Hong Kong, Macao, and Taiwanese entrepreneurs), and private enterprises, all with annual sales revenue in excess of 5m RMB, accounted for 7.76%, 15.39%, and 3.33%, respectively. Industrial non-SOEs with annual sales revenue below 5m RMB accounted for as much as another 35.82%. In 1999, the last year for which the following data are available, individual-owned and private enterprises alone accounted for 18.18% of industrial gross output value, up from 0% in 1978.[225] In most industrial sectors, industrial SOEs are thus likely to face fierce competition. The latest response to this competition is the announced future industrial SOE reform strategy; the government sees no further important role for industrial SOEs in the most competitive sectors.

A second way the momentum for industrial SOE reform has been locked in is through China's WTO accession in December 2001. WTO succession has locked in the trend of opening up industrial sectors to non-state

---

[225] See *Statistical Yearbook 2000*, p. 409; *Statistical Yearbook 2001*, p. 49; *Industrial Yearbook 2001*, p. 49.

enterprises, particularly to foreign enterprises. This happens through a reduction in import tariffs and import restrictions, as well as through foreign investment in these industrial sectors in China. Joint ventures between industrial SOEs and foreign companies are a favored approach to advance industrial SOE reform, including reform of the large and medium industrial SOEs.

Obstacles to Industrial SOE Profitability

When arguing for the inferiority of industrial SOEs, the literature focuses on corporate governance issues, as earlier reported in the introductory chapter. Thus, industrial SOEs lack a hard budget constraint. Industrial SOEs in China also suffer from three idiosyncrasies, namely differential social responsibilities, high capital intensity, and some remaining price distortions; given the information asymmetry between enterprise managers and owners, the state finds it impossible to distinguish between policy-induced losses and losses due to managerial incompetence.

These obstacles are clearly relevant to China's industrial SOEs. A hard budget constraint would impose a credible threat of exit. Removing the idiosyncrasies in order to achieve a level playing field would remove the information-asymmetry of managers and owners as to whether losses are policy-induced or operational in nature. Stronger institutions that resolve the corporate governance problems in industrial SOEs are desirable. Yet, perhaps, the importance of these factors has been overstated, or it has diminished in recent years.

Few large enterprises in Western countries have a truly hard budget constraint. Long-Term Capital Management in the U.S. was saved through the intervention of the Federal Reserve Bank in 1998. The Airbus Consortium in Europe is routinely subsidized, for example in its research operations, through the European Union. Amtrak in the U.S. appears to enjoy a rather soft budget constraint. Governments across "market" economies, but perhaps especially in the European Union, intervene when the failure of large enterprises threatens to lead to large lay-offs.

In China, the 1994 tax reform instituted a clear demarcation of government vs. enterprise funds. Since 1994, enterprises pay circulation taxes and corporate income taxes on their profit. Profit is no longer handed over to governments, except in the case of a few large SOEs which have special arrangements with the central government. Banks are increasingly under pressure to reach market-based lending decisions; the credit crunch in recent years is usually attributed to the reluctance of banks to extend new loans to the riskier enterprises among their customers. Explicit government subsidies to loss-making enterprises have fallen sharply over the years. Holding companies (or state asset management companies) may redistribute funds among their individual enterprises, but serve as a buffer between government and enterprises; the holding companies themselves supposedly operate in financial independence from the government. The budget constraint of industrial SOEs in China thus appears to have hardened over time and perhaps hardened to an extent where the issue of a hard vs. soft budget constraint has lost some of its importance.

Of the three idiosyncrasies, price distortions are likely to have become a minor issue. As seen in Chapter 3, approximately 90% of all prices are by now market determined. The government, or its surrogate in the form of holding companies or associations, may still be interfering in the price-setting mechanism but the extent of interference does not seem to warrant making price distortions the crux of industrial SOE reform. Differential social responsibilities are increasingly being removed through the establishment of the enterprise-external social security network. Progress on this social security network has been rapid enough that this problem could be off the list of most severe industrial SOE deficiencies soon.

What remains of the SOE idiosyncrasies is the high capital intensity of industrial SOEs. Industrial SOEs' capital intensity is higher than that of non-SOEs across all sectors. But the sectoral classification at a single digit level is not very sophisticated. Within one sector, industrial SOEs could be located in sub-sectors that require high capital intensity. What the data across sectors reveal is that non-SOEs are avoiding high capital intensity sectors, while SOEs are not. This suggests that the current high capital intensity of industrial SOEs is in part a historical remnant. It may reflect the deeply rooted tendency of socialist economies to overinvest, with governments encouraging investment at the expense of consumption. If the capital intensity of China's industrial SOEs were excessive by international standards, WTO accession is likely to help identify which industrial SOEs need to write off excessive assets and the government may continue to respond with reform measures.

Other aspects of corporate governance are also not as important as often made out. One aspect is direct interference by governments in the management of industrial SOEs. In a 1998 random sample of large and medium industrial SOEs that had run losses two years in a row, the "responsible" persons in 758 (of 950 sampled) SOEs answered, among others, a closed question on the main three reasons for the losses. Out of the nine possible answers (which included "others" as a possible answer), "administrative interference" was the answer least frequently chosen as the prime cause of the losses. (For six SOEs, it was the most important reason; for 18 SOEs the second-most important reason, and for 16 SOEs the third-most important reason.) The top three reasons were a lack of funds, faltering sales, and the social burden.[226] While the survey results may not be perfectly objective and do not provide a measure of the control aspect of corporate governance, they still indicate that, from the point of view of industrial SOE managers, current corporate governance procedures do not pose much of a constraint on economic decision-making within industrial SOEs.

From the point of view of the owners, the corporate governance problem in the form of weak supervision appears more severe (Chapter 8). But Peter Nolan and Wang Xiaoqiang (1999) note the continued direct involvement of the quasi-owners (the government) in enterprise development and interpret this involvement positively: "It is the bureaucrats [...] who are restructuring state industry, withdrawing the state from downstream areas of competitive light and processing industries, concentrating instead on upstream areas of natural monopolies and capital intensive industries. It is the bureaucrats who are restructuring SOEs, by allowing small SOEs to shrink, and expanding large SOEs autonomy through careful, persistent, institutional experimentation. It is the bureaucrats at both the local and national level who mobilize resources that the market would be unable to organize, such as technical transfer from multinational firms." (p. 191)

---

[226] On the survey, see *China Infobank* (13 May 1998). The question reported here was only one among several, and the survey and its interpretation appear highly professional. The author(s) do not dwell on the administrative interference issue. The article does not state who organized the survey; given its scope and quality, perhaps it was the SETC.

Perhaps there is no one perfect model of corporate governance, but a range of models each appropriate in a particular economic environment. Thus, Colin Mayer (1996), in a review article on differences in corporate governance in different countries and the performance of these corporate governance systems, concludes that there is no one superior corporate governance system, such as a capital market-based external control system vs. a main bank-based internal control system. He advocates competition between different systems rather than harmonization and notes that each has its own advantages and disadvantages: "One interpretation of the evidence is that the main differences in financial systems may concern the formulation, implementation and adaptation of corporate strategy rather than incentives, disciplining, finance and investment. Insider systems are superior at implementing policies which require the development of relations with several stakeholders. Outsider systems are better at responding to change." (pp. 28f.) One could, following Colin Mayer, argue that China, growing out of the plan, has numerous stakeholders among which a balance has to be struck. China is not at a development stage when it needs rapid innovation beyond worldwide best practices, a requirement that might favor an outsider system.

On Kit Tam (1999) goes further and for the case of China argues that "corporate governance development is not about a choice between different stylized models, but it should primarily be concerned with objectives and directions what will best serve the country's economic and social circumstances and aspirations." And "the new design should be performance-oriented and not just focused on confirming to static criteria designed to minimize agency costs." (p. 3)

If one accepts that the objectives of SOEs need not always be pure profit maximization and may furthermore be highly enterprise specific, then outsiders lack the means to evaluate management performance. In such case, the bottom line for distinguishing between good and bad management is the extent to which managers spend their time collecting rents from the government (for their enterprises or for themselves), rather than on resolving standard enterprise issues such as production, sales, or financing problems. Evidence of the extent of distraction from normal enterprise management tasks is not readily available in the form of hard data, but the incentives for managers to collect rents can be examined.

Management Distractions

Industrial SOE managers face a variety of moral hazards. If the government is willing to turn the debt of some enterprises into equity, and if mangers prefer equity to debt (as seems the case, perhaps because it creates some scope for the accumulation of new debt in the future), then industrial SOE managers have little incentive to avoid costly debt. They have every incentive to spend time convincing government officials that this particular industrial SOE has too much debt and deserves a debt-equity swap.

If the government pays for the bad loans of bankrupt industrial SOEs, banks have little incentive to monitor their borrowers, and industrial SOE debt therefore comes with little monitoring. This allows managers to misuse enterprise loans for purposes that benefit their enterprise or themselves; case-by-case evidence on the misuse of bank loans is plentiful in the Chinese press.[227] The preferential policies that take effect in the case of policy bankruptcies furthermore create incentives for industrial SOE management to adopt high-risk development strategies.

If external supervision is poor or lacking altogether, industrial SOE managers can easily be tempted to misappropriate funds or to strip the enterprise of its assets.[228] In many instances, the whole work unit, seeing no future for their enterprise, happily participates in turning public property into private property. In other instances, the manager steals for him/herself. With labor remuneration still not differentiating much between management and workers, industrial SOE managers may be easily tempted.

Enterprise managers are further preoccupied with their own personal administrative ranks. Thus, managers are reported to be interested above all in maintaining if not improving their administrative rank, because that rank determines the ease with which they are able to transfer into a government or Party position should the management position become

---

[227] See, for example, the twice monthly magazine *Caijing*.

[228] While asset stripping between 1950 and 1990 may have been equivalent to up to 30% of total state investment funding (Russell Smyth, 2000, p. 3), Russell Smyth concludes that asset stripping has not reached East European or Russian proportions. Asset stripping in the case of China therefore does not dominate the corporate governance discussion. (Also see Chapter 5.)

untenable or undesirable. The rank also has numerous everyday implications, such as what level of classified documents the manager will obtain, or to what type of housing s/he is entitled. One consequence, for example, is that rank bickering hampers cooperation and mergers between enterprises. (A lower-rank enterprise cannot easily take over a higher-rank enterprise.) Any form of rank demotion is to be avoided at all costs. The existence of the rank issue implies that managers may focus less on improving enterprise performance than on marketing themselves to the relevant government or Party cell.[229]

According to the latest regulation issued by the SETC on 13 March 2001, the administrative ranking of SOE management has supposedly ended. This should make the interchange of government and enterprise personnel more difficult, encouraging professional SOE management. Yet, how long it will take to end the ranking of enterprise managers in practice, and whether ranks will then not live on as implicit accessories, is another question.

The distractions of industrial SOE management from managing their enterprises could be countered through appropriate supervision mechanisms. But as seen in Chapter 8, except in the case of a few very large central industrial SOEs, genuine supervision may be non-existent. The tradition of unified leadership does not allow for true checks and balances. While the Chinese Communist Party in one form or another is always involved in management appointment and removal, the Party itself is not subject to any external checks. The only, partial exception are the originally 39 (by now 42) large industrial backbone SOEs for which the management is appointed by the CCPCC Enterprise Work Committee. In these cases, a newly established CCPCC Enterprise Work Commission for Discipline Inspection inspects the enterprises on behalf of the Party Commission for Discipline Inspection. But the Party Commission for Discipline Inspection is not in a position to supervise routinely the (as of 2000) 53,489 industrial SOEs in China. And even the Party Commission for Discipline Inspection is ultimately part of the same Chinese Communist Party and subject to its unified leadership.

---

[229] See Han Xu (1999) on the rank and other management problems in SOEs.

Industrial SOEs thus remain under the vague control only of a secretive organization that itself is beyond (or side-steps) the rules of the state. As seen in Chapter 8, Party primacy has hollowed out the institutional arrangements laid out for companies in the Company Law. A final check on the Chinese Communist Party through an electorate does not exist.

China's industrial SOEs thus may outlive their idiosyncrasies and experience an increasingly hard budget constraint, but anything close to a hard supervisory constraint is not in sight. While this need not be a fatal weakness of industrial SOEs, it is by now perhaps the most important weakness. The World Bank (1996b), quoted above, thought effective control by government or workers over enterprises and their managers crucial if privatization were not to occur. The evidence of effective control in the form of rigorous management appointment and supervision mechanisms is lacking for all but the largest of China's SOEs.

Peter Nolan and Godfrey Yeung (2001) note the successful military style management methods in two very large firms that they studied, Shougang and Sanjiu, and posit that "in the transition to a market-oriented economy, the military style of traditional communist culture is a potentially valuable institutional force to assist the struggle to modernize and do battle in the marketplace. It can help avoid the institutional problems of the typical Western firm, such as the principle/agent struggle, free-riding and bureaucratic hierarchy, which arise because the employees are motivated primarily by individual economic interests." (p. 449) But their sample of cases is highly biased in that they chose two very large, successful firms rather than unsuccessful firms (which might already have gone out of business). Charismatic and dedicated enterprise leadership may substitute for external controls, but as the data on the profitability of industrial SOEs reveal, Chinese Communist Party's manager selection mechanisms have not consistently yielded such leadership for all of China's large and medium industrial SOEs, let alone the small industrial SOEs.

Summing Up

The objective of this book was to let the data on China's industrial SOEs speak out on the reasons for the decline in industrial SOE profitability over the reform period, the performance of industrial SOEs relative to non-SOEs, the characteristics of industrial SOE profitability, and the success or failure of the most recent industrial SOE reform measures. As it turned out, industrial SOE profitability declined throughout the first two decades of reform for sound economic reasons; non-SOEs fared no better. Competition and growth in labor remuneration are two of the key causes to explain the decline in industrial SOE profitability, as are a series of reform shocks. The rather constant gap in profitability between industrial SOE and non-SOEs can be explained by just two factors, which in turn appear due to historical and policy reasons. Profitability differs widely across industrial SOEs depending on sector, size, and location. Profitability also differs widely across individual SOEs in each industrial sector, indicating a lack of exit.

The 1998–2000 SOE reform program has been broadly successful in improving industrial SOE profitability and is currently being quietly continued. The government is still deeply involved in the economy. But pervasive production planning has given way to macroeconomic targets, "scientific management," and a variety of discretionary measures—from interference in pricing mechanisms to debt equity swaps and administrative orders on the closure of excess capacity. Wide acceptance of the need for industrial SOE reform, a responsive government and bureaucracy, and continued pressure for reform imply that industrial SOE reform will continue to move forward.

One consequence of the increasing liberalization of the industrial sector is the gradual equalization of profit rates across sectors, in particular in the most recent period 1997 through 2000 (if the two government monopolies of petroleum and natural gas extraction and tobacco processing are excluded from the analysis). Another consequence is the rapid growth of the non-state economy in industry, in particular of individual-owned and private enterprises. Perhaps the non-state economy in industry would have grown even faster in the absence of government-imposed restrictions. But even so, with the non-state economy accounting for two-thirds of economy-wide industrial value-added today, much of the state economy has been relegated to "backbone" and "key" enterprises in "important" sectors. These transformations in the industrial sector reflect gradual processes towards a market economy.

From the point of view of continued economic growth and macroeconomic stability, privatization of the remaining industrial SOEs appears questionable. Despite their shortcomings, especially in the management appointment and supervision mechanisms, the large and medium industrial SOEs currently still have a role to play. These industrial SOEs will continue to be under pressure to improve their performance, not least from government bureaucrats facing up to the challenges that the process of transition generates.

Industrial SOE reform is inevitably helped along by China's consistently high economic growth rates. At an 8% growth rate, output doubles every nine years. This implies that problems accumulated in the past will only be half their current size in nine years' time. Since industrial SOE output in most years has been growing less rapidly than the industrial output of the non-state economy, it also implies that the share of industrial SOEs in economy-wide industrial value-added is likely to fall even further from its year 2000 level of 34.82%. As industrial SOEs continue to enter joint operations with other domestic enterprises and joint ventures with foreign enterprises, or turn into companies with increasingly non-state participation, the concept of industrial SOEs as government-run and government-protected enterprises may eventually lose its relevance altogether.

References

If Chinese author names in the original source are rendered in Chinese characters or in pinyin translation, below the family name is listed first, followed by the given name.

Academy of Social Sciences (Chinese Academy of Social Sciences Economic Research Institute). *Zhongguo gaige kaifang yilai jingji dashiji yao 1978–1998* (Compendium of major economic events since the beginning of the reforms 1978–1998). Beijing: Jingji kexue chubanshe, 2000.

Ash, Robert F., and He Liping. "Loss-Making and the Financial Performance of China's Industrial Enterprises: Data From the New Accounting and Statistical System." *Journal of Contemporary China* 7, 17 (March 1998): 5–20.

Asian Wall Street Journal. Daily newspaper, Hong Kong.

Beijing tongji nianjian 1996 (Beijing Statistical Yearbook 1996). Beijing: Zhongguo tongji chubanshe, 1996.

Black, Bernard, Reinier Kraakman, and Anna Tarassova. "Russian Privatization and Corporate Governance: What Went Wrong?" *Stanford Law Review 52*, no. 6 (July 2000): 1731–1808.

Blayney, Steven. "Reforming China's Asset Appraisal Regime." *International Financial Law Review 18*, no. 7 (July 1999): 27–29.

Board of Governors. *Balance Sheets for the U.S. Economy.* Washington, D.C.: Board of Governors of the Federal Reserve System. (Regularly updated on the Internet.)

Byrd, William A (ed.). *Chinese Industrial Firms under Reform.* Oxford: Oxford University Press, 1992.

Cao Yuanzheng, Qian Yingyi, and Barry R. Weingast. "From Federalism, Chinese Style to Privatization, Chinese Style." *Economics of Transition* 7, no. 1 (1999): 103–131.

CCPCC (Chinese Communist Party Central Committee).
____. 14 Nov. 1993. "Zhonggong zhongyang guanyu jianli shehui zhuyi shichang jingji tizhi ruogan wenti de jueding" (CCPCC decision on various issues in the establishment of the socialist market economic system). Passed by the Third Plenum of the Fourteenth CCPCC. In *China Infobank*.
____. 24 Jan. 1997. "Zhonggong zhongyang guanyu jinyibu jiaqiang he gaijin guoyou qiye dang de jianshe gongzuo de tongzhi" (Circular on further strengthening and improving the establishment of the Party in SOEs). In *China Infobank*.
____. 17 April 1997. "Zhongguo gongchandang dangyuan lingdao ganbu lianjie congzheng ruogan zhunze (shixing)" (Trial anti-corruption standards for Chinese Communist Party members in leading positions). In *China Infobank*.
____. 9 June 1998. "Guanyu qieshi zuohao guoyou qiye xiagang zhigong jiben shenghuo baozhang he zai jiuye gongzuo de tongzhi" (On conscientiously providing a basic living guarantee to laid-off staff and workers and creating re-employment opportunities). Issued in cooperation with the State Council. In *China Infobank*.
____. 22 Sept. 1999. "Zhonggong zhongyang guanyu guoyou qiye gaige he fazhan ruogan zhongda wenti de jueding" (CCPCC decision on some important issues in the reform of SOEs). Passed by the Fourth Plenum of the Fifteenth CCPCC. In *China Infobank*.
____. 1 Dec. 1999. "Zhonggong zhongyang guanyu chengli zhonggong zhongyang qiye gongzuo weiyuanhui ji youguan wenti de tongzhi" (CCPCC on the establishment of the CCPCC Enterprise Work Committee and related questions). Pp. 122–125 in CCPCC General Office Regulations Office, 2001.
CCPCC Commission for Discipline Inspection.
____. 29 June 2000. "Guanyu zhongyang guanli de guoyou zhongyao gugan qiye jijian jiancha jigou zhuyao lingdao ganbu renmian shenpi chengxu de guiding" (Regulation on the appointment and dismissal approval procedure for the main leading cadres in the disciplinary and examination institutions in important backbone SOEs under central administration). P. 283 in CCPCC General Office Regulations Office, 2001.
CCPCC General Office.
____. 29 June 1999. "Guoyou qiye ji guoyou konggu qiye lingdao renyuan renqi jingji zeren shenji zanxing guiding" (Temporary regulation on the auditing of the performance of leading personnel of state-owned and state-controlled enterprise over their employment period). Issued jointly with the State Council General Office. In *China Infobank*.

_____. 23 June 2000. "Shenhua ganbu renshi zhidu gaige gangyao" (Outline on deepening the reform of the cadre and personnel system). Pp. 261–271 in CCPCC General Office Regulations Office, 2001.

CCPCC General Office Regulations Office (together with CCPCC Disciplinary Committee Regulations Office, and CCPCC Organization Department General Office). *Zhongguo gongchandang dangnei fagui xuanbian* (Selected internal regulations of the Chinese Communist Party). Beijing: Falu chubanshe, 2001.

CCPCC Organization Department.

_____. 15 Aug. 1995. "Guanyu jiaqiang guoyou qiye lingdao banzi jianshe de yijian" (Suggestions on strengthening the leadership of SOEs). Issued jointly by the CCPCC Organization Department, the SETC, and the Personnel Ministry. In *China Infobank*.

_____. 3 March 1997. "Guanyu zuohao guoyou qiye lingdao banzi kaohe jianshe gongzuo de tongzhi" (On well establishing the SOE leadership assessment). In *China Infobank*.

CCPCC Organization Department Research Office. *Zuzhi gongzuo yanjiu wenxuan* (Selected documents in the research of personnel organization matters). Volume 1. Beijing: Dangjian duwu chubanshe, 2001.

Chai, Joseph C.H., and George Docwra. "Reform of Large and Medium State Enterprises: Corporatization and Restructure of State Ownership," Chapter 7 in Maurice Brosseau, Kuan Hsin-chi, and Y.Y. Kueh, eds., *China Review 1997* (Hong Kong: The Chinese University Press, 1997), pp. 161–180.

Chen Aimin. "Inertia in Reforming China's State-owned Enterprises: The Case of Chongqing." *World Development 26*, no. 3 (March 1998): 479–495.

Chen Kuan, Wang Hongchang, Zheng Yuxin, Gary H. Jefferson, and Thomas G. Rawski. "Productivity Change in Chinese Industry: 1953–1985." *Journal of Comparative Economics 12*, no. 4 (Dec. 1988): 570–591.

Chen Qingtai. "Guanyu guoyou qiye gaige de xingshi he tujing" (On the shape and future of SOE reform). *Zhonggong zhongyang dangxiao baogaoxuan*, no. 3 (12 April 1998): 2–20.

Cheng Chu-yuan. *China's Economic Development: Growth and Structural Change*. Boulder, Colorado: Westview Press, 1982.

Cheng, Yuk-shing, and Dic Lo. "Explaining the Financial Performance of China's Industrial Enterprises: Beyond the Competition-Ownership Controversy." *The China Quarterly*, no. 170 (June 2002): 413–440.

China Infobank. Internet source (www.chinainfobank.com); includes databases on Chinese laws and regulations as well as on news items. Individual news items are listed below.

_____. 8 Jan. 1998. "1998 nian zhongguo guoyou qiye gaige zhanwang" (Outlook for SOE reform in 1998).
_____. 13 March 1998. "Zhongguo gan san nian gong ke guoqi tuokun guan" (China puts three years of effort into making SOEs pass the grade).
_____. 13 May 1998. "Zhongguo guoyou kuisun qiye fuzeren ruhe kandai kuisun wenti" (How the responsible persons in loss-making SOEs view the losses).
_____. 21 Sept. 1998. "Zhongguo 13 jia qiye huyu jizhi e'xing jingzheng" (13 enterprises appeal to resist malignant competition).
_____. 8 Dec. 1998. "Guojia jiwei jiage si fuzeren jiu 'Guanyu zhichi dijia qingxiao gongyepin bu zhengdang jiage xingwei de guiding' banbu shishi da jizhe wen" (A leading staff of the SDPC Price Bureau answers reporter's questions regarding the implementation of the 'Regulation on curbing the irregular price behavior of low-price dumping of industrial products'). Xinhua she news item.
_____. 19 April 1999. "Xin biaozhun xianshi zhongguo you dazhongxing qiye 10177 jia" (According to the new standard China has 10177 large and medium enterprises). Xinhua she news item.
_____. 24 May 1999. "Zhongguo guojia jiwei jiagesi sizhang Bi Jingquan zhuanwen shuo muqian jiangjia jingzheng you qi biranxing" (Bi Jingquan, head of the SDPC Price Bureau, writes that the current competition in the reduction in prices is necessary).
_____. 16 Aug. 1999. "Zhongguo jiwei diaocha fan dijia qingxiao caidian jiangjia zui yinren guanzhu" (The SDPC's investigation of low-price dumping in color TV sets attracts much attention). In *Xianggang dagong bao*.
_____. 8 Jan. 2001. "Zhongguo guoqi gaige yu tuokun sannian mubiao jiben shixian" (China's targets for SOE reform and three-year reversal of difficulties have basically been achieved).
_____. 17 Jan. 2001. "Zhongguo 2000 nian jinrong tiaokong mubiao shixian" (Realization of China's year 2000 financial adjustment targets).
_____. 25 June 2001a. "Zhongguo guojia jingmaowei shenhua guoyou qiye gaige yanjiuzu" (SETC research group on deepening SOE reform).
_____. 25 June 2001b. "Guojia jingmaowei yanjiu baogao biaoming: zhongguo you san da yinsu cu guoyou qiye san nian tuokun" (SETC research report shows that three big factors allowed SOEs to in three years escape their difficulties).
_____. 31 May 2002. "Zhongguo shebao jijin zhuangkuang ji qianjing" (Current state and future of China's social security fund).
_____. 15 July 2002. "Shandong chongxin quanding 297 jia (te)daxing qiye" (Shandong newly defines 297 (especially) large enterprises).

China Markets Yearbook 1999. Hong Kong: City University of Hong Kong Press, 1999.

China Markets Yearbook 2000. Hong Kong: Asian Information Resources Limited, 2000.

China Markets Yearbook 2001. Beijing: Foreign Languages Press, 2001.

China News Digest. E-mail newsletter also available at: http://www.cnd.org/CND-Global/.

China's Industrial Markets Yearbook 1997. Hong Kong: City University of Hong Kong Press, 1997.

China Textile Association (Zhongguo fangzhi zonghui).

_____. 5 March 1998. "Quanguo yasuo taotai 1000 wan luohou mianfang ding he fenliu anzhi zhigong guihua shishi yijian" (Suggestions on implementing the outline of nationwide reducing and replacing 10m backward cotton spindles and dismissing and re-employing staff and workers). Issued in cooperation with the SETC and the SDPC. In *China Infobank*.

Chow, Gregory C. *Understanding China's Economy*. Singapore: World Scientific, 1994.

Deutsche Bundesbank. *Jahresabschluesse westdeutscher Unternehmen 1971 bis 1996* (Annual reports of West German enterprises 1971 through 1996). Deutsche Bundesbank, 1999.

Dewenter, Kathryn L., and Paul H. Malatesta. "State-owned and Privately Owned Firms: An Empirical Analysis of Profitability, Leverage, and Labor Intensity." *American Economic Review 91*, no. 1 (March 2001): 320–334.

Di Na. "Guoying gongye qiye qiankui jing ren" (The hidden losses in industrial SOEs are startling). *Jingji yanjiu cankao*, no. 22 (20 March 1992): 2–8.

Ding Xueliang. "The Illicit Asset Stripping of Chinese State Firms." *The China Journal 43* (Jan. 2000): 1–28.

Djankov, Simeon, and Peter Murrell. "Enterprise Restructuring in Transition: A Quantitative Survey." *Journal of Economic Literature 40*, no. 3 (Sept. 2002): 739–792.

Dollar, David. "Economic Reform and Allocative Efficiency in China's State-owned Industry." *Economic Development and Cultural Change 39*, no. 1 (1990): 88–105.

Dougherty, Sean M., and Robert H. McGuckin. "The Effect of Ownership Structure and Jurisdictional Governance on Productivity in Chinese Firms." Economics Program Working Paper Series #01-02, The Conference Board, 15 Feb. 2001.

Economic Planning Agency (Government of Japan). Kokumin keizei keisan nempuo (Annual report on national accounts). Tokyo: Economic Planning Agency, 1999.

The Economist. Weekly news magazine, London.

Fan Gang, and Wing-Thye Woo. "State Enterprise Reform as a Source of Macroeconomic Instability: The Case of China." *Asian Economic Journal 10*, no. 3 (1996): 207–224.

Fan Hengshan. "Guoyou xiao qiye gaige: jinzhan yu wenti" (Reform of small SOEs: progress and problems). *Jingji yanyiu cankao*, no. 13 (7 Feb. 1997): 33–38.

Financial Statistics 1952–1996. Zhongguo jinrong tongji 1952-1996 (China financial statistics, 1952–1996). Beijing: Zhongguo caizheng jingji chubanshe, 1997.

Financial Yearbook. Zhongguo jinrong nianjian (Almanac of China's Finance and Banking). Beijing: Zhongguo jinrong chubanshe. Various years.

FM (Finance Ministry).

_____. 26 April 1984. "Guoying gongye, jiaotong yunshu qiye chengben guanli shishi xize" (Detailed implementing instructions on cost administration in state-owned industrial, communication and transport enterprises). In ZHRMGHGFLQS, Vol. 1: 1839–1847.

_____. 5 Jan. 1985. "Guoying gongye qiye kuaiji zhidu" (State-owned industrial enterprise accounting system). First revision (original version issued 18 Sept. 1980). In *China Infobank*.

_____. 19 May 1986. "Guoying qiye guding zichan zhejiu shixing tiaoli shishi xize" (Implementing instructions for the trial stipulations on fixed asset depreciation in SOEs). In *China Infobank*.

_____. 7 March 1987. "Guanyu guoying gongye, jiaotong qiye zi 1987 nian 7 yue 1 ri qi quanmian zhixing fenlei zhejiu de tongzhi" (Circular on state-owned industrial and communication enterprises fully implementing depreciation according to asset category beginning 1 July 1987). In *China Infobank*.

_____. 21 April 1989. "Guoying gongye qiye kuaiji zhidu" (State-owned industrial enterprise accounting system). Second revision (original version issued 18 Sept. 1980). In *China Infobank*.

_____. 19 Jan. 1990. "Guoying qiye jiti guding zichan zhejiu zhongxin xiang youhui zhengce zai 1990 nian dao qi hou ruhe chuli de tongzhi" (Circular on how to handle preferential depreciation rates once they are due to expire in 1990). In *China Infobank*.

_____. 5 June 1992. "Guanyu renzhen qingli he chuli yusuan nei guoying gongjiao qiye qiankui de tongzhi" (Circular on seriously cleaning up and resolving the latent losses in budgetary state-owned industrial and communication enterprises). In *China Infobank*.

_____. 28 Oct. 1992. "Guanyu qingchan hezi di yi qi shidian de guoying qiye zijin sunshi kuisun guazhang deng wenti de caiwu chuli tongzhi" (Circular on how the first batch of trial SOEs for cleaning up assets should handle the losses to assets and the losses in production in their financial accounts). Issued jointly with the People's Bank of China and the office of the State Council leading group for cleaning up assets. In *China Infobank*.

_____. 30 Dec. 1992. "Gongye qiye caiwu zhidu" (Industrial enterprise financial system). In PRC FM General Office, 1999, Vol. 1: 407–417.

_____. 31 Dec. 1992. "Gongye qiye kuaiji zhidu" (Industrial enterprise accounting system). In PRC FM General Office, 1999, Vol. 1: 417–459.

_____. 17 May 1993 "Guanyu guanche shishi xin de qiye caiwu zhidu youguan zhengce xianjie wenti de tongzhi" (Circular on some problems in the implementation of the new enterprise financial system related to policy issues). In ZHRMGHGFLQS, Vol. 4: 1187–1189.

_____. 30 May 1993. "Quanmin suoyouzhi gongye qiye xin jiu kuaiji zhidu xianjie youguan tiaozheng wenti de chuli guiding" (Regulation on how to handle some problems in changes in accounts between the new and old accounting system for state-owned industrial enterprises). In ZHRMGHGFLQS, Vol. 4: 1066–1075.

_____. 10 June 1993. "Guanyu gongye qiye kuaiji zhidu ruogan wenti de buchong guiding" (Supplementary regulation on some issues of the SOE accounting system). In PRC FM General Office, 1999, Vol. 1: 461–463.

_____. 6 Sept. 1993. "Guoyou qiye zhexing xin de qiye caiwu zhidu youguan wenti de jieda" (Answers to some questions on the implementation of the new enterprise accounting system), in PRC FM General Office, 1999, vol. 1, 464f.

_____. 27 Aug. 1994. "Guanyu tingzhi zhexing qiye yi liuli zai touzi tui 40% suodeshui guiding de tongzhi" (Circular on ending the return of 40% of income taxes if enterprises use retained profit for investment). Issued jointly with the State Commission for Economic Restructuring, SETC, State Tax Bureau, and State Council Law Office. In ZHRMGHGFLQS, Vol. 5: 220.

_____. 11 Feb. 1995. "Caizhengbu guanyu zhongyang qiye zai difang xingban qiye suodeshui ruku jici youguan wenti de pifu" (FM reply on the question of who obtains the income taxes of enterprises set up in a locality by a central enterprise). In *China Infobank*.

_____. 17 July 1995. "Caizhengbu guanyu caizheng bumen jianshi xuanpai zanxing guiding" (Temporary regulation on the selection and dispatch of supervisors by the finance departments). In *China Infobank*.

_____. 21 Oct. 1997. "Guanyu jiaqiang guoyou qiye caiwu jiandu ruogan wenti de guiding" (Regulation on some issues in strengthening the supervision of SOE property). In *China Infobank*.

_____. 1 June 1999. "Guoyou zibenjin xiaoji pingjia guize" (Rules on the SOE capital achievement evaluation) and "Guoyou zibenjin xiaoji pingjia caozuo xize" (Detailed operating rules on the SOE capital achievement evaluation). Issued jointly with the Personnel Ministry, the SETC, and the SDPC. In *China Infobank*.

_____. 26 April 2000. "Guanyu jinyibu zuohao guoyou qiye xiaoji pingjia gongzuo de tongzhi" (On further improving the achievement evaluation in SOEs). Issued jointly with the SETC, the CCPCC Enterprise Work Committee, and the Labor and Social Security Ministry. In *China Infobank*.

_____. 23 March 2001. "Guanyu shenru kaizhan qiye xiaoji pingjia gongzuo jiaqiang guoyou qiye jiandu guanli de tongzhi" (On further developing the enterprise achievement evaluation work and on strengthening SOE supervision and administration). Issued jointly with the SETC, the Labor and Social Security Ministry, and the SDPC. In *China Infobank*.

Gao Shangquan. "Jiakuai qiye gaige bufa, zhuanhuan qiye jingying jizhi" (Accelerate the pace of reform, transform the enterprise management mechanism). *Jingji tizhi gaige neibu cankao*, no. 6 (1992): 3–18.

_____. *China's Economic Reform*. New York: St. Martin's Press, 1996.

Groves, Theodore, Hong Yongmiao, John McMillan, and Barry Naughton. "Autonomy and Incentives in Chinese State Enterprises." *The Quarterly Journal of Economics 109*, no. 1 (Feb. 1994): 183–209.

Han Xu. "Gaige guoyou qiye lingdao ganbu guanli zhidu" (Reforming the SOE leadership cadre administration system). *Neibu canyue*, no. 32 (18 Aug. 1999): 8–15.

Hay, Donald, Derek Morris, Guy Liu, and Yao Shujie. *Economic Reform and State-Owned Enterprises in China, 1979-1987*. Oxford: Clarendon Press, 1994.

Holz, Carsten A. "Contractionary Investment Policies in China 1988/89: Accounting for the Implementation Difficulties and Successes." *The China Quarterly*, no. 160 (Dec. 1999): 81–118.

_____. "Identifying the Patterns of Profitability Across Chinese State-owned Enterprises: Which Industrial State-owned Enterprises in China Are Profitable?" *Journal of Asian Business 17*, no. 2 (2001): 33–62.

_____, and Lin Yi-min. "The 1997-1998 Break in Industrial Statistics: Facts and Appraisal." Contribution to symposium on China's statistics. *China Economic Review 12*, no. 4 (2001a): 303–316.

_____, and Lin Yi-min. "Pitfalls of China's Industrial Statistics: Inconsistencies and Specification Problems." *The China Review 1*, no. 1 (Fall 2001b): 29–71.

_____. "Institutional Constraints on the Quality of Statistics in China." *China Information 16*, no 1 (2002a): 25–67.

_____. "The Impact of Competition and Labor Remuneration on Profitability in China's Industrial State-owned Enterprises." *Journal of Contemporary China 11*, no. 32 (Aug. 2002b): 515–538.

_____. "The Impact of the Liability-Asset Ratio on Profitability in China's Industrial State-owned Enterprises." *China Economic Review 13*, no. 1 (2002c): 1–26.

_____. "Long Live China's State-owned Enterprises: Deflating the Myth of Poor Financial Performance." *Journal of Asian Economics 13*, no. 4 (July/August 2002d): 493–529.

_____. "Fast, Clear and Accurate:" How Reliable Are Chinese Output and Economic Growth Statistics?" Forthcoming in *The China Quarterly*, no. 173 (March 2003): 122–163.

Hu, Albert Guangzhou. "Ownership, Government R&D, Private R&D, and Productivity in Chinese Industry." *Journal of Comparative Economics 29*, no. 1 (March 2001): 136–157.

Huang Yiping, and Ron Duncan. "How Successful Were China's State Sector Reforms?" *Journal of Comparative Economics 24*, no. 1 (Feb. 1997a): 65–78.

_____, and Ron Duncan. "Which Chinese State-owned Enterprises Make Losses?" *The Asia Pacific Journal of Economics & Business 1*, no. 2 (Dec. 1997b): 41–52.

_____, Wing-Thye Woo, and Ron Duncan. "Understanding the Decline of the State Sector." *MOCT-MOST 9*, no. 1 (1999): 1–15.

_____, and Ron Duncan. "Did Competition Drive Down the Profitability of China's State-owned Enterprises?" *MOCT-MOST 9*, no. 1 (1999): 49–60.

Hussain, Athar, and Nicholas H. Stern. "Comment on 'How Industrial Reform Worked in China: The Role of Innovation, Competition, and Property Rights' by Jefferson and Rawski," in Michael Bruno and Boris Pleskovic, eds., *Proceedings of the World Bank Annual Conference on Development Economics 1994* (Washington, D.C.: The World Bank, 1995), pp. 156–162.

Industrial Census 1995. Zhonghua renmin gongheguo 1995 nian di san ci quanguo gongye pucha ziliao huibian (The data of the third national industrial census of the People's Republic of China in 1995). Volume 1 (general, sectoral data), Volume 2 (state-owned, foreign-funded, and township enterprises), and Volume 3 (regional data). Beijing: Zhongguo tongji chubanshe, 1997.

Industrial Yearbook. Zhongguo gongye jingji tongji nianjian (Statistical Yearbook of China's Industrial Economy). Beijing: Zhongguo tongji chubanshe. Various years. In 1986 titled *Zhongguo gongye jingji tongji ziliao 1986* (Statistical Material on China's Industrial Economy 1986). Beijing: Zhongguo tongji chubanshe, 1987.

Internal Revenue Service. *Corporation Income Tax Returns: 1991 Statistics of Income*. Washington, D.C.: U.S. Government Printing Office, 1994.

Investment Data 1950–1985. Zhongguo guding zichan touzi tongji ziliao 1950–1985 (Statistical Material on China's Investment in Fixed Assets). Beijing: Zhongguo tongji chubanshe, 1987.

Investment Yearbook. Zhongguo guding zichan touzi tongji nianjian (Statistical Yearbook of China's Investment in Fixed Assets). Beijing: Zhongguo tongji chubanshe. Various years. (First edition is *Zhongguo guding zichan touzi tongji nianjian 1950–1995* (China investment in fixed assets statistics 1950–1995). Beijing: Zhongguo tongji chubanshe, 1997.)

Jefferson, Gary H. "Growth and Productivity Change in Chinese Industry: Problems of Measurement," in M. Dutta, ed., *Asian Economic Regimes: An Adaptive Innovation Paradigm*, Research in Asian Economic Studies Vol. 4 (Part B) (Greenwich, Connecticut: JAI Press, 1992), pp. 427–442.

_____, Thomas G. Rawski, and Zheng Yuxin. "Growth, Efficiency, and Convergence in China's State and Collective Industry." *Economic Development and Cultural Change* 40, no. 2 (Jan. 1992): 239–266.

_____, and Thomas G. Rawski. "Enterprise Reform in Chinese Industry." *Journal of Economic Perspectives* 8, no. 2 (Spring 1994): 47–70.

_____, and Thomas G. Rawski, "How Industrial Reform Worked in China: The Role of Innovation, Competition, and Property Rights," in Michael Bruno and Boris Pleskovic, eds., *Proceedings of the World Bank Annual Conference on Development Economics 1994* (Washington, D.C.: The World Bank, 1995), pp. 129–156.

_____, and Thomas G. Rawski. "The Paradox of China's Industrial Reform," in A.E. Safarian and Wendy Dobson, eds., *East Asian Capitalism: Diversity and Dynamism*, Hong Kong Bank of Canada Papers on Asia Vol. 2 (Toronto: University of Toronto Press, 1996), pp. 45–90.

_____, Thomas G. Rawski, and Zheng Yuxin. "Chinese Industrial Productivity: Trends, Measurement Issues, and Recent Developments." *Journal of Comparative Economics* 23, no. 2 (Oct. 1996): 146–180.

_____. "China's State Enterprises: Public Goods, Externalities, and Coase." *American Economic Review* 88, no. 2 (May 1998): 428–432.

_____, Inderjit Singh, Xing Junling, and Zhang Shouqing. "China's Industrial Performance: A Review of Recent Findings," Chapter 6 in Gary H. Jefferson and Inderjit Singh, eds., *Enterprise Reform in China: Ownership, Transition, and Performance* (Oxford: Oxford University Press, 1999), pp. 127–152.

_____. and Thomas G Rawski. "China's Industrial Innovation Ladder: A Model of Endogenous Reform," Chapter 3 in Gary H. Jefferson and Inderjit Singh, eds., *Enterprise Reform in China: Ownership, Transition, and Performance* (Oxford: Oxford University Press, 1999), pp. 65–88.

_____, Thomas G. Rawski, Wang Li, and Zheng Yuxin. "Ownership, Productivity Change, and Financial Performance in Chinese Industry." *Journal of Comparative Economics 28*, no. 4 (Dec. 2000): 786–813.

JHTZJGFGQS. *Zhonghua renmin gongheguo jihua touzi jiage fagui quanshu* (PRC planning, investment and price law and regulations compendium). Beijing: Zhongguo jiancha chubanshe, 1995.

Jiang Zemin. "Gaoju Deng Xiaoping lilun weida qizhi, ba jianshe you zhongguo tese shehui zhuyi shiye quanmian tuixiang er shi yi shiji" (Hold high the mighty banner of Deng Xiaoping theory, and advance the establishment of socialism with Chinese characteristics into the 21st century). 12 Sept. 1997. *Jinrong shibao*, 22 Sept. 1997.

_____. "Quanmian jianshe xiaokang shehui, kaichuang zhongguo tese shehui zhuyi shiye xin jumian" (Fully develop a moderately well-off society, initiate a new phase of socialism with special Chinese characteristics). 8 November 2002. *Jinrong shibao*, 18 Nov. 2002.

Jingji tizhi gaige neibu cankao (Internal Reference News on the Reform of the Economic System). Issued twice a month by the State Council's Commission for the Reform of the Economic System; in 1994 renamed *Gaige neican* (Internal Reform News).

Jinrong guizhang zhidu xuanbian (Selected financial rules and regulations). Beijing: Zhongguo jinrong chubanshe, two volumes per year.

Kong Xiang, Robert E. Marks, and Wan Guanghua. "Technical Efficiency, Technological Change and Total Factor Productivity Growth in Chinese State-Owned Enterprises in the Early 1990s." *Asian Economic Journal 13*, no. 3 (Sept. 1999): 267–281.

Labor and Social Security Ministry (Laodong he shehui baozhang bu).

_____. 25 Nov. 1999. "Guanyu qingli shouhui qiye qianjiao shehui baoxianfei youguan wenti" (On problems related to the collection of overdue enterprise social security contributions). In *China Infobank*.

_____. 6 Nov. 2000. "Jinyibu shenhua qiye neibu fenpei zhidu gaige zhidao yijian" (Guiding suggestions on further deepening the enterprise-internal distribution system). *Zhonghua renmin gongheguo guowuyuan gongbao*, no. 2 (20 Jan. 2001): 41–44.

Lardy, Nicholas R. *China's Unfinished Economic Revolution*. Washington, D.C.: Brookings Institution Press, 1998.

Laurenceson, James, and J.C.H. Chai. "The Economic Performance of China's State-owned Industrial Enterprises." *Journal of Contemporary China 9*, no. 23 (March 2000): 21–39.

Li Bo. "Shiyou gongye shi nian gaige de huigu yu fansi" (Critical review of ten years of reform in the petroleum industry). *Jingji yanjiu cankao ziliao*, no. 194 (18 Dec. 1989): 2–19.

Li Chun and Chen Yongqi. "Jiaqiang guoyou qiye lingdao banzi jianshe" (Strengthen the establishment of the SOE leadership team). *Neibu canyue*, no. 46 (24 Nov. 1999): 2–10.

Li, David D., and Liang Minsong. "Causes of the Soft Budget Constraint: Evidence on Three Explanations." *Journal of Comparative Economics 26*, no. 1 (March 1998): 104–116.

Li Hong. "A Testing Road for Chinese Industry: the Enterprise Responsibility System (ERS)," Chapter 9 in Glenville Jenkins and Michael Poole, eds., *New Forms of Ownership: Management and Employment* (London: Routledge, 1990), pp. 151–162.

Li Xianzong and Zhang Yongguo. *Xin caiwu guanli shiwu* (Handbook on the new financial administration). Beijing: Zhongguo shenji chubanshe, 1995.

Lin, Justin Yifu, Cai Fang, Li Zhou. "Competition, Policy Burdens, and State-Owned Enterprise Reform." *American Economic Review 88*, no. 2 (May 1998): 422–427.

_____, Cai Fang, Li Zhou. "Fair Competition and China's State-owned Enterprise Reform." *MOCT-MOST 9*, no. 1 (1999): 61–74.

_____, Cai Fang, Li Zhou. *State-owned Enterprise Reform in China*. Hong Kong: The Chinese University Press, 2001.

Lin, Yi-min. *Between Politics and Markets: Firms, Competition, and Institutional Change in Post-Mao China*. Cambridge: Cambridge University Press, 2001.

_____, and Zhu Tian. "Ownership Restructuring in Chinese State Industry: An Analysis of Evidence on Initial Organizational Changes." *The China Quarterly*, no. 166 (June 2001): 305–341.

Lo, Dic. "Reappraising the Performance of China's State-owned Industrial Enterprises, 1980–1996." *Cambridge Journal of Economics 23*, no. 6 (Nov. 1999): 693–718.

Lyons, Thomas P. 1990. "Planning and Interprovincial Co-ordination in Maoist China." *The China Quarterly*, no. 121 (March 1990): 36–60.

Market Yearbook. Zhongguo shichang tongji nianjian (China Market Statistics Yearbook). Beijing: Zhongguo tongji chubanshe. Various years.

Mayer, Colin. "Corporate Governance, Competition and Performance." OECD Economic Studies no. 27 (1996/II): 7–34.

McGuckin, Robert H., Sang V. Nguyen, Jeffrey R. Taylor, and Charles A. Waite. "Post-reform Productivity Performance and Sources of Growth in Chinese Industry: 1980-85." *Review of Income and Wealth 38*, no. 3 (Sept. 1992): 249–266.

McMillan, John, and Barry Naughton. "How to Reform a Planned Economy: Lessons From China." *Oxford Review of Economic Policy 8*, no. 1 (Spring 1992): 130–143.

Megginson, William L., and Jeffrey M. Netter. "From State to Market: A Survey of Empirical Studies on Privatization." *Journal of Economic Literature 39*, no. 2 (June 2001): 321–389.

Mok, Vincent Wai-Kwong. "Industrial Productivity in China's State-owned Enterprises: the Textile Industry in Guangzhou, 1979–1993." *Journal of Contemporary China 5*, no. 11 (March 1996): 57–67.

Morris, Derek. "The Reform of State-owned Enterprises in China: The Art of the Possible." *Oxford Review of Economic Policy 11*, no. 4 (Winter 1995): 54–69.

National State Asset Administration Bureau.

_____. 1 June 1995. "Guoyou zichan guanli bumen jianshi xuanpai zanxing guiding" (Temporary regulation on the selection and dispatch of supervisors by the state asset administration departments). In *China Infobank*.

National Statistics Office of Korea. Database "KOSIS," accessible on the internet.

Naughton, Barry. "Implications of the State Monopoly Over Industry and Its Relaxation." *Modern China 18*, no. 1 (Jan. 1992): 14–41.

_____. *Growing Out of the Plan: Chinese Economic Reform, 1978–1993*. Cambridge: Cambridge University Press, 1995.

NBS (National Bureau of Statistics, prior to 1998 "State Statistical Bureau"). *Zhongguo niandu guonei shengchan zongzhi jisuan fangfa* (Calculation of China's annual domestic gross product). Beijing: Zhongguo tongji chubanshe, 1997.

_____ (Division for Industry and Transportation). *Xinbian gongye tongji gongzuo zhinan (New guide to industrial statistics)*. Beijing: Zhongguo tongji chubanshe, 1999.

_____ (National Accounts Division). *Zhongguo guonei shengchan zongzhi hesuan lishi ziliao (zhaiyao)* (Abstract of China's historical GDP data). Beijing: Zhongguo tongji chubanshe, 1998.

Nolan, Peter. "Large Firms and Industrial Reform in Former Planned Economies: the Case of China." *Cambridge Journal of Economics* 20, no. 1 (Jan. 1996): 1–29.

———, and Wang Xiaoqiang. "The Chinese Army's Firm in Business: The Sanjiu Group." *Developing-Economies* 36, no. 1 (March 1998): 45–79.

———, and Wang Xiaoqiang. "Beyond Privatization: Institutional Innovation and Growth in China's Large State-Owned Enterprises." *World Development* 27, no. 1 (Jan. 1999): 169–200.

———. *China and the Global Business Revolution*. New York: Palgrave, 2001.

———, and Godfrey Yeung. "Big Business with Chinese Characteristics: Two Paths to Growth of the Firm in China Under Reform." *Cambridge Journal of Economics* 25, no. 4 (July 2001): 443–465.

NPC (National People's Congress).

———. 4 Dec. 1982. "Zhonghua renmin gongheguo xianfa" (PRC Constitution). In ZHRMGHGFLQS, Vol. 1: 3–16.

———. 2 Dec. 1986. "Zhonghua renmin gongheguo qiye pochanfa (shixing)" ((Trial) PRC bankruptcy law). In *China Infobank*.

———. 13 April 1988. "Zhonghua renmin gongheguo quanmin suoyouzhi gongye qiyefa" (PRC SOE Law). In ZHRMGHGFLQS, Vol. 1: 1145–1150.

———. 29 March 1993. "Zhonghua renmin gongheguo xianfa" (PRC Constitution). In ZHRMGHGFLQS, Vol. 4: 3–18.

———. 15 March 1999. "Zhonghua renmin gongheguo xianfa xiuzheng'an" (Revisions to the PRC Constitution). In ZHRMGHGFLQS, Vol. 10: 3f.

———. 25 Dec. 1999. "Zhonghua renmin gongheguo gongsifa" (PRC Company Law). In *Zhonghua renmin gongheguo guowuyuan gongbao*, no. 2 (20 Jan. 2001): 25–46.

———. 15 March 2001. "Guanyu 2000 nian guomin jingji he shehui fazhan jihua zhixing qingkuang yu 2001 nian guomin jingji he shehui fazhan jihua de jueyi" (Implementation of the 2000 national economic and social development plan and decision on the 2001 national economic and social development plan). In *Zhonghua renmin gongheguo guowuyuan gongbao*, no. 13 (10 May 2001): 14–25.

———. 6 March 2002. "Guanyu 2001 nian guomin jingji he shehui fazhan jihua zhixing qingkuang yu 2002 nian guomin jingji he shehui fazhan jihua de jueyi" (Implementation of the 2001 national economic and social development plan and decision on the 2002 national economic and social development plan). In *Zhonghua renmin gongheguo guowuyuan gongbao*, no. 10 (10 April 2002): 14–21.

OECD. *Reforming China's Enterprises*. Paris: Organisation for Economic Cooperation and Development, 2000.
Parker, Elliott. "Are Wage Increases in Chinese State Industry Efficient? Productivity in Nanjing's Machine-Building Industry." *Contemporary Economic Policy 17*, no. 1 (Jan. 1999): 54–67.
PBC (People's Bank of China).
_____. 18 April 1990. "Zhongguo renmin yinhang guanyu tiaozheng cundaikuan lilu de juti guiding de tongzhi" (People's Bank of China specific regulations on adjusting deposit and credit interest rates). In *China Infobank*.
_____. 6 Oct. 1997. "Zhongguo renmin yinhang guanyu heli queding liudong zijin daikuan qixian de tongzhi" (People's Bank of China circular on rationally determining the duration of working capital loans). In *China Infobank*.
_____. 7 Oct. 1997. "Zhongguo renmin yinhang guanyu xiafa 'yintuan daikuan zanxing banfa' de tongzhi" (People's Bank of China circular promulgating the 'syndicated loan temporary measures'). In *China Infobank*.
Perkins, Dwight H. "Summary: Why Is Reforming State Owned Enterprises So Difficult?" *China Economic Review 4*, no. 2 (Fall 1993): 149–151.
Perkins, F.C. "Productivity Performance and Priorities for the Reform of China's State-Owned Enterprises." *The Journal of Development Studies 32*, no. 3 (Feb. 1996): 414–444.
Perkins, Frances. "The Costs of China's State-owned Enterprises." *MOCT-MOST 9*, no. 1 (1999): 17–33.
PRC FM General Office (People's Republic of China Finance Ministry General Office). *Xianxing caiwu kuaiji zhidu quanshu* (Compendium of the current financial and accounting system). Two volumes. Beijing: Zhongguo caizheng jingji chubanshe, 1999.
PRC FM Tax Office. *Zhongguo shuishou zhidu* (China's tax system). Beijing: Qiye guanli chubanshe, 1996.
Price Yearbook. Zhongguo wujia nianjian (Price Yearbook of China). Beijing: Zhongguo wujia nianjian bianjibu. Various years.
Provincial statistical yearbooks of all 30 (31) provincial-level entities covering the individual years 1993 through 1998. Beijing: Zhongguo tongji chubanshe. For Hebei, industry data are found in the *Heibei jingji (tongji) nianjian* (Hebei Economic (Statistical) Yearbook). For Fujian, the *Fujian gongye jingji tongji nianjian* (Fujian Industrial Economy Statistical Yearbook) was also consulted in addition to the provincial statistical yearbook.
Qi Yu, Hu Linhui, and Miao Qingwang. *Zuzhi gongzuo chuangxin yanjiu* (Innovations in organizational work). Beijing: Zhonggong zhongyang dangxiao chubanshe, 2002.

Qian Yingyi. "Reforming Corporate Governance and Finance in China," Chapter 7 in Masahiko Aoki and Hyung-Ki Kim, eds., *Corporate Governance in Transitional Economies: Insider Control and the Role of Banks* (Washington, D.C.: The World Bank, 1994), pp. 215–252.

_____. "Enterprise Reform in China: Agency Problems and Political Control." *Economics of Transition 4*, no. 2 (Oct. 1996): 427–447.

Raiser, Martin. "Evaluating Chinese Industrial Reforms: SOEs between Output Growth and Profit Decline." *Asian Economic Journal 11*, no. 3 (Sept. 1997a): 299–323.

_____. "How Are China's State-owned Enterprises Doing in the 1990s? Evidence from Three Interior Provinces?" *China Economic Review 8*, no. 2 (Fall 1997b): 191–216.

Rawski, Thomas G. "Progress Without Privatization: The Reform of China's State Industries," Chapter 2 in Vedat Milor, ed., *Changing Political Economies: Privatization in Post-Communist and Reforming Communist States* (Boulder: Lynne Rienner Publishers, 1994a), pp. 27–52.

_____. "Chinese Industrial Reform: Accomplishments, Prospects, and Implications." *American Economic Review 84*, no. 2 (May 1994b): 271–275.

_____. "Reforming China's Economy: What Have We Learned?" *The China Journal*, no. 41 (Jan. 1999): 139–156.

Riskin, Carl. *China's Political Economy: The Quest for Development Since 1949*. Oxford: Oxford University Press, 1991.

Sachs, Jeffrey D., and Wing-Thye Woo. "Understanding China's Economic Performance." *NBER Working Paper* 5935 (Feb. 1997).

_____. Interview with *Harvard China Review 1*, no. 1 (Summer 1998): 12–29.

SC (State Council).

_____. 13 July 1979. "Guanyu tigao guoying gongye qiye guding zichan zhejiu lu he gaijin zhejiu fei shiyong banfa de zanxing guiding" (Temporary regulation on raising the depreciation rate of state-owned industrial enterprises and improving the use of the depreciation funds). In ZHRMGHGFLQS, Vol. 1: 1828.

_____. 15 Dec. 1982. "Guojia nengyuan jiaotong zhongdian jianshe jijin zhengji banfa" (Collection method for the state energy and communication key construction fund). In ZHRMGHGFLQS, Vol. 1: 1831f.

_____. 5 March 1984. "Guoying qiye chengben guanli tiaoli" (Stipulation on cost administration in SOEs). In ZHRMGHGFLQS, Vol. 1: 1835–1839.

_____. 3 May 1984. "Guowuyuan pizhuan caizheng bu guojia jiwei guanyu renzhen zhuahao qiye niukui zengying gongzuo de baogao de tongzhi" (State Council circular approving of the FM and State Planning Commission's report on seriously turning enterprise losses into profit). In *China Infobank*.

_____. 28 June 1984 (revised 3 July 1985) "Guoying qiye jiangjinshui zanxing guiding" (Temporary regulation on bonus taxes in SOEs). In ZHRMGHGFLQS, Vol. 1: 665f.

_____. 18 Sept. 1984. "Guoying qiye di er bu ligaishui shixing banfa" (Trial measures for SOEs' second stage of switching from profit surrendering to taxes). In ZHRMGHGFLQS, Vol. 1: 627–630.

_____. 26 April 1985. "Guoying qiye guding zichan zhejiu shixing tiaoli" (Trial stipulations on depreciation in SOEs). In ZHRMGHGFLQS, Vol. 1: 1857–1860.

_____. 27 Feb. 1988. "Quanmin suoyouzhi gongye qiye chengbao jingying zerenzhi zanxing tiaoli" (Temporary stipulations on the management responsibility system of SOEs). In ZHRMGHGFLQS, Vol. 1: 1174–1177.

_____. 26 March 1990. "Guowuyuan guanyu zai quanguo fanwei nei kaizhan qingli 'sanjiaozhai' gongzuo de tongzhi" (State Council circular on beginning the work to clean up the 'triangular debt' nationwide). In *China Infobank*.

_____. 16 May 1991. "Guowuyuan guanyu jinyibu zengqiang guoying dazhongxing qiye huoli de tongzhi" (State Council circular on further strengthening state large and medium enterprises). In *China Infobank*.

_____. 28 April 1992. "Guanyu shenru kaizhan qiye niukui zengying gongzuo de tongzhi" (Circular on thoroughly unfolding the work on turning enterprises' losses into profit). In *China Infobank*.

_____. 11 May 1992. "Guowuyuan pizhuan jingmaobu, guowuyuan shengchanban guanyu fuyu shengchan qiye jinchukou jingyingquan youguan yijian" (State Council approval of the SETC and State Council Production Office suggestions on giving production enterprises import-export rights). In *China Infobank*.

_____. 9 Feb. 1993. "Guowuyuan qingli sanjiaozhai lingdao xiaozu guanyu quanguo qingli sanjiaozhai gongzuo qingkuang de baogao de tongzhi" (Report of the State Council leading group for cleaning up the triangular debt on the nationwide work in cleaning up triangular debt). In *China Infobank*.

_____. 3 May 1993. "Qingchan hezi banfa" (Cleaning up assets measure). Implementing instructions were issued on 14 May 1993. In *China Infobank*.

_____. 15 Dec. 1993. "Guowuyuan guanyu shixing fenshuizhi caizheng guanli tizhi de jueding" (State Council decision on the fiscal system with separate taxes). In *China Infobank*.

_____. 23 April 1994. "Guowuyuan pizhuan guojia jiwei guanyu tiaozheng yuanyou, tianranqi, chengpinyou jiage qingshi de tongzhi" (State Council approval of the SPC circular on adjusting the prices of raw petroleum, natural gas, and petroleum end products). In *Price Yearbook 1995*, pp. 91–93.

_____. 24 July 1994. "Guanyu guoyou qiye caichan jiandu guanli tiaoli" (Regulation on SOE property supervision). In *China Infobank*.

_____. 25 Oct. 1994. "Guowuyuan guanyu zai ruogan chengshi shixing guoyou qiye pochan youguan wenti de tongzhi" (State Council circular on some issues in the trial bankruptcy of SOEs in selected cities). In China Infobank.

_____. 6 March 1995. "Guowuyuan bangongting zhuanfa guojia jingmaowei guanyu shenhua qiye gaige gaohao guoyou dazhongxing qiye yijian de tongzhi" (State Council General Office passing on the suggestions by the SETC on how to deepen enterprise reform and to strengthen large and medium state enterprises). In *China Infobank*.

_____. 12 July 1995. "Guowuyuan zhuanfa guanyu jiang bufen qiye 'bogaidai' zijin benxi yu'e zhuan wei guojia zibenjin yijian de tongzhi" (State Council circular passing on the suggestions on turning into equity some enterprises' loans obtained under the 'scheme to turn budget appropriations into loans'). In *China Infobank*.

_____. 27 Feb. 1997. "Guowuyuan pizhuan caizhengbu guanyu jiaqiang guoyou qiye caiwu jiandu yijian de tongzhi" (State Council approval of the Finance Ministry suggestions on strengthening the supervision of SOE property). In *China Infobank*.

_____. 2 March 1997. "Guowuyuan guanyu zai ruogan chengshi shixing guoyou qiye jianbing pochan he zhigong zai jiuye youguan wenti de buchong tongzhi" (Supplementary State Council circular on SOE mergers and bankruptcy and staff and worker re-employment in certain cities). In *China Infobank*.

_____. 27 Feb. 1998. "Guanyu fangzhi gongye shenhua gaige tiaozheng jiegou jiekun niukui gongzuo youguan wenti de tongzhi" (On some issues in strengthening the reform of the textile industry, adjusting the structure, resolving the problems and turning losses into profit). In *China Infobank*.

_____. 7 May 1998. "Guowuyuan xiang guoyou zhongdian daxing qiye paichu jicha tepaiyuan fang'an" (Outline of the State Council special inspectorate for key large SOEs). In *China Infobank*.

_____. 4 July 1998. "Caizhengbu zhineng peizhi neishe jigou he renyuan bianzhi guiding" (Functional adjustments, departments, and personnel numbers of the Finance Ministry). In *China Infobank*.

_____. 9 July 1998. "Guowuyuan jicha tepaiyuan tiaoli" (State Council special inspectorate regulation). In *China Infobank*.

_____. 17 July 1998. "Guowuyuan bangongting guanyu yinfa renshibu zhineng peizhi neishe jigou he renyuan bianzhi guiding de tongzhi" (State Council General Office circular on the functions, institutions, and personnel arrangement of the Personnel Department). In *China Infobank*.

———. 22 March 2000. "Guoyou qiye jianshihui zanxing tiaoli" (Temporary regulation on the SOE supervisory board). In *China Infobank*.

———. 28 May 2000. "Guanyu qieshi zuohao qiye lituixiu renyuan jiben yanglaojin anshi zu'e fafang he guoyou qiye xiagang zhigong jiben shenghuo baozhang gongzuo de tongzhi" (On conscientiously making timely and full basic pension payments and guaranteeing a basic living allowance for laid-off workers of SOEs). In *China Infobank*.

———. 20 Nov. 2000. "Guanyu jinrong zichan guanli gongsi tiaoli" (Stipulation on the financial asset management companies). In *China Infobank*.

———. 10 Jan. 2001. "Guowuyuan bangongting zhuanfa jianshebu deng bumen guanyu zhongyang suoshu gongcheng kancha sheji danwei tizhi gaige shishi fang'an de tongzhi" (Circular on the system reform of central engineering design units, issued by the Construction Ministry and other ministries, and passed on by the State Council General Office). In *China Infobank*.

———. 6 June 2001. "Jianchi guoyougu chouji shehui baozhang zijin guanli zanxing banfa" (Temporary measures on reducing state shares and building up social security funds). In *Zhonghua renmin gongheguo guowuyuan gongbao*, no. 23 (20 Aug. 2001): 33f.

———. 13 Dec. 2001. "Quanguo shehui baozhang jijin touzi guanli zanxing banfa" (Temporary measure on investment administration of the national social security fund). Issued jointly by the Finance Ministry and the Labor and Social Security Ministry, and approved by the State Council. In *China Infobank*.

———. 2 Jan. 2002. "Quanguo shehui baozhang jijin lishihui zhineng peizhi neishe jigou he renyuan bianzhi guiding" (Regulation on the functions of the board of directors of the national social security fund, the fund's institutional organization, and staff). In *China Infobank*.

———. April 2002. (State Council News Office) "Zhongguo laodong he shehui baozhang zhuangkuang" (The state of labor and social security in China). In *Zhonghua renmin gongheguo guowuyuan gongbao*, no. 19 (10 July 2002): 39–46.

SC Law Office (Guowuyuan fazhi ju fagui bianmu shi). *Zhonghua renmin gongheguo xin caiwu kuaiji zhidu daquan* (People's Republic of China new accounting system). Beijing: Zhongguo wujia chubanshe, 1993.

SDPC (State Development and Planning Commission; formerly State Planning Commission).

———. 15 Nov. 1998. "Guanyu jianyi jiuzheng zhongguo nongji xiehui nongyong che fenhui zuzhi zhiding nongyong che shichang xiaoshou 'hangye zilu jia' wenti de han" (Suggestions on redressing some of the issues raised by the 'sectoral self-discipline price' for the market sale of agricultural vehicles as determined by the China agricultural machinery association's agricultural vehicle branch). In *Price Yearbook 1999*, p. 99.

———. 16 Nov. 1998. "Guanyu zhizhi dijia qingxiao gongyepin bu zhengdang jiage xingwei de guiding" (Regulation on curbing the irregular price behavior of low-price dumping of industrial products). Issued jointly with the SETC. In *Price Yearbook 1999*, pp. 122–124.

———. 16 Jan. 1999. "Guanyu renzhen zuohao zhizhi dijia qingxiao gongzuo ji kaizhan dui dijia qingxiao jinxing jiancha de tongzhi" (On conscientiously curbing low-price dumping and launching investigations into low-price dumping). In *China Infobank*.

———. 18 Jan. 1999. "Guanyu panding dijia fanxiao de chengben yiju wenti de fuhan" (Response on how to determine the cost basis in the case of low-price dumping). In *China Infobank*.

———. 3 Aug. 1999. "Guanyu zhizhi dijia qingxiao xingwei de guiding" (Regulation on curbing low-price dumping behavior). In *China Infobank*.

SEC (State Economic Commission).

———. 5 April 1988. "Dazhongxiao xing gongye qiye huafen biaozhun" (Classification standard for large, medium and small industrial enterprises). Issued jointly with the State Planning Commission, State Statistical Bureau, Finance Ministry, and Labor and Personnel Ministry. In JHTZJGFGQS, pp. 682–695.

———. 8 July 1988. "'Dazhongxiao xing gongye qiye huafen biaozhun' de buchong tongzhi" (Supplementary circular to the classification standard for large, medium and small industrial enterprises). In JHTZJGFGQS, p. 695.

SETC (State Economic and Trade Commission; formerly State Economic Commission).

———. 5 April 1995. "Guoyou qiye zichan jingying zerenzhi zanxing banfa" (Temporary measures on the SOE asset management responsibility system). Issued jointly with the Labor and Social Security Ministry. In *China Infobank*.

———. 18 April 1995. "Guanyu jiandu jigou dui guoyou qiye paichu de jianshi gongzuo guifan" (Some standards for supervisory institutions in sending members of supervisory boards to SOEs). Issued jointly with the National State Asset Administration Bureau. In *China Infobank*.

———. 13 July 1995. "Guojia jingmaowei jianshi weipai zanxing guiding" (Temporary regulation on the SETC dispatching supervisors). In *China Infobank*.

_____. 24 July 1996 "Guanyu jianli qiye niukui zengying gongzuo mubiao zerenzhi yijian" (Suggestions on establishing targets for enterprises to turn losses into profit). Issued jointly with the Finance Ministry, People's Bank of China, and State Statistical Bureau; approved by the State Council. In *China Infobank*.

_____. 28 Nov. 1997. "Guojia jingmaowei fu zhuren Chen Qingtai tan guoyou qiye zenyang sannian zouchu kunjing" (SETC deputy head Chen Qingtai talks about how the SOEs can leave their difficulties behind within three years). In *China Infobank*.

_____. 17 Aug. 1998. "Guanyu bufen gongye chanpin shixing hangye zilu jia de yijian" (Suggestions on the use of sectoral self-discipline prices for some industrial products). In *China Infobank*.

_____. 11 Feb. 1999. "Guanyu chushou guoyou xiaoxing qiye zhong ruogan wenti yijian de tongzhi" (Suggestions regarding some issues in the sale of small SOEs). Issued jointly with the Finance Ministry and the People's Bank of China. *Zhonghua renmin gongheguo guowuyuan gongbao*, no. 9 (7 April 1999): 297–301.

_____. 26 April 1999. "Guanyu 1999 nian guoyou qiye lingdao ganbu lianjie zilu gongzuo de yijian" (Suggestions on the efforts to promote honesty and self-discipline among SOEs' leading cadres in 1999). Issued jointly with the Supervision Ministry. In *China Infobank*.

_____. 9 Aug. 1999. "Guanyu jiaqiang kuisun qiye lingdao banzi de jianshe de tongzhi" (On strengthening the establishment of the leadership team in loss-making enterprises). Issues jointly with the Personnel Ministry. *Zhonghua renmin gongheguo guowuyuan gongbao*, no. 32 (14 Oct. 1999): 1426–1428.

_____. 1 Sept. 2000. "Guanyu jiaqiang guoyou zhongdian qiye jishu zhongxin jianshe gongzuo de yijian" (Suggestions on establishing technology centers in state-owned key enterprises). In *China Infobank*.

_____. 28 Sept. 2000. "Guoyou dazhong xing qiye jianli xiandai qiye zhidu he jiaqiang guanli jiben guifan (shixing)" (Trial basic standards for the establishment of the modern enterprise system and for strengthening administration in large and medium SOEs). Transmitted by the State Council Office. In *China Infobank*.

_____. 13 March 2001. "Guanyu shenhua guoyou qiye neibu renshi, laodong, fenpei zhidu gaige de yijian" (Suggestions on deepening SOEs' personnel, labor, and distribution system). Issued jointly with the Personnel Ministry and the Labor and Social Security Ministry. *Zhonghua renmin gongheguo guowuyuan gongbao*, no. 7 (10 March 2002): 23–25.

_____. Oct. 2001. "'Shiwu' gongye jiegou tiaozheng guihua gangyao" (Outline of the adjustment in the industrial structure during the tenth Five-Year Plan). In *China Infobank*.

Seventeen Years of Reform. Gaige kaifang shiqi nian de zhongguo diqu jingji (Seventeen years of reform and opening in China's regional economy). Beijing: Zhongguo tongji chubanshe, 1996.

Shaanxi tongji nianjian 1996 (Shaanxi Statistical Yearbook 1996). Beijing: Zhongguo tongji chubanshe, 1996.

Shandong government.

———. 7 Jan. 1995. "Shishi 'guoyou qiye caichan jiandu guanli tiaoli' banfa" (Measures to implement the SOE property supervision regulation). In *China Infobank*.

Shi Dong. "Pochan zhibian" (Bankruptcy innovations). *Caijing*, no. 60 (20 May 2002): 20–28.

Smyth, Russell. "Asset Stripping in Chinese State-Owned Enterprises." *Journal of Contemporary Asia 30*, no. 1 (2000): 3–16.

SOE Escape Difficulties Research Group (Guoqi tuokun yanjiu keti zu). "Guoyou dazhong xing kuisun qiye: san nian tuokun?" (Can the large and medium-sized SOEs escape their difficulties in three years' time?). *Zhongguo tongji*, no. 7 (1999). 35f.

Solinger, Dorothy. "Why We Cannot Count the 'Unemployed.'" *The China Quarterly*, no. 167 (Sept. 2001): 271–288.

Song Qun, Lian Zhiming, Wang Dongjiang, Liu Wen, and Lu Guorong. "Analysis of Losses Incurred by State-owned Industrial Enterprises Included in the State Budget, and Proposed Countermeasures." *Chinese Economic Studies 26*, no. 1 (Fall 1992): 56–87.

SPC (State Planning Commission).

2 April 1987. "Guanyu daxing gongye lianying qiye zai guojia jihua zhong shixing danlie de zanxing guiding" (Regulation on large industrial joint enterprises turning into extra-plan enterprises under the state plan). Originally passed on 20 March 1987, revoked in 2000. In *China Infobank*.

27 April 1994. "Guojia jiwei guanyu zuohao yuanyou, tianranqi, chengpinyou, huafei jiage tiaozheng gongzuo de tongzhi" (Circular on well implementing the adjustment of raw petroleum, natural gas, petroleum end product, and chemical fertilizer prices). In *Price Yearbook 1995*, pp. 94–97.

State Price Bureau.

27 March 1993. "Guojia wujiaju guanyu xiada <1993 nian chengpinyou 'pingzhuanggao' ji tongyi jihuanei gaojia chengpinyou jiage shixing fang'an> de tongzhi" (Circular on the trial scheme for switching from 'general [planned] price to high [planned] price,' and unifying different categories of planned high prices for petroleum end products). In *Price Yearbook 1994*, pp. 235–238.

Statistical Abstract. Zhongguo tongji zhaiyao (A Statistical Survey of China). Beijing: Zhongguo tongji chubanshe. Various years.

Statistical Yearbook. Zhongguo tongji nianjian (China Statistical Yearbook). Beijing: Zhongguo tongji chubanshe. Various years.

Steinfeld, Edward S. *Forging Reform in China*. Cambridge: Cambridge University Press, 1998.

Stiglitz, Joseph E. "Why Financial Structure Matters." *Journal of Economic Perspectives* 2, no. 4 (Fall 1988): 121–126.

_____. "Quis Custodiet Ipsos Custodes?" *Challenge* 42, no. 6 (Nov/Dec 1999): 26–67 (obtained via PROQUEST, with pages numbered 1 through 20).

Supreme People's Procuratorate.

_____. 18 July 2001. "Guanyu gongtong zuohao guoyou qiye zhong tanwu huilu fanzui yufang gongzuo de tongzhi" (On jointly performing well the preventive work regarding corruption, bribery and crime in SOEs). Issued jointly with the CCPCC Enterprise Work Committee and SETC. In *China Infobank*.

Tam, On Kit. *The Development of Corporate Governance in China*. Cheltenham, UK: Edward Elgar, 1999.

TCFA Update. Published by the China Finance Association. Available at: http://www.china-finance.org.

Tenev, Stoyan, and Zhang Chunlin. *Corporate Governance and Enterprise Reform in China: Building the Institutions of Modern Markets*. Washington, D.C.: World Bank and International Finance Corporation, 2002.

Tidrick, Gene, and Chen Jiyuan. *China's Industrial Reform*. Oxford: Oxford University Press, 1987.

Township Enterprise Yearbook. Zhongguo xiangzhen qiye nianjian (Township and Village Enterprise Yearbook of China). Beijing: Zhongguo nongye chubanshe. Various years.

Wang Xiaozu, Xu Lixing Colin, and Zhu Tian. "Is Public Listing a Way Out for State-Owned Enterprises? The Case of China." Mimeo. September 2001.

Wang Zheng, and Yang Wenli. *Shuijin jisuan yu kuaiji hesuan* (Tax and accounting calculations). Beijing: Zhongguo jingji chubanshe, 1997.

Woo, Wing-Thye, Wen Hai, Jin Yibiao, and Fan Gang. "How Successful Has Chinese Enterprise Reform Been? Pitfalls in Opposite Biases and Focus." *Journal of Comparative Economics* 18, no. 3 (June 1994): 410–437.

World Bank. *China: Reform of State-Owned Enterprises*. Report No. 14924-CHA. Washington, D.C.: World Bank, 1996a.

_____. *World Development Report 1996: From Plan to Market*. New York: Oxford University Press, 1996b.

_____. *China's Management of Enterprise Assets: The State As Shareholder.* Washington, D.C.: World Bank, 1997.

_____. *China: Weathering the Storm and Learning the Lessons.* Washington, D.C.: The World Bank, 1999.

Wu Bangguo. "Zhidao guoyou qiye kua shiji gaige he fazhan de ganglingxing wenjian." (Program for SOE reform and development in the new century). *Zhonggong zhongyang dangxiao baogaoxuan,* no. 14 (20 Oct. 1999): 1–15.

Wu Guoheng. *Dangdai zhongguo tizhi gaige shi* (A history of system reform in contemporary China). Beijing: Falu chubanshe, 1994.

Wu Tianlin. "Jiakuai guoyou qiye zhidu jianshe bufa" (Accelerate the pace of the establishment of an SOE system). *Jingji tizhi gaige neibu cankao,* no. 17 (1993): 16f.

Wu, Yu-shan. *Comparative Economic Transformations: Mainland China, Hungary, the Soviet Union, and Taiwan.* Stanford: Stanford University Press, 1994.

Xiang Zhi. "Fenshui zhi yihou guoqi chushou fangshi fasheng bianhua" (Changes in the sales method of state-owned enterprises after the establishment of the central-local tax separation). *Gaige neican,* no. 10 (1995): 37f.

Xiao Geng. "Managerial Autonomy, Fringe Benefits, and Ownership Structure: A Comparative Study of Chinese State and Collective Enterprises." *China Economic Review 2,* no. 1 (Spring 1991): 47–73.

Xinbao (Hong Kong Economic Journal). Daily newspaper, Hong Kong.

Xu Xiaonian, and Wang Yan. "Ownership Structure, Corporate Governance, and Corporate Performance: The Case of Chinese Stock Companies." Policy Research Working Paper 1794, The World Bank Economic Development Institute, June 1997.

Yu Lixin. "Zhongguo qiye de kunjing he chulu" (The difficulties of China's enterprises and solutions). *Gaige neican,* no. 10 (1994): 29–35.

Yu Xiaoyun. "Liu wen guoqi" (Six questions on the SOEs). *Zhongguo tongji,* no. 7 (July 2001): 19–21.

Zhang Anming, Zhang Yimin, and Ronald Zhao. "Impact of Ownership and Competition on the Productivity of Chinese Enterprises." *Journal of Comparative Economics 29,* no. 2 (June 2001): 327–346.

_____. "Profitability and Productivity of Chinese Industrial Firms: Measurement and Ownership Implications." *China Economic Review 13,* no. 1 (2002): 65–88.

Zhang Tai. "Jinyibu shenhua guoyou qiye gaige de ruogan sikao" (Some thoughts on further deepening the SOE reform). *Jingji yanjiu cankao,* no. 52 (13 July 2001): 2–5.

Zhang Weiying. "China's SOE Reform: A Corporate Governance Perspective." Working paper, Guang Hua School of Management, Peking University, 1999.

Zhao Xiaojian, Hu Yifan, Huang Peijian, Zhu Xiaochao. "Shiye zhi you" (The Sorrows of Unemployment). *Caijing*, no. 68 (20 Sept. 2002): 26–53.

Zhang Zuocai. "Wo guo qiye caikuai zhidu de gaige yu fazhan" (Reform and development of China's financial and accounting system). *Zhonggong zhongyang dangxiao baogaoxuan*, no. 14 (20 Oct. 1999): 16–21.

ZHRMGHGFLQS. *Zhonghua renmin gongheguo falu quanshu* (PRC Law Compendium). Changchun: Jilin renmin chubanshe, first volume published in 1989 (approximately one volume per year, since 2000 two volumes per year).

Zhu Tian. "China's Corporatization Drive: An Evaluation and Policy Implications." *Contemporary Economic Policy 17*, no. 4 (Oct. 1999): 530–539.

Index

A

Accounting system
  revisions   31, 72
Accounts receivable   71, 90, 137
Administrative charges
  definition   71
Administrative rank   286, 313
Ash, Robert   6, 197
Asset stripping   138

B

Bad loans   257, 262, 293, 312
Bankruptcy   273–276
  data   260, 264
  law   258
  leading group   259, 260
  Liaoning   264
  limitations   260, 262, 263
  policy bankruptcies   259
  sectoral focus   260
Black, Bernard   299
Blayney, Steven   138
Board of directors   268, 279, 280, 283
Bogaidai. *See* Switching from budget appropriations to loans
Bonus payments   78
Budget constraint   7, 297, 308, 309
  industrialized countries   308
Byrd, William   10

C

Cai Fang   7, 164
Cao Yuanzheng   7, 197, 304
Capital intensity   8, 308, 309
  causes of high   190–193
  current assets   191
  definition   186
  fixed assets   191
  impact on SOE
    profitability   186–190
  summary of differences between
    SOEs and non-SOEs   290, 291
  time trend   187
CCPCC Commission for Discipline
  Inspection   279
CCPCC Enterprise Work
  Committee   209, 278, 282, 313
Chai, Joseph   2, 6, 33
Chen Aimin   8, 10
Chen Jiyuan   10
Chen Kuan   2, 34
Chen Qingtai   77, 79, 132
Chen Yongqi   280, 281
Cheng, Chu-yuan   105

343

Cheng Yuk-shing 6
Chow, Gregory 2
Circulation taxes
  differences across ownership
    forms 180–186
  summary of differences between
    SOEs and non-SOEs 291
Company system 245
Competition 6, 77
  impact on labor
    remuneration 122
  importance in economic
    transition 297
  malicious 129, 270–273
  market share as proxy 100
  potential impact on labor
    remuneration 103, 104
  summary of impact on
    profitability 290
  theoretical impact on
    profitability 105, 106
Conglomerates 80, 239, 282, 287,
  306
Corporate governance 6, 9, 308–
  314
  beneficial government
    involvement 310
  choices 311
  enterprise survey on administrative
    interference 310

D

Dang guan ganbu 279
Data sources 39–42
Debt-equity swap 158, 159, 160,
  257, 262
Deng Xiaoping 75
Depreciation 83, 119, 137, 186
  data derivation 43–47

period 74
  share in value-added 86
Deutsche Bundesbank 143
Dewenter, Kathryn 298, 307
Di Na 81
Ding Xueliang 138
Directly reporting industrial
    enterprises
  classification 21
  definition 16
  output share in all industry 22, 23
Djankov, Simeon 299
Docwra, George 6
Dollar, David 2
Dougherty, Sean 2
Duncan, Ron 2, 6, 33, 96, 164

E

Economies of scale 216, 220, 239,
  291, 298, 305
Efficiency 2, 3
Electricity 184, 227, 228, 234, 236,
  241
Employment
  dismissals 249, 252–255
  link with profitability across
    sectors 230–232
  reduction in overstaffing 262
Enterprise classification 17
Enterprise contract responsibility
    system 79
Equalization of profit rates 197
  across provinces 205
  across sectors 201, 233, 242,
    315
Ex-factory price index of industrial
    products 58, 60, 63, 65, 67,
    70, 75, 76, 77, 166, 167

F

Fan Gang 6, 33, 96, 97, 98, 100, 101, 102, 113, 114, 115
Fan Hengshan 247
Financial charges
 definition 71
Fiscal burden 263, 264
Fixed assets
 data problems 34
 revaluation 76
 valuation 137
Food processing 223, 224, 227, 228, 230, 231, 236, 242, 292
Funds profitability rate
 definition 33

G

Gao Shangquan 10, 79, 260
Getihu
 definition 16
Government interference in management 270–273, 284
Government response to reform challenges 305–307
Gross profit
 definition 33
Groves, Theodore 2

H

Han Xu 313
Hay, Donald 10
He Liping 6, 197
Hidden losses 70, 81, 91
Holz, Carsten 18, 20, 23, 38, 40, 41, 62, 266
Hu, Albert 303
Hu Linhui 280
Huang Yiping 2, 6, 33, 96, 164
Hussain, Athar 97

I

Idiosyncrasies
 three SOE 7, 308, 309
Import tariffs 77, 106
Individual-owned enterprises. *See* Getihu
Industrial SOEs
 and economy-wide surplus 56, 243
 coverage in provincial statistical yearbooks, 1998–2000 27, 29–31
 definition 13–19
 importance of large and medium 298
 irrelevance of concept of 316
 objectives 269, 270, 281, 294, 311
 reform gains 305
 reform pressures 307, 308
 reform process 305
 regional classification 27
 sectoral classification 26–28
 self-constraint 272
 three-year reform program summary 245
 turning around large and medium 247
Industrial state-owned and state-controlled enterprises
 definition 15–19
Industry
 definition 25
Intangible assets 136, 138
Inter-enterprise arrears 90, 136, 137

Interest rates
  deposit rate indexation   68, 75
  on working capital loans   67
Intermediate competition indicator
  contribution to profitability   123, 125–127
  definition   99, 100
  link to profitability   104
  shortcomings   100
Intermediate labor remuneration indicator
  contribution to profitability   123, 125–127
  definition   101, 102
  link to profitability   104
Internal Revenue Service   143
Inventories   65, 66, 69, 70, 71, 74, 76, 79, 82, 89, 91, 100, 106, 136, 148, 151, 152, 159, 192
  U.S.   137
Investment cuts   62

J

Jefferson, Gary   2, 5, 6, 14, 33, 34, 95, 96, 97, 296, 297, 305
Jiang Zemin   2, 244, 266, 287, 299, 303

K

Kong Xiang   2
Kraakman, Reinier   299

L

Labor remuneration
  definition and data derivation   47–54
  excessive   6
  excessive, definition   97
  excessive, reasons   130
  summary of impact on profitability   290
Land use rights   136, 138
Lardy, Nicholas   1, 14, 134, 135, 136, 163, 296
Laurenceson, James   2, 33
Leadership team   273, 274, 275, 278, 279, 280
Li Chun   280, 281
Li, David   7
Li Hong   10
Li Xianzong   90
Li Zhou   7, 164
Liability-asset ratio
  accounting link to profitability   155
  across ownership forms   142
  definition   131
  domestic comparison   142
  Germany   143
  indirect effects on profitability   147
  international comparison   143, 144
  Japan   143
  Korea   143
  measures to reduce   256–258
  stabilization   141
  summary of impact on profitability   290
  time trend   134–139, 159
  U.S.   143
Liang Minsong   7
Lianxiang konggu youxian gongsi   302
Lin, Justin Yifu   7
Lin, Yi-min   10, 18, 20, 23, 38, 40, 41, 247, 266

Lo, Dic   6, 33, 148, 224
Loss-making SOEs
　comparison with profitable SOEs, five provinces   179
　exit   178, 238, 239, 258–260
　improvements due to external factors   247
　management evaluation   275
Losses per unit of gross profit   59, 165
　definition   37
　SOEs vs. non-SOEs   168
　time trend, non-SOEs   165, 167–169
　time trend, SOEs   60, 165, 166, 168, 169
Low-price dumping   270–273, 284
Lyons, Thomas   210

M

Malatesta, Paul   298, 307
Management
　anti-corruption standards   278
　appointment   279, 280, 294, 313, 314
　appointment and Chinese Communist Party   278–281
　audit   278, 282
　distractions   312–314
　evaluation   273–278, 282, 286
　limitations to supervision   314
　reform   286, 287
　scientific   245, 267, 286, 315
　supervision   273–278, 294, 312–314
Market prices
　share of producer goods sold at, time trend   68
　share of retail sales at, time trend   68
Market share
　as a measure of state control   202–204
　industrial SOEs, time trend   68
　of largest enterprises in each sector   107, 202
　relationship with intermediate competition indicator   113
Mayer, Colin   311
McGuckin, Robert   2
McMillan, John   297
Megginson, William   298
Miao Qingwang   280
Modern enterprise system   244–246, 267, 286, 296
Modigliani-Miller theorem   132, 155
Mok, Vincent   2
Moral hazard   81, 208, 254, 312
Morris, Derek   297
Murrell, Peter   299

N

Naughton, Barry   6, 33, 95, 96, 97, 98, 105, 107, 108, 297
Neoclassical growth theory   2
Net taxes on production
　definition   83
　vs. sales-related taxes   85
Netter, Jeffrey   298
Nolan, Peter   298, 310, 314
Non-business expenses
　definition   76
Non-productive assets
　and capital intensity   192

Non-SOEs
  definition   15

O

OECD   7, 267, 269
Operating surplus   9, 57, 86–91
  comparison with profit time
    trend   86, 87
  definition   82
  definitional link to profit   88, 89
  economy-wide   84, 86
  shortcomings   91
  time trend   83–87
  U.S.   87

P

Parker, Elliott   97
Pensions
  definition and data derivation   52–54
Perkins, Dwight   298, 301
Perkins, F.C.   2
Perkins, Frances   6
Petroleum   184, 223, 224, 227, 228, 230, 231, 232, 233, 234, 236, 237, 241, 292
Price distortions   8, 308, 309
Price liberalization
  impact on profitability   218
Production cost reduction index   63, 64
Profit
  definition   31–33
  incentives to misreport   78–82
Profit per unit of equity   59, 165
  definition   36
  SOEs vs. non-SOEs   168
  time trend, non-SOEs   165, 167
  time trend, SOEs   59, 60, 165, 166
Profit per unit of sales revenue   59, 168
  definition   37–38
  SOEs vs. non-SOEs   168
  time trend, non-SOEs   167, 168
  time trend, SOEs   59, 60, 166, 168
Profitability
  across ownership forms   169–174
  best- and worst-performing sectors   226–233
  clusters (of sectors)   225
  definition   35–38
  impact of sectoral differences on provinces   233–237
  patterns across sectors, provinces, size, and ownership level   212–221
  preliminary data for 2001   284
  reasons for differences according to enterprise size   207, 208
  reasons for differences across ownership levels   210–211
  reasons for differences across provinces   204–206
  reasons for sectoral differences   200
  result of government pricing policies   216, 236
  summary of differences between SOEs and non-SOEs   290–291
  summary of patterns across sectors, provinces, size, and ownership level   292
  variation across enterprise size   208, 209

variation across ownership
    levels   211
variation across provinces   202,
    205
variation across sectors   200–202
vs. total factor productivity   5
why it matters   3–5
Profitability trends
    SOEs   61
    SOEs vs. non-SOEs   165–169
Property rights reform   7, 265–270,
    296, 299
    acceptance of private sector   265–
        267
    privatization of large and medium
        industrial SOEs   300–304
Public goods   296
Purchasing price index of raw
    materials, energy and power   63,
    67, 77
Pure SOE
    definition   16

Q

Qi Yu   280
Qian Yingyi   7, 164, 197, 265, 304

R

R&D   298, 303
Raiser, Martin   2, 6, 33, 96, 205
Rawski, Thomas   1, 2, 6, 14, 33, 81,
    96, 97, 105, 296, 305
Re-employment service center   253,
    260
Resolution trust companies   81,
    256, 262, 293
Resource tax   184, 235

Retrenchment and adjustment
    period   58, 70, 306
Return on assets   59, 165
    definition   36, 37
    SOEs vs. non-SOEs   168
    time trend, non-SOEs   165, 167
    time trend, SOEs   59, 60, 165, 166
Return on equity. *See* Profit per unit
    of equity
Riskin, Carl   210

S

Sachs, Jeffrey   1, 96, 113, 163, 296
Sales fees
    definition   71
Sales revenue
    composition, industrial SOEs   64
Sales-related taxes. *See* Net taxes on
    production
Sectoral associations   130, 271
Sectoral classification   28
Sectoral policies 2001–2010   285
Self-discipline prices   271–273,
    284
Shareholding companies
    appointment regulations   268
    company law   268, 269
    definition   14
Shi Dong   259, 264
Shifting financial burdens   263
Size classification of
    enterprises   207
Small industrial SOE reform   247–
    249, 265–267
Smyth, Russell   138, 312
Social responsibilities   8, 308
Social return on assets   59, 165
    definition   36, 37

time trend, non-SOEs   165, 167
time trend, SOEs   59, 60, 165, 166
Social security system
   national fund   225
   pensions   254, 255
   reform   254, 255
Social welfare payments
   definition and data derivation   50–54
Solinger, Dorothy   253
Song Qun   6, 197
Special inspectorate   277, 278, 282, 287
State asset administration
   reform   287
State asset management
   companies   269, 270, 297, 305, 309
Steinfeld, Edward   7, 10, 164, 211
Stern, Nicholas   97
Stiglitz, Joseph   132, 265, 297
Stock cooperatives   247, 266, 299
Stock market   283, 284
Subsidies   47, 50, 52, 65, 68, 83, 89, 90, 92, 93, 160, 309
Supervisory board   268, 275, 276, 277, 280, 281, 283
Survey data
   evaluation   40, 41
Switching from budget appropriations to loans   80, 139

T

Tam, On Kit   7, 164, 265, 269, 311
Tarassova, Anna   299
Tenev, Stoyan   7
Tenth Five-Year Plan   285

Textiles   223, 224, 227, 228, 230, 231, 236, 242, 249, 260, 261, 292, 293
Three reforms and one enhancement   244
Tidrick, Gene   10
Tobacco   181, 184, 223, 224, 227, 228, 230, 231, 232, 233, 234, 236, 241, 242, 292
Total factor productivity   2, 3, 5
Triangular debt   75, 80, 90, 207
Turnover ratio   64, 66, 75
Two guarantees   253

V

Value-added
   composition   84
   data derivation   42, 43

W

Wages
   definition and data derivation   47, 50
   relationship to intermediate labor remuneration indicator   120–122
Wang Xiaoqiang   298, 310
Wang Xiaozu   283
Wang Yan   283
Wang Zheng   185
Weingast, Barry   7, 197, 304
Woo, Wing-Thye   2, 6, 33, 34, 96, 97, 98, 100, 101, 102, 113, 114, 115
World Bank   7, 82, 131, 268, 269, 296, 300, 314
WTO   93, 307, 309
Wu Bangguo   210, 285

Wu Guoheng   210
Wu Tianlin   138
Wu, Yu-shan   10

X

Xiang Zhi   210
Xiao Geng   2
Xu Lixing   283
Xu Xiaonian   283

Y

Yang Wenli   185
Yeung, Godfrey   314
Yu Lixin   80, 138
Yu Xiaoyun   246

Z

Zhang Anming   2, 6
Zhang Chunlin   7
Zhang Tai   248
Zhang Weiying   81, 296
Zhang Yimin   2, 6
Zhang Yongguo   90
Zhang Zuocai   73
Zhao Ronald   2, 6
Zhao Xiaojian   255
Zheng Yuxin   2
Zhu Tian   6, 7, 164, 247, 283
Zhuada fangxiao   244